For the past twenty years, [...] involved with the refugee question in Southeast Asia. A speaker of Thai, Khmer and Mandarin Chinese, he started in 1979 with the Indochina Refugee Action Centre in Washington, DC. This was followed by three years (1982–85) as Programme Coordinator at Phanat Nikhom in Thailand for the Consortium (World Education, Save the Children and World Learning). In 1986 he returned to Washington to join the staff of the US Committee for Refugees as a Senior Policy Analyst, a position he held for six years. In 1992, he received a grant from the John D. and Catherine T. MacArthur Foundation to return to Southeast Asia to research refugee repatriation. From 1994 to 1996 he served as a Senior Fellow at Chulalongkorn University's Asian Research Centre for Migration. Educated originally at Haverford College, Pennsylvania, he is currently an Associate at the Centre for Refugee and Disaster Studies at the Johns Hopkins University School of Hygiene and Public Health in Baltimore, Maryland.

He is the author of various publications, including *Double Vision: A History of Cambodian Refugees in Thailand* (Chulalongkorn University, 1996); *Something Like Home: The Repatriation of Cambodian Refugees in Thailand* (USCR, 1994); and *Sri Lanka: Island of Refugees* (USCR, 1991).

About the Book

'Terms of Refuge is the definitive work on the greatest international refugee undertaking in half a century, written by someone who was a part of it, who lived and who breathed its essence.'
ROGER WINTER, Director, US Committee for Refugees

'Courtland Robinson has produced the most comprehensive and complete account of the Indochinese refugee exodus ever written. This landmark work will be "must" reading for anyone interested in this extraordinary humanitarian saga. I cannot recommend it highly enough.'
ROBERT P. DEVECCHI, Adjunct Senior Fellow, Council on Foreign Relations, New York

'Courtland Robinson provides a perceptive, solidly documented survey of the complexities of the Indochinese refugee outflow of the 1970s and 80s, of the tragedies that provoked and attended it and the varied, often callous, responses of the countries called upon to offer temporary or permanent asylum.'
HENRY KAMM, author of *Dragon Ascending: Vietnam and the Vietnamese and Cambodia: Report from a Stricken Land.*

'Courtland Robinson has written the most informative and comprehensive study of the international community's response to the Indochinese refugee to date. Not only does this book tell us a lot about past refugee policy. but there are many lessons here for future decision-makers regarding finding appropriate solutions to refugee problems elsewhere in the world.'
PROFESSOR GIL LOESCHER, University of Notre Dame

Other Zed Titles in its
Politics in Contemporary Asia Series

Asia has come to prominence in recent years because of its economic dynamism, despite the dramatic financial collapse of 1997. But the decade-long economic success of this highly diverse continent has been dependent on the maintenance of effective government. It can also lead, as the Zed Books Series on *Politics in Contemporary Asia* shows, to the downplaying of the region's many political problems in the areas of ethnicity, religious identity, democratic control and human rights.

C. Beyrer, *War in the Blood: Sex, Politics and AIDS in Southeast Asia*

Chorbajian, Donabedian and Mutafian, *The Caucasian Knot: The History and Geopolitics of Nagorno-Karabagh*

P. Donnet, *Tibet: Survival in Question*

S. Goldenberg, *Pride of Small Nations: The Caucasus and Post-Soviet Disorder*

J. Goodno, *The Philippines: Land of Broken Promises*

S. Gopal (ed.), *Anatomy of a Confrontation: Ayodhya and the Rise of Communal Politics in India*

P. Marsden, *The Taliban: War, Religion and the New Order in Afghanistan*

G. Ogle, *South Korea: Dissent within the Economic Miracle*

J. Pettigrew, *The Sikhs of the Punjab: Unheard Voices of State and Guerrilla Violence*

A. Rashid, *The Resurgence of Central Asia: Islam or Nationalism?*

M. Smith, *Burma: Insurgency and the Politics of Ethnicity*

J. Taylor, *Indonesia's Forgotten War: The Hidden History of East Timor*

For full details of this list and Zed's other Asia titles, as well as our subject catalogues, please write to:
Marketing Department,
Zed Books, 7 Cynthia Street, London N1 9JF, UK
or email Kirby@zedbooks.demon.co.uk
Visit our website at: http://www.zedbooks.demon.co.uk

Terms of Refuge

The Indochinese Exodus
& The International Response

W. COURTLAND ROBINSON

Zed Books Ltd
LONDON & NEW YORK

Terms of Refuge was first published by
Zed Books Ltd, 7 Cynthia Street, London N1 9JF, UK,
and Room 400, 175 Fifth Avenue, New York, NY 10010, USA
in 1998

Published in Burma, Cambodia, Laos and Thailand by
White Lotus Co. Ltd, GPO Box 1141, Bangkok 10501, Thailand

Cover designed by Andrew Corbett.
Laserset by Long House, Cumbria, UK.
Printed and bound in the United Kingdom
by Biddles Ltd, Guildford and King's Lynn

Distributed exclusively in the USA by
St Martin's Press, 175 Fifth Avenue
New York, NY 10010, USA.

A catalogue record for this book
is available from the British Library.
ISBN 1 85649 609 0 Cased
ISBN 1 85649 610 4 Limp

Library of Congress Cataloging-in-Publication Data
Robinson, W. Courtland (William Courtland), 1955–
    Terms of refuge : the Indochinese exodus and the international
response / W. Courtland Robinson.
        p.   cm.
    Includes bibliographical references and index.
    ISBN 1-85649-609-0 (hc.). – ISBN 1-85649-610-4 (pbk.)
    1. Refugees–Indochina. 2. Office of the United Nations High
Commissioner for Refugees.   I. Title.
HV640.5.I5R63   1998
325'.21'09597–dc21   98-27305
                                                              CIP

Portions of the text have been published, in substantially different form, in the following publications:
'Laotian Refugees in Thailand: The Thai and US Response, 1975–1988', in Joseph J. Zasloff and Leonard Unger (eds), *Laos: Beyond the Revolution*, St Martin's Press, New York, 1988.
'"Unhappy Endgame": Hmong Refugees in Thailand', *Refugee Reports*, Vol. 13, No. 8, August 1992.
Something Like Home Again: The Repatriation of Cambodian Refugees in Thailand, US Committee for Refugees, Washington, DC, 1993.
Double Vision: A History of Cambodian Refugees in Thailand, Institute of Asian Studies, Chulalongkorn University, Bangkok, 1996.

The two maps (pages xii and xiii) are drawn from ©ADC Worldmap, Chulalongkorn University and ©UNHCR Environmental Database. The boundaries and names shown and the designations used on these maps do not imply official endorsement or acceptance by the United Nations.

Contents

Tables

Foreword

SADAKO OGATA

UNITED NATIONS HIGH COMMISSIONER FOR REFUGEES

For UNHCR, Indochina has a very special significance. Throughout most of the 1970s and 1980s, the three countries of the region – Cambodia, Laos and Vietnam – were a byword for armed conflict, political turmoil and mass refugee movements. During that period, more than three million people fled from their homes and sought refuge in other Asian states. Many failed to survive the hazardous journey into exile. Those who succeeded in reaching a country of first asylum frequently found that they were obliged to spend many years in a closed camp or detention centre. And those who were eventually resettled in one of the industrialized states were confronted with the difficult task of adapting to a completely new language, culture and way of life.

Despite the human suffering that the Indochinese exodus entailed, *Terms of Refuge* is a story of hope and positive human achievement. Today, more than 20 years after the first Vietnamese boat people set to sea, the countries of Indochina have undergone significant changes. The refugee camps that were once scattered throughout Southeast Asia have been closed. Practically all of the refugees and asylum seekers who could not be resettled have gone back to their own country. Many of those who were admitted to countries such as the USA, Canada, Australia and France have now become fully fledged citizens of their adopted state. And while poverty, persecution and political instability have not yet been banished from Southeast Asia, the states of the region are no longer affected by the large-scale human rights violations and population displacements which they experienced in previous decades.

Terms of Refuge is also of considerable relevance to the management and resolution of refugee problems in other parts of the world. Its cogent analysis confirms the need for states scrupulously to respect the right of asylum and other refugee protection principles. The book underlines the importance of pursuing comprehensive approaches to refugee problems, involving countries of origin, countries of asylum and the donor states. It reveals the way in which humanitarian activities and negotiations can contribute to the resolution of longstanding political conflicts, both within and between states. And it demonstrates the influential role which public opinion, pressure groups and advocacy organizations can play in shaping the international response to a regional refugee crisis.

The original idea for this book came from an informal discussion amongst UNHCR colleagues in April 1994, held in a sidewalk cafe in Haiphong, Vietnam. During that meeting, we became acutely aware of the need to record the remarkable story of the Indochinese exodus and all those who were involved in or affected by it. At the same time, we recognized the need to learn as many lessons as possible from the Indochinese experience and to see how those lessons could be applied to other and future refugee crises. It was for these reasons that UNHCR agreed to support the research of Courtland Robinson, one of the world's leading authorities on refugee issues in Asia.

Mr Robinson's work represents a major contribution to our understanding of refugee issues, and will be of great value to scholars of modern Asian history. At the same time, this book tells an intensely moving and human story. *Terms of Refuge* describes the dangerous circumstances which prompted so many people to abandon their homes and to set out for unknown destinations abroad. It pays tribute to the many UNHCR and NGO staff who worked so hard to protect those refugees and to help them find solutions to their plight. And at a time of continued crisis in many parts of world, it reaffirms the need for us all to show solidarity with the victims of violence, armed conflict and human rights abuses. The vast majority of Indochina's refugees have now been able to resume a peaceful and productive life. We look forward to the day when people in every part of the world can live safely in their own homes.

Acknowledgements

As this book is the outgrowth of nearly two decades of involvement with Indochinese refugee issues, I am indebted to an almost impossibly long list of individuals and institutions who shaped my thinking and supported my work. In terms of institutional benefactors, I must first thank the UN High Commissioner for Refugees for the support (and the freedom) to write this book. I am also grateful to the John D. and Catherine T. MacArthur Foundation and to the Ford Foundation for research and writing grants that enabled me to document the flight and return of Cambodian refugees in Thailand.

For giving me employment and an opportunity to witness first-hand the unfolding events of the Indochinese exodus, I am indebted to the Indochina Refugee Action Center, the Consortium (World Education, Save the Children and World Learning), the US Committee for Refugees, and Chulalongkorn University's Asian Research Center for Migration. My directors – Rob Stein and Le Xuan Khoa of IRAC, David Belskis of the Consortium, Roger Winter at USCR, and Supang Chantavanich at Chulalongkorn – have been invaluable and inspirational mentors.

In constructing this narrative, I have been privileged to draw on the time and ideas of literally hundreds of people. Those whom I interviewed formally or whose works I cite are listed in the bibliography and I am grateful to all of them for their cooperation and their insights. I would like to thank especially Werner Blatter, Jeff Crisp, Francois Fouinat, Lennart Hansson, Udo Janz, Dennis McNamara, and Eric Morris of UNHCR for their comments and careful reading of the manuscript. I am, of course, solely responsible for any errors of fact or judgement that remain.

To the many refugees and asylum seekers, named and nameless, who shared their stories with me, I offer my humble gratitude and hope that, in some small way, this book repays their time and their trust. For their friendship, encouragement and inspiration over the years, I am especially indebted to Rob Burrows, Vilay Chaleunrath, Cindy Coleman, Bob DeVecchi, Bill Frelick, Dennis Grace, Ginny Hamilton, Carl Harris, Le Xuan Khoa, Andy Pendleton, Lional Rosenblatt, Hiram Ruiz, Raci Say, Susan Walker and Roger Winter. Finally, I want to acknowledge the love and support of my family – my wife, Ang, who has shared so much of this work with me, and my children, Yani and Nick. It is my parents, Sally Shoemaker Robinson and James Courtland Robinson, who introduced me to Asia so many years ago and to humanitarian endeavour, and it is to them that I dedicate this book.

Abbreviations & Acronyms

AALCC	Asian-African Legal Consultative Committee
ACNS	American Council for Nationalities Service
APA	Anti-Piracy Arrangement
ARC	American Refugee Committee
ASEAN	Association of Southeast Asian Nations
ATV	Affected Thai Villages
AVS	Agency for Volunteer Service
BCAR	British Council for Aid to Refugees
CADP	Center for Assistance to Displaced Persons
CAMA	Christian and Missionary Alliance
CARERE	Cambodian Resettlement and Reintegration Programme
CEIC	Canada Employment and Immigration Commission
CGDK	Coalition Government of Democratic Kampuchea
CNE	Comité National d'Entraide
CPA	Comprehensive Plan of Action
CPAF	Cambodian People's Armed Forces
CPR	Coalition for Peace and Reconciliation
CRC	Cambodian Red Cross
CSDPT	Coordination of Services to Displaced Persons in Thailand
CWS	Church World Service
Disero	Disembarkation Resettlement Offers
DK	Democratic Kampuchea
DPPU	Displaced Persons Protection Unit
EAO	Ethnic Affairs Officer
EC	European Community
ECIP	European Community International Programme
ESL	English as a Second Language
EVI	Especially Vulnerable Individual
FTA	France Terre d'Asile
FUNCINPEC	National United Front for an Independent, Neutral, Peaceful and Cooperative Cambodia
HIAS	Hebrew Immigrant Aid Society
IATF	Interagency Task Force
ICC	International Control Commission
ICCB	International Catholic Child Bureau
ICEM	Intergovernmental Committee for European Migration
ICG	Informal Consultative Group
ICK	International Conference on Kampuchea
ICRC	International Committee of the Red Cross
ILO	International Labour Organization
INS	Immigration and Naturalization Service
IOM	International Organization for Migration
IRC	International Rescue Committee

IRIC	Indochinese Refugee Information Centre
IRO	International Refugee Organization
JVA	Joint Voluntary Agency
KISA	Khmer Intelligence Security Agency
KPNLF	Khmer People's National Liberation Front
KPRC	Kampuchean People's Revolutionary Council
LIRS	Lutheran Immigration and Refugee Service
LPDR	Lao People's Democratic Republic
MAA	Mutual Assistance Association
MLSW	Ministry of Labour and Social Welfare
MOI	Ministry of Interior
MOLISA	Ministry of Labour, War Invalids and Social Affairs
NARV	Nordic Assistance to Repatriated Vietnamese
NEZ	New Economic Zone
NGO	Non-governmental Organization
NSC	National Security Council
ODP	Orderly Departure Programme
OFPRA	Office Français de Protection des Refugiés et Apatrides
OPS	Office for Project Services
ORP	Orderly Return Programme
ORR	Office of Refugee Resettlement
OSRSG	Office of the Special Representative of the Secretary General of the United Nations for the Coordination of Cambodian Humanitarian Assistance Programmes
PERKIM	Malaysian Muslim Welfare Organization
PRK	People's Republic of Kampuchea
PRPC	Philippine Refugee Processing Centre
PSB	Public Security Bureau
PSU	Provincial Support Unit
RASRO	Rescue at Sea Resettlement Offers
ROKU	Regional Office Kampuchean Unit
ROVR	Resettlement Opportunities for Vietnamese Returnees
RPG	Refugee Policy Group
RRTC	Regional Resettlement Transit Centre
SCORRI	Select Committee on Refugee Resettlement and Immigration
SNC	Supreme National Council
SOC	State of Cambodia
SRV	Socialist Republic of Vietnam
UNBRO	United Nations Border Relief Operation
UNDP	United Nations Development Programme
UNHCR	United Nations High Commissioner for Refugees
UNICEF	United Nations Children's Fund
UNRRA	United Nations Relief and Rehabilitation Administration
USCC	United States Catholic Conference
USCR	United States Committee for Refugees
VGP	Vulnerable Groups Programme
Volag	Voluntary Agency
WFP	World Food Programme
WHO	World Health Organization
YMCA	Young Men's Christian Association

Map 1. *Laotian, Cambodian and Vietnamese Camps in Thailand*
Source: ADC Worldmap, Chulalongkorn University; UNHCR Environmental Database.

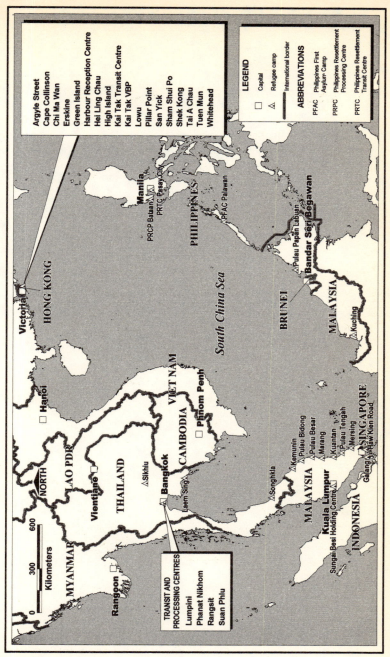

Map 2. Vietnamese Boat People Camps in South East Asia, 1980s to 1990s
Source: ADC Worldmap, Chulalongkorn University; UNHCR Environmental Database.

CHAPTER 1

—

Introduction

In the panicky last days of April 1975, Nguyen Thu Huu recalled many years later, 'the only way I could think to keep calm was by going to work.'[1] A captain in the South Vietnamese Air Force, Thu reported each morning to his post at Tan Son Nhut air base outside of Saigon. He watched each day as the US transport planes filled up and flew off with American citizens, family members, friends, foreign diplomats, and assorted camp followers. Each day, he checked to see if his name was on the lists of those cleared for departure. Word was out that the Americans were taking 'high-risk' Vietnamese but no one was sure exactly what that meant. One US official offered vaguely that 'The kind of people who know us are the kind of people who would be in trouble.'[2] With the North Vietnamese forces on the outskirts of the city, Thu both feared he was that kind of people and hoped the Americans agreed. On 29 April, he crouched in his barracks as communist rockets shelled the air base and shut down the evacuation from Tan Son Nhut. The last Americans would leave late that night by helicopter from the roof of the US embassy. On 30 April, tanks of the National Liberation Front stormed the gates of the presidential palace as soldiers pulled down the red and yellow stripes of the Saigon regime and waved the Democratic Republic of Vietnam's yellow star on a field of red.

'I did not want to stay and see what happened next,' Thu said,

> so at the beginning of May I went to Ha Tien, got on a fishing boat and left Vietnam. We reached Thailand in a few days. I found my way to the US embassy in Bangkok. They sent me to the UN High Commissioner for Refugees (UNHCR). I went to see UNHCR and they sent me to a local Christian church. The church referred me to the YMCA. When I got there, I found about 100 other Vietnamese who had also escaped by boat and were rescued by a Danish ship.

If Thu had not been on anyone's list in Saigon, he most certainly was an unexpected guest in Bangkok.

In August the Thai authorities ordered Thu and his group to enter a 'displaced persons' camp south of the city. By September, he said, 'There were about 1,000 of us: soldiers, teachers, carpenters, goldsmiths, a lot of

1

young men, a lot of children, Buddhist monks, Catholic nuns and priests, government officials, prostitutes, farmers and fishermen. All kinds of people.' Thu said he saw very little of the Americans or UNHCR for a time. 'There was much uncertainty in the camp. A lot of people had expected to be resettled. I had expected it when I went to the US embassy and instead they referred me to UNHCR.' By the end of the year, Thu was growing desperate. He approached an American official who was visiting the camp and asked what he should do. 'He advised me to go to Australia,' said Thu.

Thu took the American man's advice and was approved for admission to Australia. By March 1976 he was in Melbourne, where he got a scholarship to study social work at Melbourne University. In 1981 he came to America to visit some friends from his days in the Bangkok camp. One was working with a voluntary agency in Michigan, helping to resettle unaccompanied minors. Thu went back to Australia and one year later immigrated to the United States on a professional worker's visa. For the next ten years, he worked with unaccompanied minors, first in Michigan and later in Virginia. In 1992 UNHCR invited him back to Thailand to help interview unaccompanied minors for repatriation or resettlement. 'Generally, I counselled people to go back. But I tried to persuade UNHCR to accept more for resettlement with relatives overseas if the relatives were willing to take them and the parents in Vietnam were having trouble. So nobody liked me.'

Nguyen Huu Thu came back to Vietnam in October 1993 as country director of an American non-profit organization working with returnees in and around Saigon, since renamed Ho Chi Minh City after the founder of the Vietnamese Communist Party. 'Twenty years later,' said Thu, 'my new office is one hundred yards from my old barracks at Tan Son Nhut.'

Over the last twenty years, more than three million people left their homes in Vietnam, Laos and Cambodia, many with their lives in obvious peril and others fleeing fear, hunger and uncertainty. Some came seeking to rejoin relatives overseas or to start a life of new opportunity. Others waited only for a chance to go home again in peace. They ran the gamut from generals and ministers to farmers and fishermen, highland tribespeople to the urban elite, students and housewives, warriors and draft dodgers, elderly grandparents and small children, extended families and unaccompanied minors. They left on foot, on large freighters and small fishing boats, by oxcart and airplane, swimming rivers and stealing through jungles.

Most of these have been resettled in other countries, including 1.4 million in the United States, 260,000 in China, 200,000 in Canada, 185,000 in Australia, and 130,000 in France. Roughly half a million people have returned home. What these figures do not count are the unregistered movements back and forth across borders nor the tens of thousands who suffered and died along the way as a result of piracy, pushbacks, drownings, banditry and abuse.

The Indochinese exodus spanned three decades, through two ground-breaking international conferences and a third war in Indochina. Refugee camps the size of small cities have been built and dismantled. Refugee families enough to people a small country have been picked up from those camps and resettled throughout the world. Repatriation programmes – ranging from massive convoys moving 10,000 per week to modest trickles of hundreds per year – have been set in train. The international response has given rise to such innovative measures as the Orderly Departure Programme, anti-piracy and sea rescue efforts, and ambitious reintegration projects for returnees. It has also been party to more than its share of callous brutality, political manipulation, bureacratic incompetence, indifference and inertia.

The Indochinese camps in Southeast Asia are mostly closed or closing. An eight-year initiative known as the Comprehensive Plan of Action (CPA) has brought an end to the exodus of Laotian and Vietnamese asylum seekers and provided the means for the continued resettlement of refugees and special immigrants as well as the safe return home of those found not to meet international refugee criteria. The Cambodian civil war ended in 1991 with a fragile and somewhat piecemeal peace that enabled 360,000 refugees on the Thai–Cambodian border to return home. Political conflict in 1997 spawned a new exodus of Cambodian refugees but the death of the infamous Khmer Rouge leader, Pol Pot, in April 1998 held out at least some hope that Cambodia might finally lay its tragic past to rest.

It is a timely moment to look back and take stock of these events. How did the Indochinese exodus and the international response evolve? What were the decisive turning points or roads not taken? How do we chart the legacy of the last twenty years for the international refugee regime, for the countries involved and for the refugees and migrants themselves? How do we measure the achievements and failures? What has been left behind in Asia and what lessons can be drawn or models taken for use in other refugee situations around the world? It has been said that the Indochinese programme put UNHCR on the map. What roles has it played and what contributions did it make to resolving the dilemmas of the Indochinese exodus? And, in turn, what impact did that have on UNHCR?

Origins of the International Refugee Regime

'Refugees', noted Louise Holborn in her two-volume study of UNHCR, 'are an anomaly in a nation-state system.'[3] It is not surprising, then, that the first initiative toward an international refugee response came in the wake of the First World War as the new era of the nation-state began to emerge from the crumbling edifices of empire. In February 1921, a group of private relief agencies in Geneva made an appeal that the League of Nations appoint a Commissioner for Refugees to assist the 800,000 Russian refugees then scattered throughout Europe. On 20 August of the same year, the League appointed Dr Fridtjof Nansen, a Norwegian explorer and humanitarian, to the post of High Commissioner, a position he held until 1929.

With a threadbare budget and an even more limited mandate, Nansen worked tirelessly to bring relief and a proper solution to the plight of the refugees then languishing in Europe. In his first address to the Assembly of the League of Nations, he spoke plainly of the problems both he and the refugees were facing:

> Let the League of Nations come to their help and let us have no hypocrisy. Let us look at the facts as they are. The governments are at this moment not in a position to give £5 million sterling. They cannot rake up that sum which is merely half of what it costs to build a battleship. The food lies there in America but no one will fetch it. Is it possible that Europe can sit calmly and do nothing to bring food across and so save the people on the other side? I cannot believe it![4]

Among Nansen's most innovative and enduring initiatives was the creation of a Certificate of Identity, better known as the Nansen Passport, which offered Russian and other refugees both legal status in their country of residence and permission to travel. When Nansen died in 1930, the Office of the High Commissioner was temporarily renamed the Nansen Office, partly to honour his ground-breaking achievements and partly, one suspects, because governments could not agree on a more permanent name or broader mandate. Indeed, from 1930 to 1947, no fewer than five refugee organizations were created and disbanded, even as the League itself was dissolved and reconstituted as the United Nations.[5]

In November 1943, nearly two years before the UN charter was formally ratified at the San Francisco Opera House, 44 nations established the United Nations Relief and Rehabilitation Administration (UNRRA), making it, according to Holborn, 'the first UN agency to deal in a comprehensive way with refugees and displaced persons.'[6] At the Yalta Conference in February 1945, the big powers agreed to large-scale repatriation of displaced persons to the Soviet Union and UNRRA was tasked with the job. In all, UNRRA helped more than seven million war refugees to return to their countries of origin, not all of them voluntarily.[7] Among the nearly two million displaced persons who were returned to the Soviet Union by Allied Forces were 'a number of large groups who did not wish to be handed over to the Red Army. These mainly covered persons from countries or territories which had been annexed by the Soviet Union and who did not want to return.'[8] A number of those repatriations, wrote former UNHCR official Gervase Coles, 'had to be carried out by force, with not a few suicides.'

With the end of the Second World War, East–West relations deteriorated. The Cold War had begun and the United Nations was to become a strategic battlefield. As historian and refugee specialist Gil Loescher notes in his 1993 study *Beyond Charity*, 'Repatriation touched on the fundamental ideological conflicts dividing East and West. The core of the conflict concerned the rights of people to choose where they wanted to live, to flee from oppression, and to express their own opinions.'[9] The United States grew increasingly critical of UNRRA operations and refused to fund it beyond 1947. In its place, the American government worked to establish the International Refugee Organization (IRO), which, as Loescher notes had as its chief function not repatriation but the resettlement of refugees and displaced persons uprooted by World War II and its aftermath.... The Soviet Union favored the retention of UNRRA, both because of the aid it channeled to Eastern Europe and because its limited mandate – which favored repatriation over resettlement – accorded well with the official Soviet view that all those resisting repatriation were criminals or traitors.[10]

During the IRO's brief four-year existence, total expenditures ran to more than $400 million, of which the United States covered $250 million. Of the 1.6 million people assisted by the organization, more than one million were resettled in third countries – the bulk of them in the United States, Canada, Australia, Latin America and Israel – while only 73,000 chose to repatriate. Despite the IRO's successes in finding permanent homes for most of the displaced, by 1950 about 400,000 'hard-core' still remained in camps in Europe.[11]

It had become apparent to many of the Western nations that refugees were not simply vestigial remnants of the Second World War but a far more intractable, and growing, problem. But exactly whose problem they were, what solutions they required and who would pay for them were matters of some disagreement. The IRO had served its purpose, but what sort of agency should be created to take its place? The United States, suggests Holborn,

> as the dominant spokesman for the states of overseas resettlement, sought a strictly defined agency with narrow authority and limited function which would be temporary (lasting three years), require a small staff and little financing, and which would seek to achieve very limited objectives, notably the protection of the remaining IRO refugees until they were permanently settled and assimilated.[12]

The West European countries wanted, in effect, just the opposite. The United States, moreover, preferred to work outside the bounds of an increasingly polarized United Nations, at least when it came to refugee activities, while the West Europeans sought a permanent agency housed within the UN system.

On 14 December 1950 a fledgling organization, the United Nations High Commissioner for Refugees, was born, full of promise and compromise. Placed under the authority of the UN General Assembly, the office was established as a temporary body (the term of the first High Commissioner was limited to three years) to be financed largely by voluntary contributions.[13] But if UNHCR had been given a limited organizational structure, its mandate was large. The Statute of UNHCR gave it the responsibility 'of providing international protection, under the auspices of the United Nations, to refugees ... and of seeking permanent solutions for the problem of refugees by assisting Governments and ... private organizations to facilitate the voluntary repatriation of such refugees, or their assimilation within new national communities'.[14]

The definition for refugee established by statute encompassed not only refugees covered by the terms of the IRO constitution and other previous agreements but also 'Any other person who is outside the country of his nationality … because he has or had well-founded fear of persecution by reason of his race, religion, nationality or political opinion and is unable or, because of such fear, is unwilling to avail himself of the protection of the government of the country of his nationality'.[15] This gave UNHCR its own working definition of refugee. In July 1951 a small number of countries acceded to the Convention relating to the Status of Refugees, which gave states a common definition of the term. In this case, the definition of refugee both gained and lost. For the purposes of the Convention, a refugee was any person who,

> As a result of events occuring before 1 January 1951 and owing to well-founded fear of being persecuted for reasons of race, religion, nationality, membership of a particular social group or political opinion, is outside the country of his nationality and is unable, or owing to such fear, is unwilling to avail himself of the protection of that country.[16]

Membership of a particular social group was added to the other four reasons for a well-founded fear of persecution – race, religion, nationality or political opinion – but this now wider safety net could only be cast backwards in time to events occuring before January 1951. Some states further restricted the terms to events occurring in Europe. It was not until 1967 that a Protocol removed these temporal and geographical restrictions, though not all signatories to the 1951 Convention acceded to the 1967 Protocols.[17]

The first UN High Commissioner for Refugees, Dr G. J. van Heuven Goedhart, began his term with an annual budget of $300,000, a staff of 33 in Geneva, no field offices, and responsibility for nearly half a million refugees in Europe along with scattered numbers elsewhere. 'I found three empty rooms in the Palais des Nations,' he wrote, 'and I had to start from scratch.'[18] In 1952, the General Assembly finally authorized UNHCR's first appeal for funds, a modest $3 million. It would take three full years to raise that amount. The most conspicuous hold-out was the United States which, through most of the 1950s, sought to maintain a separate, almost unilateral, structure for refugee programmes outside the United Nations. In 1951, the United States and its allies established the Intergovernmental Committee for European Migration (ICEM). As Loescher writes, 'ICEM inherited the resettlement function of the IRO and was generously financed. It was established outside the United Nations, was administered almost exclusively by American directors, and was composed entirely of nations friendly to the United States.'[19] From 1952 to 1955, the US government spent $45 million on the United States Escapee Program to resettle refugees from the communist bloc while contributing a mere $500,000 toward the UNHCR budget. 'While creating and developing its own refugee institutions,' suggests Loescher, 'the United States treated the UNHCR almost as a sideshow.'[20]

In November 1956, however, Soviet troops crushed a brief uprising in Hungary and, before the borders were sealed, more than 200,000 Hungarians had slipped into neighbouring Austria and Yugoslavia. New refugee High Commissioner Auguste Lindt earned high marks from East and West alike for coordinating an international response that, within two years, managed to resettle nearly 200,000 Hungarians in third countries and negotiate the safe and voluntary return of another 18,000.[21]

In the wake of its first international success, UNHCR found itself called upon more and more frequently in times of crisis. In 1957, for the first time, the UN General Assembly authorized UNHCR to use its 'good offices' to assist Chinese refugees in Hong Kong even though they were not 'of concern' to the agency.[22] Two years later, another UN resolution extended the use of UNHCR's 'good offices' to all refugees 'who do not come within the competence of the United Nations'. In 1975, Resolution 3454 of the General Assembly affirmed 'the essentially humanitarian character of the activities of the High Commissioner for the benefit of refugees and *displaced persons*' (emphasis added).[23]

In mid-1975 UNHCR was still a rather small organization with no more than a few hundred employees and a worldwide budget of $50 million. Nevertheless, under the leadership of its fourth High Commissioner, Prince Sadruddin Aga Khan, UNHCR's special operations budget had grown thirty-fold since 1966 as it coordinated such significant relocations as the repatriation of ten million former residents of East Pakistan (mostly Bengalis) to the new state of Bangladesh in 1971, the return of 150,000 southern Sudanese refugees and displaced persons in 1972, and the resettlement of thousands of Asians thrown out of Uganda by President Idi Amin in the same year.[24]

In 1973, following the Paris peace agreements on Vietnam and Laos, UNHCR began to make overtures to the various parties – north and south, communist and otherwise – offering humanitarian aid to the millions of people internally displaced by war. At the end of 1973, the provisional Lao government estimated that at least 890,000 people had been internally displaced by hostilities. In South Vietnam alone, displaced persons and war refugees cumulatively numbered more than 10 million since 1954.[25]

In October 1974 UNHCR established a regional office in Vientiane, Laos, and in November that year it opened a branch office in Hanoi. With an estimated three million internally displaced persons in Cambodia, UNHCR hoped to establish an eventual presence in Phnom Penh as well. Although access to Cambodia would be five long years away, UNHCR undertook multi-million dollar projects to rehabilitate families uprooted by war in Laos and Vietnam.

No Middle Ground

In 1975, even as UNHCR was preparing to expand its presence in Southeast Asia, the United States was in a rush to disentangle itself from 15 years of conflict in Indochina that had killed 60,000 Americans and wounded 300,000 more, cost in excess of $100 billion, and deeply divided the country. The government was willing to evacuate a credible number of Vietnamese colleagues and their dependents, along with a token number of Cambodians and Laotians. Few people in the country, however, seemed eager to bring home reminders of the Indochinese tragedy or to involve themselves in its aftermath.

The upshot of all this was that when Nguyen Huu Thu showed up in Bangkok, he was not on anyone's agenda. The United States bucked him to UNHCR who bucked him to a local church who sent him to a hotel. When it got around to classifying Thu, the government of Thailand called him a displaced person although under Thai law he was an illegal immigrant. The United States was not prepared at the time to resettle Thu – or many of the thousands of other Indochinese who had begun drifting into Bangkok or camping on the borders – but it insisted from the outset that he was a refugee, not only to point the blame at the new communist regimes but to elicit international help in sharing the burden of assistance. UNHCR chose to call Thu and his like 'displaced persons outside of Indochina', partly because it saw Thu as an evacuee and thus an American responsibility and partly because it saw little or no reason at the time why he could not return.

Through all the twists and turns of the Indochinese exodus and the international response – and despite the consensus that sometimes was achieved in the pursuit of solutions – these views never were fully reconciled. The countries of asylum, the countries of resettlement and the countries of origin all held their own convictions as to what meaning the exodus carried and their own ways of acting and reacting to it. UNHCR, at times, simply bent to the prevailing winds and, at other times, sought to reshape fundamentally the terms of the debate. More often than not, the debate focused on the terms of refuge in Southeast Asia – how to define a refugee, how to preserve asylum, how to protect refugees and asylum seekers from abuse, how and in what measure to employ resettlement or promote repatriation, and, ultimately, how to bring the programme to some humane end.

Frequently, the terms took shape in stark dichotomies – *bona fide* refugee vs economic migrant, push factor vs pull factor, screened in vs screened out, resettlement vs repatriation. As simplistic, even misleading, as these contrary pairings could be, they revealed a disturbing truth: in the search for refuge in Southeast Asia, there was virtually no middle ground.

Notes

1 Author's interview with Nguyen Thu Huu, Ho Chi Minh City, 28 March 1996.
2 In James Fenton, 'The fall of Saigon', *The Best of Granta Reportage* (London: Granta Books, 1993), p. 84.
3 Louise W. Holborn, *Refugees: A Problem of Our Time* (Metuchen: The Scarecrow Press, 1975), p. 5.
4 Cited in Poul Hartling's Foreword to Yefime Zarjevski, *A Future Preserved: International Assistance to Refugees* (Oxford: Pergamon Press, 1988), p. xii.

5 These organizations included the International Nansen Office (1931–8), the Office of the High Commissioner for Refugees Coming from Germany and Austria (1933–9), the Office of the High Commissioner for Refugees Under the Protection of the League of Nations (1939–46) and the Intergovernmental Committee on Refugees (1938–47). See Holborn, *Refugees: A Problem for Our Time.*

6 *Ibid.*, p. 24.

7 Rosemarie Rogers and Emily Copeland, *Forced Migration: Policy Issues in the Post-Cold War World* (Medford, Mass: Tufts University, 1993) p. 33.

8 Gervase Coles, *Voluntary Repatriation: A Background Study*, Prepared for the Round Table on Voluntary Repatriation, San Remo, Italy, July 16–19, 1985. p. 30.

9 Gil Loescher, *Beyond Charity: International Cooperation and the Global Refugee Crisis* (New York and Oxford: Oxford University Press, 1993) p. 49.

10 *Ibid.*, p. 50.

11 Zarjevski, *A Future Preserved*, p. 9.

12 Holborn, *Refugees: A Problem for Our Time*, pp. 62–3.

13 See Zarjevski, *A Future Preserved*, p. 11.

14 UN High Commissioner for Refugees, *Collection of International Instruments Concerning Refugees* (Geneva: UNHCR, 1988) p. 5.

15 *Ibid.*, p. 7.

16 *Ibid.*, p. 11.

17 As of mid-1997, 131 UN member states were signatories to the UN Convention and Protocol relating to the Status of Refugees (three to the Convention only), and 54 were non-signatories. See US Committee for Refugees, *World Refugee Survey 1997* (Washington, DC: USCR, 1997) p. 9.

18 In Zarjevski, *A Future Preserved*, p. 76.

19 Loescher, *Beyond Charity*, p. 62.

20 *Ibid.*, p. 63.

21 For a discussion of the Hungarian refugee crisis of 1956, see Valerie O'Connor Sutter, *The Indochinese Refugee Dilemma* (Baton Rouge: Louisiana State University Press, 1990) pp. 23–49.

22 Zarjevski, *A Future Preserved*, p. 16. At the time, Taiwan was recognized by the UN as the legal government of China. Thus, the refugees theoretically had the protection of the Chinese government and, as such, were not considered to be 'of concern' to UNHCR.

23 *Ibid.*, p. 17.

24 See Zarjevski, *A Future Preserved*.

25 US Congress, Senate, Committee on the Judiciary, *Relief and Rehabilitation of War Victims in Indochina: One Year After the Ceasefire*, A Study Mission Report Prepared for the Use of the Subcommittee to Investigate Problems Connected with Refugees and Escapees, 93rd Congress, 2nd Session, 27 January 1974, p. 7. See also Louis A. Wiesner, *Victims and Survivors: Displaced Persons and Other War Victims in Viet-Nam, 1954–1975* (New York: Westport Press, 1988).

First Flight

Cambodia collapsed so suddenly that Thida Khus was a refugee before she even knew it. The Khmer mother of three had come to Thailand at the beginning of 1975 so her husband could take a faculty position in Bangkok. 'It didn't occur to us', she said, 'that we would be gone from Cambodia for a long time.'[1] In fact, her father owned a sawmill just over the Thai border in the village of Nimit. Thida was planning to go back for a family wedding when she heard the news that Phnom Penh had fallen. On 17 April 1975, the Communist Party of Kampuchea – more commonly known as the Khmer Rouge – captured Cambodia's capital city and launched a sweeping social revolution that would leave up to two million people dead and millions more displaced in its wake.[2]

The period 1968–75 had witnessed the exponential growth of Cambodian communist forces and an escalation of conflict nationwide. In 1970, the tortuous efforts by Cambodia's head of state, Prince Norodom Sihanouk, to maintain his country's neutrality in the face of the encroaching Vietnam War came to an end when he was ousted in a right-wing coup. The United States threw its weight behind General Lon Nol and his Khmer Republic while the North Vietnamese bolstered their support for the Khmer Rouge. The five-year civil war that ensued was both brutal and brutalizing. An estimated 500,000 people died and two million were uprooted.[3]

When the Khmer Rouge marched into Phnom Penh, they found a city swollen to four times its normal size with refugees. Some were fleeing the US saturation bombing that had laid waste their crops and villages; some came looking for food and shelter; and some, no doubt, already were fleeing the harsh regimen of the Cambodian communists. Beginning on 17 April the Khmer Rouge marched an estimated four to five million people out of Phnom Penh and the provincial townships. Many of the evacuees were told that the move was only temporary to avoid the threat of US retaliatory bombing. But on the day of Phnom Penh's 'liberation', Pol Pot, the elusive leader of the new Democratic Kampuchea, had issued an eight-point directive to his assembled cadres:

1 Evacuate people from all towns.

2 Abolish all markets.

3 Abolish Lon Nol regime currency and withhold the revolutionary currency that had been printed.

4 Defrock all Buddhist monks and put them to work growing rice.

5 Execute all leaders of the Lon Nol regime beginning with the top leaders.

6 Establish high-level cooperatives throughout the country with communal eating.

7 Expel the entire Vietnamese minority population.

8 Dispatch troops to the borders, particularly the Vietnamese border.[4]

Between 170,000 and 270,000 ethnic Vietnamese who were long-time residents of Cambodia were expelled in 1975.[5] Substantial numbers of Cambodians and ethnic Chinese residents took advantage of this expulsion to flee into Vietnam. Ha Duong Hui, a Chinese-Cambodian, was forced to evacuate Phnom Penh along with all the other city-dwellers. He was marched south to Takeo province. 'After a few weeks there,' he said, 'we were told to register our province of origin. I lied and said mine was Svay Rieng on the Vietnamese border. Once we got there, we were allowed to move on. I crossed the border into Vietnam in October 1975.'[6] Ha and his family made their way to Ho Chi Minh City. 'We heard that a lot of Cambodian refugees were living in a pagoda in Cholon,' the Chinese section of the city. 'There were a few hundred people when we arrived. We put our mats down and slept on the floor.'

Just days before the fall of Phnom Penh, the last American officials had evacuated the city in Operation 'Eagle Pull', taking with them into Thailand about 800 high-ranking Cambodians in the Lon Nol government. In the chaotic weeks before and after the Khmer Rouge victory, several thousand more Cambodians streamed toward the Thai border. François Ponchaud, a Catholic missionary in Cambodia (and among a group of foreigners evacuated into Thailand at this time) wrote: 'Most of these people were officers, officials, Chinese merchants or rich Khmer families. As they had been too involved with the Khmer Republic, they knew they would lose everything on the arrival of the Khmer Rouges.'[7]

Shortly after their takeover, the Khmer Rouge had announced on the radio that 'Our policy is not to allow foreigners to remain in our country.'[8] Among the first groups of refugees into Thailand were several foreign nationalities as well as ethnic and religious minorities, including Cambodian Muslims (also known as Cham), Indians, Pakistanis, and ethnic Thais. On 3 May about 600 foreigners who had been detained by the Khmer Rouge at the French Embassy in Phnom Penh drove across the Poipet bridge into Thailand.

'We went to the border to try to find our families,' said Thida.

We witnessed the arrival of the foreigners. I had cousins who married Frenchmen just to get out. My brother came out in April. My parents sent word, saying,

'Everything is OK. Now there is peace.' They stayed behind with another brother. My husband still thought things would get better, so we waited to go back to Cambodia. At first there were just rumours, then later we began to hear more clearly what was happening – the killings, the torture, the starvation. It cost money – up to $2,000 – for someone to get your family out for you. Very few got out. We had people looking for my family but the Khmer Rouge had moved them. We had no idea if they were alive or dead.

By the end of 1975, just over 17,000 Cambodian refugees had entered Thailand and were living in camps and temple sites from Surin to Trat. 'As the months passed,' wrote François Ponchaud,

> the greater became the flow of refugees and the lower the social level. Towards the end of 1975, the arrivals consisted of soldiers who had escaped extermination, workers and peasants whose motives were not ideological: they fled to save their lives as the iron discipline then in force prescribed death for any fault; furthermore there was a lack of food and medicaments and the conditions of life were such as to make this the only possible decision. In most cases, they had to leave their families behind, eke out a living in the forest for many weeks and cross a frontier which had been mined before arriving in Thailand in a state of utter physical and mental exhaustion. With the few belongings still in their possession taken from them by the Thai frontier police, sometimes beaten and imprisoned, they then joined the refugee camps.[9]

The Flight of the Hmong

Ever since 1954, when the French withdrew from Indochina and the three independent states of Cambodia, Laos and Vietnam were established, civil wars and internal conflicts had flared in all three countries. The Geneva Accords of 1954 – which had partitioned Vietnam temporarily into North and South, pending elections – had declared both Laos and Cambodia 'neutral' in the global Cold War and its local manifestation across their eastern borders. In Laos, not in Cambodia, leftist insurgents – the *Neo Lao Hak Sat* or Lao Patriotic Forces (better known as the *Pathet Lao*) – were provided a regroupment area in the provinces of Sam Neua and Phong Saly pending a political settlement, though all foreign military forces were banned from the country except for a small French mission in Vientiane. Thus, although Laos was not partitioned like Vietnam, it was a divided country nonetheless, and its 'neutrality' was a matter of international, though hardly internal, consensus.

A new set of Geneva Accords in July 1962 reaffirmed the neutrality of Laos, although the term was fast losing any semblance of reality. A tripartite government, composed of communist, royalist and neutralist parties, sat ineffectually in Vientiane, headed by Prince Souvanna Phouma, even as civil war raged in the Laotian countryside and foreign forces penetrated its sovereign borders on every side. North Vietnamese troops, present in Laos since at least 1959, were running men and war materiel down the Ho Chi Minh Trail into South Vietnam and the United States was flying in CIA operatives, Green Berets and Thai paramilitary units to train and arm a highland ethnic minority, the Hmong, in guerrilla warfare. Soviet airplanes dropped supplies to the Pathet Lao and Chinese labourers built roads in the north.

In January 1961 the CIA-run Operation Momentum began training a group of 1,000 Hmong, handpicked by their leader, Vang Pao, then a major in the Royal Lao Army. By the end of the year, the Hmong 'secret army' had grown to 10,000 men and, at its peak in 1967, to nearly 40,000.[10] By that time, however, US military objectives in Laos had been taken over by the enormous build-up in neighbouring Vietnam. Only two years after the first ground troops had entered the war, US armed forces in Vietnam numbered 431,000 and growing. The strategic interest in Laos, for the Americans, now lay in pinning down as many North Vietnamese troops as possible and thwarting movements on the Ho Chi Minh Trail. Increasingly, the Americans came to rely on massive air power and pitched battles. The small-scale guerrilla tactics of the Hmong were making them irrelevant; as the new face of the conflict forced them more and more into conventional warfare, they were becoming cannon fodder.

Hmong losses during the war were catastrophic. Between 18,000 and 20,000 were killed in combat, as many as 50,000 civilians were dead or wounded and, by 1973, 120,000 Hmong – nearly half of the entire population – were refugees in their own land.[11] In January 1973, the four parties to the Vietnamese conflict agreed to a ceasefire and terms for national reconciliation.[12] One month later, representatives of the Vientiane Government and the Pathet Lao signed a peace agreement in Vientiane, calling for a ceasefire, the withdrawal of all foreign armed forces, and the establishment of a Provisional Government of National Union.

As the US forces withdrew, however, the 'ceasefire war' intensified in Vietnam. In Laos, as more and more territory fell into the hands of the advancing Pathet Lao and North Vietnamese, the Hmong began looking for a way to counter the threat, or for a way out. But, either way, the Americans were making no commitments.[13] In the early days of Operation Momentum, CIA advisers had talked of Sayaboury province, west of the Mekong River and sharing a mountainous land border with Thailand, as a fall-back option, but nothing had ever come of it. By spring of 1975, with the Hmong stronghold of Long Cheng surrounded and a communist victory in Laos all but certain, the United States agreed to evacuate Vang Pao and his senior military officers along with their families.

On 13 and 14 May US transport planes carried about 2,500 Hmong out of Long Cheng and into Thailand, while thousands more crowded desperately onto the airstrip. 'The first announcement from Vang Pao was that women and children would go to Thailand and the men would fight back,' recalled Boua Yang, a major in the Hmong forces.[14] 'Later, quietly, Vang Pao told his colonels to go with their families. There was no plan to fight but there was no plan for everybody to leave either. By the second day, people were fighting and pushing to get onto the C-130s. Thousands were left waiting.'

Boua Yang and his family made it onto the last flight out of Long Cheng. 'We flew straight to the US airbase at Udorn and from there we were taken on trucks to Nam Phong,' a Thai military camp 50 miles farther to the south. 'Some Thai soldiers were there to meet us and the people who had come on the first day,' he said. 'I didn't see any Americans.'

When Pao Herr reached Long Cheng, he said, 'I saw the last planes leave as thousands of people were lined up crying. After a time, we started to realize that was it, so we picked up our belongings, regrouped and began to think about how to get across the river.'[15] Pao Herr had a student ID card which enabled him to get his family past the Pathet Lao checkpoint at the Hin Heup bridge and into Vientiane. (Two weeks later, the soldiers would fire on a group of several hundred unarmed Hmong trying to cross this same bridge, killing four to eight people and scattering thousands more who were massing in the area.)[16] Once in Vientiane, Pao Herr went out and scouted the Mekong River, looking for a safe place to cross. 'We paid a taxi driver a lot of money to take us out of town, jumped in a boat I had arranged to have waiting and crossed the river to Nong Khai.'

In Thailand, he found twenty to thirty other Hmong families sheltering in a Buddhist temple, Wat Samaky. 'We had no idea what would happen but the Thai people took care of us very well,' Pao Herr remembers. 'One family even offered us a bedroom to sleep in overnight.' They spent a week in Nong Khai before being transferred to the Nam Phong camp.

Hmong continued to pour into Thailand, along with other highland ethnic groups and lowland Lao with links to the Vientiane Government. In mid-June a group of 5,000 Hmong crossed the mountains into Nan Province from Sayaboury. According to one report, they were all suffering from 'malnutrition, malaria and a variety of related disease and ailments.'[17] By August, an estimated 12,000 Hmong, Mien and other ethnic minorities were living in Nan province in two camps, Pua and Sop Tuang. The population in Nong Khai was close to 11,000, including 7,000 Hmong, 2,000 Thai Dam, 500 Nung and about 1,400 lowland Lao who were former soldiers or government officials.[18] All told, counting Nam Phong and a small camp for lowland Lao in Ubon, Laotian refugees in Thailand numbered more than 36,000 in August 1975 and 54,000 by the end of the year. And these figures counted only those who sought assistance in the camps; an equal number were believed to be living on their own or with friends and relatives throughout northeastern Thailand.

The First Wave of Vietnamese

On 2 September 1945, within weeks of the Japanese surrender to the Allied forces, Ho Chi Minh proclaimed an independent Democratic Republic of Vietnam. But the French, who had been driven out of Indochina by the

Japanese a few years earlier, moved quickly to reassert control of their former colonies in Cambodia, Laos, and Vietnam. From 1946 to 1948, about 50,000 Vietnamese, mainly from the North but several thousand of whom had been living in Laos or Cambodia, escaped the First Indochina War by fleeing into Thailand. Pridi Phanomyong, founder of the Free Thai Movement and an elder statesman in Thai government from 1944 to 1947, openly sympathized with the anti-French movements. His government permitted the Viet Minh, Ho Chi Minh's nationalist revolutionary movement, to open an office in Bangkok and made no move to halt rebel shipments through Thailand.[19]

In November 1947, however, the Pridi government was overthrown in a military coup and Thai politics began a nearly 30-year swing toward the right. The military-backed governments of Phibun Songkhram and his successors aligned themselves with the Western powers and against communism, be it of Chinese or Indochinese extraction. Not coincidentally, the Chinese and Vietnamese communities in Thailand fell under strong suspicion of subversion, from which it took decades to free themselves.

The 1954 Geneva Accords, which partitioned Vietnam at the 17th parallel into a communist North and republican South, also provided a 300-day grace period for civilians to move freely into or out of either zone. Despite what one observer called 'administrative obfuscation' from the government of Vietnam in the South and a 'propaganda campaign' carried out by the United States, between 130,000 and 140,000 Viet Minh supporters moved North, most of them transported by Polish and Soviet ships.[20] Likewise, those wishing to go South faced what a Canadian member of the International Control Commission (ICC) called 'comprehensive North Vietnamese propaganda and police and administrative measures to dissuade or restrain them'.[21] Despite the obstructions, a total of 928,000 civilians moved south in 1954–55 along with 120,000 military and quasi-military personnel. South Vietnamese figures showed that, of the civilians, 98 per cent were ethnic Vietnamese and the other two per cent were highland minorities (principally Nung); 85 per cent were Catholics and the remainder Buddhists and Protestants; 76 per cent were farmers, 10 per cent were fishermen and the remaining 14 per cent were artisans, small businessmen, students, government employees and professionals.[22]

In his study of Vietnamese war refugees from 1954 to 1975, Louis Wiesner asks the question, 'Why would almost a tenth of the population of North Vietnam, attached to their land, homes, possessions, jobs and associations, leave all these behind after a victory which made the Viet Minh so popular in the country that, in the opinion of at least one historian, they would have won in any free elections?'[23] First, the French Union forces were required to withdraw, along with the National Army of Vietnam, which brought out many family dependents as well as those associated with the French presence. Second, 'many Catholics were persecuted for practising their religion and others feared that they would be.' Others may have had 'reasons to hate and fear the Communists, especially if they had been wealthy or had collaborated with the French'. Still others complained of hard work without pay, high taxes and 'intense Communist indoctrination'. Finally, Wiesner adds the factor of 'overpopulation of the North, which for generations had pushed Vietnamese down to the underpopulated South'.[24]

The impact of this southern exodus on both governments and the widening rift between them, he suggests, was enormous.

> Many – some say too many – of South Vietnam's civilian and military leaders in subsequent years sprang from the refugees, especially the Catholics. The religious balance of Vietnam as a whole was drastically altered by the exodus. In the North, the number of Catholics declined from 1,133,000 to 457,000 while the number in the South jumped from 461,000 to 1,137,000, or one in every 9.6 inhabitants. In 1956, the Diocese of Saigon had more practicing Catholics than Paris or Rome and about the same number as New York City. However, the transfer of so many strongly anti-Communist Catholics and others who were embittered by their treatment at the hands of the Viet Minh was a significant factor in the polarization of the two parts of Vietnam and the unwillingness of the leaders on both sides to reach a compromise solution of their conflict.[25]

Shortly after Ngo Dinh Diem, a Catholic patrician, became president of the Republic of Vietnam in October 1955, he began a series of ambitious social engineering schemes designed to consolidate control through population relocations. Much of his attention was focused on the Central Highlands, straddling the strategic border zone between North and South, and home to an estimated one million people from 20 different ethnic groups. The land development programme sought to reclaim supposedly unused land in the highlands, along with millions of hectares in the Mekong Delta, for settlers from overcrowded urban areas. At the same time, Diem's highlander resettlement programme moved tens of thousands of Montagnard families out of their mountain homes, ostensibly to regroup them in more secure areas but mainly to free up more land for Vietnamese settlers.[26]

North Vietnam, it so happened, had many of the same plans for the Central Highlands with virtually the same motives: 'to move surplus populations, including troublesome elements (who in the North were private traders, vagrants and petty thieves) from the coastal plains; strengthen control in areas that were inhabited by the less patriotic ethnic minorities, ultimately producing a Vietnamese majority; increase security in the very regions that had been used by the Viet Minh as sanctuaries during the French war; and open up previously uncultivated land.'[27]

As the conflict escalated in the early 1960s and National Liberation Front forces (otherwise known as the Viet Cong) penetrated deeper into the South, the Diem regime borrowed a page from the British efforts against communist insurgency in Malaya and instituted a 'strategic hamlet' programme. Operation Sunrise, which began in October 1962, aimed to relocate villages in contested areas inside fortified perimeters. Once behind these bamboo barricades, the resolve of the villagers to resist the communists would likewise be fortified through self-defence training and government-funded development programmes.

Designed to build popular support for the South Vietnamese government, the 'strategic hamlet' programme probably weakened it overall as hundreds of thousands of villagers were forced into new settlements and saw their old homes burned behind them. By mid-1963, the Diem government was claiming that more than eight million people, including 200,000 Montagnards, were living in about 6,000 completed hamlets.[28]

President Diem was assassinated in November 1963 and the 'strategic hamlets' programme collapsed with his government. As Wiesner writes, 'This was the last nationwide governmental attempt to fit the South Vietnamese people into the Procrustean bed of rigid dogma until the Communists, after their victory of 1975, tried it their way.'[29]

But the massive displacements caused both by military destruction and by civilian design were taking their toll. By the time the first US ground troops landed in Danang in March 1965, more than half a million Vietnamese were refugees within their own country. Each year added hundreds of thousands more to the lists of refugees, evacuees and war victims. By 1973, when the Paris Peace Accords were signed and the last US forces were withdrawn, a total of about ten million people had been displaced in South Vietnam since 1954.

In 1975, the People's Army of Vietnam launched a final offensive against the South. By March, PAVN troops had taken Ban Me Thuot and Danang and were pushing hard toward Saigon, driving more than two million panicked soldiers and civilians in front of them. When Saigon fell at the end of April, more than half of the entire South Vietnamese population had been uprooted at least once in the previous two decades.

Three days after the last Americans had been evacuated from Phnom Penh on 12 April, Senator Edward M. Kennedy, chairman of the Senate Subcommittee to Investigate Problems Connected with Refugees and Escapees, called a hearing to discuss the government's evacuation plan for Vietnam. The ranking witness for the Administration was Philip C. Habib, Assistant Secretary of State for East Asian and Pacific Affairs, who insisted on discussing details only in a confidential, 'executive session' with the committee members. Otherwise, he said, 'you create … fears on the part of the people concerned'.[30] In other words, talking publicly about a big evacuation might make it more so.

Once behind closed doors, Habib sketched out the Administration's plan, such as it was. First priority in the evacuation went to an estimated 3,839 American citizens and their dependants, followed by 1,870 foreign dependants and about 1,000 members of foreign diplomatic missions. 'Now, we get into the big number,' said Habib: 'Vietnamese who work for any element of the US mission.' These numbered 17,600 and, counting their dependants, up to 130,000. Finally, he said, 'there is another element that is in a high-risk category for which, frankly, we don't have a figure'. Habib included in this category 'government officials and the military and the police and security authorities'. The total 'benchmark figure' for the evacuation, Habib told the Senate, was 200,000.[31]

On 21 April South Vietnam's President Nguyen Van Thieu resigned, with a bitter condemnation of the United States for abandoning its ally. The following day, the Senate Judiciary Committee approved parole for more than 150,000 Indochinese, including 50,000 'high-risk' Vietnamese and the evacuation began in earnest.[32] As the Pentagon positioned more than two dozen aircraft carriers, destroyers and merchant marine vessels off the Vietnamese coast, civil and military authorities on Guam prepared temporary facilities for 50,000 refugees.

During the next week, more than 7,500 people a day were flown out of Saigon's Tan Son Nhut airport to Clark Air Force Base in the Philippines or directly to Guam. On 29 April, when North Vietnamese rocket attacks on Tan Son Nhut halted the fixed-wing evacuation, the US launched Operation 'Frequent Wind' which carried nearly 7,000 by helicopter to aircraft carriers waiting off shore. In all, the United States directly evacuated by air or boat about 65,000 Vietnamese. Another 65,000 Vietnamese got out on their own.

> Many had access to planes or boats or were armed and could commandeer transportation. Vietnamese air force pilots took their planes, loaded them with family, girlfriends, or mistresses, or hired out space at more than $10,000 per person and flew to US bases in Thailand. Vessels of the Vietnamese navy evacuated families of crew members and friends and headed for Subic Bay in the Philippines. Other Vietnamese fled by sea in small fishing boats, barges, rafts, and floats and were picked up by friendly ships. Still others fled overland through Laos and Cambodia to Thailand.[33]

On 18 April President Gerald Ford had formed a Special Interagency Task Force for Indochina Refugees, charged with the coordination of 18 federal agencies responsible for evacuating the refugees, providing them with temporary care and securing their resettlement either in the United States or in other countries. Gradually, the Task Force's 'Operation New Life' began to register the more than 140,000 who had been brought to Guam. Frances Fitzgerald, author of the Pulitzer Prize-winning book, *Fire in the Lake: The Vietnamese and the Americans in Vietnam*, wrote in the *New York Times* magazine,

> What figures there were indicated that about half of the adults spoke some English, a quarter had university educations, a third were Catholics and the population as a whole was very young. Of those who answered the Task Force questionnaire, about a sixth were former US Government employees (10,000 people) and there were as many enlisted men (7,000) as there were officers. The survey did not, of course, register the number of prostitutes, dope dealers or generals, and it did not show that the population included almost all the inhabitants of one fishing village and a Saigon rock band.[34]

A team of researchers in Camp Pendleton – one of the four military bases in the continental US where the Vietnamese were housed pending their resettlement with sponsors – discovered something else about the evacuees: the majority of heads of household had lived in North Vietnam prior to 1954.[35]

Overall, it was estimated that only about 55,000 of those accepted for US resettlement fell within the parole guidelines. 'The bulk of the escapees', concluded Wiesner,

> were soldiers, small merchants, farmers, fishermen, housemaids, bar girls, and others who by no stretch of the imagination could be characterized as high-risk.... That it brought out many thousands who were not seriously at risk is understandable and not a tragedy. What is harder to understand and to excuse is that so many genuinely endangered people were left behind.[36]

Asked in mid-April what the United States would do if 200,000 Vietnamese were evacuated, Philip Habib replied, 'We would hope that the international machinery would take them and spread them around the world if they come out.'[37] In hopes of spreading some of the refugees around the world, the Task Force had invited UNHCR to maintain a presence in Guam and in the processing camps in the United States.

The international machinery responded only sluggishly, however. Canada resettled about 2,000 from Guam and another 1,000 were taken by France or other European countries. The prevailing sentiment was that the refugees were an American responsibility. Even Vietnam seemed to agree. Shortly after arriving in Guam, some evacuees insisted that they had never intended to leave Vietnam and wished to return immediately. The Task Force referred the matter to UNHCR who asked for time to take the matter up with the new authorities in the South. Neither the US State Department nor the Vietnamese Foreign Ministry were keen on the idea.

The list of would-be returnees, many of them former military, grew to nearly 2,000 and at the end of August, as a gesture of impatience, some of the group burned their barracks at Camp Asan on Guam and US marshalls were sent in to restore order. As Julia Vadala Taft, former director of the Task Force recalls,

> They were demonstrating, making Molotov cocktails, threatening to cut off their fingers and mail them to President Ford. It was a mess. Finally, I decided that our program was intended to bring in people voluntarily. We could not make them stay. We had this Vietnamese cargo ship, the *Thuong Tin I* and decided we would put them on it. The State Department was not pleased and neither was UNHCR. UNHCR wanted Vietnam to give its OK first but basically it did not want to disturb Vietnam and offered nothing in the way of assistance. We developed a system on Guam where we provided a safe place to interview each person privately. People could say whether they wanted to go back or not: Door A, they went back to camp, Door B, they went to the boat.... The US government stocked the ship, the refugees painted it and set sail in October 1975. UNHCR felt it would become the Flying Dutchman.[38]

On 16 October, the *Thuong Tin I* left Guam with 1,546 people aboard.

Eight days later, it sailed into Cam Ranh Bay where the Provisional Revolutionary Government permitted the returnees to disembark but denounced the unilateral US action. 'We found out about one year later', said Taft, 'that most of the group was placed in re-education camps.' In a May 1976 interview with *Le Monde*, a senior Vietnamese official said, 'We are investigating each case in order to find out what their intentions are.' One news report indicated that a naval lieutenant, Vu Tien Hai, had been executed as a spy shortly after his arrival.[40]

The International Response

By the middle of 1975, Indochinese refugees in Thailand were living in 21 temporary camps along the Lao and Cambodian borders and on the coast. In July of that year, the Thai government signed an initial agreement with UNHCR, under which Thailand pledged to provide temporary assistance to the new arrivals – including food, shelter, clothing and medical care – while UNHCR sought international contributions of cash, materials, equipment and services. In August, UNHCR launched an appeal for $12.4 million to cover needs through the end of 1976. The basic agreement was extended many more times but its limits were established at the outset:

> the High Commissioner and the Government have agreed to collaborate in a program for the purpose of providing humanitarian aid to Displaced Persons from Cambodia, Laos and South Vietnam.... [T]he two parties have also agreed to collaborate in seeking durable solutions, including in particular voluntary repatriation and resettlement in other countries.[41]

Notably absent from this agreement, and from all the other agreements UNHCR signed with other governments in the region, were any commitments to provide asylum, protection and possibly local settlement for any of these displaced persons outside their country. There is no mention of refugees at all. The only nod toward protection was the qualification of return as 'voluntary'.

At the time of the initial exodus of Indochinese in 1975, not one country in Asia had acceded to the 1951 Convention or the 1967 Protocol. It is hardly likely that Thailand or any of the other Southeast Asian countries, even if pressed by UNHCR, would have acknowledged a fundamental obligation to offer asylum to Indochinese in 1975. UNHCR, in any event, was not pressing the point. Its sights at the time were set on voluntary repatriation.

In June 1975, two months after the fall of Saigon, the Liaison Bureau of the Provisional Revolutionary Government of South Vietnam sent a letter to UNHCR saying that it was willing, on a case by case basis, to take back 'those Vietnamese who had recently been induced to leave their country by false propaganda or who had been taken abroad against their will and who wished to be repatriated.' The next day, High Commissioner Sadruddin Aga Khan held a press conference to announce receipt of the offer. He said that

> based on our experience, voluntary repatriation can be the happiest of solutions, though it is seldom the easiest.... I would like to express a note of caution that solutions for all will not be found overnight. Unlike many situations that my Office has faced in the past, this was not a mass exodus across a frontier to a neighbouring country. The Vietnamese situation is much more complex. Different groups in different situations are involved and it will take time to sort it out. However, it has been our experience that while these operations might begin slowly, they gain momentum as the return begins.[42]

When Prince Sadruddin arrived in Thailand for a week-long visit in September, he announced confidently that 'This present emergency should not last.'[43] From what he could see at the time, the 60,000 Indochinese in Thailand and the 12,000 Vietnamese scattered throughout the region were an aftermath of the US evacuation which was itself an aftermath of war. Those who were not resettled in the United States or other countries would soon be able to go home. The US government, however, saw things somewhat differently.

In November 1975, at a meeting of the Third Committee of the UN General Assembly in New York, Prince Sadruddin updated member states about the three special operations his office had undertaken to assist displaced Indochinese inside and outside their country. The first involved a $12 million programme to rehabilitate families uprooted by war in Vietnam and Laos. Through an arrangement with the Provisional Government of National Union, UNHCR had transported more than 35,000 people from Vientiane to their home areas in the Plain of Jars and provided them with agricultural equipment and rice through the next harvest. In North Vietnam, UNHCR was distributing yarn for textile production and machinery for poultry breeding.

Rehabilitation projects in the South, however, had been put on hold with the displacement of over two million people in March and April 1975. As the North Vietnamese Army pushed toward Saigon, UNHCR, UNICEF and other international organizations mounted an emergency relief operation to bring in more than 22,000 tons of food, medicine, clothing and temporary shelter material. By September, the emergency was over but the new government of a unified Vietnam was seeking continued UNHCR assistance in helping those displaced by war to return to their homes.

Finally, Prince Sadruddin noted, UNHCR had been called upon 'to assist with the voluntary repatriation and resettlement of thousands of displaced persons from Cambodia, Laos and Vietnam'. All these efforts, he emphasized, 'must be seen in totality, as distinct yet interrelated humanitarian actions, designed to assist those who had been most seriously uprooted by war and its consequences'.[44] The US representative, Haugh, preferred to see these operations as distinct. He commended the High Commissioner for his 'excellent' report, then proceeded to drop rather large hints about what he found missing from the discussion.

'The refugee', noted Haugh

> fled from his homeland as an individual who had been deprived of his human rights and it was noteworthy that the High Commissioner directed his program of international protection and material assistance to the refugee as an individual and that each project was geared to the rehabilitation of the refugee and the restoration of his faith and hope in humanity.

The United States clearly was preoccupied with Thailand, whose 70,000 Indochinese, Haugh said, presented UNHCR 'with a grave challenge.... Although many of those refugees would be remaining in Thailand, there was a compelling need to locate resettlement opportunities in third countries for large numbers whose local integration would not prove feasible.' Even more so than with the Vietnamese, America wanted to share the Laotian and Cambodian burdens around. 'The problem in Thailand', said Haugh, 'could be resolved only through the effective response of the international community as a whole.'

Finally, Haugh stressed

> that the increased scope of UNHCR's material assistance program and the repeated calls upon the High Commissioner to use his 'good offices' in special situations should not be allowed to impede or to infringe upon the High Commissioner's first priority, which was to provide effective international protection for refugees.

The United States clearly wanted to establish that the Indochinese in Thailand and elsewhere were not displaced persons outside their countries, but refugees. The point, in an obvious sense, was political: these people were not fleeing an old conflict, the Americans were saying, but a new fear of reprisal at the hands of the communist regimes and that should be acknowledged by UNHCR and the international community. Helping the refugees was not necessarily interrelated with assisting the displaced persons in Indochina. If Prince Sadruddin's comments avoided mention of refugees, notably absent from Haugh's discussion was any reference to repatriation.

The United States had another motive at the same time, which was perhaps more tactical than ideological. Refugees were UNHCR's main concern, its stock in trade. An appeal to protect and provide durable solutions for refugees was more likely to attract a broad international response than one which couched the issue in terms of a special operation for displaced persons. The United States had already contributed $8.6 million to UNHCR's initial appeal for $12.4 million for Thailand and had accepted 10,000 for resettlement above and beyond the 130,000 absorbed in the initial evacuation. Henceforth, Haugh was suggesting, the world might look to the United States to take the lead but other countries must do their share.

Outside of Thailand, UNHCR's main job in Southeast Asia in 1975 was locating the several thousand Vietnamese who had landed in half a dozen different countries, offering temporary assistance and getting them resettled as quickly as possible. In Hong Kong, on 4 May, a Danish container ship, the *Clara Maersk*, offloaded 3,743 boat people rescued in the South China Sea. That same day, on the Malaysian island of Pulau Perhentian, 47 Vietnamese came ashore. Shortly thereafter, Indonesia found its first boat people on Pulau Laut. Singapore permitted transit of nearly 2,000 in the wake of the US evacuation and even offered permanent settlement to 110 fishermen. The Vietnamese rejected the offer, preferring to seek resettlement in the West.

The first boat people that landed in the Philippines – aside from the thousands of evacuees who transited the US military bases at Subic and Clark on their way to the United States – included 2,600 Vietnamese dependants of Filipino overseas workers. A Catholic group, the Daughters of Charity, formed the Center for Assistance to Displaced Persons (CADP) to help these common-law wives and their children establish themselves. 'They had no marriage documents, no status,' said Sister Pascale Le thi Triu, a Vietnamese nun who directed CADP. 'Some found their husbands had wives back in the Philippines. Some of the women were placed in jail for bigamy. The men ran faster and went back abroad.'[45]

As the months wore on, small boats kept turning up from time to time. It was by no means a crisis but President Ferdinand Marcos wanted it stopped. In August 1975, just after a boatload of 84 people arrived on Palawan island, Marcos commanded the Philippine Coast Guard to re-provision the boat with fuel, food and water and order it 'to sail to Hawaii'.[46] A local cleric alerted the Catholic Bishops Conference of the Philippines, whose appeal to Marcos caused him to rescind the order. The Philippines made threats occasionally but never turned away another boat.

Throughout most of 1975, as UNHCR was coming to terms with the first wave of the exodus, it relied heavily on local counterparts for assistance. CADP not only provided emergency relief and advocacy in the Philippines but helped process cases for overseas resettlement. In Malaysia, it was the Malaysian Red Crescent Society that came to the rescue of the first Vietnamese boats, winning a UNHCR Nansen Medal in 1977 for what Prince Sadruddin called its 'profoundly humane attitude'.[47] Indonesia enlisted its national Red Cross.

In Thailand, the Ministry of Interior formed the Operations Center for Displaced Persons in June 1975 but both the national and international relief effort got off to a very slow start. As one assessment put it,

> No local or international relief agencies were prepared for such an influx of refugees into Thailand – and Thai authorities, not without some justification, assumed that the United States would accept the major responsibility for the refugees. Moreover, the small regional office of the UNHCR had neither the staff nor the funds to immediately respond to the growing refugee crisis.... At least through August of 1975, relief efforts were ad hoc at best and nonexistent in

many areas. Conditions among the refugees became increasingly desperate. And as their numbers increased squalid refugee shanty-towns popped up in the border areas and elsewhere.[48]

If there was a relief effort at all in the summer of 1975, it was due mainly to the work of a number of private agencies, both Thai and international. In early July, a group of seven voluntary organizations met in Bangkok to discuss the growing refugee problem. On 19 September, a group of ten agencies formed the Committee for the Coordination of Services to Displaced Persons in Thailand (CCSDPT).[49] Through regular weekly or monthly meetings and close cooperation with the Thai government, UNHCR and the International Committee of the Red Cross, CCSDPT proved invaluable in reducing duplication of efforts and covering gaps. In little more than one year, its member agencies had contributed $2.7 million in services and supplies to the burgeoning refugee populations.

'Without the contributions of the voluntary agencies,' concluded a 1976 report from the US Senate, 'especially in the early days, and their effective efforts to coordinate their work, the refugee situation today in Thailand would be far more desperate, and many thousands of refugees would have died of neglect.'[50] The question was: what next?

In May 1975, at the urging of the United States, UNHCR had issued a worldwide appeal for commitments to resettle the Indochinese displaced outside their country. Twenty-four countries responded positively, with pledges ranging from a few families to several thousand people. By the end of the year, Canada had resettled 5,200 Vietnamese, France had taken 4,500, Malaysia had resettled 1,200 Cambodian Muslims and Australia had absorbed 700. At the small end of the scale, Iran took 16 and the Ivory Coast resettled 10. On top of the 134,000 Indochinese already resettled as part of the evacuation, the US government was shortly to approve admission of an additional 11,000 Indochinese stranded in the region. But of all those resettled as of December 1975, only about 5,000 had been taken from Thailand, leaving 80,000 scattered along the kingdom's borders, still waiting for a solution.

From the beginning of the Indochinese exodus, UNHCR had favoured the solution of voluntary repatriation but it soon became apparent that this was not a hugely popular option either with the refugees or the new governments in their countries of origin. The next best thing was local settlement and UNHCR offered Thailand various inducements to pursue the idea. In November 1976, Prince Sadruddin proposed a scheme under which UNHCR would continue feeding the refugees if Thailand agreed to let them settle permanently. The Thai government rejected the proposal. UNHCR's March 1977 appeal for $12.35 million to assist refugees in Thailand earmarked $2 million for self-help projects in the camps, which UN officials hoped would be a stepping-stone to local integration. However, the continued high rate of influx forced UNHCR to spend the bulk of its funds on food, medical care and new construction. By September of that year, less than 1 per cent of the budget for self-reliance projects had been spent or even committed.

The United States, too, had been hopeful that many of the refugees in Thailand, who numbered 100,000 at the end of 1977, would be absorbed locally. 'With the passage of time,' said one government report,

> voluntary repatriation has ceased to be an immediately realistic alternative. Overseas resettlement helps Thailand. But local settlement is clearly inevitable for a substantial number of the refugees. For several categories of refugees, local settlement is not only the more realistic but perhaps also the more humane solution.

The report singled out Hmong and Cambodian farmers as well as Lao shopkeepers and tradesmen. It continued:

> The [Thai] government has always recognized the need for some local settlement and has agreed, in principle, with UNHCR's proposals for the local settlement of refugees; the only question is timing. The Thai government has progressively encouraged self-sufficiency among the refugees in camp but has shied away from implementing local settlement as long as the influx of people continues. Rightly or wrongly, the Thais have feared that moving on a program of local settlement would simply encourage a heavier influx.[51]

In May 1978, on a trip to Thailand, US Vice-President Walter Mondale pledged $2 million to support local settlement for Indochinese refugees. A Thai inter-agency committee examined the proposal seriously and, in mid-May, Prime Minister Kriangsak Chomanand confirmed that 'We are examining how many persons we accept for local settlement.' Additional international funding, he suggested, could be persuasive. 'Though we want to help them, we cannot afford to hurt ourselves financially.'[52] The Ministry of Interior's 1978 annual report on Indochinese displaced persons, likewise, held the door open if only slightly.

> While it is easy to suggest all displaced persons be permitted to resettle in Thailand, even if funding were on hand, political and national security matters coupled with the shortage of arable land makes it impossible for us to consider this alternative. Thailand still has hundreds of thousands of landless farmers; in addition we are experiencing difficulties in assimilating the more than 70,000 Vietnamese refugees who came to our country in 1945. We are, however, in spite of these two major obstacles, studying the possibility of permitting some of the displaced persons to resettle here.[53]

In early September 1978 former Danish prime minister and the new High Commissioner for Refugees, Poul Hartling, stopped in Thailand on his first tour of Southeast Asia. He praised Thai generosity in sheltering the refugees and pledged $25 million in aid for the year. Following a two-day inspection of the camps in Nong Khai, Aranyaprathet, and Laem Sing, Hartling suggested that some refugees were not likely to be resettled in France or the United States; local settlement for them could be a 'necessity'.[54]

Chinese from Vietnam

In 1975, the Vietnamese economy was in desperate shape, with more than eight million unemployed in the South alone. Virtually overnight, the US infusion of $700 million in annual foreign aid dried up. Both sides in the conflict, moreover, had come to rely on massive food aid from their backers. Agricultural production had declined and the country faced a food deficit of more than six million tons. Adding to these problems were the large numbers of refugees and migrants who had flocked to the cities during the war, seeking safety and opportunity. Saigon alone was home to four million people, one-fifth of the population in the South.[55]

In order to increase food production, Hanoi reasoned, it was necessary to reclaim lands abandoned during the war. To reclaim the land, it was necessary to redeploy some of the labour force. This would involve moving people from the North to central and southern Vietnam and from the cities to the countryside. But the massive population relocation programmes that Vietnam launched in 1975 had as much (if not more) to do with politics as economics.

Soon after the Provisional Revolutionary Government took power in the South, it began to promote a 'Return to the Village' programme, targeting the war refugees in Saigon and other cities. In order to participate in the programme, however, the villages had to have arable land and a good revolutionary record. Its former residents, moreover, had to want to return. Those who were landless when they left or had grown used to life in the cities were not likely to be lured back with a promise of free transportation and a three-month supply of rice.

In July 1976, when North and South were officially reunified as the Socialist Republic of Vietnam, relocation efforts shifted into a higher gear. Earlier that year, in April, the Fourth Party Congress had approved the development of New Economic Zones (NEZs) as the keystone of a new, five-year development plan. In this phase of relocations, the movements were by no means all voluntary and the targets were not all former peasants. One government directive listed some of the groups slated for rural resettlement: 'The unemployed or semi-employed; traders; those who have capital; students who cannot pursue their studies; officers, officials and personnel of the old regime; relatives of those undergoing reeducation; the Chinese; members of religious minorities; and skilled machinery workers.'[56]

In early May 1975 the revolutionary authorities had ordered all low-ranking soldiers and policemen (non-commissioned officer and below) as well as former civil servants and members of political parties to attend a three-day term of re-education. At the end of the session, each person wrote a paper demonstrating his or her understanding of the new political realities and then was issued a re-education release certificate. Several weeks later, the government issued another communique, this time inviting senior military officers and high-ranking government officials to report to designated localities in Saigon by June 15 to undergo one month of re-education.

More than one million people undertook the three-day re-education course and were promptly released. As many as 200,000 were held for several years or more, and perhaps 40,000 were detained for up to twelve years, without trial or sentence, in conditions of punishing deprivation. For many prisoners, the very arbitrariness of the terms of their detention was especially cruel. 'Once, I asked a cadre when I might be released,' related one former prisoner, 'and he answered, "When you are well re-educated in your thoughts, you will be released." I asked him, "How do I know when I am well re-educated?" He answered: "That's easy. When you are released, then you will know that you have been well re-educated." '[57] The family members of re-education camp prisoners not only waited out the years in the same uncertainty but generally were blacklisted by the communist authorities, which led to confiscation of property, denial of citizenship rights as well as education and employment opportunities, and removal to NEZs. By early 1977, demographer Jacqueline Desbarats estimates that 850,000 were relocated to NEZs. Of the 700,000 moved from Saigon, by now officially renamed Ho Chi Minh City, about 400,000 had returned to home villages while the rest went to NEZs:

> Most NEZs were very primitive, and life was extremely harsh. People who escaped from the NEZs described the conditions as uniformly bad. Officially, settlers were supposed to receive 6 months' worth of food supplies, some seeds and tools and a hut. But most of the time, they found no housing facilities whatsoever, and sometimes no source of drinking water. These urban dwellers lacking farming skills, resentful of their new assignments, often malnourished because of delays in the distribution of government food supplies, existed on the edge of starvation. Lack of medicines increased the incidence of disease. Malaria and dysentery were rampant, pneumonia and skin diseases widespread. Mosquitoes and poisonous snakes added to the difficulties of NEZ life. Shortages of all kinds and poor sanitary conditions caused such hardship and deprivation that death rates rose, particularly among young children and the aged.[58]

Not all the NEZs were equally bad – some even were reserved for families of communist cadres – but some of the most marginal and insecure zones were those established hard by the Cambodian border. As cross-border conflicts between Vietnam and the Khmer Rouge escalated throughout 1977 and 1978, relocation to NEZs in Tay Ninh, Long An, and Song Be could prove both difficult and dangerous.

As the new socialist system pressed down, boat departures picked up in mid-1977 after a near two-year lull. By the end of the year, more than 15,600 Vietnamese had reached the shores of first asylum countries in Southeast Asia. Malaysia got the most – an omen of things to come – followed closely by Thailand, which had 5,300 Vietnamese arriving by boat and overland through Laos and Cambodia.

Boat outflows continued to rise dramatically throughout 1978. UNHCR figures for September showed 7,300 Vietnamese arrivals in Southeast Asia, the highest monthly total since the end of the Vietnam War. About 70 per cent of the boat people were Vietnamese of Chinese origin. In October 1978, the number of boat people arriving in the region nearly doubled to 14,000, including 10,000 to Malaysia alone. The boats had grown larger, too, from an average of 35 to 40 people per boat in September to between 180 and 400 in October. Along with the arrival figures and the size of the boats, evidence mounted that the refugees on board were both pawns and players in a lucrative and well-organized racket involving Hong Kong syndicates and Vietnamese officials who were charging an average of $2,000 in gold per person to leave the country.

In September 1978, a tramp steamer, the *Southern Cross*, beached itself on a reef off the Indonesian island of Pengibu. Authorities permitted the 1,252 Vietnamese on board to disembark, accepting the captain's story that he had rescued the refugees from smaller boats at sea. Later investigations revealed that this '900-ton, Honduras-registered, uninsured rust bucket was … the first large foreign vessel explicitly chartered to go to Vietnam and pick up refugees.'[59]

On 15 October another freighter, the *Hai Hong*, left Singapore empty. Nine days later, it rendezvoused off the Vietnam coastline with a flotilla of smaller boats and picked up 2,500 passengers who had paid a smugglers' syndicate a total of $5 million boat fare. The ship's original destination was Hong Kong but bad weather forced it south to Indonesia where it anchored temporarily. On 8 November the Indonesian Navy forced the *Hai Hong* to depart its territorial waters and, later that day, the 1,500-ton freighter reached Port Klang, Malaysia. There began a tense, two-week stand-off as Malaysian officials demanded that the boat return to sea while UNHCR and several Western embassies urged that the *Hai Hong*'s cramped and suffering cargo be allowed ashore for resettlement.

On Friday, 10 November, UNHCR's regional representative, Rajagopalam Sampatkumar, was able to go alongside the ship (no visitors were permitted on board) and interview five of the Vietnamese passengers. The following Monday, Sampatkumar called on the Malaysian Foreign Ministry and presented an *aide memoire* to a senior official saying that, based on the interviews,

> the 2,500 Vietnamese on board the *Hi Hong* [*sic*] are considered to be of concern to the Office of the UNHCR.… UNHCR appeals to the Government of Malaysia to treat humanely these unfortunate 2,500 Vietnamese, many of whom are children and minors under the age of 17 and not to force the ship to leave Malaysian territorial waters. UNHCR on its part wishes to convey … its assurances to provide care and maintenance for these refugees and arrange for their early resettlement in a third country.[60]

Sampatkumar told the Foreign Ministry that allegations of people paying large sums of money to leave their country was not an issue in determining whether they were of concern to UNHCR. In his cable to UNHCR Head-quarters, he warned,

> It is generally believed by all those concerned with the boat people problem that

Hi Hong is only one of several such ships [with] large numbers of Vietnamese leaving home country.... High Commissioner may wish to consider possible repercussions that a long line of ships in future can have in not only countries of first asylum but also in resettlement countries.

On 14 November 1978 UNHCR Headquarters cabled back a reply:

We basically consider Sampatkumar's reaction correct and suggest that also in future, unless there are clear indications to the contrary, boat cases from Vietnam be considered *prima facie* of concern to UNHCR... Consent of authorities of country of departure or fact that permission to leave obtained through bribe or even official exit taxes have no impact on refugee status. In fact this applied in number of previous instances where states had interest in getting rid of dissidents or potential opponents. Such persons usually face danger if forced to return.[61]

The full import of this cable could not have been known at the time but UNHCR was establishing a precedent and a policy that would obtain for Vietnamese asylum seekers for a full decade: in the future, boat people were to be considered *prima facie* of concern, a decision giving them *de facto* refugee status, the protection of UNHCR, and an opportunity to seek a durable solution – either voluntary repatriation, local settlement, or third-country resettlement.

It was not simply to get them safely off the boat and onward to resettlement that UNHCR declared them refugees. What Sampatkumar heard from the *Hai Hong* passengers, especially from the ethnic Chinese, were compelling stories of official harassment, property confiscation, and forced relocation to NEZs. In a move to hasten the socialist revolution in the South and gird the country for the coming clash with China, Hanoi had reached the decision that Vietnam's 1.5 million ethnic Chinese were, at worst, reactionary fifth columnists and, at best, expendable.

On 24 March 1978 the government radio station announced: 'The policy of terminating all bourgeois tradesmen's business will be carried out in a unified manner throughout [Ho Chi Minh City] and all southern provinces, regardless of nationality or religion.'[62] In fact, the hammer came down first and hardest in Cholon, the Chinatown of Ho Chi Minh City and a 'strong capitalist heart beating inside the Socialist body of Vietnam'.[63] The same day, 30,000 youth volunteers accompanied by soldiers conducted a house-to-house search, confiscating hidden gold bars and dollar bills, inventorying property for state appropriation, and closing businesses. By mid-June, the authorities had relocated nearly 16,000 people to three NEZs outside the city.[64]

In the weeks prior to the crackdown in Cholon, thousands of Chinese residents in North Vietnam had begun to stream across the border into China. This northern exodus comprised not bourgeois traders principally but labourers: miners, fishermen and dockworkers in particular. Its origins lay in Vietnamese efforts that began in late 1977 to clear the border and other strategic areas (like Haiphong harbour) of ethnic Chinese.

Chen Hui Hua was working in Haiphong harbour, doing 'coolie labour', as he called it. Born in Vietnam, his parents had come from China in 1930. 'When the Americans were in Vietnam, China helped Hanoi,' he said. 'But in 1975–76, we heard that Vietnam was moving toward Russia and away from China. From that time on, the Vietnamese began to mistreat the Chinese more and more.'[65]

> It began with work. Some Chinese were dismissed or transferred to bad jobs. In Haiphong, the Vietnamese used to call us friend or comrade. Now, they started to insult us. I felt very depressed. One day, some people came and dumped a load of rubble and sand right on the path in front of my house. One of them said, 'He is leaving. He will go and his house will be mine.' They didn't drive us out but they did things that made it impossible to stay. Most did not want to leave and some did not want to go to China. We thought there would be no work, no housing, no fuel. At last, we had to go. I lost my job in Haiphong harbour. No explanation. It was not like we were dismissed. It was like we had disappeared.

Chen Hui Hua took his family by train to the Chinese border then walked across. The Vietnamese took his money and the Chinese took his ID. 'I had nothing,' he said.

By late May 1978 the People's Republic of China was publicly charging Vietnam with 'expelling large numbers of Chinese,' citing a figure of 72,000. That soon grew to 100,000, then 130,000 by mid-June. Declaring that 'our great socialist motherland is a mountain of support for overseas Chinese,' on 15 June, Beijing sent two ships to Vietnam 'to bring home persecuted Chinese'.[66]

Vietnam fired back, accusing China of 'gunboat diplomacy': 'This is the height of arrogance. The South China Sea is not China's own pond. Haiphong and Ho Chi Minh City are not Chinese ports where Chinese ships can come and go as they please.' Hanoi insisted that 'almost all Chinese residents have taken up Vietnamese citizenship and become Vietnamese of Chinese origin.'[67] China was meddling in Vietnam's internal affairs.

There was a large element of truth in both positions. Unfortunately, the increasingly shrill debate over definitions only obscured the issues and, as historian Michael Godley put it, 'deepened the semantic chasm into which real people fell'. China wanted the right to protect the interests of *huaqiao*, or 'overseas Chinese', without insisting that they necessarily were Chinese nationals. Vietnam claimed that most of the ethnic Chinese were Vietnamese nationals but said they were free to leave, while 'Those who stay on in Vietnam will be treated like all other foreign residents.'[69] On 12 July 1978, with more than 160,000 refugees now in Guangxi and Yunnan provinces, China sealed its land border.[70] Two weeks later, the Chinese ships went home empty. But the southern exodus was just beginning and those ships were filled to bursting.

When the Panamanian-registered freighter, *Tung An,* dropped anchor in Manila Bay in late December 1978, carrying 65 tons of fish meal, 40 tons of raw rubber and 2,300 Vietnamese asylum seekers, the Philippine authorities ordered everyone – and everything – on board to sit tight. The government of President Ferdinand Marcos was worried about security and the risk of being saddled with unwanted refugees. As the weeks went by, the cargo, so to say, ripened. Some time in January, the story goes, President Marcos paid a birthday visit to Cardinal Jaime Sin, spiritual leader of the powerful Catholic Church in the Philippines. Asked what he wanted for a gift, Cardinal Sin reportedly replied, 'I am sure the people out there in the harbour would like a bath.'[71] As Werner Blatter, UNHCR's representative in Manila, later recalled, 'After protracted negotiations, the government agreed to anchor a Navy boat beside the *Tung An*. All the people from the *Tung An* were allowed to spend a couple of days on the Navy ship. However, after this bathing ceremony, everybody went back on the *Tung An*.' People eventually were allowed to disembark but only when they had received a confirmed resettlement offer. By April 1979, scarcely half of the passengers had left the ship and Marcos again threatened seriously to send it back to sea, relenting ultimately to US pressure. The last Vietnamese finally left the *Tung An*, according to Blatter, some time in 1980.[72]

In Hong Kong, the crisis began on 19 December 1978 with the arrival of 3,300 boat people aboard the *Huey Fong*, also of Panamanian registry. After a month of delays and debate, while the ship waited outside the mouth of the harbour, the Hong Kong government reluctantly allowed the Vietnamese to disembark though it arrested the captain of the *Huey Fong* along with 10 other men and put them on trial for conspiracy and racketeering. As the trial unfolded, it became clear that the Socialist Republic of Vietnam was 'morally if not legally, an unindicted co-conspirator'.[73]

International syndicates were supplying the ships but, at least since July 1978, officials of the Cong An, the Public Security Bureau, had been collecting the bulk of the fees charged for departure. In the case of the *Huey Fong*, adults paid 12 taels of gold each (one tael was worth about $250 in late 1978) of which 10 allegedly went to the Vietnamese authorities and two went to organizers. Fees, and the official cut, varied depending on the province, the size of the boat, and the age of the passengers. But there was no question that the Vietnamese government was involved in the business of exporting its Chinese population as 'pacesetter and coordinator' and, apparently, profiteer.[74]

'The communists decided that they couldn't change our attitudes,' one Chinese-Vietnamese merchant said. 'Since we refused to go to the countryside to produce as farmers and sooner or later would have fled anyway, they decided it [*sic*] might as well collect our gold and let us go.'[75]

Eventually, all the refugees on board the big freighters were resettled. But the lessons were painful and profound for all concerned. The asylum countries discovered that the boat departures were organized and on the rise. They also learned that hard hearts could drive hard bargains. UNHCR and the Western countries realized that – lacking other durable solutions – temporary haven for the boat people would have to be purchased, on a one-to-one ratio if necessary, with resettlement offers.[76] The boat refugees found out that the journey could be long and difficult, but a new life in the West was waiting for those who survived. The organizers learned that big ships drew too much attention and began to abandon them for smaller vessels, often with deadly consequences for those on board. Within the space of one 11-day period, six boats capsized off the Thai and Malaysian coastlines, taking more than 400 lives.[77]

At the end of 1978 a total of 61,729 boat refugees were in camps in nine countries throughout Southeast and East Asia. By far the largest number – 46,286 – were in Malaysia, followed by 4,810 in Hong Kong. Thailand came third with 3,608. Excluding the 130,000 people evacuated to the United States in the spring of 1975, nearly 149,000 Indochinese had been resettled by January 1979. America and France had combined to take more than 110,000.[78]

On 11–12 December in Geneva, 38 governments attended a consultative meeting on Indochinese refugees called by UNHCR, hoping to generate new resettlement and funding pledges and perhaps some new ideas as well. Siddhi Savetsila, Secretary-General of the National Security Council and head of the Thai delegation, came with an old complaint. 'For each displaced person that leaves Thailand,' he pointed out, 'two new ones enter the country.'[79] Thailand, he noted, was unique in shouldering the burden not only of boat refugees from Vietnam but also land refugees from Cambodia and Laos. Although the Cambodian influx had receded, more than 56,000 Laotians entered refugee camps in 1978, bringing Thailand's overall total to 140,000. On a proportional basis, the resettlement of land cases was lagging far behind the boat people.

The Vietnamese delegate to the conference, Vo Van Sung, reminded participants that Thailand was not the only country with a problem of overlooked land refugees: 'First there are 131,000 Cambodians,' he said, who had fled to Vietnam since Pol Pot took power. 'There are then 26,309 citizens of another country who have had to leave Cambodia to take refuge in Vietnam and who are not yet accepted by their own country, China. There are then 268,350 Vietnamese who have lived for a long time in Cambodia but had to leave three years ago. That makes in all 426,459 people, without speaking of the 1,235,000 Vietnamese who live in frontier regions and who had to leave them because of events.'[80]

The 'events' to which the Vietnamese delegate innocuously referred was a violent border war that had flared for nearly two years between Vietnam and its communist neighbour. Systematic Khmer Rouge attacks had begun in January 1977 on six or seven Vietnamese border provinces. As assaults continued, refugees brought stories of fierce fighting and Khmer Rouge atrocities.

On 24 September 1977 Cambodian soldiers attacked a Vietnamese village in Tay Ninh province, killing several hundred people. As journalist Nayan Chanda described the carnage, drawing on eyewitness accounts, 'In house after house bloated, rotting bodies of men, women and children lay strewn about. Some were beheaded, some had their bellies ripped open, some were missing limbs, others eyes.'[81]

In October 1977 Vietnamese ground troops launched a brief probing operation into Cambodia's Svay Rieng province. Then, in late December, Vietnamese infantry and artillery combined for a massive, multi-pronged assault into the Cambodian interior. When they withdrew in early January 1978, the Vietnamese brought with them about 60,000 Cambodian refugees. Vietnam already was hosting more than 60,000 Khmer and Chinese-Cambodian refugees who had fled in or been forced out in 1975 and 1976.

Most of the first wave were city people – shopkeepers, petty traders, and manufacturers. The new arrivals 'were a different kind of refugee', Chanda observed after a visit to Ben Sanh camp in Tay Ninh. 'And Vietnam had something different in mind than humanitarian concern in giving them asylum.'[82] What it sought was the formation of a rebel army to front a Vietnamese invasion of Cambodia. Supplied with rice from UNHCR in the refugee camps and training from the Vietnamese, able-bodied men and women joined the Khmer Salvation Front, making them 'the first in a long series of Khmer refugee-warriors.'[83]

Less than two weeks after the refugee conference concluded, on 25 December 1978, Vietnamese invasionary forces pushed across the Cambodian border. On 7 January 1979, with the Khmer Rouge army offering only fitful resistance and the population none at all, the Vietnamese entered Phnom Penh and the following day, Khmer Salvation Front broadcasts announced the liberation of Cambodia and the installation of an eight-member Revolutionary Council headed by Heng Samrin. The People's Republic of Kampuchea was in power and the Khmer Rouge were on the run. For most of the next decade, the Cambodian conflict would add a violent new twist to the Indochinese refugee saga and increasingly polarize the humanitarian response.

Notes

1 Author's interview with Thida Khus, Phnom Penh, 28 August 1995.
2 The nation known since 1993 as the Kingdom of Cambodia has had many names in the last half century. This study employs the name Cambodia as a generic term for the country while Kampuchea is used in reference to particular governments or political parties or in quotations from other sources.
3 The figure of 500,000 deaths is from David Chandler, *The Tragedy of Cambodian History* (New Haven: Yale University Press, 1991), p. 215. The figure of two million internally displaced is from Judith Banister and Paige Johnson, 'After the nightmare: the population of Cambodia', in Ben Kiernan, ed., *Genocide and Democracy in Cambodia* (New Haven: Yale University Southeast Asian Studies, 1993), p. 72.

4 Cited in Ben Kiernan, *How Pol Pot Came to Power* (London: Verso, 1985), pp. 415–16.

5 The figure of 170,000 was generally used by UNHCR and the higher one was cited by Vietnamese officials. It is possible that the Vietnamese government's figure includes some of an estimated 200,000 ethnic Vietnamese who were expelled or fled racist pogroms during the Lon Nol regime, 1970–75.

6 Author's interview with Ha Duong Hui, Song Be, Vietnam, 26 March 1996.

7 François Ponchaud, 'Indochinese refugees in Thailand', International Catholic Migration Commission, 1977, p. 1.

8 *Keesing's Contemporary Archives*, 1975, p. 27470.

9 Ponchaud, 'Indochinese refugees in Thailand,' p. 1.

10 For recent histories of the Hmong and the CIA 'secret war' in Laos, see Roger Warner, *Back Fire: the CIA's Secret War in Laos and Its Link to the War in Vietnam* (New York: Simon and Schuster, 1995) and Jane Hamilton-Merritt, *Tragic Mountains: the Hmong, the Americans and the Secret Wars for Laos, 1942–1992* (Bloomington and Indianapolis: Indiana University Press, 1993).

11 The number of combat losses is from Arnold R. Isaacs, *Without Honor: Defeat in Vietnam and Cambodia* (New York: Vintage Books, 1984) p. 169. Civilian casualties are cited in Hamilton-Merritt, *Tragic Mountains*, p. 334. Internal displacement figures are from Gary Y. Lee, 'Minority policies and the Hmong,' in Martin Stuart-Fox, ed., *Contemporary Laos: Studies in the Politics and Society of the Lao People's Democratic Republic* (Queensland: University of Queensland Press, 1982), p. 203. These figures appear to cover mainly those Hmong who fought with, or at least fled to, the side of the royalist Lao and the Americans. Significant numbers of Hmong in the northeastern provinces either actively sided with the Pathet Lao or at least remained in communist-controlled territory during the war.

12 The 'Agreement on Ending the War and Restoring Peace in Vietnam,' otherwise known as the Paris Peace Accords, were signed on 27 January 1973 by the United States, the Republic of Vietnam, the Democratic Republic of Vietnam and the Provisional Revolutionary Government of Vietnam. Article 2 called for a ceasefire and the halt of all US military activities against the DRV. Article 12 stated that 'immediately after the ceasefire, the two South Vietnamese parties will achieve national reconciliation and concord, end hatred and enmity, prohibit all acts of reprisal and discrimination against individuals or organizations that have collaborated with one side or the other'.

13 At a Congressional hearing on Laos in 1969, a US senator had asked William Sullivan, former Ambassador to Laos, 'Do you see any obligation on the part of the United States for the safety or well-being of General Vang Pao and his people?' Sullivan replied, 'No formal obligation upon the United States, no.' In Hamilton-Merritt, *Tragic Mountains*, p. 226.

14 Author's interview with William Boua Yang, Bangkok, 4 June 1996.

15 Author's interview with Pao 'Paul' Herr, Bangkok, 4 June 1996.

16 Warner, *Back Fire*, p. 350.

17 Twelve-page mimeograph report titled 'Thailand: April–August 1975'. The report is unsigned but was probably written by a private relief agency official then working with Indochinese refugees in Thailand.

18 Several prominent families of the Thai Dam and Nung minorities had collaborated with the French in Vietnam. In 1954, about 10,000 Thai Dam (or Black Thai, so called because of their distinctive ethnic dress) were evacuated to Laos along with a smaller number of Nung.

19 Peter A. Poole, *The Vietnamese in Thailand: A Historical Perspective* (Ithaca and London: Cornell University Press, 1970), pp. 39–42. In both direct and indirect ways, Poole suggests, this movement of Vietnamese refugees was encouraged by Thai officials.

20 Wiesner, *Victims and Survivors*, p. 3. This included armed soldiers, political cadres and dependents.

21 W.T. Delworth, 'Vietnamese refugee crisis 1954/55', in Howard Adelman, ed., *The Indochinese Refugee Movement: The Canadian Experience* (Toronto: Operation Lifeline, 1980), p. 61. In addition to Canada, the other two members of the ICC, charged with monitoring implementation of the Geneva Accords, were Poland and India.

22 Bui Van Luong, 'The role of friendly nations', in Richard A. Lindholm, ed., *Vietnam: The First Five Years* (East Lansing: Michigan State University Press, 1959), p. 49.

23 Wiesner, *Victims and Survivors*, p. 7.

24 *Ibid.*, pp. 7–9.

25 *Ibid.*, p. 17.

26 *Ibid.*, pp. 20–25.

27 *Ibid.*, p. 301. The effect of these relocation schemes, combined with the effects of war, was devastating to the highland people and their cultures. As anthropologist Gerald Hickey writes, 'The Vietnam War exacted its toll, and one of the most tragic and little-known consequences was the decimation and destruction it brought to the highland people. By war's end in 1975, around 85 per cent of their villages were either in ruins or abandoned.... Of the estimated one million highlanders, between 200,000 and 220,000 had died. But a great many were not killed by bullets or bombs. They perished because their world was shattered.' Gerald Cannon Hickey, *Shattered World: Adaptation and Survival Among Vietnam's Highland Peoples During the Vietnam War* (Philadelphia: University of Pennsylvania Press, 1993), p. 261.

28 Wiesner suggests that the figure was probably only half that amount, and that about 20 per cent of these people had been relocated from their homes. *Victims and Survivors,* p. 347.

29 *Ibid.*, p. 55.

30 US Congress, Senate, Committee on the Judiciary, Indochina Evacuation and Refugee Problems, Part II: The Evacuation, Hearings before the Subcommittee to Investigate Problems Connected with Refugees and Escapees, 15, 25 and 30 April 1975, 94th Congress, 1st Session (Washington, DC: GPO, 1975), p. 23.

31 *Ibid.*, p. 30.

32 At that time, the US Immigration and Nationality Act of 1965 established a numerical limit on the annual admission of refugees from 'Communist or Communist-dominated' countries or from the Middle East, though it also allowed the Attorney General discretion to parole any number of aliens into the country 'for emergent reasons or for reasons deemed strictly in the public interest'. Though not expressly required to do so by law, the Attorney General normally consulted with Congress before exercising this parole authority in the case of large-scale admissions.

33 Gil Loescher and John A. Scanlan, *Calculated Kindness: Refugees and America's Half-Open Door, 1945–Present* (New York: The Free Press, 1986), p. 111.

34 *New York Times*, 28 December 1975. See also Reginald P. Baker and David S. North, *The 1975 Refugees: Their First Five Years in America* (Washington, DC: New

Transcentury Foundation, 1984).

35 William T Liu, Maryanne Lamanna and Alice Murata, *Transition to Nowhere: Vietnamese Refugees in America* (Nashville: Charter House Publishers, 1979), p. 32.

36 Wiesner, *Victims and Survivors*, pp. 340–4.

37 US Congress, Senate, Committee on the Judiciary, *Indochina Evacuation and Refugee Problems, Part II: The Evacuation*, p. 32.

38 Author's interview with Julia Vadala Taft, Washington, DC, 16 April 1996.

39 Cited in US Congress, Senate, Committee on the Judiciary, *Aftermath of War: Humanitarian Problems of Southeast Asia,* A Staff Report Prepared for the Use of the Subcommittee to Investigate Problems Connected with Refugees and Escapees, 94th Congress, 2nd Session (Washington, DC: GPO, 1976), p. 41.

40 *Christian Science Monitor,* 11 May 1976.

41 Agreement between the United Nations High Commissioner for Refugees and the Government of the Kingdom of Thailand, 22 December 1975.

42 In Gervase Coles, *Voluntary Repatriation*, pp. 147–8.

43 *Bangkok Post,* 7 September 1975.

44 United Nations General Assembly, Thirtieth Session, Third Committee, New York, 17 November 1975. Quotes are from a provisional summary record and should not be taken as verbatim.

45 Author's interview with Sr. Pascale Le thi Triu, Manila, 21 November 1995.

46 Center for Assistance to Displaced Persons, Program Report, 2 February 1993, p. 1.

47 Instituted in 1954, the Nansen Medal has been awarded by UNHCR, as a rule annually, in honour of Dr Fridtjof Nansen for outstanding service to the cause of refugees. UNHCR, *The Nansen Medal and its Recipients: Thirty Years in Retrospect* (Geneva: UNHCR, 1984).

48 US Congress, *Aftermath of War*, pp. 28–9.

49 The organizations were Christian and Missionary Alliance (CAMA) Services, Inc., World Vision, Food for the Hungry, World Relief Committee, Scandinavian Pentecostal Mission, Thai Baptist Mission, Norwegian Relief Services, Young Men's Christian Association (YMCA), Save the Children Fund, and the Overseas Missionary Fellowship. By 1980, at the peak of the refugee crisis in Thailand, CCSDPT had 49 member agencies, 25 of whom were headquartered in the United States. For a history of CCSDPT in the early years, see Clifford Olson, *Associations and Committees Serving Voluntary Agencies at the Country Level: A Study of Eight Organizations in Five Countries* (International Council of Voluntary Agencies, March 1981), pp. 5–30.

50 *Aftermath of War*, p. 34.

51 US Congress, Senate, Commitee on the Judiciary, *Humanitarian Problems of Southeast Asia, 1977–8,* 95th Congress, 2nd Session (Washington, DC: GPO, March 1978), p. 16.

52 *The Nation,* 14 May 1978.

53 Thai Ministry of Interior, *A Call for Humanity: Displaced Persons from Indochina in Thailand* (Bangkok: MOI, Operation Center for Displaced Persons, 1978), p. 15.

54 *Bangkok Post,* 7 September 1978.

55 Jacqueline Desbarats, 'Population relocation programs in socialist vietnam: economic rationale or class struggle?' *Indochina Report*, No. 11 (April–June 1987), pp. 4–5.

56 In *ibid.*, p. 14.

57 In Lesleyanne Hawthorne, ed., *Refugee: The Vietnamese Experience* (Melbourne:

Oxford University Press, 1982), p. 153.

58 *Ibid,.* pp. 26, 35.

59 Barry Wain, 'The Indochina refugee crisis', *Foreign Affairs* (Fall 1979). In US Congress, Senate, Committee on the Judiciary, *Hearing on the Refugee Crisis in Cambodia, October 31, 1979,* 96th Congress, 1st Session (Washington, DC: GPO, 1979), p. 212. See also Barry Wain, *The Refused: The Agony of the Indochina Refugees* (New York: Simon and Schuster, 1981).

60 Cable from Regional Office Malaysia, to UNHCR Geneva, 13 November 1978.

61 Cable from UNHCR Geneva to Regional Office Malaysia, 14 November 1978.

62 In Nayan Chanda, *Brother Enemy: The War After the War* (New York: Harcourt Brace Jovanovich, 1986), p. 241.

63 Comment by Hong Ha, economics editor of *Nhan Dan*, to Nayan Chanda, *ibid.*, p. 234.

64 Michael Godley, 'A summer cruise to nowhere: China and the Vietnamese Chinese in perspective,' *The Australian Journal of Chinese Affairs*, No. 4 (1980). p. 38. See also Ramses Amer, *The Ethnic Chinese in Vietnam and Sino-Vietnamese Relations* (Kuala Lumpur: Forum, 1991).

65 Author's interview with Chen Hui Hua, He Cheng, People's Republic of China, 1 November 1995.

66 In Godley, 'Summer cruise to nowhere,' pp. 36, 39.

67 Vietnam News Agency, 5 June 1978. *Ibid.*, pp. 39, 50. Vietnam levelled another charge: 'Why has [China] shown such touching concern for a handful of comprador capitalists of Chinese stock in Cholon, Vietnam while not saying one word about the fate of hundreds of thousands of laboring Chinese residents in Kampuchea who were really persecuted, ostracized and evicted.' *Vietnam News Agency*, 6 June 1978. *Ibid.*, p. 51

68 *Ibid.*, p. 50.

69 Vietnam News Agency, 5 June 1978. In *ibid.*, p. 50.

70 Godley suggests that on the same day China closed its border, Vietnam had presented 'a passenger list made up of 1,507 ethnic Chinese, supposedly from Kampuchea and desperate for a place on the evacuation ship'. *Ibid.*, p. 51. These were the wrong kind of persecuted Chinese and China turned them down.

71 Author's interview with Bill Applegate, Manila, 22 November 1995.

72 Author's communication with Werner Blatter, 18 April 1997.

73 Wain, *The Refused*, p. 103.

74 *Ibid.*

75 Charles Benoit, 'Vietnam's "Boat People" ' in David W. P. Elliot, ed., *The Third Indochina Conflict* (Boulder: Westview Press, 1981), p. 153.

76 Although the United States came to offer a significant number of admissions to Indochinese refugees, it had the critical advantage of being a long step removed from the boat influx. In late November 1978, when US Attorney General Griffin Bell announced a US commitment to admit another 21,875 Southeast Asian refugees, including 2,500 from Malaysia, he said that if a boatload of 5,000 refugees entered New York harbour without food or water, saying they wanted to stay in America, 'I guess I would have to tell the Immigration Service to push them off.' *The Nation*, 30 November 1978.

77 *Bangkok Post,* 5 December 1978.

78 US General Accounting Office, *The Indochinese Exodus: A Humanitarian Dilemma* (Washington, DC: General Accounting Office, April 1979), pp. 5, 103.

79 *Bangkok Post*, 12 December 1978.

80 *The Nation*, 15 December 1978.
81 Chanda, *Brother Enemy*, p. 194.
82 *Ibid.*, p. 215.
83 Aristide R. Zolberg, Astri Suhrke and Sergio Aguayo, *Escape from Violence: Conflict and the Refugee Crisis in the Developing World* (Oxford: Oxford University Press, 1989), pp. 170–71.

CHAPTER 3

— ⌐ —

The Year of Leaving Dangerously

By the start of 1979, China–Vietnam relations had moved in a brief space of years from communist solidarity through cautious rivalry to bitter enmity. Having lost the race with China to win diplomatic recognition from the United States, Vietnam had signed a 25-year treaty of friendship and cooperation with the Soviet Union.[1] At the end of a triumphant visit to the United States in January, Chinese leader Deng Xiaoping told a press conference in Washington, 'We call the Vietnamese the Cubans of the Orient. If you don't teach them some necessary lessons, their provocations will increase.'[2]

In the early morning of 17 February, the Chinese People's Liberation Army launched a thunderous artillery barrage across the Vietnamese border followed by a wave of 85,000 Chinese foot soldiers. Sixteen days later, having briefly captured all five provincial capitals in the border region, Chinese troops declared victory in this 'pedagogical war' and withdrew. Chinese casualties, by their own estimates, numbered 20,000. The destruction on the Vietnamese side was substantial. One official account listed 'four towns seriously damaged, 320 rural communities affected … and 904 schools, 691 day-nurseries, 430 hospitals and health stations and 42 logging-camps destroyed'.[3] As Nayan Chanda put it, 'Whether the Chinese taught a lesson or the Vietnamese learned one, this was one war that nobody won.'[4] Some of the biggest losers, as usual, were the refugees.

Even after China closed its border in July 1978, the refugee flow from the North had continued at a rate of about 8,000 per month. Roughly half came across the border at Dongxing Pass while others used Youyiguan (Friendship) Pass or came by boat to the port of Beihai. The process at this time generally required obtaining a passport at the Chinese Embassy in Hanoi, although some people reportedly were expelled at more remote checkpoints along the border. By the end of 1978, China's refugee population had grown to 200,000.[5]

In the first few months of 1979, the departure policies that the Vietnamese government had imposed on the Hoa in the South beginning in July 1978 came north. In March and April, said one man, neighbourhood cadres

39

called representatives from each Hoa family in Hanoi. 'The cadre gave us
two choices. We could remain in Vietnam and be relocated to the mountains, or we could leave....We were never expelled outright. We spoke of it
rather as being "cleverly chased away".' This time, however, their departure
would have semi-official sanction. Said another man, the cadre 'told us we
would be allowed to buy a seaworthy boat, fix its hull and motor and bring
along a mechanic and helmsman. We could also take along sufficient food,
water, fuel and medicine. These were big advantages over trying to flee
illegally.'⁶

These advantages, however, did not come free. For ethnic Chinese
throughout the country, semi-legal departure meant going through the Cong
An or Public Security Bureau (PSB).

> For the refugee trade, PSB officers sometimes recruited passengers directly. But
> in the South, they relied heavily on intermediaries to do their legwork. Refugees
> paid the intermediary in gold after he had settled the matter with the PSB. They
> often had to hand over what was called an application or registration fee – about
> 2 taels of gold for an adult – when their names were first submitted to the PSB.
> The rest of the payment, looked upon as an exit fee, was usually made near
> embarkation. The final terms tended to average between 5 and 8 taels of gold per
> adult, half price for children.... Kids under 5 or 6 were not charged at all. The
> intermediary received about 2 taels of gold per adult as his fee for organizing the
> exercise and linking up with a boat owner, or alternatively, purchasing a boat
> himself. A typical split: 50 per cent of the proceeds for the government, 40 per
> cent for the boat, fuel and provisions, with 10 per cent left over for the boat
> owner and organizer.⁷

In the North, fees tended to be lower than in the South both because of
lower income levels and because the PSB worked more directly with the
would-be refugees, thus avoiding the costs of the middleman. Movements
into China continued in the first half of 1979 apparently for a combination
of reasons: some had relatives there, some could not afford the exit fees for
the boat departures, and some said they were forced into China by the
Vietnamese.

Li Chong Sheng, a worker in a brick factory in Mang Cai said 'In April
1979, the police made me go to Dongxing where there is a small river
between the two countries. They took my money and my wristwatch and
forced me at gunpoint to go across. So I came to China with nothing. I had
to borrow my younger brother's clothes.' By July 1979, another 50,000
refugees had crossed into China, bringing the total to a quarter of a million.

Vietnam had a different version of events, one that made no mention of
expulsions. According to an article, 'Those who leave', written in 1979 by
Nguyen Khac Vien, 'This is the way things happen:

> A rich merchant wants to leave Vietnam. Against payment of a handsome amount
> of cash – 2,000–3,000 US dollars on an average – a clandestine organization will
> take him and his family to a coastal port where they will hide in one of the
> hundreds of fishing boats that put out to sea every day. At sea, they are picked

up by ships which will take them to neighboring countries. For an 'intellectual', especially a technician with good qualifications, the journey will be free of charge, for the point is to perform a 'brain drain' to the detriment of Vietnam and simultaneously raise a political hullabaloo.[9]

The article acknowledged that 'There may be cadres who have availed themselves of the situation to get their palms greased, but this is not government policy.'[10] The best evidence that the pay-as-you-go policy was set at the very highest levels of government comes from the recently published memoirs of Bui Tin, former deputy editor of *Nhan Dan*, the Communist Party daily, who has been living in voluntary exile in France since 1990. 'Plan 2, the exodus of the boat people,' Bui Tin writes, was approved by the Ministry of Interior, which controlled the Public Security Bureau. It 'was so organized that they all had to contribute gold to the national treasury. Each person leaving had to hand over from 3 to 5 taels of gold.' The head of the Cong An in Bien Hoa province was later sentenced to death 'for organizing this network. But who knows how many others took advantage of it,' Bui Tin asks, 'and still remain unpunished?'[11]

Vietnam's failure to acknowledge any government complicity in 1979 is hardly surprising. But 'Those who leave' was also misleading in saying that 'intellectuals' left for free. In fact, these people generally paid a premium to depart as it was government policy to deny even legal departure to 'holders of important economic and administrative responsibilities'.[12] Interviews with refugees suggest that, other than young children or the disabled, the only ones not charged by the organizers were the boat owners, crew, and those invited to serve as navigators or mechanics for the journey.

The article was right, of course, in saying that the departures raised a 'political hullabaloo', though that was not likely the intent of the organizers as it could only jeopardize their profit margins. But the arrival of the *Hai Hong* and the other big boats dubbed part of 'Rust Bucket Tours, Inc.' galvanized international awareness that the exodus from Vietnam had changed. Not only was it bigger and more organized but, perhaps most significantly, it was less the residue of a war that ended in 1975 and more the product of the class struggle – and regional conflicts – that began the same year.

But even as this awareness generated new sympathies in some quarters, it raised old antipathies in others. The fact that Vietnam seemed to be engaged in the wholesale export of its ethnic Chinese population set off alarms throughout the region, especially Malaysia and Indonesia, whose ethnic balances were a matter of profound political sensitivity.

In early 1979, a political cartoon on the front page of the Indonesian daily, *Kompas*, showed a caricature of Foreign Minister Mochtar Kusumaat-madja holding a slant-eyed monkey whose pockets were stuffed with money and on whose head perched a conical Vietnamese hat. In the background stood a spindly Indonesian farmer clutching a hoe. The caption went, 'Don't cuddle the monkey while your children are crying.'[13]

As anthropologist Judith Strauch has noted, 'Eruptions of hostility directed at overseas Chinese are nothing new' in Southeast Asia:

> A pogrom in Manila in 1603 took 20,000 Chinese lives; a massacre of somewhat lesser proportions occurred in Batavia (Jakarta) in 1740; there were riots against Chinese in Saigon in 1919, in Haiphong in 1927, in Kuala Lumpur in 1969, to name only a few. Nor is mass flight unprecedented: the Indonesian ban on alien business and residence imposed in rural areas in 1959–60 led to the repatriation to China of some 100,000 Chinese.[14]

Not mentioned in this list is the extraordinary violence in Indonesia in 1965 following an attempted left-wing coup, in which an estimated 300,000 ethnic Chinese were killed.[15]

Strauch pointed out that Malaysia had offered asylum to 120,000 Muslim refugees from the southern Philippines who had settled in the East Malaysian state of Sabah and had offered permanent resettlement to several thousand Cambodian Muslims. Thus, 'the government's assertions that ethnicity plays no role in its firm denial of resettlement to any of the boat people', she said, 'are less than credible.'[16] Within four weeks of the *Hai Hong*'s arrival, Malaysia's National Security Council ordered the creation of the Federal Task Force on Vietnamese Illegal Immigrants, usually known as Task Force VII or Task Force 'Seven'. Its three roles, according to the Task Force's last director, were (1) to stop landings by the boat people and, if they could not be stopped, to see that they were safely handed over to the UNHCR so they would not cause security problems; (2) to look after these people temporarily, and (3) to see that they were resettled.'[17]

The 'touch base' policy, in fact, had been in place since the beginning of Vietnamese boat arrivals. One UNHCR official posted to Kuantan, Malaysia in 1976–77 said, 'The security forces were trying systematically to push all the boats back, but there was a gentleman's agreement that if I got there first, they would be allowed to stay. I can't say how many I lost but I know I won hundreds' of these races.[18]

Task Force VII records show that in 1975, a total of seven boats carrying 1,342 people were 'assisted out' while 27 boats with 1,460 people landed.[19] This suggests that the push-backs were targeted at bigger boats (or at least boats carrying larger numbers of Vietnamese) or that the smaller boats were better able to evade detection and reach shore. It would appear that UNHCR lost the race to a total of 15 boats in 1976 and 1977, when about 900 people were sent back out to sea.

In 1978, Vietnamese arrivals in Malaysia ballooned to more than 63,000, with nearly 40,000 of those coming in the last three months of the year. Push-backs, likewise, jumped to 4,959. Arrivals in Malaysia then showed a decline to 54,000 in 1979 while neighbouring Indonesia experienced a nearly 20-fold increase from about 2,800 in 1978 to almost 49,000. It was not Vietnamese navigators who had changed their course but the Malaysian Navy doing it for them. Task Force VII recorded a total of 51,422 people in 386 boats 'assisted out' of Malaysian waters in 1979, most of them in the first half of the year.

UNHCR officials in the region believed that most of the Vietnamese pushed off by Malaysia ultimately ended up in Indonesia, although the process for tracking boats was hampered by the fact that the numbers were so large and UNHCR staff in Indonesia focused most of their attention on rescuing the people who fetched up on isolated outer islands. In May 1979 alone, nearly 13,500 people were refused asylum in Malaysia and pushed back out to sea. UNHCR records indicated that between 20 and 40 out of the 100 boats that subsequently landed in Indonesia may have been attacked by pirates.

According to Adnan Nala, an Indonesian national who started working with Vietnamese refugees in 1976 and was hired by UNHCR in 1979,

> At one point we had up to 1,500 people per day arriving in Indonesia. We chartered a helicopter to look for boats reported to have been pushed off from Malaysia. It was a flotilla down below. One boat came in with over 500 people on board. We pulled out 12 bodies. I remember many times jumping on a boat of new arrivals and shouting in Vietnamese, 'Does anyone need any help?' They couldn't even answer because most were exhausted, dehydrated, and suffering from exposure. There were so many deaths, rapes at sea, robberies.[20]

In June 1975 the Thai Cabinet had established a policy toward Indo-chinese refugees that seemed to shut the door and leave it slightly open at the same time: 'It is undesirable to allow displaced persons seeking asylum in this Kingdom to stay here. Those that come should be pushed out again as soon as possible. When this cannot be done, they must be confined in displaced persons' camps.'[21] Another Cabinet resolution in August 1977 re-asserted the point: 'There should be detention for the existing displaced persons population and preparation for the return of those who enter, once it becomes possible to send them back.' For boat arrivals, the directive was crystal clear:

> In the event that people sneak into the country by boat, officials should detain the escapees and either force or tow the boat out of territorial waters immediately. If a boat has already reached shore, it should be helped with repairs, food, engine oil, medicines, and other necessary equipment. Then the boat should be towed out of Thai waters without delay (no more than 30 days after its arrival).[22]

Until the end of 1978, Thai naval patrols did occasionally turn away refugee boats but made no systematic effort to enforce the push-back policy. In early 1979, however, as the flows increased — and no doubt aware of Malaysia's actitivies — Thailand stepped up push-backs. 'In the past three months,' admitted a Royal Thai Navy spokesman in June 1979, 'several thousand Vietnamese boat people who intended to come to Thailand were towed back to sea.' Spotter aircraft from the Sattahip naval base were flying missions three times a day, he said. 'If they spot a refugee boat they report to the patrol boat to intercept them.'[23]

One month before the Cabinet decision of August 1977, Thailand and UNHCR had signed an agreement that 'a distinction must be made between persons who qualify as being within the competence of UNHCR and those who leave their country of nationality or habitual residence for reasons of personal convenience, for example economic migrants or persons who are not *bona fide* refugees.' From 15 November 1977 only those who could establish to the satisfaction of a Thai immigration official that they were fleeing persecution would be permitted to enter a UNHCR refugee camp, while those who were screened out would be placed in Thai detention centers pending their repatriation. If they could be persuaded to go peacefully, the Cabinet guidelines had suggested, they should be turned back immediately.

Here again, the new policies were not applied with much rigour at first. By the end of 1977, Thai authorities had placed 64 Laotian and Cambodian new arrivals in detention while 3,200 had entered UNHCR camps in the previous two months. As one US government assessment concluded, 'Many local officials, when faced with an actual situation, follow a humanitarian policy. A few provincial officials along the Mekong [River], however, do make determined efforts to discourage refugee arrivals. Nonetheless, most of the recent Lao and Cambodian refugees have been allowed to stay.'[25]

In January 1979, anticipating a new refugee influx in the wake of the Vietnamese invasion of Cambodia, High Commissioner for Refugees Poul Hartling had cabled Thai Prime Minister Kriangsak Chomanand with an offer of additional financial aid. Thailand did not respond immediately to the offer. Said one senior Thai official,

> Thailand realizes that among those leaving Cambodia in the present circumstance, there will be some *bona fide* refugees. But Thailand also has a serious concern for its internal security. Now that the struggle is between communist factions, some coming to Thailand will inevitably be communists. Therefore all new arrivals will be strictly screened by Thai military authorities and Border Patrol Police. For this purpose, new arrivals will be kept in a special camp, perhaps in Buriram or Trat.[26]

At this point, UNHCR was supporting four refugee camps for Cambodians who had entered Thailand between 1975 and 1978. Aranyaprathet camp (also known as Ban Thai Samart) was the largest with 7,400 residents, Lumpuk camp held 4,700, Kamput camp housed 1,900 and Mairut camp held 500. Residents of these camps, who soon came to be known as the 'Old Khmer', were recognized as de facto refugees by UNHCR – and by Thailand as well – and were permitted to seek third-country resettlement. Thailand was not prepared to mix the 'New Khmer' with the old, however; indeed, it was not at all sure just what to do with them.

As in the earliest days of Cambodian arrivals in mid-1975, makeshift camps and detention centres sprang up along the border in Buddhist temples, police stations and small villages. Arrivals in the first two months of 1979 were light, roughly 400 in January and about 1,500 more in February.

But as the numbers increased in March and screening proved an ineffective parrying tactic on the border, Thai officials shifted to less subtle measures of deterrence.

Said Prem Tinsulalonda, then army commander-in-chief,

> The UNHCR feels we have to assist all the incoming refugees but we think we have had enough trouble and need not increase the size of the burden.... If the refugees are sick, we will give them medical treatment. If they are hungry, we will feed them. And when they have recovered, they will be pushed back across the border.'[27]

Push-back at Preah Vihear

By late April, as Vietnamese troops pressed their attack on the retreating Khmer Rouge forces, between 50,000 and 80,000 Cambodians – many of them Khmer Rouge soldiers and cadres – had reached the border at the Thai village of Khlong Hat, south of Aranyaprathet. After rejecting an initial attempt to cross, the Thai military permitted most of the group – led by 8,000 armed Khmer Rouge soldiers – to enter Thai territory on 24 April and walk south for 40 kilometres before re-entering Cambodia two days later at Ban Laem. Reporters and relief officials who witnessed this forced march of hungry and frightened men, women, and children said it was clear – and Cambodian survivors later confirmed this – that many of the civilians were being held against their will. Near Khlong Hat, Thai soldiers 'stumbled on the bullet-riddled bodies of a number of refugees who tried to break away'.[28]

UNHCR field officers reported that 6,000 Cambodians were forced out of Ta Phraya district from 21–26 April and, from 18–23 May another 1,000–3,000 were sent back from around the village of Nong Chan.[29] The three-week reprieve on push-backs from late April to mid-May was probably in anticipation of a visit by UN Secretary General Kurt Waldheim. If so, the ploy backfired. UNHCR and International Committee of the Red Cross (ICRC) officials persuaded Waldheim to visit Wat Koh camp, where one month earlier Thai officials had removed 1,700 people and sent them back across the border. After hearing the anguished appeals of their friends and relatives, Waldheim appealed to Kriangsak to let the refugees stay.

By the middle of May at least 15,000 people had spurted through the briefly open window to seek sanctuary in Thailand. Most of the new arrivals were ethnic Chinese from Cambodia. Another 20,000 were reported to have gathered in Battambang, awaiting clearance to leave by the Vietnamese.[30] Signs were growing of a mass exodus to the Thai–Cambodian border.

Shortly after the Chinese invasion of Vietnam, the ethnic Chinese community in Cambodia, which had suffered grievously under the Khmer Rouge, were swiftly and adversely affected by several policy pronouncements from the new government. In February and March, according to Cambodia scholar Stephen Heder, 'the Vietnamese began to attempt a step by step evacuation of the market towns'. The first step was to restrict access only to those employed in the provincial administration; others had to move a kilometre or more from the city centre. This regulation, says Heder, 'seemed to be more strictly enforced against Chinese than against Khmer, unless they had plenty of gold to pay off Vietnamese military officials and/or Salvation Front cadres.'[31]

In April, May and June 1979, the authorities 'announced that towns were to be cleared, markets closed, and people organized for agricultural production.... Again, the Chinese found that these regulations seemed primarily aimed at them.' Tens of thousands decided, at that point, that 'it would not be out into the countryside for them, but out, if possible, to Thailand'.[32]

By late May, an estimated 15,000 ethnic Chinese had crossed into Thailand and perhaps 15,000 to 20,000 more were waiting in Battambang and Sisophon. Vietnamese authorities had arranged transportation for many of them all the way from Phnom Penh. The average 'transport fee' to the Thai border was 2,500 baht (then about $125) per person. Said one refugee in Wat Koh, 'Heng Samrin's Khmer ... hate the Chinese and would beat [us] and steal what rice we had. The Vietnamese were friendly. But no one is fooled. They only helped us as long as we were leaving.'[33]

An alarming feature story in the 20 May edition of the *Bangkok Post* linked the organized exodus of ethnic Chinese from Cambodia to the expulsions from Vietnam itself, which, at its peak one month later, would see 2,000 boat people per day struggling ashore in Malaysia, Thailand, Indonesia and other countries throughout Southeast Asia. 'Famine and an anti-Chinese campaign by Vietnamese invaders', the article warned, 'means at least 100,000 new Cambodian refugees in 1979. Some experts are already predicting one million.'

Prime Minister Kriangsak had squeaked through national elections in May and his patchwork coalition held the slimmest of majorities in Parliament. Opposition leaders and voices in the military were calling for tighter controls along the border and a stronger stance against the Vietnamese threat. Something had to be done. Somebody pushed the panic button.

Sari Touv had arrived at Nong Chan in May with her mother, brother and niece. The camp, she said, 'was rather confused and disordered but we thought that we would not stay there for a long time, that we would be rescued and resettled in a third country.' But early in the morning of 8 June 1979, she said,

> we were all surprised and puzzled to see numerous buses standing outside of the camp. A troop of Thai soldiers forced us to get on the buses. They said that we would be taken to Bangkok and would wait there to be resettled. A crowd of refugees were getting on the buses until they were full. By that time, I had an intuition so my family stayed in the back of the crowd of people.
>
> Sure enough, before day broke, Thai soldiers surrounded us and coerced us to get on the buses. This time, my family could not avoid going so we simply packed up some food and water and a plastic cloth with us in case we needed it. We got on the bus with reluctance and a gloomy mind. Some Thai citizens

came near the buses and gave each of us a packet of cooked rice through the windows.

The bus drove the whole afternoon and into the night along a way with forests on both sides. The road seemed to be sloping up inch by inch. At dawn, all the buses stopped and the soldiers who were waiting there bullied us to get off and go into the forest. Then they said, 'Go forward and down. There is your country.' As soon as they finished saying this, they raised their guns, pointed the muzzles to the sky and fired. Then they pointed their guns at us.[34]

The soldiers had brought them to the Thai–Cambodian borderline at Preah Vihear, an ancient Khmer ruin sitting atop the steep and desolate Dang Rek mountains. 'All of us were stampeded into the forest,' said Sari, 'and could not help going straight forward.

About half a mile farther, we realized that we were on a mountain when we came to a cliff from which we had to climb down. At the sight of the vast forests below and the steep cliff, we involuntarily stopped our paces. But in a few minutes, we heard the sound of a volley of shots and the screaming of people far behind.

The rainy season had been coming in which made the ground and rocks slippery. We took off our shoes and clambered down barefoot. However, our legs and arms were cut by the thorns and the sharp blades of the wild grass. We could only grit our teeth, endure the pain and go on. My brother took care of my mother. I took care of my niece. There were so many people who slipped down and rolled over the cliff.

Farther down, I heard the sound of explosions and people below me shouted that there were buried mines all the way down. Landmines below and Thai soldiers up above. They were coming near the cliff and giving us a volley of shots again. Some of us shouted back to them that we could not go forward, because mines were scattered everywhere. The answer was a long continuous barrage directed straight down. There were more people who died behind us. We could not help resuming our steps.

The explosions, the dead people, all the terrible scenes filled me with despair. When the night came on, and we were so exhausted, we stopped and rested to drink and eat something. The night was impenetrably dark in the forest and none of us wanted to move for fear of the buried mines. At midnight, it began to rain. We could only sit and hunch up our knees in front of us as it was so cold. My poor niece snuggled on my lap and I hugged her tightly. I took a plastic cloth to cover my head and our bodies. I could not help breaking into tears.

It took three days to empty Nong Chan. Then the soldiers moved to Wat Koh. One eyewitness there gave this account:

There were about 6,000 people. The UNHCR together with the American, French, and Australian Embassies, attempted a last-minute rescue operation. They had permission from the Thai Supreme Command to take out about 900 people for resettlement in third countries. However, they had 25 buses available to take people to a temporary transit camp. Local officials gave permission for all the buses to be filled. UNHCR and Embassy officials were not allowed in to the camp, but had to stand at the entrance and call out names from their lists. There were many problems.

Firstly, the names often could not be pronounced properly due to translation from Chinese to English. Secondly, some had already escaped fearing they would be sent back. Thirdly, many did not come forward as they feared that the buses would be coming to take them back to Cambodia. Finally, 20 buses were filled with 1,500 people, and then the military stopped them taking any more. The convoy moved off, and all the foreigners were made to leave the area. The whole area was then sealed off by a special detachment of troops…. Half an hour after the buses left another convoy of buses arrived. The authorities tried to trick the refugees into getting on the buses by telling them that they, too, were being taken to the transit camp to await resettlement in third countries.

However, the refugees knew what was in store for them, and they refused to get on the buses. They all sat down in a big mass on the ground. Then the soldiers moved in with sticks. They started beating the people on the edge of the crowd and carrying them onto the buses one by one. The children were screaming and completely terrified. Finally, after many people had been beaten and carried onto the buses, the rest of the people were too afraid to resist further and they climbed onto the buses.[35]

The last-minute rescue efforts appear to have saved at least 1,500 people. All were offered resettlement overseas or transferred to a UNHCR camp. The other Wat Koh refugees were pushed down the mountainside. By 15 June more than 42,000 Cambodians – about two-thirds of them ethnic Chinese – had been rounded up from Nong Chan, Wat Koh, and other sites and forced back into Cambodia. Then, just as suddenly as they had started, the push-backs stopped and the crowds dispersed through the mine-infested plains below.

Sari Touv and her family walked for fifteen days. During that time, she said, 'many people died from overexhaustion and some people died while walking around to find water and trod on the mines. During the day, we walked over the corpses, at night we sat near them.'[36] On the sixteenth day, they encountered Vietnamese soldiers clearing a path through the mines. The soldiers gave them food and water and led them south to a collection point to wait for other survivors.

Outside of Kompong Thom, one of the refugees said,

the war of race began. The Vietnamese separated the ethnic Chinese people from the group and made them stay there beside the [Steng Sen] riverbank. They said that the ethnic Chinese people were from the city and had no farmland to go back to, that it didn't make sense to let these people go anywhere else and since this place needed manpower they would stay there.[37]

Sari Touv said she was told to

go back to the home of our birthplace to take part in the farming. My house was in Phnom Penh, but we could not go back. My family were Chinese descendants and had been extremely discriminated against. So my family decided to go to Battambang. We earned our living there by sewing for people for a few months. When we had enough energy, we looked for a chance to escape to Thailand again.[35]

By late June, however, perhaps 8,000 people still remained in the desolate no-man's land below Preah Vihear. Alarmed at reports of disease and starvation among the group, the Swedish government tried to mount an emergency relief effort through the Swedish Red Cross but was rebuffed by Khmer Rouge representatives in Peking and the Heng Samrin government's ambassador in Hanoi.[39] Following belated interventions by the United States and UNHCR, Thailand permitted about 2,000 people to re-enter the country in July.

Survivors' estimates of the death toll vary from several hundred to several thousand. The worst casualties, no doubt, were suffered by the first to go down the mountain and the last to escape the plains below. Most in the first group died from mines and those in the last from starvation, dehydration, and disease.[40]

One day after the push-backs began, the ICRC issued an urgent appeal that they cease. 'I believe that if these people are pushed back into Kampuchea against their will,' said Francis Amar, the head of delegation in Bangkok, 'they may lose their lives. If not, they will face the same situation which they found serious enough to drive them to leave their country in the first place.'[41] Amar was ordered to leave Thailand. 'This is our business,' Kriangsak said angrily. 'It is done to protect the national interest.'[42]

What did UNHCR have to say about the single largest instance of forced repatriation since the agency was established in 1951? In a press statement released on 11 June, High Commissioner Hartling expressed 'deep concern' at the reports and urged the Bangkok office to follow up with diplomatic missions in order to prevent further push-backs 'particularly of cases [with] a reasonable chance of resettlement'. 'This', wrote UNHCR official Dennis McNamara later, 'was to be the full extent of its official response ... UNHCR's remarkable failure to formally or publicly protest the mass expulsions of Cambodians from Thailand during 1979 must be seen as one of the low points of its protection history.'[43]

As for the US reaction, journalist William Shawcross described it as 'weak'. Morton Abramowitz, then US Ambassador to Thailand, told him, 'We asked the Thais to stop. They refused. We took the view that if the government had been forced to stop in midstream, Kriangsak could have been brought down by the military. Also we hoped that the refugees would be able to get back. We didn't realize how awful the geography was.'[44]

Some evidence suggests that the expulsion was planned and ordered by the Thai military rather than by the Prime Minister, though he opted to endorse it after the fact. Military strategists told Richard Nations of the *Far Eastern Economic Review* that, according to Vietnamese deserters, orders had come from Hanoi 'to push three categories of undesirables out of Kampuchea: Pol Pot's soldiers, civilian Khmers who refuse to collaborate, and ethnic Chinese'. With the first two categories, Thailand could afford to be flexible. The Khmer Rouge soldiers could be expected to go back on their own and the Khmer civilians could be sent on for resettlement or sent home whenever it suited.

But the expulsion of ethnic Chinese from Cambodia could not stand, the Thai officers said. 'They are the natural commercial class and administrators. If they are driven out of the country they will inevitably be replaced by Vietnamese through the sheer necessity of restoring the country.' Alluding to the strong business links between ethnic Chinese communities on both sides of the Thai–Cambodian border, another officer added, 'They are not Peking's Fifth Column as Hanoi suspects, but ours.'[45]

In the first six months of 1979, Thailand's House Refugee Affairs Committee reported, a total of 154,925 Cambodians had fled into Thailand. By the end of June, 108,719 had been pushed back.[46]

The 1979 International Conference on Indochinese Refugees

By the middle of 1979, more than 700,000 people had left Vietnam and found permanent resettlement or temporary safe haven in other countries. This included the 130,000 Vietnamese evacuated to the United States in April 1975, 235,000 who had fled north into China, 277,000 who had fled Vietnam by boat since mid-1975, and 21,000 who had fled overland into Thailand. More than 17,000 of the land Vietnamese had been resettled by the end of June, along with 82,000 boat people, leaving nearly 200,000 Vietnamese in camps throughout the region.[47]

Thailand, moreover, had been on the receiving end of an exodus of more than 160,000 Laotian refugees since 1975. In addition, 375,000 Khmer and ethnic Vietnamese had fled Cambodia during the Pol Pot years and an estimated 150,000 Cambodians had crossed, successfully and otherwise, into Thailand since January 1979. To this figure of nearly 1.4 million people should be added the tens of thousands who had slipped clandestinely across borders or died in the effort. 'All in all,' concluded Barry Wain, 'it was one of the great population shifts in history. And it was continuing.'[48]

It was not simply continuing but accelerating. Laotian arrivals in Thailand had averaged more than 4,700 per month throughout 1978 and the early part of 1979, the highest level in nearly four years. The Vietnamese boat flow, too, was in full spate. In four months from March to June, arrivals in the region totalled 148,105, nearly twice the number of all boat people resettled since 1975. By the end of June, Malaysia had 75,000 boat refugees, Hong Kong 59,000, Indonesia 43,000, Thailand 9,500, the Philippines 5,000, and smaller numbers were scattered in at least half a dozen other countries.

But even as the Indochinese exodus gained pace, it ran a growing risk of collapsing under its own weight. Following a meeting in Bali at the end of June, the foreign ministers of the five-member Association of Southeast Asian Nations (ASEAN)[49] issued a joint communique, warning that they 'have reached the limit of their endurance and have decided they would not accept any new arrivals'. As for those 'illegal immigrants/displaced persons/refugees' already being given temporary shelter, the foreign ministers gave notice that if they could not be resettled or returned in a timely fashion, "the ASEAN countries would send [them] out'.[50]

Two weeks earlier, Malaysia's outspoken deputy prime minister, Mahathir Mohamad, had been somewhat less diplomatic when a local daily, *The Star*, reported that he had given an order to 'shoot on sight' any Vietnamese found trying to enter Malaysian territory. Other government officials later tried to dismiss the comment as a misunderstanding – one suggested that Mahathir had said 'shoo on sight' – but the threat to asylum was taken very seriously.

Following the December 1978 consultative meeting, UNHCR had noted in a summary that 'there can be no humane or durable solutions unless governments grant at least temporary asylum in accordance with internationally accepted humanitarian principles'. As a corollary, the consultations had noted that 'existing facilities in countries of first asylum in Southeast Asia were already overloaded and that for such countries, temporary asylum depended on commitments for resettlement in third countries and the avoidance of residual problems in the area'.[52] But the meeting had summoned an all too grudging international response. Resettlement numbers no sooner were pledged than they were over-subscribed and money no sooner committed than it was spent. New funding pledges amounted to only $12 million and new resettlement places to no more than 5,000.[53] Six months later, arrival rates were skyrocketing and asylum was on the brink of collapse.

On 30 June 1979, UN Secretary General Waldheim issued a formal invitation to 71 nations to attend a Meeting on Refugees and Displaced Persons in Southeast Asia to be held in Geneva on 20–21 July. The impetus for the meeting, the first of its kind in the United Nations, came from British Prime Minister Margaret Thatcher, who was seeking to relieve the burden of her country's tiny colony, Hong Kong, then struggling to accommodate an influx of more than 56,000 people in the first six months of 1979.

'A grave crisis exists in Southeast Asia,' said UNHCR's Poul Hartling in a background note prepared for the July meeting. For 'hundreds of thousands of refugees and displaced persons ... fundamental right to life and security is at risk'. Of the more than 550,000 Indochinese who had sought asylum in Southeast Asia since 1975, 200,000 had been resettled and 350,000 remained in the countries of asylum. In the first half of 1979, refugee camps had taken in 155,000 new arrivals while 54,000 had departed for resettlement in the same period. Despite a doubling of worldwide resettlement commitments within the past nine months, said Hartling, 'the problem has clearly run ahead of the solutions'.[54]

'The numbers involved in Southeast Asia are not unmanageable,' Hartling insisted. Indeed, had he been less diplomatically inclined, the High Commissioner could have pointed out that China and Vietnam had absorbed far higher numbers with far fewer complaints. 'The difficulties arise,' he said, 'rather from the historical and political complexities of the problem and the uncertainties of the future. It is these factors which have inhibited durable solutions.' In short, the ASEAN countries wanted little to do with

Vietnamese refugees and even less if they were ethnic Chinese. Thailand might have been more tolerant of the Laotians and Cambodians if they were not crossing the borders by the tens of thousands.

In 1979, Hong Kong's concerns about too many Chinese-Vietnamese had to do both with balance and sheer bulk. In late 1974, Hong Kong's law-making body, the Legislative Council, had decreed that illegal immigrants caught trying to enter the territory from mainland China would be summarily returned. From 1975 to 1977, only about 4,000 Chinese were arrested and sent back but the number of deportations grew to 8,000 in 1978 and simply exploded to 89,000 in 1979. It is both ironic and telling that, during the same five-year period, the pattern of Vietnamese arrivals almost exactly matched that of Chinese deportations. It was not simply that Hong Kong had a population of 5.5 million people living on scarcely 1,000 square kilometres of real estate but that 98 per cent of those people were Chinese and largely unsympathetic to a two-faced policy that permitted Vietnamese to stay but sent Chinese back home.[55]

'There is now no way in which the problem can be resolved by piecemeal measures,' Hartling argued. 'No single action, however generous, will suffice.'[56] The only way that countries in the region might be persuaded to offer local settlement would be if they had some assurance that the outflow was under control. That would require both international resettlement and some efforts to check, or redirect, the flow at its source. Without such assurances, even temporary asylum could not be secured.

Hartling laid out three priorities for coordinated international action. The first objective was that 'wise and humane measures are taken by those concerned … in order that the exodus does not continue in the present appalling manner'. Hartling did not name names but he was referring, no doubt, to Vietnam and the state-sanctioned expulsion/exodus of its ethnic Chinese population which had replaced the coal industry as Vietnam's top source of foreign exchange, with projected earnings of $3 billion.[57]

The High Commissioner for Refugees then cast his attention on the first asylum countries though, again, he mentioned no names: 'Every humanitarian principle requires that refugees not be turned away and forced into situations that further endanger their lives.' Malaysia and Thailand were the principal offenders in this case, although Singapore's navy was also interdicting boats and turning them away.

Third, and most explicitly, Hartling called for a reduction of the backlog of 350,000 cases awaiting resettlement in Southeast Asia. 'This means', he said, 'exceeding the rate of arrivals, which, it is most earnestly to be hoped, will decline.'[58] At the end of June, resettlement countries had absorbed 197,000 Indochinese refugees (not counting the 130,000 evacuated to the United States or the 235,000 in China) of whom 180,000 had gone to four countries: America, France, Australia and Canada. The United States, in particular, was still looking to further 'internationalize' the burden-sharing.

In all, 65 governments accepted Waldheim's invitation to Geneva. Vice-

President Walter Mondale headed the US delegation while China and the Soviet Union were represented by their deputy Foreign Ministers. All of the ASEAN countries were in attendance, as was Japan and virtually all of Western Europe. Of the three countries of origin, only Vietnam was invited. The Heng Samrin regime was not recognized by the United Nations and Vietnam would not sit down with the Khmer Rouge. Laos thus could not be invited or China would have protested.

Despite strident appeals from China and Singapore to address the 'root causes of the exodus', most delegations focused on the humanitarian aspects of the crisis as they had been urged to do by the UN organizers. At the ASEAN ministerial meeting in Bali, Singapore's foreign minister, Sinnathamby Rajaratnam, had warned, 'If we keep it at the humanitarian level, then the consequences will be disastrous for us and irreversible.' The exodus from Vietnam, he said, was a dangerous weapon aimed at the region. 'Each junkload of men, women and children sent to our shores is a bomb to destabilize, disrupt, and cause turmoil and dissension in ASEAN states. This is a preliminary invasion to pave the way for the final invasion.'[59] Singapore could afford to posture – as of November 1978, it had set a cap of 1,000 on the number of boat people permitted on its territory at any one time, and that only on the condition of a guarantee of resettlement. The other members of ASEAN, however, were desperate for solutions and felt they could not afford to alienate Vietnam.

Vice-President Mondale 'set the emotional tone of the discussions,' as one observer put it,

> by referring in his address to the failure of the Evian Conference forty-one years earlier to provide international sanctuary to the persecuted Jews of Germany and Austria. On that occasion, thirty-two nations had 'failed the test of civilization' and he strongly urged the participants at Geneva to follow the US lead in doubling their resettlement quotas for Indochinese refugees to ensure that such a failure would not be repeated.[60]

It was not only a potent appeal but a neat rhetorical trick to cloak a comparison of Vietnam to Nazi Germany in a criticism of international inaction and a call for renewed commitments.

Unlike the December 1978 consultation, the international commitments made in June 1979 were wide-ranging and generous. Although participant countries signed no resolutions, a report from the Secretary General summed up the new initiatives arising from the meeting:

- It was agreed that resettlement should proceed on a larger and faster scale. Worldwide resettlement pledges increased from 125,000 in May 1979 to 260,000 for 1979 and 1980. The United States doubled its monthly quota from 7,000 to 14,000 for an annual total of 168,000.

- The government of Vietnam gave assurances that it would 'cooperate with UNHCR in expanding the present seven-point program designed to bring departures within orderly and safe channels'. This was in reference to a Memorandum of Understanding signed by UNHCR and Vietnam on 30 May 1979, which spelled out steps for the orderly departure from Vietnam of 'family reunion and other humanitarian cases.'

- The governments of Indonesia and the Philippines each pledged to establish regional processing centres to help move refugees more quickly on to resettlement. The site in the Philippines was to hold 50,000 refugees and the Indonesian site 10,000.

- New pledges to UNHCR totalled about $160 million in cash and in kind. This far exceeded the amount UNHCR had received for Indochinese programmes since 1975.

- 'Finally,' noted the report from the Secretary General, 'the general principles of asylum and non-refoulement were endorsed.'[61]

As with many successful international meetings, most of the major agreements had been made in advance. At an economic summit of industrialized nations in Tokyo in late June, US President Jimmy Carter's announcement of his decision to double resettlement numbers had encouraged Japan to double its funding of the 1979 UNHCR budget from 25 to 50 per cent of the total. Tokyo, moreover, pledged $6.5 million to cover half of the costs of the regional processing centres.

From August 1975 to the beginning of January 1979, the United States had contributed nearly $58 million, or 52 per cent of the total. All told, only 19 donor governments covered the entire contribution of $112 million. At the end of 1978, UNHCR was facing a deficit of some $8 million. In 1979, assistance for Indochinese was shifted from a UNHCR special programme to its general programme to which 64 governments normally made contributions.

As a report from the US General Accounting Office noted at the time, although

> this change creates a greater potential for financing of the program and acceptance of refugees for resettlement, it may not necessarily achieve such results. The general program is funded by voluntary contributions, and ... donors tend to earmark their contributions. Therefore, the burden of funding the Indochinese refugee program may continue to fall on the United States and the former special program contributors.[62]

The United States did remain the largest contributor in terms of resettlement numbers but Japan became the largest financial donor and, following the July 1979 meeting, international commitments broadened significantly. The Indochinese, for better or worse, were now a mainstream refugee programme and not just an extra-curricular UNHCR activity.

In terms of resettlement, Canada raised its pledge dramatically from 8,000 to 50,000 by the end of 1980. Australia committed to an additional 14,000 on top of the 22,000 already resettled. France had taken more than 50,000 by mid-1979 but agreed to take 5,000 more boat people. Germany pledged 10,000 places. The United Kingdom agreed to take 10,000 Vietnamese from

Hong Kong, which only partly satisfied the territory's governor, Sir Murray MacLehose, who had said at the conference:

> The people of Hong Kong ask why proportionately more resettlement places are given to other places of first asylum. This year, 35 per cent of the boat refugees in the region came to Hong Kong but it only received 13 per cent of the resettlement places. Or, putting it differently, 66,000 arrived this year, but only 5,500 have been resettled. Hong Kong's record as a place of first asylum is unique. But on past experience, you cannot blame people in Hong Kong for drawing the conclusion that help would be greater if policies were harsher.[63]

In early 1979, when it became apparent that Malaysia had taken burden-sharing into its own hands and was forcefully redistributing boat people to its neighbours, Indonesia's Foreign Minister Mochtar Kusumaatmadja had proposed a safer alternative in the form of a regional processing centre. The basic idea of these centres was to relieve the burdens of overcrowded first asylum countries by removing some of their refugee population to another site in the region where they could complete their processing for permanent resettlement in a third country. At the ASEAN ministerial meeting in Bali, Mochtar had confirmed Indonesia's commitment to make available an island site capable of holding 10,000 people. Not to be outdone, Philippines Foreign Minister Carlos Romulo offered a site with a capacity of 7,000 people. In July, the Philippines trumped their own offer (and stole some of Indonesia's thunder) by pledging an additional site with a capacity of 50,000.

By August 1979 UNHCR had negotiated a $650,000 contract with the Indonesian government to build five kilometres of asphalt road and a pier capable of receiving ships of up to 200 tons on Galang Island in the Riau Archipelago. More than one year and $7 million later, UNHCR had a regional processing centre operating on Galang. Construction began in December 1979 for the Philippine Refugee Processing Center (PRPC) in Morong, Bataan with an initial phase inaugurated in October 1980. Although the population of the PRPC never exceeded 17,000 at any one time, in its 14-year history, nearly 340,000 passed through Bataan on their way to countries of resettlement. The Galang centre processed more than 55,000 before it was phased out in 1987.

The regional processing centres and the pledges of mass resettlement covered those who had already left their countries. As for those who had not yet left, Vietnam made two commitments at the 1979 meeting, one covering legal departures and the other, more controversially, illegal departures. On 12 January 1979, as rust buckets packed to the scuppers with people still sat in harbours around the region, the Vietnamese government sent a message to UNHCR that it 'is prepared, as of today, to grant exit visas to all Vietnamese who, by written request, express the desire to leave'. Furthermore, 'in order to find a solution to the question of "boat people" which has created problems to neighbouring countries in Southeast Asia, Vietnamese government also invites UNHCR to assist it in this field by providing transportation and a country willing to receive those persons wishing to leave'. While the message spoke of accelerating family reunion cases, it made it clear that not all Vietnamese would be permitted to leave, noting three exceptions:

1 Those who have military obligations,

2 Those who are in possession of state secrets or who occupy important posts in the field of production, and who are irreplaceable for the moment, and

3 Those who, at the present, are on trial.[64]

Days after receiving the message, Deputy High Commissioner for Refugees Dale de Haan convened an informal meeting of interested governments in Geneva to discuss the Vietnamese initiative. Views were decidedly mixed. Japan welcomed the prospect of an 'orderly movement of people from Vietnam'. Canada wondered what steps, if any, the Vietnamese government was prepared to take to stop the 'quasi-legal' outflow. France said the announcement 'had given rise to a very delicate situation. It might be interpreted to mean that if people do not like the regime then they might be assisted to leave the country. If this were the case, it could lead to contagion, which could be dangerous.' France had maintained diplomatic ties with Vietnam and, given its long colonial and post-colonial involvement with the country, saw itself as first in line to receive a potentially limitless supply of family reunion cases. 'It would be better,' suggested the French representative, 'if people could be kept within the region, accepted by neighbouring countries in a spirit of regional solidarity'.[65]

Thailand feared that international attention would be diverted to Vietnamese boat people and family reunion cases while 'land cases in Thailand, which had continued to increase in number, might be forgotten'. The United States, conspicuously, made no comment.

In late February 1979 de Haan led a UNHCR delegation to the region, stopping first in Hanoi. In discussions with the Vietnamese on legal departure, 'it was understood that the movement of persons would comprise family reunion cases and special humanitarian cases'. As for those ineligible to leave, Vietnam assured UNHCR that it would 'pursue a policy of flexibility to avoid separating families' and, as token of this, agreed to waive travel restrictions for those with military obligations.[66]

On 30 May 1979 UNHCR and Vietnam signed a seven-point Memorandum of Understanding, laying the foundation for what was to become known as the Orderly Departure Programme (ODP). The key agreement was that 'Authorized exit of those people who wish to leave Vietnam and settle in foreign countries – family reunion and other humanitarian cases – will be carried out as soon as possible and to the maximum extent.' The selection of these people would be made 'on the basis of the lists prepared by the Vietnamese government and the lists prepared by the receiving countries.

Those persons whose names appear on both lists will qualify for exit.' The cases of those whose names appeared on only one list – the vast majority at the beginning – would be subject to discussions, either between the two governments concerned or between Vietnam and UNHCR.[67]

If some governments had reservations about orderly departure, so too did some people within UNHCR who saw it as 'essentially an immigration program, albeit with refugee links'.[68] Others, both within and outside UNHCR, questioned Vietnamese motives: was this a ploy to enhance its international standing? Would ODP provide Vietnam with more legitimate means of exporting undesirable elements, like the ethnic Chinese? Would the programme distract attention and resources from the needs of people already in asylum?

By July, however, the boat flows from Vietnam had grown so large that more governments began looking for means to address the movement at its source. UNHCR's de Haan, who played a key role in establishing the programme, said Vice-President Mondale was 'very supportive' of ODP and helped warm the United States to the idea. 'The beauty of ODP', said de Haan, 'was that each government could make its own arrangements even while operating under the umbrella of UNHCR. The Vietnamese had people it wanted to get out and the US had people it wanted to get in. The lists were very important. They were criticized and laughed at but they worked eventually.'[69]

By the end of June, UNHCR had arranged its first charter flights out of Ho Chi Minh City but ODP remained small and plagued with start-up problems for some time. By December 1979, just under 2,000 Vietnamese departed directly from their country for resettlement overseas. By the end of 1980, only 6,700 people had departed Vietnam via legal channels, most of them going to France.

The government of Vietnam made another pledge in Geneva regarding departures. In his closing statement to the assembled delegates, Secretary General Waldheim said, following extensive consultations, the government of Vietnam had authorized him to say that 'for a reasonable period of time, it would make every effort to stop illegal departures'.[70] The French delegation had proposed that Vietnamese authorities impose a six-month moratorium on clandestine departures, a suggestion which garnered strong support from the ASEAN countries and, privately, some of the resettlement countries as well.

UNHCR officials say the proposal was put forward without their consultation and generated 'widespread reservations' within the organization by those who saw it 'as a potential invitation to governments to impose strict controls in order to deter potential refugees'.[71] In his closing statement summarizing the meeting's many accomplishments, Poul Hartling made no mention of the moratorium.

In 1948, the General Assembly had adopted the Universal Declaration of Human Rights which proclaimed that 'Everyone has the right to leave any country, including his own.'[72] Now 65 member states, and the Secretary

General himself, endorsed suspending that right. Waldheim had admitted the dilemma at the outset of the meeting:

> The United Nations of course stands for the proposition that individuals wishing to leave their country have the right to do so. At the same time, as a practical matter, we obviously do not wish to see an exodus of persons anywhere in the world who depart from their countries in a manner which would put their lives in jeopardy.[73]

Vietnam cracked down hard on the now 'illegal' boat departures, arresting thousands and even executing some accused of violence in their escape. Almost overnight, Vietnamese boat arrivals in the region plummeted, from 56,941 in June to 17,839 in July and 9,734 in August. In the last quarter of 1979, arrivals averaged only 2,600 per month. That decline, coupled with the substantial increase in worldwide resettlement numbers, persuaded the ASEAN countries to open their shores again.

Although the international meeting produced no binding resolutions, the Secretary General's report had noted that 'the general principles of asylum and non-refoulement were endorsed'. These endorsements, however, were both informal and conditional. As the report also noted, 'while the countries of initial arrival were expected to respect fully the principle of first asylum for refugees coming there by land and sea, they in turn expected an assurance that they would not be burdened with the residual problems and that no refugees would stay in their countries for more than a specified time'.[74]

In a brief submitted to the Ministry of Foreign Affairs, Malaysia's Task Force VII noted that, since the 1979 conference,

> Malaysia has ceased all measures to regulate entries on Vietnamese refugees. Our country gave the assurance that as long as the influx of refugees is not sudden and unmanageable as similar to early 1979 and the government of Vietnam takes necessary measures to stop the attempts by its citizens to leave Vietnam and third countries continue to accept the refugees for resettlement in their countries seriously, Malaysia will continue to avail itself as temporary transit for all Vietnamese refugees that arrive in Malaysia. This Open Door Policy is obviously conditional and temporary in nature. Whether or not Malaysia would revert to regulating the entry of refugees entirely hinges on the serious cooperation of all concerned and affected.[75]

Hartling had said that the refugee problem could not be resolved by 'piecemeal measures' and that 'no single action, however generous, would suffice'. The Geneva meeting brought four important new measures into play – massive third-country resettlement, regional processing centres, promotion of orderly departures and a moratorium on illegal departures. He also had urged that 'the prospects of repatriation – on a voluntary basis – must constantly be explored' and said UNHCR was fully prepared to help governments in this regard, but he had no takers.[76] As ODP struggled to get going and boat people managed to evade the coastal patrols and embark on the South China Sea, their hopes of finding temporary asylum hung squarely on the 'single action' of third-country resettlement.

Ships of Mercy, Ships of Prey

In his background note prepared for the Geneva meeting, Hartling observed that 'many thousands of boat cases have been rescued on the high seas by passing vessels'. He also noted that 'Regrettably ... persons have been lost at sea not only when rescue was not at hand but also as a result of disregard of distress signals.'[77] Ships that rescued boats at sea often faced long and costly delays at ports of disembarkation, particularly if they were flying the flag of a state that would not guarantee resettlement. Increasingly, it seemed that ship captains were choosing not to stop and help. From 1975 to late 1978, for example, UNHCR figures show that ships from 31 different countries rescued a total of 186 boats carrying 8,674 people. During this period, 110,000 boat people left Vietnam and reached the safety of an asylum country. In the first seven months of 1979, when boat arrivals climbed to more than 177,000 in the region and push-backs were at their peak, only 47 boats were rescued with 4,593 people aboard. About half of the rescues, moreover, were made by ships from only three countries: Norway, the Netherlands and the United Kingdom.

In August 1979, UNHCR convened a meeting in Geneva on the subject of rescue at sea, where it was agreed that new instructions were needed for ships operating in the South China Sea along with special resettlement arrangements for those rescued. Out of these discussions came a programme known as Disero (Disembarkation Resettlement Offers) under which a number of countries jointly agreed to guarantee resettlement for any Vietnamese refugee rescued at sea by merchant ships flying the flags of states that did not resettle refugees.[78]

The new commitments appeared to have almost immediate effect. In the last five months of 1979, a total of 81 boats carrying 4,031 people were rescued at sea, even though arrivals dropped to about 28,000 for the period. This meant that more than 14 per cent of boat arrivals were rescued at sea in the latter half of 1979, as against only 2.5 per cent in the calamitous first half of the year.

The question of how many people died in the boat exodus has been asked many times but remains largely a matter of conjecture. Estimates range from 10 per cent to 70 per cent and these, in turn, vary depending on the period of departure and the routes employed. The northern flow to Hong Kong probably was the safest while the small boat flow to Thailand and Malaysia, particularly at its peak in 1979, was the most dangerous. Bruce Grant, in *The Boat People: An 'Age' Investigation*, cites an 'experienced western official' as saying 10–15 per cent of those leaving on small boats were lost at sea.[79] Barry Wain also accepts a figure of around 10 per cent.[80]

Grant cites a figure of 500 documented cases of drowning as a result of Malaysian push-backs but says that 'the overwhelming proportion of more than 40,000 Indochinese towed out to sea by the Malaysian navy in the first six months of 1979 returned to Malaysia or landed in Indonesia'.[81]

UNHCR officials and other observers generally agree, as one put it, that while 'Malaysia's policies may have been cruel … there are very few stories of personal cruelty by Malaysian officials – shootings, rape, beatings, etc.'[82] There were exceptions. In late March 1979, a boatload of 237 Vietnamese on board the *MH-3012* were intercepted by a Malaysian Navy patrol boat near the Thai maritime border. The Vietnamese were towed south for 36 hours then cut loose and told to head for Indonesia. By this point, according to a UNHCR report on the incident, the Malaysian officials knew the boat's engine and water pump were broken and that a newborn baby was on board.

The *MH-3012* drifted for four days, during which ten people died of dehydration. On 31 March another Malaysian Navy boat, the *Renchong*, encountered the Vietnamese boat and tried to tow it south again. 'When the Vietnamese refused to tie the rope to their boat,' said the UNHCR report, 'naval officers fired shots and one Vietnamese, Hua Trac Thanh, was hit in his left arm.'[83] After taking Thanh and several sick people on their boat, the crew of the *Renchong* began towing the Vietnamese craft at high speed 'in a zig-zag manner. As the navy towed it, the boat started taking on water and capsized. Women and children were screaming as their boat was pulled to pieces.'[84] The *Renchong* reportedly circled the wreckage for half an hour taking photographs before it began picking up survivors who, by that time, numbered only 124.

By July 1979, Malaysian push-backs had effectively stopped but, as Vietnamese boat people were discovering to their horror, the sea held other dangers: Thai fishermen were finding that the defenceless refugee boats were easy prey for plunder. On 19 October 1979, author Nhat Tien left Vietnam on a boat bound for Malaysia. Among the 81 passengers were writers, artists, reporters, university professors, former re-education camp prisoners, priests and nuns, but the largest number were students from Saigon University 'who were of that age where one is held responsible for military duty'.[85]

On the third day out, their engine died and the boat drifted. On the tenth day, Nhat Tien writes, 'we came upon a fishing boat and that was when we learned we had entered the Gulf of Siam:

> These fishermen instituted our first shakedown, confiscating all our jewelry, watches and some clothing they took a fancy to. Afterwards, they repaired our engine, lent us their battery to get us started and directed us toward the Thai mainland…. Our happiness did not last long, for the next evening we were approached by two fishing vessels, whose occupants rushed aboard our boat to search us again…. When they found nothing of value to steal, the fishermen of one boat were furious and tried to ram us…. Finally, one boat left and the other connected a cord to us and towed us to Ko Kra Island, about 5-6 sea hours from Pakpanang district in Nakhon Si Thammarat province in Thailand…. We were all pleased to be setting foot on land even though it was a deserted island…. We lay down on a beach covered with stone and coral and slept the first peaceful night since our leaving.[86]

On the evening of the second day, Nhat Tien's group spotted a Thai Navy vessel coming in their direction. They waved an SOS flag and soon the boat anchored and several men in uniform came ashore. They jotted down some information on refugees and then left, promising to return. They never did. 'The night after the navy boat left,' Nhat Tien continued, 'we experienced our first night of terror.

> As dusk fell, a band of Thai fishermen bearing rifles, hammers and knives came to us with torches. They gave us a thorough search, took some clothing and then went away. Just after they were gone, another band came to take their place, searching us everywhere and this continued until midnight. All in all, there were three bands that did this. The last one, completing their search, drove all the men and youths into a cave and stood guard over it while they took the women away to rape them.... We could do nothing but gnash our teeth and swallow our anger and shame beneath the barrels of their guns. That was the only way we could be sure no one died. It was nearly dawn when the incident ended. The women were brought back to us and lay on the coral exhausted. Many were sobbing, collapsing in grief and humiliation in the arms of their loved ones.
>
> Following that painful and frightening night, we began organizing the concealment of the women.... Some of our women went into the jungle to lie in the cold and damp for entire days in thick brush full of snakes and insects whose bite could make you swell up and drive a sharp pain through to your brain. Others climbed precariously on the smooth rocky slopes to hide in the trees.... But the fishermen who came were well-acquainted with the geography of the island so they did not cease looking both day and night. Women were pulled out of some spots and beaten, then gang raped cruelly by as many as ten fishermen at a time.

As the weeks passed, three more refugee boats were brought to the island. The 34 people on the last boat were tossed into the sea at night several hundred yards from shore. Sixteen people, including four women and three children, drowned before they could reach the island. On 18 November a Thai marine police launch reached Ko Kra, carrying a doctor and a UNHCR field officer, Ted Schweitzer, from Songkhla camp. A helicopter pilot for an oil company had spotted the refugees two days earlier and told Schweitzer, whose first mssion to the island rescued 157 Vietnamese. He would make at least two dozen return trips during his four remaining months at Songkhla, rescuing 1,250 refugees.

Schweitzer's rescue of the first group of 157 boat people also led to the arrest and conviction of seven Thai fishermen, who received jail sentences averaging 16 years each for rape and robbery. But the piracy problem only got worse. In 1981, the first year that UNHCR kept such statistics, 77 per cent of all Vietnamese boats reaching Thailand were attacked, most of them more than once. A total of 571 deaths were reported, along with 599 rapes and 243 abductions.[87] This was after UNHCR had provided a patrol boat to the Thai Navy and the United States had funded a bilateral effort to increase sea and air surveillance. One can only guess what the statistics might have shown for 1979 and 1980, when arrival rates in Thailand were equally high and intervention was a matter of isolated acts of kindness and courage.

In mid-December 1979, a small fishing boat slipped out of Vung Tau harbour with 94 people aboard, all Vietnamese. According to their leader, Kieu Van Cuong, the passengers had paid a total of 90 taels of gold for construction and provisioning of the boat. They also paid three local officials in the village of Phuoc Loc a total of 9 taels in order to cover their escape. Kieu told a UNHCR interviewer that there was 'intensive patrolling and public announcements on punishment of boat leaders, owners and organizers' but he also said there were rumours spreading in Saigon that 'those who have paid will be allowed to leave from now on'.

Their original destination was Malaysia as it was the closest country but they 'wandered on the sea because of engine troubles and loss of direction'. Kieu reported 'no attack by Thais'. The boat reached Malaysia after dark on 23 December. It was not turned away. After one week in a transit camp, the 27 families from Saigon and environs were admitted to Pulau Bidong, Malaysia's overcrowded island camp. Their trip had been happily uneventful and no media were on hand to record their arrival, now almost a matter of routine. Attention, in any event, had shifted to the Thai–Cambodian border, where the Indochinese crisis and the plight of refugees were taking on larger, more complex and dangerous dimensions.

Notes

1 See Chanda, *Brother Enemy*, pp. 263–362.
2 In *ibid.*, p. 354.
3 Nguyen Khac Vien, 'Those who leave', in *Southern Vietnam: 1975–1985* (Hanoi: Foreign Languages Publishing House, 1985), p. 235.
4 Chanda, *Brother Enemy*, pp. 361.
5 Pao-min Chang, *Beijing, Hanoi, and the Overseas Chinese* (Berkeley: Institute of East Asian Studies, University of California, 1982), p. 52.
6 Benoit, 'Vietnam's "boat people"', pp. 152, 157.
7 Wain, *The Refused*, p. 87.
8 Author's interview with Li Chong Sheng, Dong Feng Forest Farm, Guangxi Province, 4 November 1995.
9 Nguyen Khac Vien, 'Those Who Leave', p. 254.
10 *Ibid.*, p. 268.
11 Bui Tin, *From Cadre to Exile: Memoirs of a North Vietnamese Journalist* (Chiang Mai: Silkworm Books, 1995), p. 102.
12 Nguyen Khac Vien, 'Those who leave', p. 273.
13 Author's interview with Adnan Nala, Galang, Indonesia, 7 October 1995. See also Judith Strauch, 'The Chinese Exodus from Vietnam: Implications for the Southeast Asian Chinese', Cultural Survival, Occasional Paper 1, December 1980: p. 1.
14 Judith Strauch, 'The Chinese exodus from Vietnam', p. 1.
15 Keith St. Cartmail, *Exodus Indochina* (Auckland: Heinemann, 1983), p. 246.
16 *Ibid.*, p. 6.
17 Author's interview with Rear Admiral Dato Yaacob Bin HJ Daud, Kuala Lumpur, 25 September 1995.
18 Author's interview with François Fouinat, Geneva, 12 February 1996.
19 'Statistik Pendatang Haram Vietnam (1975–1983)': this document was provided

to the author in September 1995 by Dato Abdullah bin Samsuddin, former director of Task Force VII.

20 Author's interview with Adnan Nala, Galang, Indonesia, 7 October 1995.

21 In Kosol Vongsrisart, Vanchai Julsukont, Cletus Rego and Jack Reynolds, eds, *The Indochinese Refugees (Thailand)* (Bangkok: Office for Human Development of the Federation of Asian Bishops' Conferences, 1980), p. 48.

22 Nayaporn Penpas, 'Khambanyai ruang panha phuopayop lae pholopniikhao-muang' ('A lecture on the problem of displaced persons and those who flee into the country'), Sathaban Jitwittaya Khwammankhong (Institute of Security Psychology), 25 November 1987, p. 21. Translation by the author.

23 *The Nation*, 19 June 1979.

24 In Committee for the Coordination of Services to Displaced Persons in Thailand, 'Seminar on Displaced Persons in Thailand, Nakorn Pathom, September 22, 1977' (Bangkok: CCSDPT, 1977), p. 35.

25 US Central Intelligence Agency, *The Refugee Resettlement Problem in Thailand* (Washington, DC: National Foreign Assessment Center, May 1978), p. 2.

26 Lt Col Kamol Prachuopmoh, Asst. Dir. of MOI Operations Center for Displaced Persons. Comments made at the MOI/CCSDPT Conference on Relief of the Indochina Displaced Persons Problem in Thailand, Bangkok, 19 January 1979.

27 *The Nation*, 20 April 1979.

28 *Bangkok World*, 25 April 1979.

29 Dennis McNamara, 'The politics of humanitarianism: a study of some aspects of the international response to the Indochinese refugee influx (1975–1985)'. Unpublished manuscript, Section II, p. 44.

30 *Bangkok World*, 16 May 1979.

31 Stephen Heder, *Kampuchean Occupation and Resistance,* Asian Studies Monograph No. 027, Institute of Asian Studies, Chulalongkorn University (January 1980), p. 23.

32 *Ibid.*, p. 24.

33 *Far Eastern Economic Review*, 25 May 1979.

34 From an unpublished series of interviews collected by the Khmer Section of JVA Thailand in July 1981. Hereinafter referred to as 'Preah Vihear Interviews.'

35 In Georgina Ashworth, *The Boat People and the Road People* (London: Quartermaine House, 1979).

36 'Preah Vihear Interviews'.

37 *Ibid.* Heder (*Kampuchean Occupation and Resistance*, p. 26) also reports this.

38 'Preah Vihear Interviews'.

39 See *Far Eastern Economic Review*, 3 August 1979.

40 See Henry Kamm, 'Cambodians starving in forest', *International Herald Tribune*, 26 June 1979.

41 In Hanna Sophie Greve, *Kampuchean Refugees, 'Between the Tiger and the Crocodile'*, PhD Dissertation, University of Bergen, 1987, Vol. I, p. 70.

42 *Bangkok Post*, 12 June 1979.

43 McNamara, 'The politics of humanitarianism,' Section II, p. 47, Section V, p. 21.

44 William Shawcross, *The Quality of Mercy* (New York: Simon and Schuster, 1984), p. 92.

45 *Far Eastern Economic Review*, 29 June 1979.

46 *Bangkok Post*, 18 July 1979.

47 See Congressional Research Service, *World Refugee Crisis: The International Community's Response* (Washington, DC: US Government Printing Office, August 1979), p. 141.

48 Wain, *The Refused,* p. 80. Wain estimated that by mid-1979, 20,000 Cambodians and 40,000 Laotians had slipped undetected into Thailand and that 110,000 Indochinese refugees 'had died fleeing all these countries'.

49 The five members of ASEAN were Thailand, Malaysia, Indonesia, Singapore and the Philippines. A sixth member, Brunei, joined later.

50 'Joint Communique Issued at the Twelfth ASEAN Ministerial Meeting; Bali, Indonesia; 28–30 June 1979', in Thai Ministry of Foreign Affairs, *Documents on the Kampuchean Problem: 1979–1985* (Bangkok: 1985), p. 78.

51 Wain, *The Refused*, pp. 196–7.

52 UNHCR, 'Consultative Meeting with Interested Governments on Refugees and Displaced Persons in Southeast Asia', Summing-Up by UNHCR, Annex I, in Note by the High Commissioner for the Meeting on Refugees and Displaced Persons in Southeast Asia, 9 July 1979. Hereinafter referred to as 'UNHCR Note-1979'.

53 Loescher and Scanlan, *Calculated Kindness*, p. 139.

54 'UNHCR Note-1979', p. 1.

55 Lui Ting Terry, 'Undocumented migration in Hong Kong', *International Migration Review*, Vol. 21, No. 2, 1983: pp. 262–3.

56 'UNHCR Note-1979', p. 6.

57 Chang, *Beijing, Hanoi, and the Overseas Chinese*, p. 57.

58 'UNHCR Note-1979', p. 7.

59 In Sutter, *The Indochinese Refugee Dilemma,* pp. 144–5.

60 McNamara, 'The politics of humanitarianism', Section II, p. 73.

61 UNHCR, 'Meeting on Refugees and Displaced Persons in Southeast Asia, Convened by the Secretary-General of the United Nations at Geneva on 20 and 21 July, 1979, and Subsequent Developments', 7 November 1979. Hereinafter referred to as 'Secretary-General Report-1979'.

62 US General Accounting Office, *The Indochinese Exodus: A Humanitarian Dilemma*, p. 19.

63 In Leonard Davies, *Hong Kong and the Asylum-Seekers from Vietnam* (London: Macmillan, 1991), p. 7.

64 Annex to letter from Poul Hartling to missions of Executive Committee countries in Geneva, 22 March 1979.

65 UNHCR, Note for the File, 'Meeting with Representatives of Interested Governments on Refugees and Displaced Persons in Southeast Asia', 16 January 1979. Quotes should not be considered verbatim.

66 Letter from Poul Hartling to missions of Executive Committee countries in Geneva, 22 March 1979.

67 The 30 May 1979 Memorandum of Understanding is included in the Appendices of a November 1986 report by Migration and Refugee Services, US Catholic Conference, *The Orderly Departure Program: The Need for Reassessment.*

68 McNamara, 'The politics of humanitarianism', Section II, p. 84.

69 Author's interview with Dale de Haan, Washington, DC, 17 April 1996.

70 'Secretary-General Report-1979', p. 6.

71 McNamara, 'The politics of humanitarianism', Section II, p. 78.

72 UNHCR, *Collection of International Instruments Concerning Refugees,* p. 101.

73 In Wain, *The Refused*, p. 229.

74 'Secretary-General Report-1979', pp. 5–6.

75 'Vietnamese refugees in Malaysia'. This mimeographed document, with statistics that are current as of June 1983, was provided to the author in September 1995

by Dato Abdullah bin Samsuddin, former director of Task Force VII.

76 'UNHCR Note-1979', p. 9.

77 *Ibid.*, p. 4.

78 The countries participating in the Disero programme included Canada, France, New Zealand, Sweden, Switzerland and the United States. In 1985, the RASRO (Rescue at Sea Resettlement Offers) programme was introduced, which shared out resettlement guarantees for refugees rescued by small resettlement countries with large merchant fleets.

79 Bruce Grant, *The Boat People: An 'Age' Investigation* (Harmondsworth: Penguin Books, 1979), p. 81.

80 Wain, *The Refused*, p. 83.

81 Grant, *The Boat People*, p. 81.

82 Author's interview with Lennart Hansson, Bangkok, 21 October 1995.

83 In Wain, *The Refused*, p. 205.

84 Hansson interview.

85 Nhat Tien, Duong Phuc and Vu Thanh Thuy, *Pirates on the Gulf of Siam* (San Diego: Boat People SOS Committee, 1981), p. 79.

86 *Ibid.*, pp. 81–2.

87 US Committee for Refugees, *Vietnamese Boat People: Pirates' Vulnerable Prey* (Washington, DC: February 1984), p. 6.

CHAPTER 4

Cambodians on the Border

In January 1979, following the Vietnamese occupation of neighbouring Cambodia, Thailand found itself at a difficult crossroads. While some countries in the region had begun to speak metaphorically of the boat people as a Vietnamese invasion, Thailand feared it might be facing the real thing. Thai political scientist Sukhumbhand Paribatra argues that Hanoi's armed intervention in Cambodia

> presented a 'clear and present danger' to Thailand at the very time that the latter was no longer assured of direct military assistance from the US. The stationing in Cambodia and Laos of between 200,000 to 250,000 Vietnamese troops, well-supplied with Soviet military hardware and backed by the growing Soviet naval presence in the region, was … perceived by the Thais as a threat in a number of ways, ranging from psychological intimidation, subversion and incursion to invasion and outright colonization.[1]

To counter the Vietnamese threat, Thailand moved closer to China and the Khmer Rouge. Years after the event, a Thai diplomat revealed that on 14 January 1979, Prime Minister Kriangsak Chomanand met secretly with two senior Chinese officials who had just flown into U-Taphao airbase. At that meeting, 'Kriangsak agreed to allow the use of Thai territory to supply the Khmer Rouge and … help Khmer Rouge leaders to make foreign trips through Thailand.'[2] In return, China agreed to withdraw support for the Communist Party of Thailand and to provide the Thai military with favourable terms in arms sales.[3]

Throughout 1978, both despite and because of the growing boat exodus, Thailand and most of its ASEAN partners had been inclined to seek closer relations with Vietnam in order to stem the outflow. After the Vietnamese invasion of Cambodia and the subsequent Chinese incursion into Vietnam, positions within ASEAN began to polarize, with Thailand and Singapore moving toward the Chinese side while Malaysia and Indonesia sought to acknowledge the legitimate security interests of both Thailand and Vietnam. Cambodia had long been seen as a buffer zone by its two more powerful neighbours. Now that middle ground was occupied and it was time to take sides.

For the United States, the choice by that point was clear. As Elizabeth Becker wrote in her 1986 study of Cambodia, *When the War Was Over*,

> The invasion proclaimed the new China–US alliance of interests and ensured that China continue to hold sway over affairs in Indochina, this time on the side of the West. To that end, National Security Adviser [Zbigniew] Brzezinski was of considerable help.... Brzezinski said, 'I encouraged the Chinese to support Pol Pot. I encouraged the Thai to help the DK [Democratic Kampuchea]. The question was how to help the Cambodian people. Pol Pot was an abomination. We could never support him but China could.' The result was a policy that the United States continued to follow during the subsequent Republican administration. The United States 'winked, semipublicly,' in Brzezinski's words, while encouraging China and Thailand to give the Khmer Rouge direct aid to fight against the Vietnamese occupation.[4]

As the Vietnamese swept across Cambodia and the Khmer Rouge retreated, up to half the country also went on the move. Initially, most Cambodians were content to stay within their borders to head for home, search for relatives, and look for food. Some thought of escape or temporary safety and began to move toward Thailand. By the middle of the year, despite the brutal push-backs by Thai authorities in June, more than 100,000 Cambodians were massing at the border.

On 21 September 1979, the same day that the UN General Assembly voted to recognize Democratic Kampuchea as the legitimate government of Cambodia, Thai officials called a meeting with four international organizations – the International Committee of the Red Cross (ICRC), the United Nations Children's Fund (UNICEF), the World Food Programme (WFP) and UNHCR – to discuss relief strategies. At the meeting, Thai officials

> stressed that their borders would still remain closed to the refugees, but that aid organizations could deliver aid to the border and hand it over to Khmer Rouge representatives. Aid would also be administered to displaced Thai villagers along the border. The Thais decided that the aid organizations could provide food, medicines, blankets, and tarpaulins. The responsibilities were designated as follows: WFP would purchase and deliver relief supplies to government warehouses; UNICEF was responsible for delivering the supplies to the border and eventually monitoring the distributions; ICRC would conduct the distributions and provide medical services. Prime Minister Kriangsak specified that ICRC and UNICEF should jointly coordinate the border relief program. They were henceforth referred to as the Joint Mission.[5]

In July 1979, representatives from the People's Republic of Kampuchea (PRK) had approached the World Food Programme with a request for 100,000 tons of food. But Phnom Penh had three requirements for an expanded aid operation: (1) assistance plans, including shipment schedules and distribution plans, must be approved by the government; (2) distribution must be through official or national Red Cross channels; and (3) UNICEF and ICRC should not provide aid through any other channels than those mentioned above.[6] In short, Phnom Penh wanted no international aid going to the Khmer Rouge or anyone else who could not or would not take it from the government.

The Joint Mission submitted readily to the first two conditions, but disagreement on the final issue bedevilled the operation on both sides of the border throughout its 15-month tenure and beyond. Both ICRC and UNICEF had mandates to provide humanitarian aid in a neutral and impartial manner, while China and Thailand, in particular, were insistent that the Khmer Rouge be fed. Some major Western donors like the United States, while supporting aid through Phnom Penh, also wanted aid at the border, as a gesture of solidarity with Thailand and a signal of doubt that the Cambodian authorities could do the job alone.

In October 1979 UNICEF and ICRC had issued a joint appeal for $110 million to deliver 165,000 tons of food – along with medical supplies, educational materials, and seeds – to 2.5 million Cambodians still inside their country. The needs were enormous, according to Joint Mission representatives:

> It is reported that 80–90 per cent of children are malnourished. Malaria, dysentery, intestinal parasites and respiratory diseases are endemic and have taken a heavy toll of those weakened by hunger. The cumulative effect of malnutrition and communicable diseases is particularly severe for young children; it is reported that the number of children under the age of five in the country is abnormally low. It is estimated that only about 50 doctors remain to care for some 4 to 4.5 million persons. Hospitals are bare of equipment and drugs and health care institutions of any kind are few; where they exist, they are packed to twice normal capacity. Orphanages are overflowing and the school system remains to be re-established. Reports are that perhaps only 10–20 per cent of land normally under cultivation has been planted ... and rice is in such short supply that little, if any, will be available for the forthcoming planting season.[7]

The lingering devastations of the Khmer Rouge and the growing unease at the continued Vietnamese presence were compelling Cambodians to uproot themselves in ever larger numbers, searching for a little more food and a little better security.

Thailand's Open Door Policy

By early October 1979 an estimated 100,000 Cambodians were living in two sprawling encampments, Nong Samet and Mak Mun, controlled by non-communist resistance forces loosely known as the Khmer Serei (Free Khmer). Farther south on the border, below the town of Aranyaprathet, a more desperate group of Cambodians had begun massing. Their numbers, by mid-October, were nearing 30,000. These were the refugees whose appalling condition journalist William Shawcross described in *The Quality of Mercy*:

> Daily, awful spindly creatures, with no flesh and with wide vacant eyes stumbled out of the forests and the mountains into which the Khmer Rouge had corralled them. They had malaria, they had tuberculosis, they had dysentery, they were dehydrated, they were famished, they were dying.[8]

Vietnamese attacks on other Khmer Rouge sanctuaries nearby brought the refugee total south of Aranyaprathet to more than 60,000. To the north, tens of thousands more Cambodians began crossing the border at Nong Samet.

On 17 October Prime Minister Kriangsak flew out from Bangkok for a two-day inspection of the border. When he returned to the capital, he announced a new approach toward Cambodian refugees, which came to be known as Thailand's 'open door policy'. Its commitments essentially were three:

- However large the influx of displaced persons, no one will be turned back. Entry into Thailand for Kampuchean distressed civilians will be unimpeded.

- Temporary asylum will be given to displaced persons until they can return to their homeland after the fighting has ceased, or until they are resettled in third countries.

- If the displaced persons choose to be repatriated, they will be repatriated voluntarily with the knowledge of the UNHCR.[9]

New arrivals would be transferred to three temporary camps under Thai military control – Sa Kaeo, Kamput, and Surin – before being moved to a 'national refugee centre' to be built at Mairut, capable of holding 300,000 people.[10]

At the 21 September meeting Thai officials were conspicuously silent about a role for UNHCR at the border which, after all, was closed to refugee arrivals. UNHCR was to continue serving the 'Old Khmer' who had arrived in Thailand prior to January 1979 but, on the border, it was odd-man-out. Thailand by now associated the agency explicitly with international resettlement, an option it did not want to make available to the border Khmer.

As for the new camps, Thailand's initial thinking was to solicit international funding for these centres while retaining control of their construction and operations. But on 22 October, Colonel Sanan Kajornklam of the Thai Supreme Command telephoned Martin Barber, a UNHCR programme officer in Bangkok, and invited UNHCR to establish a 'holding centre' for up to 90,000 Cambodians at Sa Kaeo, 60 kilometres west of the border. The Thai military had decided that the original idea was 'impractical' according to Barber and now wished UNHCR to set up and run the camps, though they still would be under military supervision.[11] In dealing with the new influx of Cambodians, Thailand chose to give authority for the holding centres to the military, specifically the Joint Operations Centre of the Supreme Command, citing as a reason that 'among the Kampucheans fleeing to Thailand, a number of them are combatants. So to put them under control in safe areas, the Thai military has to get involved.'[12]

Within two days, the first buses from the border had rolled into Sa Kaeo, churning the former rice field into a quagmire, and pictures of the emergency 'were being beamed to most of the television sets in the Western world'.[13] By the end of the month, more than 30,000 people had crowded into the muddy fields of Sa Kaeo, all from Khmer Rouge border sites south of Aranyaprathet. Two weeks after the camp opened, more than 400 people had perished from the lingering effects of disease and starvation.[14]

In response to this influx and the appeal for help from the Thai government, UNHCR's Hartling dispatched a special mission to Thailand headed by Zia Rizvi, who had been one of Sadruddin Aga Khan's key advisers and now was recalled from 'exile' in Rome to become UNHCR's senior regional coordinator for Southeast Asia. UNHCR also pledged nearly $60 million to meet the needs of up to 300,000 Cambodian refugees and created a special Regional Office Kampuchean Unit (ROKU), headed by Martin Barber, to coordinate the work in the holding centres.

In mid-November 1979, Thai authorities asked UNHCR to establish another camp, this one for an estimated 300,000 or more Cambodians living in the area of Nong Samet, Mak Mun and other Khmer Serei encampments. Khao I Dang, named for a nearby mountain, was far better situated than Sa Kaeo, with more space and better drainage. After four days of intensive preparatory work, Khao I Dang was opened on 21 November, but only 4,800 people arrived on the first day.[15] The numbers climbed steadily though unspectacularly to about 28,000 by the end of the month, but it became clear that many people were in no rush to abandon the border camps. Some, as it turned out, were being held back.

Most of the arrivals north of Aranyaprathet reached the border in far better shape than those to the south who had spent the previous ten months in the evacuation columns of the Khmer Rouge. They had not been force-marched to the Thai border but came on their own – singly, in families, or in larger groups – for a world of reasons. Some came for food or medicine, some came looking for family members, some were running from the Vietnamese, some were still running from the Khmer Rouge, some came to fight, some came to escape the fighting, some came to trade or smuggle, some were simply following someone else. They were farmers and factory workers, rich merchants and landless peasants, Khmer and ethnic Chinese, Buddhist monks and common bandits. Some came for a few days and some came looking for a whole new life.[16]

When word reached the Khmer Serei camps of the pending move to Khao I Dang, many residents were sceptical and the warlords who ran the camps were furious. A number of refugees had just made their way back to the border after having been pushed back at Preah Vihear five months earlier. No one wanted to relive those experiences. Some feared that Khao I Dang was a Thai prison, where they would be enslaved or killed. The Khmer Serei warlords nurtured the fear and rumour-mongering, since a move to Khao I Dang reduced the headcount for food aid, which they were diverting in substantial amounts.

On 8 December, following an outbreak of factional infighting in Mak Mun, the Thai army ordered Khmer Serei troops to pull away from the border and allow civilians to enter Khao I Dang if they wished. By this time, UN officials estimated that about 750,000 Cambodians were gathered along the border. In addition, about 60,000 new arrivals were now in Khao I Dang, 37,000 in Sa Kaeo, 2,600 in Kamput, 2,800 in Mairut II, and about 2,000 unaccompanied minors in Khao Larn. The 'Old Khmer' remained in UNHCR-funded camps operated by the Ministry of the Interior. These included 5,000 in Aranyaprathet, 6,000 in Mairut I, 3,500 in Surin, and 800 in Buriram detention centre.[17]

Then, on 24 January 1980, Thailand abruptly reversed course again and closed its doors to new Cambodian arrivals. By then, Khao I Dang held 112,000 people, making it the second largest Cambodian city in the world after Phnom Penh. All told, the number of Cambodian refugees in Thailand exceeded 157,000, by no means an insignificant figure, but less than half what Kriangsak expected when he opened Thailand's doors scarcely three months earlier.

It is likely that Thai officials never meant the policy to be more than temporary. National Security Council official Khachadpai Burusapatana described the 'two stages' of Cambodian arrivals in 1979. In the first stage, from January to October,

> particularly during January to May ... the Vietnamese forces had drastically wiped out Pol Pot forces in Western Cambodia resulting in the influx of approximately 150,000 Cambodians into Thai territory. As rainy season approached, the situation in Cambodia had calmed down; authorities gradually sent the Cambodians back into safe places [sic] in Cambodia.

In the second stage, said Khachadpai, 'after the end of the rainy season in September, Vietnamese soldiers had resumed wiping out Pol Pot forces'. In his inspection tour of the border in October, Kriangsak 'had witnessed the misery of these Cambodians.... The Prime Minister felt very sorry and sympathetic and realized that if these Cambodians were sent back under this condition, they would not be able to survive.'[18]

As one observer put it, 'refugee policy has always been at least one part State interest and at most one part compassion' and Thailand was no exception.[19] As Khachadpai's analysis makes plain, the compassion of the open door policy was motivated by the strategic interest in seeing Pol Pot's forces survive to fight another day. When the Vietnamese dry season offensive flared but did not fully ignite, Thailand closed the border again.

Seen in this light, the open door was never intended as a permanent policy shift but merely a brief season of respite.

In their 1983 study of the Cambodian relief effort, *Rice, Rivalry, and Politics*, Linda Mason and Roger Brown suggest that with the establishment of Sa Kaeo, the relief operation 'split into two distinct spheres – the holding centers within Thailand and the volatile no-man's-land called simply "the border".'[20] But it was not until Thailand's open door began to close that the distinction became real, for some no less than a matter of life or death.

In March 1980, Thai Foreign Minister Siddhi Savetsila reiterated that Cambodians already in Thailand would continue to be granted temporary asylum and that any repatriation would be voluntary and 'with the approval and knowledge of the UNHCR'. But for those still on the border, Siddhi said, 'it is preferable to let them remain on the Kampuchean side of the border.'[21]

UNHCR figures show a total of 43,608 Cambodian arrivals in Thailand in 1980. Many of these came in January, before the border was closed, but others begged or bribed their way into Khao I Dang. By the middle of the year, the camp population had climbed to its all-time high of 140,000. Security tightened as the year waned, however, and in all of 1981 new Cambodian arrivals in Thailand officially totalled only 16. For most of the next decade, the holding centres – Khao I Dang, in particular – and the border camps would occupy their own erratic orbits, close to touching but worlds apart.

The question was asked at the time and many times since: why was UNHCR not responsible for all Cambodians at the border instead of only those who entered the 'holding centres' during the brief period of the open door? At a 1995 conference in Tokyo, Zia Rizvi offered seven answers to that question:

1 It is UNHCR's established policy that refugees must not be allowed to become a source of tension between their country of origin and the country of asylum and, consequently, must be removed away from the border.

2 UNHCR felt that by keeping an increasing number of Cambodians at the border, a 'human buffer' was being created between Thailand and Cambodia and that, eventually, the Cambodians at the border would be caught in crossfire.

3 UNHCR did not want its policy of holding centers to be weakened by this diversion, thereby decreasing pressure on the Thais.

4 The border was not clearly delineated and straddling could create uncertainty as to where the refugees were and problems of territorial jurisdiction could arise.

5 There was a strong presence of the military forces on both sides of the border, creating an atmosphere of insecurity for the refugees. Also,

weapons were easily available and the law-and-order situation was precarious.

6 No guarantees were being offered by anyone regarding the safety or welfare of the border people and it seemed that they were going to be used as political pawns by those who were, understandably, against the Vietnamese presence in Cambodia.

7 The border encampments could be easily penetrated by the Khmer Rouge and could serve as excellent recruitment grounds.[22]

In fact, in late December 1979, UNHCR had sent a cable to Waldheim in New York, offering to be the United Nations' 'executing agency' and 'focal point' in Thailand. The cable spelled out three conditions for a UNHCR presence on the border: that the camps be moved away from the border, that they be demilitarized, and that UN access should be unrestricted. As one UNHCR official said later, 'I think we laid out those conditions because we did not want to go to the border'.[23] Dale de Haan, then Deputy High Commissioner, urged Poul Hartling to press for a lead agency function.

> I was an advocate of us doing the UNICEF role. We were involved in Indochina. UNHCR had a program in Laos. It had a program in Vietnam and Vietnam occupied Cambodia. We were cooperating closely with ICRC. I saw this as a preventive measure – humanitarian intervention. It made sense but there was strong opposition to that in UNHCR.[24]

Hartling, by and large, felt that UNHCR already had its hands full and Rizvi did not want to jeopardize relations with the Indochinese states by getting too involved with the resistance.

But even if UNHCR had been uniformly supportive of the lead agency idea, it would have faced stiff opposition from outside. Those reluctant to see an enhanced role for UNHCR on the border included the United States, Thailand and UN Secretary General Waldheim, as well as ICRC and UNICEF.[25] Morton Abramowitz, then US Ambasssador to Thailand, said later,

> The principal problem with UNHCR ... was that they showed insufficient concern about the problem and insufficient willingness to go out and provide services to the refugees.... It had a mentality which saw itself as a small agency providing protection against refoulement, staffed by people who had been working for 30 years on European problems and were totally unprepared for this new thing ... handling large emergencies. It was an organization not equipped to handle the responsibility it was seeking.[26]

As Rizvi noted, 'Interestingly, UNICEF together with ICRC accepted to do what UNHCR was reluctant to do, thus creating the unusual situation whereby UNHCR was left minding children in the holding centers while UNICEF was busy taking care of refugees at the border.'[27] But UNICEF did not have a refugee protection mandate and UNHCR's reluctance to get involved with the border left several hundred thousand civilians at the mercy of men with guns, subject to all kinds of abuse and unable freely to seek asylum or be safe from the risk of expulsion.

Repatriation and Relocation

When the 'holding centres' were established, it was Thailand's policy – endorsed by UNHCR over the objections of the United States – that no third-country resettlement should be available in these new camps in order to reduce the 'magnet effect'. Thus, although overseas resettlement in 1979 had reduced the numbers of Cambodian refugees in Thailand by more than 17,000, fully as much as the previous four years combined, this involved mainly the remnants of the 'Old Khmer' caseload. For the new arrivals, both Thailand and UNHCR wanted to promote repatriation, although through different means and for different ends.

In February 1980 UNHCR's Regional Coordinator for Southeast Asia, Zia Rizvi, had met with officials of the Phnom Penh regime to discuss assistance for returnees inside Cambodia. Foreign Minister Hun Sen told him that more than 200,000 refugees had come home by that point, mostly from Vietnam but also from Thailand and Laos; he was seeking food aid and longer-term reintegration assistance. Meanwhile, the Khmer Rouge had been moving hundreds of people out of the holding centres clandestinely, at night, often aided by the Thai military.[28]

From February through April, UNHCR had engaged the services of Milton Osborne, an Australian academic and Cambodia scholar, to assess perspectives on repatriation in the holding centres. Osborne concluded that almost two-thirds of the people 'expressed an interest in returning' but only when there was peace. He also made clear his grave concerns at the prospects of involuntary repatriation from Sa Kaeo.[29] As Rizvi later told Shawcross,

> I decided that if [repatriation] had to take place, it had better be done under our control, in daylight. I told Siddhi that there must be a formal voluntary repatriation, which must be done like UNHCR repatriations all over the world. My main concern was not to have a repetition of the forced repatriation of June 1979, to Preah Vihear. It was quite possible. After all, the same military commanders were still along the border.[30]

In March, UNHCR entered into discussions with Thai authorities to provide a mechanism for ensuring the voluntary status, if not the safety, of a cross-border return. At a meeting on 6 May the Thai government and UNHCR concluded a 15-point agreement on voluntary repatriation, though they declined to make this public until nearly five weeks later. Following an announcement in the camps of the repatriation option, those wishing to return to Cambodia would be asked to sign (or thumbprint) a confidential statement witnessed by UNHCR and Thai officials. Volunteers would have the choice of one of four crossing points.

The first, Ban Sangae, was a Khmer Serei camp about 40 kilometres to the north of Aranyaprathet and the farthest of the four points from the holding centres. The second, Prasat Sarokok, was the site of a Khmer temple ruin, where in mid-June, the Thai military had ordered an estimated 70,000 people to be moved from the Khmer Serei camp of Nong Samet. The third crossing point, Nong Chan, was the principal conduit for the 'landbridge' cross-border relief operation and the fourth, Tap Prik, was south of Aranyaprathet, across from the Khmer Rouge strongholds at Phnom Malai.

Voluntary agencies had agreed to provide the returnees with rice, seeds, hoe heads, fishing nets, and a small medical kit. The programme would begin in Sa Kaeo and Khao I Dang, to be followed by Kamput and Mairut. Movements would start taking place, according to the agreement, around mid-June. Thai military sources at the border explained that 'the Sa Kaeo refugees who entered Thailand under the control of Pol Pot's guerrillas late last year will be the first to return because they are physically stronger and healthier than those in other camps.'[31]

The growing suspicion was that both the Khmer Rouge and the Thai military wanted combatants to rejoin the struggle for Cambodia and Sa Kaeo was the first place to look for fighters. Khao I Dang was not likely to have many of those but it was by far the largest and, as it were, the most respectable of the holding centres. Its participation thus was expected to lend a certain scope and credibility to the undertaking.

On 10 June, following the Thai Cabinet's approval of UNHCR's repatriation guidelines, Foreign Minister Siddhi announced plans for a 'mass voluntary repatriation of Kampuchean refugees at the border'. Although Thailand clearly had hopes of a large-scale operation, the numbers did not look promising. Relief officials in Khao I Dang confirmed at the time that only about 1,500 people actually had requested to return and another 1,500 were 'probably eager to go'.[32]

As rumours and propaganda circulated in the camps — with threats of food cut-offs, nighttime round-ups and retributions — many refugees began to fear they would be forced to leave. Khmer Rouge in Sa Kaeo began to chant a dark little tune:

Those who go back first will sleep on cots.
Those who go back second will sleep on mats.
Those who go back third will sleep in the mud.
And those who go back last will sleep under the ground.[33]

Both members of the Joint Mission, ICRC and UNICEF, were greatly disturbed at the prospective repatriation and at UNHCR's hitherto un-publicized role in it. ICRC's Bangkok delegation wrote to Thai Foreign Minister Siddhi, stating that the organization

has reservations as to whether conditions currently prevailing within Kampuchea are such that the safety and physical integrity of those wishing voluntarily to return to their homes can be considered adequate and as to whether they will be able to reach their villages.[34]

A UNICEF official expressed shock at 'the remarkable lack of clarity and depth of planning by UNHCR as to the political and social implications of this repatriation.... Rather than solving the problem of Khmer refugees in Thailand, UNHCR may only be passing the responsibility for their care to UNICEF and ICRC' across the border.[35]

The political implications were becoming clearer by the day. On a four-day visit to Thailand, Singapore's Deputy Prime Minister Sinnathamby Rajaratnam said, 'when these refugees come, we look after them. We should send them back to fight for their freedom.'[36] That same day, Phnom Penh's state news service published a statement from the PRK Ministry of Foreign Affairs condemning the repatriation as 'deliberate hostility' on the part of Thailand. The Foreign Ministry demanded 'that Thai authorities stop using the question of Kampuchean refugees and "humanitarian aid" to interfere in and wage aggression against Kampuchea'. It closed on a threatening note: 'These vile maneuvers will be crushed.'[37]

Stung and perhaps slightly unnerved by the strong feelings the repatriation plan was stirring up, the Thai Foreign Ministry issued a statement to clear up the 'misunderstandings': 'The government was requested by UNHCR to set guidelines for the voluntary repatriation of Kampucheans to their home country,' the announcement said, seeming to shift the onus to UNHCR. These guidelines – which included confidential interviews, choice of returning point, and provision of relief supplies – 'will help solve the problem in a way that means humanitarian principles will not be violated'.[38] Phnom Penh, however, was not appeased and on 15 June Hun Sen wrote to Poul Hartling, warning him that 'UNHCR collaboration with this attempt can only damage the reputation of your institution and jeopardize the good relations between the KPRC [Kampuchean People's Revolutionary Council] and UNHCR.'[39]

On the morning of 17 June 1980, 511 people boarded buses in Khao I Dang and went back to Cambodia, at least as far as the Nong Chan crossing point. Former UNHCR official Hanne Sophie Greve says the majority of returnees were young and old people 'who found life in Khao I Dang especially difficult.' Many were going back to find relatives. One 83-year-old woman told journalists, 'I want to die in the place I was born.'[40] Sa Kaeo the next day was 'a completely different scene', according to Greve:

> For the first few days, the interview area was crammed with people eager to get out. Nearly everyone, young and old, was dressed in their black pyjamas or grey or green fatigue. The *krama*, an all-purpose Kampuchean scarf, had been converted by most people into a tube containing cooked dry rice (an ideal jungle provision) and formed into a hoop that was slung over one shoulder.... [L]arge numbers did not hide the fact that they were going back to fight.[41]

The Sa Kaeo returnees chose to cross the border at Tap Prik, where they were met by a group of 100 Khmer Rouge soldiers. Hanoi radio issued another threat: 'The consequences of this repatriation will not be good for Thailand.'[42] Bangkok issued another denial on the use of force: 'If we really forced them,' said Prime Minister Prem Tinsulanond, 'the number would be more than 500. It would be tens of thousands.'[43] By 19 June a total of 2,032 people had been repatriated but the numbers from Khao I Dang had fallen off quickly.

But movements, especially from Sa Kaeo, gathered new momentum and more than 3,400 people returned in the next three days. The Voice of Democratic Kampuchea, the Khmer Rouge radio station, broadcast a briskly titled commentary, 'Our people in Sa Kaeo Camp have voluntarily returned to the fatherland in order to take part in the fight against the Vietnamese aggressors, expansionists, swallowers of territory and race exterminators': 'After receiving aid – food, seeds, and various other materials – from the humanitarian organizations, our returned people, assisted by our female combatants, moved into their beloved Kampuchean fatherland in the joyful atmosphere of a family reunion.' The only shadow to fall on this bright homecoming, the broadcast noted, was 'heavy rainfall'.[44]

In fact, the mood at Phnom Malai must have been rather bleak. Stephen Heder, a Cambodia scholar who interviewed hundreds of Cambodian refugees along the border in 1979 and 1980, concluded that the Sa Kaeo repatriation 'demonstrated how marginal Democratic Kampuchea's successes in regaining support after October 1979 [when most of the Khmer Rouge refugees had fled into Thailand] had been'. Out of nearly 24,000 people in Sa Kaeo, fewer than 7,500 people returned to Cambodia in the June repatriation, of whom Heder estimated that about 1,000 were combatants and 750 were party or Youth League cadres.

Some of these 'were true fanatics who had killed scores, maybe hundreds, in the service of a regime which had given them total power and total license'.[45] But the bulk of the Sa Kaeo returnees, much like those from Khao I Dang, were women and children who felt isolated in the camps and wanted to rejoin relatives in the Khmer Rouge zones. One woman said, 'If we stay in Sa Kaeo we will have nothing we can depend on. We don't want to go back, but to stay here is to have an empty life, a meaningless life.... There's nowhere else to go.'[46]

During 17–26 June a total of 9,090 Cambodians returned from the holding centres, including 7,464 people from Sa Kaeo and 1,626 from Khao I Dang.[47] As far as the voluntary character of the repatriation was concerned, Greve, who witnessed the situation in the camps, writes that 'I think it can be said that the vast majority were not directly forced to leave, but there was a marked indirect pressure, because of the overall problems in the camps.'[48]

Martin Barber, head of ROKU, defended the agency's role in the repatriation, though he acknowledged it caused the 'biggest storm' the unit ever faced. 'There was no choice,' he wrote later:

> The Khmers asked to return to the area of Kampuchea controlled by the internationally recognized legitimate government of their country – Democratic Kampuchea. The Thai government, as was clearly its right, insisted that they be allowed to return. UNHCR's sole function was to ensure that those who went

did so voluntarily.... From that point of view, our success lay in the 17,000 Khmers in Sa Kaeo who were able to decide not to return to the Khmer Rouge areas.[49]

The June 1980 repatriation, however, raised at least three essential questions, only one of which had to do with whether the return was voluntary or not. The second regarded the safety of the places to which people were returning: did repatriation offer returnees a 'durable solution' to their uprootedness, or only perpetuate it in more hazardous surroundings? Third was the matter of the people themselves: To what extent was it UNHCR's job to know or to care that at least some of the returnees were combatants?

It was on these latter issues that UNICEF and ICRC had questioned the foresight and the planning of their partner international organization and the Thai government. It was Vietnam, however, that delivered the ultimatum. On 23 June UNICEF sent a cable to New York, warning, 'We are concerned with the political ramifications of the repatriation effort and the possible action of the Vietnamese opposing forces to seal the border.... According to the camp leaders the opposing forces are now closing the border, and the exit trails to Kampuchea are blocked.'[50]

Early that same morning, approximately 200 Vietnamese soldiers crossed into Thailand and occupied the village of Ban Non Mak Mun. As their artillery shelled along the border, Vietnamese troops seized the refugee camps of Mak Mun and Nong Chan, forcing tens of thousands to flee toward Thailand or into the Cambodian interior. Thai military counter-attacked with ground troops, artillery, and helicopter gunships.

In two days of fighting, Thai casualties included 22 soldiers dead and more than 30 wounded. One Thai civilian was killed, a four-year-old boy in Ta Phraya district, and 27 villagers were injured. The Thai military reported 75 Vietnamese soldiers killed and seven captured. During 23–28 June the ICRC hospital in Khao I Dang treated 458 Cambodian wounded. The death toll in the border camps totalled several hundred, more of them probably from Thai artillery than Vietnamese fire. About 50,000 Cambodians were temporarily displaced inside Thailand along with 2,000 Thai villagers.

On the evening of 24 June Thai Foreign Minister Siddhi Savetsila departed Don Muang airport for Kuala Lumpur to attend the ASEAN Foreign Ministers Conference. On the first day of the meeting, the assembled ministers from the six Southeast Asian nations issued a statement condemning Vietnam's move as 'an irresponsible and dangerous act which will have far-reaching and serious consequences and which constitutes a grave and direct threat to the security of Thailand and the Southeast Asian region'.[52]

Only 124 people returned from Sa Kaeo on 26 June and the Thai–UNHCR repatriation program dwindled to a halt. The Supreme Command later called off repatriations from Kamput and Mairut, citing instability across the border.

'There are probably several reasons for the [Vietnamese] attack,' wrote Robert Ashe, a border relief worker who is credited with creating the 'landbridge' programme, which channelled a total of 44,000 metric tons of food and 23,000 metric tons of rice seed into western Cambodia from December 1979 to September 1980. 'The primary reason appears to have been their answer to the repatriation. To be sure, they were more angry about the repatriation of Khmer Rouge from Sa Kaeo to Tap Prik, but they have launched repeated unsuccessful attacks in that area in the last six months, and a further attack would have had no meaning for the Thais.'[53]

Zia Rizvi, for one, refused to acknowledge any link between the repatriation and the Vietnamese attack.[54] Indeed, UNHCR seemed blinkered to many of the profound and far-reaching ramifications that UNICEF had warned about on June 23. It would not be an overstatement to say that the repatriation and its aftermath changed the face of the border and signalled a new phase in the Cambodian refugee crisis. What had been defined principally as a relief emergency for the previous 12 months now took on more distinct political and military overtones. The ASEAN position solidified behind Thailand as the 'front-line' state, the United States upped its military aid to Thailand and the UN vote in favour of Democratic Kampuchea grew more lopsided than ever.[55]

The Vietnamese incursion also gave ICRC and UNICEF new incentive to reconsider their role in the border operation. Their headquarters gave three reasons for wanting to pull out: (1) the border relief programme was 'deeply provocative' to Phnom Penh; (2) it promoted a burgeoning black market trade in the camps; and (3) it strengthened combatants in the resistance forces, especially the Khmer Rouge.[56] Except for the second point, these were the very reasons Thailand and China – backed implicitly or explicitly by the United States and other donor countries – wanted the operation to continue.

After weeks of negotiations with Thai authorities, UNICEF resumed feeding in the Khmer Rouge camps 'with a sense of defeat and capitulation'.[57] Moreover, after several failed attempts to establish direct distribution of food rations solely to women residents, UNICEF reverted to the old system of putting the aid in the hands of the Khmer Rouge administrators. ICRC, for its part, never involved itself again in cross-border food distribution although it continued to coordinate emergency medical assistance in the camps.

At the beginning of 1981, Thai authorities had instituted a number of changes in policy in order to diminish the allure of asylum in Thailand. The so-called 'humane deterrence' policies, aimed primarily at Vietnamese and Laotians, reduced camp services to basic levels and halted resettlement interviews for new arrivals. The UNHCR-supported camps for Cambodians were already closed to new arrivals so, in the absence of any meaningful voluntary repatriation, Thailand seized upon another means to further reduce the number of Cambodians in the country. The euphemism chosen in this case was 'relocation'.

In September 1980, 314 people were transported by the Thai military from holding centres to encampments on the border. In October, the number increased to 734, then to 962 the following month. From December 1980 to November 1981, at the peak of the relocations, an average of 1,652 people returned from the UNHCR camps to the border each month. The movements tailed off after that but continued up until 1986, by which time 32,473 people had been relocated to the border. The bulk of these transfers came out of Khao I Dang and the two most popular locations on the border were Nong Chan and Nong Samet.[58] In late July 1982, following a visit by Prince Norodom Sihanouk to Khao I Dang to enlist supporters for his new government-in-exile, more than 2,000 men, women, and children were moved from Khao I Dang to the 'liberation zone' village of O'Smach. By September, more than 6,200 people had relocated to O'Smach, nearly doubling its population.

The official UNHCR position was to 'disassociate' itself from the relocations without opposing them. As Zia Rizvi explained to a briefing of foreign embassies in May 1982, 'relocation essentially means movement of people from one part of Thai territory to another part of Thai territory. Thais are not taking people to another land.' Furthermore, 'our main concern was that there should be no coercion, and on the whole our monitoring indicates that this is indeed so. There wasn't any undue persuasion of people who want to go back.'[59]

Other than UNHCR's absence from the operation, there appeared to be little to distinguish the relocations from the repatriations of June 1980. They did not principally involve transfers from a Khmer Rouge-dominated holding centre to a Khmer Rouge border camp, certainly, but the basic thrust of the movement was a return to Cambodian border zones. Even if one accepted the argument that this was simply a camp-to-camp transfer, it was a transfer out of UNHCR camps and UNHCR protection into an increasingly violent no-man's-land from which, Thailand made clear, there could be no recognized return.

UNBRO and the Border Camps

At the beginning of 1980, UNHCR was assisting more than 150,000 Cambodian refugees inside Thailand and the Joint Mission was delivering food aid to some 750,000 Cambodians gathered in some two dozen encampments along the border. Daily Joint Mission relief flights out of Bangkok were trying to push an average of 10,000 metric tons of food per month through the sluggish arteries of the Phnom Penh distribution system. To coordinate all these activities and the fundraising needed to maintain them, on 2 January 1980 the UN Secretary General appointed a special representative, Sir Robert Jackson, to act on his behalf. Australian diplomat, elder statesman and humanitarian, Jackson, by all accounts, was the best person to manage the chaotic, three-ring relief circus. He moved to Bangkok and took up the position as head of the Office of the Special Representative of the Secretary-General of the United Nations for the Coordination of Cambodian Humanitarian Assistance Programmes (OSRSG), a job even more complex and burdensome than its title.

By 1982, Cambodia had begun to recover from its crisis. It no longer needed large-scale hand-outs of food and relief supplies so much as urgent development aid. Likewise, most of the people at the border were no longer in dire need of rescue but of more durable solutions like resettlement or return. For nearly three years, the humanitarian relief effort had tried to emphasize a common goal: save the Cambodian people from extinction.[60] That mission was accomplished but the way forward showed scant common ground. Did the future of Cambodia belong to the regime in Phnom Penh and its 'irreversible' Vietnamese presence or to a motley rout of resistance fighters on the border? Humanitarian aid agencies, like the rest of the world, were being pressed more than ever to take sides. 'Political factors', regretted Sir Robert Jackson at a May 1982 donors meeting, 'have become increasingly acute in the last six to eight months.'

They would only become more so. On 22 June 1982, in Kuala Lumpur, two non-communist resistance factions – the Khmer People's National Liberation Front (KPNLF) under former Prime Minister Son Sann and Prince Norodom Sihanouk's FUNCINPEC (French acronym for the National United Front for an Independent, Neutral, Peaceful and Co-operative Cambodia) – joined with the Khmer Rouge to form the Coalition Government of Democratic Kampuchea (CGDK). The stated aims of the CGDK were 'to mobilize all efforts in the common struggle to liberate Kampuchea from the Vietnamese aggressors'. These efforts included both armed struggle and political opposition. The guerrilla war would be fought from the Thai border with Chinese arms. The political war needed a base in New York. On 28 October 1982, the UN General Assembly voted to recognize the credentials of the CGDK under the presidency of Prince Sihanouk.

As one observer has pointed out, there were only four things wrong with the Coalition Government of Democratic Kampuchea: it was not a coalition, it was not a government, it was not democratic and it was not in Kampuchea. But the special problem that the CGDK presented, particularly for UN agencies, was that it was the government of Cambodia, with recognition from the majority of the world's nations and a seat in the UN General Assembly to prove it. Notwithstanding any moral or legal arguments for recognition of the PRK or support for a vacant seat, the CGDK carried United Nations credentials and the UN agencies were obliged to give that reality its due.

Here there arose another problem: no UN agencies seemed willing or mandated to serve this misshapen entity, which straddled a border that was its own and not its own and which claimed among its citizenry not only genocidal killers but their erstwhile victims. At the end of 1981, UNICEF officially withdrew as the lead UN agency for the border relief programme, handing over its responsibilities to the WFP. The two agencies signed a transfer agreement to the effect that the humanitarian relief operations would be carried out under the overall authority of OSRSG, headed by Sir Robert Jackson. Border operations would be coordinated and monitored by the Resident Coordinator in Bangkok of the UN Development Programme (UNDP), Winston R. Prattley, who also served as WFP representative. WFP involvement would consist of delivery and monitoring of emergency food aid, with the assistance of the voluntary agencies as appropriate and assistance in coordinating overall aid to the border areas.[63]

In addition to his roles as UNDP resident coordinator and WFP representative, Prattley put on a third hat as of 1 January 1982: director of a new entity, the UN Border Relief Operation (UNBRO). Because the new operation needed staff, UNICEF agreed to a six-month loan of its Kampuchean Emergency Unit until UNBRO could hire its own people. In January 1982 UNBRO's beneficiaries numbered 290,000 in three groups:

- 155,000 Cambodians in nine camps in the border's Central sector stretching from Ban Sangae to Tap Prik. In five camps in the Central (or Northwestern) sector – Ban Sangae, Kok Tahan, Phnom Chat, Nong Samet and Nong Chan – the UN was permitted to carry out frequent headcounts and direct distribution of food. For the Khmer Rouge camps to the south of Aranyaprathet – Nong Prue, Tap Prik, and Khao Din – with an estimated 25,000 residents, food distributions were handled by Task Force 80, under the supervision of the Thai Supreme Command. The Central sector also included NW-82, a camp housing 800 Vietnamese land refugees assisted by ICRC.

- 70,000 Cambodians in the Northern and Southern sectors. The eight camps in the Northern sector – Ban Baranae, O'Bok, Naeng Mut, Chong Chom, Ban Charat, Samrong Kiat, Paet Um and Nam Yun – totalled 28,000 people from all three resistance factions. Of the three Southern sector camps comprising 42,000 aid recipients, one, Sok Sann, was affiliated with the KPNLF and two, Borai and Ta Luan, were Khmer Rouge. Headcounts were infrequent, at best, and food distributions were handled through Task Force 80.

- 65,000 Thai border residents living in villages affected by conflict also received UNBRO food aid. This too was distributed by the Thai military, not TF 80 but units of the Royal Thai Army and Marines.

The Affected Thai Village (ATV) programme began in October 1978 as a Thai government initiative known as the Self-Defence Border Village Programme which focused initially on villages affected by the conflict both with the Khmer Rouge and the Communist Party of Thailand. In the first two years of operation, the Thai government budgeted more than 100 million baht (about US$5 million) for the border village programme, the bulk of which went to the army to help 114 villages in 'risk locations' to consolidate into 64 fortified new or reconstituted villages.[64]

Security problems worsened throughout 1979: 'the presence of the refugees, the continued fighting, the raids by the resistance groups and the increased military personnel in the area' had affected villages spanning the seven border provinces from Ubon Ratchathani to Trat.[65] By the end of that year, the largest item in the ATV budget was 50 million baht to build a 123-kilometre 'strategic canal' along the central border that 'would provide an obstacle to tanks in this flat, easily over-run area and also would provide irrigation for agriculture.'[66] For the next ten years or so, the 'tank ditch' would serve as the de facto borderline between Cambodia and Thailand. Whatever development purposes it had originally were irrelevant.

Prior to 1982, all WFP food aid for the ATV programme and for Cambodian displaced persons in the Northern and Southern sector camps was deposited in Thai army warehouses. Its final distribution was undertaken by the Thai military without international monitoring. As one assessment put it bluntly, 'The organization did not know where its food was going and did not witness even the first step of the distribution.'[67] UNICEF officials estimated that less than half of the food distributed to the ATV programme in 1979–81 actually reached affected Thai villagers.[68] As for the unmonitored Cambodian food aid, most of it was going to Khmer Rouge camps. How much of it actually reached those camps and how much of that reached *civilians* in those camps was anyone's guess.

This was the structure that UNBRO inherited at the beginning of 1982 and this was the structure that persisted, with some improvements, until the beginning of 1985 when the resistance camps were driven once and for all into Thailand. For one-third of the Cambodian population and much of the affected Thai population, UNBRO could not directly monitor or verify that food was reaching its intended beneficiaries.

In July 1981, at UN headquarters in New York, an International Conference on Kampuchea (ICK) had laid out a four-point plan for a 'comprehensive political settlement' in Cambodia, including (1) an agreement to a ceasefire and UN-verified withdrawal of all foreign forces; (2) arrangements to ensure that no armed factions would disrupt free elections; (3) measures for the maintenance of law and order following the withdrawal of foreign forces and before the establishment of a new government following free elections; and (4) the holding of free elections under UN supervision.[69] It all sounded quite reasonable on paper, but who could expect the PRK to submit to UN supervision when the UN recognized only its adversaries? And who could expect the Khmer Rouge to submit to international law and free elections when it would not even permit UN food monitoring in its border camps?

The ICK Declaration also noted the 'serious problem of refugees' and declared itself 'convinced that a political solution to the conflict will be necessary for the long-term solution of the refugee problem'.[70] That sounded as much like a threat as a conviction. Either way, the message to the border populations was very clear: hunker down.

In the early morning of 31 January 1983, Vietnamese and PRK forces launched an assault on Nong Chan, a camp of 45,000 residents. As the attacks continued over several days, half of Nong Chan fled north to a temporary site just west of Nong Samet while more than 20,000 people streamed across the tank ditch, which served as the *de facto* borderline. The second round of attacks came on 31 March against the Khmer Rouge camps of Chamkar Ko and Phnom Chat. By the morning of 1 April, about 15,000 people had gathered at the tank ditch waiting for permission to cross over. Shelling at mid-morning killed five people, including one child, and persuaded Thai officials to permit entry. The crowd walked two hours to an evacuation site at a laterite pit that came to be dubbed Red Hill.

By mid-April, more than 100 people were dead and several hundred wounded. Nearly 70,000 people had been evacuated into Thailand, of whom 21,000 had re-crossed the tank ditch, and 49,000 remained in Thailand at two evacuation sites, Red Hill and Green Hill.

Aside from all the logistical problems of feeding and sheltering the suddenly uprooted population, Red Hill posed an additional one: the evacuees were from Khmer Rouge camps. Would they be permitted to stay in Thailand or sent back into Khmer Rouge hands? ICRC delegates who were monitoring the site estimated that as many as one third of the population wished to be free of Khmer Rouge control. More than two thousand petitioned ICRC and UNHCR, seeking protection. 'Everybody was sending letters,' recalls Scott Leiper, an UNBRO field officer, '"I want to escape the border, escape the Khmer Rouge." Some wanted to go to Khao I Dang. Some just wanted to get out of the Khmer Rouge camps.'[71]

High Commissioner for Refugees Poul Hartling prepared a *démarche* for Thai Foreign Minister Siddhi urging Thailand to consider favourably granting asylum to Cambodians who sought it or who entered UNHCR-assisted camps.[72] It was delayed at the insistence of ICRC and UNBRO officials who argued that, in this case, the ideal was the enemy of the good: if Thailand saw UNHCR trying to gain asylum and refugee status for anyone who crossed the border, it would no longer permit even temporary evacuations under fire. That argument won the day and UNHCR delayed the letter for several weeks until after the site was cleared.

Meanwhile, throughout the month of May, Khmer bandits had been terrorizing Red Hill. Some UNBRO officials suspected they were Khmer Rouge 'trying to intimidate the people into going back to Khmer Rouge camps on the border where they would be safe.'[73] UNBRO worked a deal with Colonel Kitti Puttiporn, head of Thailand's Task Force 80, the para-military unit in charge of camp security: give people a free choice of border camps, Khmer Rouge or non-communist, and UNBRO would assist in the return. He agreed.

On the morning of 24 May, said Leiper,

We lined up 50 buses in Wattana Nakorn waiting for a 'surprise attack' on Red Hill. When they rolled in, UNBRO staff began to announce that the buses would be leaving shortly for Sanro Changan, the KPNLF camp. Those who wanted to go should board them. The next day there would be buses going to Phnom Malai/Tap Prik. Almost immediately, there were KR people going around with their own megaphones spreading disinformation, telling people to wait and go back with them.

In the end, only about 2,700 chose Sanro Changan and the rest went to Tap Prik.[74] Among them were an estimated 2,000 soldiers. 'No one,' said Leiper, 'was allowed to stay in Thailand.'

With the dry-season offensive, UNBRO Director Winston Prattley told donors in New York,

> the Khmer civilian administration and leadership ... has rapidly given way to military or para-military leadership, whose visible and active presence has transformed most major settlements into armed camps. Weapons and military equipment are in plain evidence and are brandished amongst the UNBRO and voluntary agency personnel as they attempt to provide relief assistance. As a consequence, the control and direction of food distribution and provision of medical services has become less efficient, more precarious and often dangerous. UNBRO officials have been abused and held at gun-point. During the offensive, UNBRO and voluntary agency personnel have been subject to grave personal risk as a consequence of artillery bombardment and other military action.... Clearly, the polarization and militarization of the border encampments has drawn the United Nations system, and by extrapolation the contracted voluntary agencies, into a situation which stands in contradiction with the instructions of the Secretary-General.[75]

Amid growing insecurity and militarization, Prattley circulated a copy of his terms of reference to all voluntary agencies cooperating in the border relief programme asking them to review especially 'the directive given to me to avoid the exposure of UNBRO and associated voluntary agency personnel in any situation in which the prospect of combat or conflict appear imminent'.[76] In this regard, the terms of reference established that 'the Director will make arrangements relating to the security and safety of UNBRO personnel including those of voluntary agencies.' The document continued that 'although the Director may require UNBRO personnel to observe guidelines or co-operate in arrangements which he has established for security and safety purposes, nevertheless such personnel are free to withdraw from or decline to enter into the area of the border *between Thailand and Kampuchea* [emphasis added] if they consider that their own safety so requires.'

Just weeks after the creation of the CGDK, Colonel Sanan Kajornklam of Joint Operations Centre/Supreme Command was asked if Thailand planned to give responsibility for Cambodian refugees over to the new Cambodian government. He replied, 'The [CGDK] has just been established and does not yet have a clear framework for helping the Cambodian displaced persons in the border area so they must negotiate this through the

Thai government. In addition to that, these Cambodians are displaced persons in Thai territory so they must let aid go through the Thai government.'[77] But later in the same discussion, when Sanan was asked if new Cambodian arrivals were still entering Thailand, he answered, 'New arrivals who come in are allowed to stay only in the border area. They are not permitted to enter the country.'[78] Further on, he conceded that

> In reality, the Cambodians in the border area are living in Cambodian territory. Only some are on Thai territory – for example, Ban Nong Chan and Nong Samet. The [Thai] government is attempting to move these people back to their own country as much as possible. On this, the government will cooperate with the voluntary agencies and various international organizations in order to help these people return to their own country and become self-sufficient.[79]

The 1983 evacuation and return showed clearly how confounded the situation had become at the border: Was this repatriation? Was it voluntary? It hardly seemed to matter anymore. It was happening in a place 'between Thailand and Cambodia' that aid officials could freely withdraw from or decline to enter if their safety was in question. The freedom of the Cambodians to do likewise was another matter.

By 1984, the Vietnamese occupation of Cambodia had passed its fifth anniversary and was showing signs of wearing out its welcome. UN and voluntary agency officials pointed to impressive strides by the Phnom Penh authorities in restoring a shattered infrastructure and re-establishing primary education and basic health services in much of the country. But Vietnam's 200,000 troops stood accused of growing indiscipline and abuse in the countryside. The CGDK, moreover, estimated that as many as 640,000 Vietnamese settlers had come to live in Cambodia since 1979. The PRK countered with figures of only 56,000.[80]

Growing resentment of the Vietnamese presence, some observers felt, was driving people toward the border and giving new fuel to the resistance forces. The principal beneficiary, at least in the short term, appeared to be the Khmer Rouge. 'So far there are no positive reports about the Khmer Rouge,' one foreign diplomat told the *Washington Post* in November 1983. 'It's more that tolerance toward them has increased as intolerance of the Vietnamese has increased.' Khmer Rouge troop strength was estimated at around 40,000 with a militia of another 10,000 to 15,000. In contrast, KPNLF armed forces numbered at most 12,000 while the Sihanoukist National Army had perhaps 3,000 to 5,000 guerrillas.[81]

From May to October 1984, more than 15,000 new arrivals came to the border. UNBRO monitors noted that 33 per cent of those interviewed one month gave forced labour as a reason for coming to the border while 26 per cent said they were fleeing military conscription. But overall, the new arrivals team said interviews gave

> a continued impression of people who are coming to the border for an easier and less restricted life, where political harassment is nil [sic] and food is readily available. There continues to be a considerable proportion of arrivals from Phnom

Penh (10 per cent). Most of them were petty traders and it seems like they were drawn to Nong Samet by the flourishing trade in the camp.... There was [also] a fairly high proportion of families (20 per cent) of single women (either widowed or divorced) with young kids. These women professed that they were unable to cope alone in the village, without material assistance.

On 18 November 1984 Vietnamese/PRK forces attacked Nong Chan camp. The 1984–85 dry season offensive had begun. The civilian population of 22,000 fled into Thailand as Nong Chan was burned to the ground. In early December, camps in the north and south were attacked and evacuated. Then, on 25 December, Nong Samet was attacked and its population of 60,000 fled across the tank ditch and into Red Hill. Counting the 45,000 people still in evacuation sites from the previous dry season and the new influx, nearly 120,000 Cambodian refugees – half of the border population – were in Thailand at the end of 1984. The ICRC field hospitals at Khao I Dang and Kap Cherng were filled with 400 war-wounded.

In late January 1985, citing security concerns, Task Force 80 had moved the entire 62,000 evacuees from Nong Samet out of the Red Hill evacuation site and into an area right next to Khao I Dang. In fact, more than 5,000 people had to be moved out of one section in Khao I Dang to make room for the new site, Bang Phu. The two camps were separated by a ditch, a fence, and several hundred guards. 'It is important that all concerned realize that this is another evacuation site which happens to be situated adjacent to Khao I Dang', UNBRO's John Moore told the other relief agencies. It 'should not be considered as a holding center'.[83] But the two spheres – the holding centres and the border camps – were now quite literally touching after more than five years of separation and the shock, for some, was electric.

Throughout January, voluntary agencies in the United States were swamped with calls from anxious relatives trying to track family members. Robert De Vecchi, executive director of the International Rescue Committee, which ran resettlement programmes in the United States as well as refugee programmes in Thailand, sent out a sobering update:

> Please advise your clients and colleagues to keep inquiries about specific Khmer to a minimum. Tens of thousands of people have been relocated and more will be moved about. As to 'Bang Phu' specifically – UNBRO and ICRC are providing food, shelter and other basic services as if these people were still on the border. According to Thai sources, they are there temporarily – not as refugees – and will go back to the border when conditions warrant. As such, they are not eligible for resettlement.[84]

There is no evidence that either UNHCR or influential donors like the United States ever petitioned Thailand to allow people in Bang Phu or any of the other evacuation sites to come under UNHCR protection now that they were clearly on Thai soil. Indeed, the record suggests that all parties supported, or at least reluctantly accepted, the notion that border Cambodians in Thailand should remain 'displaced persons'. An April 1985 report prepared for the US Congress said that 'The Khmer civilians on the

Thai/Cambodian border are considered to be "displaced persons" by the UNHCR, the Thai Government, and the resettlement countries, including the United States ... Australian and Canadian officials all oppose any processing of this population for third country resettlement as refugees.'[85]

By September 1985, following the evacuation of 180,000 Cambodians from 17 border encampments from the end of 1984 – and the displacement of 55,000 Thai villagers – the border had consolidated somewhat, though it was still far from stable. Unlike previous dry-season offensives, the Vietnamese/PRK forces did not withdraw but dug into the border and began laying mines. This time, they were going to stay. In the next twelve months, UNBRO, ICRC, and the Thai government succeeded in further separating civilian populations from the military and in consolidating ten camps into eight (and eventually six) border camps, all inside Thailand.

In the years that followed, official population counts on the border rose and fell, peaking at more than 350,000 in December 1991. But the basic structure of the border camps – that is, closed camps for 'displaced persons' controlled by the Thai government, administered by the CGDK factions, and served by UNBRO along with about 14 non-governmental organizations – remained intact from 1986 until voluntary repatriation commenced in late 1991. Khao I Dang remained under the aegis of UNHCR, a world apart from the border camps. It was free from the threat of shellfire or political intimidation, certainly, but with legal entry foreclosed, thousands of unregistered Cambodians with a desperate hope for resettlement lived a perilous twilight existence under threat of extortion, physical abuse, or expulsion by Thai security.

In a twilight world of a very different sort, an estimated 60,000 to 100,000 civilians lived in resistance camps along the so-called 'hidden border' with no access to international assistance or protection. Forced relocations out of UN-assisted Khmer Rouge camps in Thailand to these military bases were to plague the border relief effort for many years.

'With the growth of the resistance groups and the intensification of conflict,' wrote Josephine Reynell in her 1989 study, *Political Pawns: Refugees on the Thai–Kampuchean Border*, 'movement from the border into Kampuchea has become increasingly difficult.'

> Not only did the Vietnamese and PRK government mine the Kampuchean side of the border but also, from the PRK's perspective, the people from the camps inevitably became associated with the resistance groups. The camp inhabitants therefore fear they would be deemed traitors and in risk of persecution if they did return. This changes their status from displaced people to *refugees-sur-place*.... Correspondingly, the [CGDK] has gained increasing control over the camp populations and the border entry posts to Kampuchea, making it very difficult for people to return to Kampuchea should they wish to do so.[86]

From 1985 to 1989 there was little movement between Thailand and Cambodia (save the forced relocations to the 'hidden border' camps and the 'liberated zones'). It was deemed traitorous by one side to go to the border and traitorous by the other side to leave it. Spontaneous return was unsafe and organized return was impossible. Resettlement opportunities declined to a handful per year. The Cambodian refugees and displaced persons were trapped in Thailand, hostage to agendas far more powerful than their own.

A Tale of Two Refugee Cities

By 1980, no fewer than 37 voluntary agencies were working in Khao I Dang, making it, for a time at least, what one observer called 'the most elaborately serviced refugee camp in the world.'[87] This attention was even more extraordinary given the fact that the camp had been closed to new arrivals since early 1980. The official ban, however, meant only that Cambodians trying to enter the camp were forced to bribe or smuggle themselves in. Some got a little help from their friends. The American Refugee Committee ran the field hospital in Nong Samet in the early 1980s. 'We would dress up people as patients, stick a fake IV in their arm, and drive them through the gates of Khao I Dang and into the hospital,' said Susan Walker, then ARC's country director. 'Some were legitimate medical cases but many just flagged us down on the road. They wanted safety from the border. They were looking for relatives. They were still reeling from the horrors of the Khmer Rouge and they wanted nothing more to do with killing and the killing fields. By 1981, resettlement fever had caught on and many began looking for a way overseas.'[88]

Once inside the camp, 'illegals' often lived for years, without registration or food rations, in hope of refugee status and in constant fear of discovery. Some spent their days behind false partitions and their nights in underground rooms dug beneath the houses of friends or family. Gradually, the luckier survivors of this degrading game of hide-and-seek would emerge into the light of legal residence. The unlucky ones were sent back to the border or simply disappeared.

A campwide registration on 9 December 1982 provided all residents of the camp – as well as later official transfers from other camps – with 'Khao I Dang cards'. These 'KDs' were entitled to all camp services and were permitted to seek overseas resettlement. On 26 August 1984, Thai authorities conducted another census and issued 'family cards' to about 4,500 former illegal residents, which permitted them to receive food and other camp services though they were initially prohibited from seeking resettlement. By the time this was granted, thousands more 'illegals' had planted themselves underground in hopes of cultivating the same fortune.

In the latter half of 1986, the Thai government insisted repeatedly that Khao I Dang too would be closed and its remaining inhabitants moved to the border. Five years after it had first instituted humane deterrence policies, Thailand again was chafing under the *status quo*. Having fallen off dramatically in 1982, annual arrivals had been steadily rising even as resettlement commitments were tapering off. In six years, Squadron Leader Prasong

Soonsiri told assembled guests at the 1986 CCSDPT conference, 'this is the first time that the number of refugees remaining in the camps at year's end was larger than at the previous year's. In 1985 the number was 130,413 compared with 128,439 in 1984.'[85] In July 1985 Thailand had begun a programme to interview new Laotian arrivals at border checkpoints, in order to distinguish *bona fide* refugees from other migrants. The Vietnamese population was no more than 5,000 and resettlement was moving people along at a satisfactory pace. But the Khmer in Khao I Dang, said Prasong, 'are the least likely to be given the opportunity to resettle in third countries'. Processing had slowed to a trickle and departures rarely exceeded 100 per month. He gave the resettlement countries an ultimatum and a deadline: decide who would qualify and who would not qualify for resettlement and announce those decisions by the end of 1986. 'Those displaced persons who are found unacceptable will be transferred to border camps under appropriate circumstances,' said Prasong, 'so that Khao I Dang Holding Center can be closed completely.' As another Thai official put it, while 1986 would be 'a year of resettlement', 1987 would be 'a year of other solutions'.[90]

The message clearly was intended to light a fire under the resettlement countries but, as the year drew to a close, Khao I Dang still held 22,500 people whose resettlement status seemed anything but resolved. They included about 13,500 'KDs', 1,900 'FCs' or family card holders, and 7,100 'RCs' or 'ration card' holders. This last group were former illegals who, following registration in a September 1985 camp survey, had been placed in the Khao I Dang Annex (the former Bang Phu site), pending a decision by the Thai government on their eligibility for resettlement.

On 31 December 1986 the Thai government issued a statement declaring that Khao I Dang had officially closed down. The camp population would be moved to the border gradually, beginning with the 'illegals' in March 1987. In New York, the Secretary-General communicated his concerns about the move to Thailand's ambassador to the UN, saying he 'fully recognizes the right of the [Royal Thai Government] to move the refugees' location within Thai territory' although 'the choice of a location should be dictated by concern for the physical safety of the refugees.... The movement plan, therefore, should not alter UNHCR's protection role vis-a-vis this population.'[91] The note was careful to point out, however, that this concern applied only to the three registered groups. The 'illegals' would have to fend for themselves.

Meakea was a 30-year-old medic with the American Refugee Committee in Site 2 before she left for Khao I Dang in late 1986. She had heard it was closing and hoped for a last chance at resettlement. Several thousand baht in bribes to Task Force 80 guards got her out of one camp and into another. She wrote to an American friend in December 1986: 'Nowaday, the situation is very dangerous; the Thai Task Force caught many of the illegal refugees, put them in jail, and after send them to another place. I'm so afraid. Everyday I escaped from the soldier so my life is full of trouble. We cannot live peacefully in KID. Every night I sleep underground for hiding, difficult to breathe, not enough oxygen for respiration.'[92]

Thailand went ahead as scheduled with its moves of the 'illegals'. In mid-February, Meakea wrote to her American friend again:

> You know the situation at KID? The legal refugees must be evacuated to the border. The illegal refugees (like me) must be caught if they don't go to admit to the police that [they are] in the camp. I'm so afraid, J—, because the soldiers are very bad for illegal refugees. Now I'm so worry about myself. I'm afraid of the word 'jail'. I don't wish to hear this word. Please pray God for me. I don't want to go back to the border.[93]

On 1 March Thai soldiers rounded up 214 Cambodian refugees in Khao I Dang, many of them weeping, and carried them off in army trucks to Site B. In late April, another 175 were sent to Site B, followed by 160 more on 28 July. It is not clear what happened to Meakea; there were no more letters after February. But by no means all of the 'illegals' were caught in Khao I Dang. Indeed, the flow into the camp only increased, so that by early August one 'illegal' in the camp estimated the numbers to be as high as 2,400.[94] As the pace of these clandestine movements increased, so too did the dangers. In July, the bodies of 32 Cambodians were found on the smugglers' routes from Site 2 to Khao I Dang.[95]

'Site 2 is a Monster'

In early 1985, when Thai authorities were preparing to send the Bang Phu residents back to the border, they made it known that any 'illegals' found in Khao I Dang would be treated in the same manner. International concern, though muted at first, deepened when it was discovered in May that some undocumented residents, along with repeat violators of camp rules, were being sent as punishment to Site 8. Still more alarming was the fact that on two separate incidents on 14 and 19 May, armed Khmer Rouge soldiers entered Site 8 and tried to remove people forcibly for military service. In the first incident, two people were reported killed and six wounded as most of the population fled the camp in panic. In the second incident, the population fled again but not before the soldiers herded up to 200 civilians onto trucks and took them away.[96]

In September 1985, stimulated by pressure from Congress and Cambodian advocates in the United States, the State Department's Arthur F. Dewey from the Bureau for Refugee Programs sent a letter to Tatsuro Kunugi, the UN Special Representative for Cambodian assistance:

> There is continuing concern in the United States that the Khmer along the border lack international protection against return to Cambodia under unsafe conditions and against physical and human rights abuses.... I remain concerned that if it is perceived that the present informal protection practices are ineffective, the pressure for a role for another international organization, especially UNHCR, will become irresistible. This is a solution that none of us, including UNHCR, wants.[97]

In UNBRO's long list of 'direct inputs' to the border camps – food distribution, monitoring, shelter, infrastructure, pharmacy, relief materials, logistics, water, anti-malaria measures, education, social services, and security coordination – there was no specific mention of protection. The monitoring responsibility referred to population headcounts, nutrition surveys, and field visits.[98] To the charge that the operation had no protection mandate, UNBRO officials often responded (1) that services themselves were a form of protection; (2) that all UN agencies had a mandate to uphold the principles of human rights; and (3) that ICRC had an explicit mandate to protect civilians in time of war. At the same time, many of these same officials were aware of the growing violence and abuse in the camps, and were often frustrated at ICRC's seeming aloofness and its strict commitment to confidentiality. Moreover, as one ICRC delegate put it, 'We are not a police force.'[99]

The Khmer camp administrations supposedly were responsible for internal security and the Thai military was responsible for security around the camp. Both were at least as much part of the problem as part of the solution. The problems at the border were legion, including forced relocation and conscription, banditry, rape, extortion and physical abuse. The perpetrators included Khmer bandits and criminals as well as camp administrators and Thai security.

By August 1987 the camp's seven square kilometres housed nearly 160,000 people and encompassed seven former resistance camps, five with their own administrations, as well as a section for Vietnamese refugees. In that month alone, more than one million pieces of thatch were distributed for housing in Site 2. One hundred million litres of water were trucked in, at a rate of 225 trips per day. The Nong Samet bakery turned out 700,000 loaves of bread for primary school children. And refugee mothers turned out 541 new-borns (the border camps had a birth rate of 50 per 1,000, among the highest in the world).

'From a logistical point of view,' said an UNBRO official, 'Site 2 is a monster.'[100] It was a monster in more ways than one. In 1986, UNBRO had reported 205 incidents of violence in the border camps. In 1987, the number had risen to 462 incidents; of these 378 had occurred in Site 2 alone.[101] UNBRO's monthly report for July 1987 recorded the following 'highlights':

July 2:   Two Khmers at Site 2 kill themselves in unrelated suicides.
July 12: Thai security guns down a Khmer man in Site 2 without warning and for no apparent reason.
July 31: Thai security beat, then shot to death a Khmer woman and her husband. Another guard set off a grenade in the Nong Chan market, wounding three Khmers.[102]

What the laconic prose of the field office's report failed to note was that the woman was pregnant, her husband was an amputee and the Task Force 80 ranger was drunk. He had beaten the couple in camp then chased them out beyond the fence and up a nearby mountainside where he shot them both to death. The Cambodians in the camp, observed one relief worker, 'need protection from their protectors'.[103]

Ever since the evacuation sites were established in 1985, UNBRO had been considering various ideas to formalize its protection role in the camps. One of the first concrete initiatives came with the documentation of incidents of violence beginning in the latter half of 1985. In January 1987, UNBRO hired its first protection officer, Phillip Scott, who also functioned as senior camp officer in Site 2. Bob Maat, a Jesuit brother who had worked on the border since 1979 and was himself an UNBRO protection officer from March 1988 to April 1989, wrote,

> To avoid 'turf wars', particular areas of jurisdiction were set up between UNBRO and ICRC. The UNBRO unit took special interest in domestic disputes and internal Khmer to Khmer problems while ICRC, still overseeing all, kept its eyes on the international incidents, in addition to all of its traditional services such as tracing, etc. There was obviously much overlapping and sharing of information, although the habitual UNBRO complaint that ICRC was too confidential was heard throughout that year.[104]

UNBRO also commissioned a private security firm, Shield Asia, to conduct a study of the border camps, especially Site 2. In August 1987, Shield Asia issued a confidential report to UNBRO:

> There is no doubt in the opinion of all the members of the survey team, that a potentially disastrous and tragic situation is in the making at Site 2. Urgent remedial work must be undertaken, if the crisis is to be averted. If this is not commenced soon, Site 2 will either explode or implode within the next eighteen months. The tensions within the overcrowded camps are beginning to come visibly to the surface and events will soon begin to take their own momentum. Domestic crimes, suicides, and confrontation with Khmer police and Task Force 80 Rangers will increase dramatically and in proportion to the growing overcrowding and decreasing hope of a viable future.[105]

Overcrowding, depression, and enforced inactivity were conjuring a witches' brew of violence in the camp. Over 80 per cent of the crimes reported in the camp, Shield Asia concluded, 'can be attributed to the physical and psychological results of overcrowding, disillusionment and depression, lack of hope and incentive, inactivity and unemployment prevailing after many years of war'. The report predicted that 'Domestic crimes, including rape, child rape and molestation of minors, incest, petty theft, actual and grievous bodily harm, gang warfare, juvenile delinquency, suicide, oppression of ethnic, religious or political minorities will assume uncontrollable proportions.' Commented one Cambodian resident,

> Normally, people need to be happy; they need to listen to things and see things; above all, they need to do those things that make their life comfortable. But living here is not comfortable at all. It is too narrow: we are too crowded here. We are like a wild dog that has been tied for too long until it becomes mean and vicious, and finally begins to bite people. Like the dog, a man becomes mean, almost crazy, from being in this camp too long.[106]

In 1988 UNBRO recorded 1,264 incidents of violence in the border camps, including 1,077 in Site 2 alone. This represented nearly three times the number in 1987 and six times the number in 1986. Beatings were the most common, followed by knife and axe attacks, suicide attempts, armed robbery, shootings, rape, and child abuse. Fifty-six per cent of all victims were women. Most of the violence was Khmer on Khmer, though all too often beatings, rape and even death came at the hands of Task Force 80.

Shield Asia offered a long list of remedial actions to stem the rising tide of violence in Site 2, including reducing the population by opening a second site, establishing youth programmes and vocational opportunities, creating a legal market, and training a Khmer police force, including a women's police unit to attend to the security needs of women and children. The recommendations were thoughtful, detailed and ambitious, but they were nothing that relief workers or the Cambodians themselves had not thought of before. The real trick would be persuading Thailand to accept the changes and the donor community to pay for them.

Patrick van de Velde, former deputy director of UNBRO, acknowledged that 'the main reason I hired [Shield Asia] was because of their connections with the Thai military'. Shield Asia's chairman of the board, Lieutenant General Yuthasak Klongrujrok, was the former dean of Chulachomklao Military Academy, the training school for the Thai army's top brass. 'He could talk to the commanders-in-chief and they would listen,' said Van de Velde. 'He had been their teacher.'[107]

Van de Velde credited this connection with bringing about one of the most tangible improvements in camp conditions – the replacement of Task Force 80 with a better-trained civilian security force known as the Displaced Persons Protection Unit (DPPU), which was deployed in July 1988. Over time, Site 2 got much of what Shield Asia recommended, including a legalized market, a Cambodian police force and expatriate security liaison officers, and more education and training programmes. Norah Niland, an UNBRO social services officer, chronicled the changes:

> Security and protection were revamped. TF 80 departed and new ground rules were established for the incoming DPPU. Protection officers were recruited and set to work documenting and following through on abuses in Site 2. A police training program was developed together with the formation of 'Justice Committees' designed to work as an independent judiciary. An ambitious education program was developed to allow 60,000 children to attend school; it was launched with a dedicated troupe of some 30 fluent Khmer-speaking teacher trainers. Community Support Services, a project covering a wide range of activities from early childhood care, agriculture and adult literacy to skills training for women, stove-making, and youth centers was geared to enhancing survival skills and offsetting the corroding impact of camp life.
>
>   To wide acclaim, a Buddhist education program was also developed for both [lay] populace and novice monks; it covered elements of human rights education and was probably the first structured monk-training program since the Khmer Rouge marched into Phnom Penh. Other important initiatives included officially

sanctioned markets where Thai merchants could exchange goods with refugees who traded rice for items which allowed some diversion from the monotony of their diet; the erosion of black market trade also meant a reduction of abuses associated with it.[108]

The number of reported 'incidents of violence' rose from 462 in 1987 to 1,269 in 1988 and then dropped to 1,003 in 1989 where it stabilized. From January 1989 until October 1991, when the camps were handed over to UNHCR, 'incidents of violence' averaged around 84 per month. Even this must be taken as a sign of progress since, in those three years, the camp population rose and UNBRO protection coverage expanded to camps beyond the Central border. One of the most significant achievements of the protection effort was the reduction of protection incidents involving Thai military and security personnel. It may be a strange sort of victory to claim that by the end of the UNBRO era, the border populations were largely safe from their Thai protectors, but perhaps it is no more perverse than the fact that the refugees' worst predators remained fellow Khmer.

The single worst protection incident in the history of Site 2 was all the more tragic because of its sheer mindlessness. In the early evening of 28 March 1991, a KPNLF soldier wandered unarmed but drunk into a wedding party at Ban Sangae. He began to pester a woman to dance but she refused. He persisted and eventually was asked to leave. The man returned with a high fragmentation grenade which he hurled into the crowd. It exploded in mid-air, killing 13 people on the spot and injuring 125 more. Five more people later died at the ICRC hospital in Khao I Dang, bringing the death toll to at least 18, including four children.[109]

For all of its changes, one thing Site 2 never got was smaller. By 1990, the population had reached 180,000 and, by 1991, it was more than 200,000. Site 2 had taken on the features and disfigurements of a permanent city. As photojournalist Kari Rene Hall put it in her book, *Beyond the Killing Fields,*

> Site 2 has hospitals, pharmacies, schools, Buddhist temples, a police force, a justice system, factories that make water jars and latrines, women's associations, libraries, bicycle-taxi drivers, and its own local newspaper. It also has brothels, gambling dens, organized cockfights, skyrocketing crime and corruption at all levels, including a thriving black market in everything from food, books and clothing to drugs and hand grenades.[110]

It seemed that people could find just about anything they wanted on the border except a safe way out.

Ban That: UNHCR Comes to the Border

From late 1979 to early 1980, Vietnamese who had escaped to Thailand by coming overland through Cambodia were moved into Khao I Dang and then on to Sikhiu for refugee processing. In March 1980, consistent with its effort to close the Cambodian border to new arrivals, the Thai government announced that Vietnamese land refugees would no longer be permitted to enter the country. In April 1980, the Thai military set up NW 9, a camp just north of Nong Samet especially for Vietnamese arrivals. ICRC assumed responsibility for their feeding and 24-hour protection. By June 1980 NW 9 held 2,700 people. The camp was abandoned in the Vietnamese attack on Mak Mun that month; for most of the next year, Vietnamese land refugees clustered haphazardly in Nong Chan and Nong Samet, as ICRC tried to negotiate their entry into refugee camps in Thailand. In 1982 the Thai military permitted the establishment of NW 82 in Nong Samet, adjacent to the American Refugee Committee ARC hospital complex. From this point on, the Vietnamese land refugees often were referred to as the 'Platform Vietnamese'. In July 1985, following the move of the Dong Ruk population into Site 2, UNBRO took over responsibility for the land Vietnamese from ICRC. Over the years, many of them suffered considerable abuse and extortion at the hands of the Cambodian resistance.[111]

Since 1979, ICRC had assisted more than 15,000 Platform Vietnamese in securing access to overseas resettlement, something that was denied the ordinary Cambodian 'displaced person'. Thus, despite the dangers of life as a Vietnamese on the Cambodian border, it was no surprise that many Cambodians tried to pass themselves off as Vietnamese. It fell to the Thai and international authorities to try to distinguish the simply fraudulent applicants from those, like the Khmer Krom from the Vietnamese Delta, whose nationality was a far more complex issue.

Even the cases of 'fraud' were far from simple. Said one woman, 'I wanted to get my children away from the border. Smuggling them into Khao I Dang was too dangerous and too expensive. So I arranged for Vietnamese lessons for the three eldest. We got them into the Platform as Khmer Krom unaccompanied minors. Now one is in America, one is in Australia, and one has settled in France. All of them are in university. I am sure their lives are better than if they had stayed in camp and come back to Cambodia.'[112]

In February 1988, following a sudden reversal of policy directed against the rising tide of Vietnamese boat arrivals, Thailand announced that boat people who arrived in Thailand after 1 January would be transferred to Site 2, where they would be deprived of opportunities to seek resettlement. On 20 April UNHCR signed an agreement with the Thai government to assume responsibility for the boat Vietnamese in Site 2. In May, a group of 800 boat people were transferred from detention centres on the east coast to a new camp, Ban That, built on the edge of Site 2.

By September, the Ban That population had grown to 3,200 boat Vietnamese. Also in Site 2, though in separate locations, were about 2,000 Platform Vietnamese, most of whom had been on the border since 1986, and another 2,200 recent Vietnamese land refugee arrivals living in Section 5 who were still awaiting screening to enter the Platform. In late July, Thailand had announced that both groups of Vietnamese would be available for resettlement interviews until 31 August, after which time they would be moved to Ban That. The government insisted that 31 August 1988 also marked the date of Khao I Dang's final, official closure. Anyone still in camp after that date would be moved to Ban That, beginning with the estimated 3,000 new 'illegals'.[113]

On behalf of the UN agencies, OSRSG head S.A.M.S. Kibria voiced concerns about the proposed Khao I Dang move to the border, saying it would not only add to the 'congested condition of Site 2, [but] the population of Khao I Dang is bound to come under various pressures which would put its safety and neutrality in danger'.[114] Some of the Platform and Section 5 Vietnamese also opposed being moved to Ban That and, in December, about 2,000 of them went on a hunger strike.

On the face of it, this reluctance to go to Ban That seemed counter-intuitive. For nearly ten years, land Vietnamese had been fighting for UNHCR recognition as refugees. Now it could be had in a new camp just a few hundred yards away and they were resisting. Resettlement would not be available in Ban That, they had been told, but then they had been told it was ending in Site 2 as well.[115] Why not take a chance with UNHCR rather than staying on the Platform?

The answer still lies partly behind a veil of misinformation, obfuscation, and bitter memories. Some say the leaders of the strike did not want to give up lucrative black market operations they had organized. Others say they were manipulated by the Nong Samet administrator, Thou Thon, for his own political interests. Certainly, in part, it was a matter of 'Better the devil you know than the devil you don't.' All the rhetoric, aimed largely at stemming the Vietnamese boat influx, was saying that Ban That was a definite dead end. Staying in Site 2 was a gamble, but such was the life of the land Vietnamese. For once, it seemed better not to link one's fate to that of the boat people.

On 28 December representatives from UNBRO, ICRC, UNHCR, and DPPU met with the strike organizers and tried to persuade them that the move was in good faith, that Ban That would not be a staging ground for forced repatriation as some rumours had it. They gave the Vietnamese until 15 January 1989 to make a decision: either go to Ban That as Vietnamese under UNHCR supervision or stay with UNBRO in Site 2 as Khmer 'displaced persons'. On 19 January following weeks of mounting tension and threats, some of the remaining Vietnamese set fire to the Platform buildings and placed the blame on DPPU. As Bob Maat wrote of the events:

> What began in relatively good faith ended up in threats of suicide, self immolation, self mutilations, hunger strikes, death threats to both UNBRO and ICRC staff members, the incineration of most of the VNLR [Vietnamese land refugee] Platform and the disruption of services to a camp of 170,000 people. A VNLR leadership of nine people, desperate, having been rejected by embassies for 5 to 7 years already, desiring a 'global solution' to get out, needing a body of people for strength, spread a most effective dis-information campaign. Truth suffered nearly mortal blows at the beginning of this hot dry season.[116]

In February more than 1,000 chose to enter Ban That, including some of the strike leaders, but about 1,000 stayed behind, victims of bad judgment and worse information. In April 1989, more than 2,800 'illegal' residents of Khao I Dang were moved to Ban That but, following a UNHCR intervention with the Thai government, the 'FCs' and 'RCs' were permitted to remain where they were. For all of its official closings – in 1980, 1986, and again in 1988 – Khao I Dang remained operational until February 1993, when only one other Cambodian camp in Thailand was still open.

By September 1990, Ban That was closed and its Vietnamese population had all moved to Panat Nikhom for resettlement processing. The 'illegals' moved back to Khao I Dang to await repatriation. The Vietnamese who fought to stay in Site 2 in hopes of improving their migration chances were among the last to leave the border. Ultimately, most of them did achieve their dream of resettlement but the lessons were painful all round, and the scenes of violence and protest proved ominous portents of things to come in other Vietnamese camps around the region.

Notes

1 Sukhumbhand Paribatra, *From Enmity to Alignment: Thailand's Evolving Relations with China* (Bangkok: Institute of Security and International Studies, Chulalongkorn University, 1987), p. 10.
2 Chanda, *Brother Enemy*, p. 349.
3 Sukhumbhand, *From Enmity to Alignment*, pp. 17ff.
4 Elizabeth Becker, *When the War Was Over: The Voices of Cambodia's Revolution and its People* (New York: Simon and Schuster, 1986), p. 440.
5 Linda Mason and Roger Brown, *Rice, Rivalry, and Politics: Managing Cambodian Relief* (Notre Dame: University of Notre Dame Press, 1983), p. 21.
6 *Ibid.*, p. 4.
7 UNICEF, 'Joint UNICEF/ICRC Emergency Relief for Kampuchea,' Information Note by the Executive Director, 2 November 1979, p. 5.
8 Shawcross, *The Quality of Mercy*, p. 170.
9 In Vitit Muntarbhorn, 'Displaced Persons in Thailand: Legal and National Policy Issues in Perspective,' *Chulalongkorn University Law Review*, Vol. 1 (1982), p. 173.
10 *Bangkok Post*, 20 October 1979.
11 Martin Barber, 'Operating a United Nations Program: A Personal Reflection,' in Barry S. Levy and Daniel C. Susott, eds, *Years of Horror, Days of Hope: Responding to the Cambodian Refugee Crisis* (New York: Associated Faculty Press, 1987), p. 29.
12 Thai Ministry of Interior, *An Instrument of Foreign Policy: Indochinese Displaced Persons* (Bangkok: Department of Local Administration, 1981), p. 41.
13 Barber, 'Operating a United Nations program', p. 29.
14 In a 15 December 1979 press release, UNHCR noted that for the week ending 4 November, an average of 32 people died every day in Sa Kaeo. This had dropped to 1.1 per day for the week ending 11 December.
15 See Shawcross, *The Quality of Mercy*, pp. 169–90, for a discussion of the construction of Sa Kaeo and Khao I Dang.
16 See Mason and Brown, *Rice, Rivalry and Politics*, p. 30, and Stephen R. Heder, 'Kampuchea: From Pol Pot to Pen Sovan to the Villages,' in Khien Theeravit and

MacAlister Brown, eds, *Indochina and Problems of Security and Stability in Southeast Asia* (Bangkok: Chulalongkorn University Press, 1983), p. 16.

17 Citing a lack of on-site water among other reasons, the Thai government ultimately scrapped plans to turn Mairut into a 'national refugee centre'. But for a time, two camps existed across the road from one another: Mairut I, the old UNHCR/MOI camp, and Mairut II, the new holding centre run by UNHCR and the Supreme Command.

18 Khachadpai Burusapatana, speech presented at the Public Affairs Institute Seminar on Refugee Research, Pattaya, Thailand, 28–29 March 1986.

19 Andrew Shacknove, 'From asylum to containment,' *International Journal of Refugee Law* Vol. 5, No. 4 (1993), p. 517.

20 Mason and Brown, *Rice, Rivalry and Politics*, pp. 34–5.

21 In Vitit Muntarbhorn, 'Displaced persons in Thailand: legal and national policy issues in perspective,' Round Table of Asian Experts on Current Problems in the International Protection of Refugees and Displaced Persons (Manila: International Institute of Humanitarian Law, 14–18 April 1980), p. 174.

22 Zia Rizvi, 'The Indochinese refugee exodus: comments on some specific aspects', *International Seminar on the Indochinese Exodus and the International Response* (Tokyo, United Nations University, 27–28 October 1995), pp. 114–15.

23 Author's interview with Dennis McNamara, Geneva, 14 February 1996.

24 Author's interview with Dale de Haan, Washington, DC, 17 April 1996.

25 McNamara, 'The politics of humanitarianism,' Section II, p. 55.

26 Author's interview with Morton Abramowitz, Tokyo, 27 October 1995.

27 Zia Rizvi, 'The Indochinese refugee exodus,' p. 115.

28 Hanne Sophie Greve put the figure at 'several thousand' out of Sa Kaeo alone (*Between the Tiger and the Crocodile*, p. 278).

29 Shawcross, *The Quality of Mercy*, p. 311.

30 *Ibid*, pp. 313–14.

31 *Bangkok Post*, 11 June 1980.

32 *The Nation*, 11 June 1980.

33 In Shawcross, *The Quality of Mercy*, p. 316.

34 *Ibid.*, p. 315.

35 *Ibid.*

36 *Bangkok Post*, 13 June 1980.

37 All quotations from SPK, 13 June 1980, in Foreign Broadcast Information Service (FBIS-APA-80-116).

38 *Bangkok Domestic Service*, 13 June 1980, (FBIS-APA-80-116).

39 *Phnom Penh Domestic Service,* 20 June 1980, (FBIS-APA-80-121).

40 Greve, *Between the Tiger and the Crocodile*, pp. 271–2.

41 *Ibid.*, p. 272.

42 *Hanoi Domestic Service*, 18 June 1980, (FBIS-APA-80-120).

43 *Bangkok Domestic Service,* 18 June 1980, (FBIS-APA-80-120).

44 *Voice of Democratic Kampuchea*, 22 June 1980, (FBIS-APA-80-124).

45 Stephen Heder, 'Kampuchea, October 1979–August 1980: the Democratic Kampuchea Resistance, the Kampuchean countryside, and the Sereikar,' unpublished manuscript, p. 77.

46 *Ibid.*

47 Ministry of Interior, *Too Long to Wait: Displaced Persons from Indochina in Thailand* (Bangkok: Operations Center for Displaced Persons, 1980), p. 33.

48 Greve, *Between the Tiger and the Crocodile,* p. 273.

49 Martin Barber, 'Resettlement in third countries versus voluntary repatriation' in Levy and Susott, *Years of Horror, Days of Hope*, p. 304.

50 In Mason and Brown, *Rice, Rivalry and Politics*, p. 151.

51 See Greve, *Between the Tiger and the Crocodile*, pp. 275–6.

52 Cited in Thai Ministry of Foreign Affairs, *The Vietnamese Acts of Aggression against Thailand's Sovereignty and Territorial Integrity* (Bangkok: 1980), p. 11.

53 Robert Ashe, 'Cross-border feeding,' mimeographed report, 8 July 1980.

54 See Shawcross, *The Quality of Mercy*, p. 318. Years later, Rizvi would insist: 'My discussions with the leadership, in Hanoi as well as Phnom Penh, both prior and subsequent to the Sakeo operation leave me in no doubt that there was no linkage but it was concocted by some to make political mileage.' Zia Rizvi, 'The Indochinese refugee exodus.' p. 116.

55 See Larry A. Niksch, 'Thailand in 1980: confrontation with Vietnam and the fall of Kriangsak', *Asian Survey*, Vol. 21, No. 2 (February 1981), pp. 224–8.

56 *International Herald Tribune*, 3 July 1980. In Mason and Brown, *Rice, Rivalry and Politics*, p. 155.

57 *Ibid.*, p. 183.

58 Unclassified State Department cable from American Embassy, Bangkok to Secretary of State, Washington, DC, March 1982.

59 'Zia Rizvi Briefing at Australian Embassy, Thursday, 20th May, 1982.' mimeograph, p. 21–2.

60 On 14 November 1979, the UN General Assembly had passed Resolution 34/22, which made an appeal 'to all states and national and international humanitarian organizations to render, on an urgent and non-discriminatory basis, humanitarian relief to the civilian population of Kampuchea, including those who have sought refuge in neighboring countries.' See Office of the Special Representative of the Secretary-General of the United Nations for the Coordination of Cambodian Humanitarian Assistance Programs (OSRSG), *Cambodian Humanitarian Assistance and the United Nations, 1979–1991* (Bangkok: United Nations, 1992), pp. 79–80.

61 In Greve, *Betweeen the Tiger and the Crocodile*, p. 615n.

62 The comment is attributed to Australian historian Ben Kiernan, in Paul Davies and Nic Dunlop, *The War of the Mines: Cambodia, Landmines and the Impoverishment of a Nation* (London: Pluto Press, 1994), p. 8.

63 WFP, Committee on Food Aid Policies and Programmes, 'Kampuchean emergency operation: an information note', Rome, April 1982: p. 2.

64 Joint Operations Center, Supreme Command, 'The assistance plan for Thai villagers affected by Kampuchean migration into Thailand,' (undated mimeograph), p. 5.

65 M. R. Narisa Chakrabongse, *The Affected Thai Village Program: 1978–1986* (Bangkok: Ford Foundation, October 1986), p. 3.

66 *Ibid.*, p. 21.

67 Mason and Brown, *op. cit.*, pp. 141–2.

68 Shawcross, *op. cit.*, p. 395.

69 In *Documents on the Kampuchean Problem*, p. 123.

70 *Ibid.*

71 Author's interview with Scott Leiper, Phnom Penh, 30 August 1995.

72 McNamara, 'The politics of humanitarianism,' p. 207.

73 UNBRO Monthly Report, May 1983.

74 Eighteen months later, in October 1984, nearly 600 people fled from the Khao Din area and relocated in Sanro Changan. All of them had moved there from

Red Hill. As reasons for leaving the Khmer Rouge area south of Aranyaprathet, they mentioned 'forced labor, shortage of food, high incidence of malaria, and severe restrictions on personal freedom'. (UNBRO Monthly Report, October 1984).

75 In Rob Burrows, *Displacement and Survival: United Nations Border Relief Operation for Cambodians in Thailand* (Bangkok: UNBRO, 1994), p. 57.

76 Letter from Winston Prattley to Susan Walker, Director, American Refugee Committee, 7 October 1983.

77 Group Discussion of Policy Implementation for Displaced Persons from Kampuchea, in *1982 Annual Conference on Indochinese Displaced Persons in Thailand* (Bangkok: CCSDPT, 1982), p. 102. Translated by the author.

78 *Ibid.*, p. 105.

79 *Ibid.*, p. 106.

80 See Ramses Amer, 'The ethnic Vietnamese in Cambodia: a minority at risk?' *Contemporary Southeast Asia*, Vol. 26, Number 2 (September 1994), p. 220. See also Marie-Alexandrine Martin, 'The Vietnamisation of Kampuchea: a new model of colonialism', *Indochina Report*, October 1984.

81 *Washington Post*, 22 November 1983.

82 UNBRO Monthly Report, July 1984.

83 Minutes of the Inter-Agency Field Meeting, Aranyaprathet, 13 February 1985.

84 Letter from Bob De Vecchi to Officers and Allocations Committee [ACVA], 28 January 1985.

85 US Congress, Senate Committee on the Judiciary, *US Refugee Program in Southeast Asia: 1985*, Report Prepared for the Use of the Subcommittee on Immigration and Refugee Policy, 99th Congress, 1st Session, April 1985, pp. 7–8.

86 Josephine Reynell, *Political Pawns: Refugees on the Thai–Kampuchean Border* (Oxford: Refugee Studies Programme 1989), p. 42.

87 John Rogge, 'Return to Cambodia', in Frederick C. Cuny, Barry N. Stein and Pat Reed (eds), *Repatriation During Conflict in Africa and Asia* (Dallas: Center for the Study of Societies in Crisis, 1992), p. 144.

88 Author's interview with Susan Walker, Bangkok, 6 July 1993.

89 Speech by Prasong Soonsiri at the 1986 CCSDPT Annual Conference, Bangkok, 11 July 1986.

90 *Washington Post*, 12 August 1986.

91 'Aide-Memoire on the Question of Khao I Dang handed to Perm. Rep. of Thailand from Mr. R. Ahmed on 29 January 1987 in New York.'

92 'Refugee Letters–Khao I Dang, 1987', CCSDPT Files.

93 *Ibid.*

94 Author's interview with Suon Sandab, Khao I Dang, 9 August 1987. He had been an intelligence officer with the KPNLF's Khmer Intelligence Security Agency (KISA) but had left Site 2 after a general had threatened his wife sexually. He too was living underground and frightened of arrest.

95 Hanne Sophie Greve, 'Evacuation sites for Kampucheans in Thailand: virtual concentration camps under international auspices?', mimeograph, 9 September 1987.

96 *Far Eastern Economic Review*, 5 June 1985. The UNBRO Monthly Report, May 1985, reported the camp evacuations.

97 Letter from Arthur F. Dewey to Tatsuro Kunugi, 4 September 1985.

98 'Origins of the structure and functions of UNBRO,' June 1986.

99 Author's interview with Dominique Buff, ICRC, Aranyaprathet, 6 August 1987.

100 OSRSG, *Cambodian Humanitarian Assistance*, p. 43.

101 Bob Maat, 'The weight of these sad times: end of mission report on the Thai–Kampuchean border,' 8 December 1979–30 April 1989, p. 17.

102 UNBRO Monthly Report, July 1987. All told, there were 47 incidents of violence reported that July, including 11 deaths.

103 Anonymous letter from 'a relief worker' to Asia Watch, 19 May 1988.

104 Maat, 'The weight of these sad times,' p. 52.

105 Shield Asia Report, August 1987.

106 In Lindsay French, Barnabas Mam and Tith Vuthy, eds, *Displaced Lives: Stories of Life and Culture from the Khmer in Site II, Thailand* (Bangkok: International Rescue Committee, 1990), p. 40.

107 Author's interview with Patrick van de Velde, Bangkok, 9 August 1995.

108 Norah Niland, 'The politics of suffering: the Thai–Cambodian border, a case study on the use and abuse of humanitarian assistance', Masters' thesis, University of Dublin, 1991, pp. 133–4.

109 See Burrows, *Displacement and Survival*, p. 106.

110 Kari Rene Hall, *Beyond the Killing Fields,* photographs by Kari Rene Hall, text by Josh Getlin and Kari Rene Hall (Bangkok: Aperture, 1992), p. 47.

111 Kim Ha, *Report on the Vietnamese Land Refugees: The Journey Through Cambodia and Life in the Refugee Camps* (San Diego: Boat People SOS Committee, 1983).

112 Author's interview with Cambodian returnee, Battambang, 23 September 1992.

113 *The Nation*, 21 July 1988.

114 Statement by Mr S. A. M. S. Kibria, Multilateral Donors' Meeting, New York, 8 September 1988.

115 On 27 November 1988 a Platform Vietnamese, Tran Sarin, had received a letter from UNHCR stating, 'As you know residents of Ban That camp are, according to the policy of the Royal Thai Government, not released for resettlement processing…. We regret that we cannot be of further assistance.' In a letter from Rev. Thomas J. Dunleavy to the US Committee for Refugees, 18 February 1989.

116 Maat, 'The weight of these sad times', p. 71.

CHAPTER 5

—

Laotian Refugees in Thailand

Even before the war in Laos was over, UNHCR was involved in efforts to help an estimated 700,000 internally displaced people, including about 150,000 Hmong, to get back to their homes. Its 1974–5 programme, budgeted at $3 million, aimed both to help people go home and provide them with transitional food aid and agricultural equipment to sustain themselves. By December 1975, when the Lao People's Democratic Republic (LPDR) was formally established, some 117,000 people had returned to their original villages. In the following year, roughly 150,000 people were transported by air, road and river, with another 121,000 moving back in 1977.

By the end of 1977, UNHCR declared that the 'return to village' phase of assistance was complete while rehabilitation was hampered by 'uneven, often slow' implementation by the local authorities and an inadequate transportation network. These were aggravated by a drought in the southern rice-producing provinces which had resulted in a food deficit of some 260,000 metric tons, six per cent of annual needs. 'A good many of the 386,000 persons who have returned under the UNHCR', concluded a 1978 UNHCR report, 'continue to depend on government-supplied rations.'[1]

In 1978, however, UNHCR committed no new funds for assistance programmes in Laos. More than $2 million remained unspent from previous allocations. 'A major reason for this slow implementation of UNHCR assistance programs,' UNHCR concluded, 'is the inability of the government to formulate and submit well defined project proposals, which is mainly due to a chronic lack of skilled manpower.'[2]

Some of the skilled manpower that had not fled across the Mekong into Thailand was languishing in a re-education camp. According to the government's own statements, in late 1975 and early 1976, between 10,000 and 15,000 people – many of them members of the administration, police or armed forces of the Royal Lao Government – were arrested and taken away for re-education, a regimen to rehabilitate 'counter-revolutionaries' through political 'seminars' and collective manual labour.

As a 1985 Amnesty International report described it, 'most of those detained for "re-education" were transported to and concentrated in heavily guarded camps far from their homes, at sites in geographically remote and sparsely populated areas of Laos that had long been under solid [Pathet Lao] control and were near the politically friendly border with Vietnam.' Sites for those considered the most politically dangerous could be found in Houa Phan, Xieng Khouang and Phong Saly provinces in the northeast and in Savannakhet in the southeast. Lower-ranking government and military officials were detained in smaller camps closer to their homes.[3] From 1980 to 1982, two UNHCR irrigation projects in the Pakse area were used as 'suon samana' or re-education camps.[4]

By mid-1982, Amnesty International estimated that perhaps 2,000 former inmates had been released and another 2,000 transferred from internment camps to heavy labour sites. But as of early 1985, despite a restructuring of the re-education system, an estimated 6,000–7,000 people still were being held, with the largest numbers in Houa Phan.[5]

Vilay Chaleunrath had completed an undergraduate degree in economics at the University of Hawaii in 1973 and returned to Laos to work as an economist for the USAID program in Vientiane. He also taught English at the Lao–American Association. 'I had originally thought that people like me would be left alone,' he said, 'but a friend of mine who had also studied overseas was arrested and that gave me a lot of uncertainty. I left the country in June 1976. At that time, you could go back and forth across the river to buy things. I asked for a pass to go buy medicine. I got to Nongkhai camp and asked to be a refugee.'[6]

For many others, especially the Hmong, leaving was not nearly so easy. Doua Thao had served for nine years as a soldier in Vang Pao's army and came to Long Cheng in hopes of being evacuated. Instead, he said,

> We fled into the jungle [around Phu Bia] and lived there until August 1977 when we crossed into Thailand. We started out with a group of 3,000. Some dropped out and many were killed. Maybe 300 reached Thailand safely. I had left with my wife and our two-year-old son. There were ten of us altogether in our group. I tied a rope around us in a long chain and we slipped into the Mekong River at night. I was swimming in front. But there was a patrol boat cruising the river. They had a flashlight and shined it on us and started shooting. My wife shouted to me, 'I think they've hit our son.' I turned around and felt for him in the dark. My fingers went into the hole in his head. They were still firing and someone yelled, 'Cut us loose or they will kill us all!' I did and then dived under the water and swam for as long as I could. I made it to the Thai side but I lost track of the others.... I learned eight months later that my wife had been captured and imprisoned. My uncle was able to get her released [by paying a bribe]. In May 1978, I snuck back across the Mekong, again at night, and brought her back with our newborn daughter. She had been pregnant when we left the year before.[7]

For highland Lao, the single biggest year for flight to Thailand was 1975, when 44,659 crossed the border. For lowland Lao, it was 1978, when UNHCR figures showed 48,781 arrivals, more than the previous three years combined. The reasons for this surge are varied: many certainly feared the possibility of re-education or regretted the loss of political, economic and religious freedoms. Other reasons included the drought and generally poor state of the economy along with what one observer described as the 'petty controls of a suspicious administration ... limitations on freedom of movement and on the sale of produce, the introduction of pricing, agriculture taxes, the obligation of civil servants to cultivate a cooperative garden and to attend political seminars, and the disappearance of benefits deriving from Lao contacts with the West'.[8] Others resented government efforts to collectivize agriculture. As one refugee told political scientist Joseph Zasloff, 'People feel that the fields and buffalo don't belong to them but to the community. They grow poorer.'[9]

Part of the 1978 surge, however, is merely a statistical artifact. A UNHCR report for 1978–9 noted that 'In addition to the 42,000 persons who were granted temporary asylum in Thailand during 1978, more than 25,000 persons who had arrived earlier and were living outside camps without UNHCR assistance were moved into the UNHCR camps by the Thai authorities.'[10] Given that lowland Lao were by far the largest group of arrivals in 1978, and that their cultural and linguistic affinities with northeastern Thais made it relatively easier for them to remain outside of camps, it can be assumed that most of the 25,000 earlier arrivals were lowland Lao.

Ubon camp, for those fleeing southern Laos, held about 14,000 people in early 1978 but saw its population rise to nearly 40,000 by early 1979. Most of them, according to Dr John O'Sullivan of Save the Children Fund who was working in the camp, were 'Lao peasants' whose state on arrival was 'extremely variable, from those in perfect health who had managed to bring many of their belongings, to those near death who had only the rags they stood in'. The exact size and composition of the camp population, said O' Sullivan, became 'one of the central issues affecting life in Ubon':

> By early 1979, the Thai camp authorities were asking UNHCR for money to feed and house 38,000 people. UNHCR felt that the estimate was too high by 6,000 and paid accordingly.... Ubon camp was unusual in that it was relatively easy for the inhabitants to come and go and they mingled easily with the peasants of the surrounding area. UNHCR themselves made one attempt to count the population but were totally frustrated by the arrival of hundreds of people in buses the night before the count started. The Lao refugees claimed that many of these were in fact their own kind who were working (illegally) away from the camp. Subsequently, UNHCR agreed to support 38,000 and for their part, the camp authorities started to issue identity cards soon afterwards. However, not even this was foolproof, as many genuine refugees failed to obtain one for various reasons. By May 1979, according to our estimates, there were certainly 40,000 dependent to some extent upon aid from within the camp. According to our Lao paramedics, perhaps 10 per cent were of Thai origin.[11]

In September 1975, on a visit to Laos, the High Commissioner for Refugees, Prince Sadruddin Aga Khan, had signed an agreement with the LPDR 'to cooperate in supporting the Laotian refugees who want to go back to their native country as soon as possible'.[12] Despite UNHCR commitments of transportation and reintegration aid, however, the records show no official returns from Thailand until 1980 when 193 lowland Lao crossed back home. There was little interest on the refugees' part in going back and little on the government's part in welcoming them home. Each side, at that point, felt it was well rid of the other.

Following a visit by High Commissioner Poul Hartling in September 1978, UNHCR halted all further activities for displaced persons inside Laos and announced a 're-orientation of UNHCR's activities towards the provinces bordering Thailand, particularly in the southern part of the country ... with a view to preventing the exodus of persons who might wish to leave Laos because of economic difficulties and chronic food shortages in some areas.' Food assistance and food production projects were begun in Savannakhet and Champassak provinces, particularly in villages where some spontaneous repatriation was taking place. An assessment of this 'exodus prevention policy' in early 1980, however, predicted gloomily that 'it appears that in 1980, more Laotians than in any previous year will have fled Laos,' adding that 'this Branch Office considers that the main causes of this exodus now have to be found in factors other than in the internal situation of the country'.[13]

Laotian movements into Thailand in 1980 exceeded 43,000 people, including 29,000 lowland Lao, despite a temporary closure of the border by Thailand, flood conditions along the Mekong in August and September, and a fire in Nong Khai in February. The UNHCR statement revealed a rather benign view of the Lao regime, at least as far as treatment of lowland Lao was concerned, and reflected a growing suspicion that the proximity of the camps, with their enticements of free food, medical care and third-country resettlement, were drawing many across the river who had little to fear by staying home. This opinion, of course, was not shared by everyone, even within UNHCR. Werner Blatter, who worked for the agency on both sides of the Thai–Laotian border, said

> If there is one group of people who has no departure mentality it must be the [lowland] Lao. Economic considerations were definitely no pull factor. The Lao, even the sophisticated class, can live on very little. Only after the monarchy was established and the regime became more and more repressive, and when the traditional Lao way of life was in serious jeopardy could many not take it any longer and left.[14]

Early Days at Ban Vinai

The myths say that the first Hmong was born from a mountain cleft. True or not, the history of the Hmong is a long search for the freedom of high places, and adamant resistance to those who might deny them. Their history places them in China more than two thousand years ago, where the Chinese called them Miao, or 'barbarian', a term that carries down to the present-day pejorative, Meo. Hmong, on the other hand, means 'free people'.

As the Chinese empire expanded southward during the Han Dynasty, the new settlers sought to grace this savage, indigenous minority with the sublimities of civilization. Those who adopted Chinese ways, who spoke Chinese, paid taxes, lived in the valleys and practised wet-rice cultivation came to be called the *shu* or 'tame' Miao. But those who stayed in the mountains and resisted acculturation were called *sheng* or 'wild' Miao. Such resistance often was met with violent suppression. In 1735, more than 18,000 Hmong reportedly were slaughtered. As Chinese colonization continued and reprisals mounted in the 1800s, the Hmong began moving south into northern Vietnam, Laos and Thailand. 'It was not independence they seem to have prized,' according to anthropologist Nicholas Tapp, 'so much as the freedom to cultivate, after their own fashion, the lands they lived on, and to pursue their own customs and traditions in a peaceable, equable way.'[15]

But peace was hard to find in the lands to the south and, just as the Hmong had fought the Chinese in Kweichou, they fought against the Vietnamese and French in Vietnam and against the Khhmu and French (and, later, the Japanese) in Laos. But as they moved to higher ground, the Hmong were left more and more to themselves. The coming of the Second Indochina War in the 1960s, however, not only brought the Hmong down from the highlands again but pitted them against the Pathet Lao, the North Vietnamese and fellow Hmong who had chosen to side with the communists. The sudden withdrawal of the Americans – along with the Hmong military leadership – in May 1975 left a scattered and vulnerable population behind.

As tens of thousands of Hmong began to make their way toward the Thai border, perhaps 60,000–100,000 regrouped in the area of Phu Bia to the south of General Vang Pao's former headquarters at Long Cheng. Some began organizing resistance movements; others were just looking for a place to hide. Said one woman who eventually sought refuge in Thailand:

> When Vang Pao evacuated Long Cheng, there were not enough airplanes to transport all of us with him. He told us, 'You know all the birds and squirrels have lived all their lives in the jungle, but they do not die. If you can't live in your village, you can go to live in the jungle.... That's why when the communists started to arrest our men and sent them to re-education camps, we fled to the Phu Bia forest. We hid and hid. We had no salt to eat, no rice to eat. If we built a fire to cook food, the communists would see smoke and attack us. We fled from place to place. When we tried to make some rice fields, the communists came and burned them all. My children started to die of starvation. Eight died. Now I have only six children living.[16]

In 1977 and 1978, Pathet Lao and Vietnamese troops launched Operation Sam Kieng ('Complete Destruction') to wipe out the last vestiges of Hmong resistance. Out of a population of about 350,000, estimates of Hmong deaths in Laos from 1975 to 1980 range from 50,000–100,000.[17] By the end of 1980, another 100,000 Hmong and other highland minorities had sought safety in Thailand.

Robert Cooper, an anthropologist who has written extensively on Hmong history and culture, served as a programme officer for UNHCR in Laos from 1980 to 1983. 'That the great majority of Hmong refugees fled because of a genuinely-felt fear of reprisal or persecution from the new regime is not called into question,' he wrote in a study published in 1986, but 'there were additional economic reasons for the Hmong to leave Laos and to leave when they did.' Not only had the war removed large areas from cultivation through bombing and chemical defoliation but

> a great many Hmong families came to rely increasingly on food drops by aircraft, handouts in the population centers, or the soldier's pay earned by adult males.... When, in 1975, the alternative means of livelihood came to an abrupt end, tens of thousands of Hmong found themselves abruptly face to face not only with the fear of the enemy's revenge but also with a situation of accumulated resource scarcity.... Had they remained in Laos, it is difficult to see how they could have avoided large-scale famine.[18]

From its beginnings in early 1976 until the end of 1978, Ban Vinai camp had maintained a fairly stable population, as new arrivals each year would be offset by resettlement. As a husband-and-wife team of relief workers, John and Jean Sibley, wrote,

> visualize an established camp of ten to twelve thousand people in a shallow valley outlined at intervals by several high-peaked hills.... Every open space in the camp is tilled with vegetable gardens. Women alone and in small groups are busy with their embroidery.... Along the two dirty, dusty roads that wind through camp are little shops selling everything the refugees can find to sell – by growing, by buying from the Thais, by making with their own hands.... Bamboo houses vary in size and style, on low stilts for the Lao, on the ground for the Hmong. Surface wells are scattered throughout the camp and much time is spent carrying water in every conceivable manner and container. There is a look of cramped but settled stability as the inhabitants await an uncertain future....
>
> But beginning in January of [1979] the settled stability was pried apart as first tens, then hundreds and, by summer, thousands of Hmong were trucked into the camp. Lean-tos were thrown up while more permanent housing was rapidly constructed. More wells were dug, and filled by the May to August monsoon rains. Food was trucked in, plus mosquito netting, charcoal, pails, cooking pots, blankets, wood and bamboo as UNHCR tried to keep up with the growing invasion. The population of the camp doubled in size over a five-month period and then, in June and July, almost doubled again. The new refugees were – too many of them – penniless, weak from hunger, malaria and its all too common companion, pneumonia. Adults wilted. Infants died.[19]

By the turn of the year, the pace of influx had declined, permitting medical teams to get out of the hospital wards and into the community to work on the preventive side of disease. The Sibleys also had time to explore a question that had been puzzling them: 'why so many were getting serious infections in the face of UNHCR supplied food rations which were supposedly meeting at least minimum standards'. They found that, 'in fact, these standards are nowhere near being met'. The standard for rice was 500 grams per day. The refugees were getting 330 grams. The standard for protein was 65 grams. Ban Vinai residents were receiving one-third that amount. In the midst of one of the best-funded relief operations in history, in a country with superb infrastructure and plentiful food supplies, the Sibleys reported that 'our chief root problem is nutrition'. The UNHCR representative, they said, 'is concerned and working on the problem because the funds are being given for meeting minimum standards, but something is happening somewhere along the line. He says the established camps are in much worse condition as regards supplies than the crisis camps at the Kampuchean border.'[20]

What was happening along the line was diversion, corruption, theft of food that at any given point may have seemed petty but whose cumulative impact was nothing less than murderous. Truck drivers paid to transport the food to the camps left their loads a few bags light. Local villagers who saw so much free food going to the camps saw nothing wrong with taking some for themselves. And along the way, as the relief supplies passed through the hands of Thai officials, they too levied their own informal duties. One refugee interviewed in Sop Tuang camp in 1978 said,

> Since the camp was first set up in 1975, the head of camp has been changed five times. The present head had been in the job for only two months. Refugees, including my own father, trust the new man who called in person on our house shortly after his arrival. He assured everyone there would be no more corruption. But I am not sure. The history of camp heads and officials has been a history of greed and violence. They have helped themselves to UNHCR food, blankets, mosquito nets and lengths of cloth. Quite openly and in broad daylight, the rice or vegetables brought into camp have repeatedly been put into official jeeps to be sold elsewhere.[21]

One of the reasons why the problem was so much more severe in the 'established camps' than in the 'crisis camps' on the Cambodian border was that, in the case of the Vietnamese, Laotian and pre-1979 Cambodian camps, UNHCR provided funds to the Thai Ministry of Interior which then handled the sub-contracts for food procurement, transport, and distribution. In the Cambodian holding centres, on the other hand, the Thai military left that job to the United Nations and the voluntary agencies.

Only days before Sadruddin's arrival in Thailand in September 1975, the *Bangkok Post* had published a highly critical article on the refugee relief effort, saying government corruption was preventing food from reaching the sprawling Laotian refugee camp of Sop Tuang and that 20 people were dying every day as a result. 'Thai officials are selling the contributed rice to the refugees at about twice market value,' said the paper. 'Most of the rice never gets to the settlement and is probably being sold on the local market to the benefit of government officials.'[22]

Charges of corruption in the Ministry of Interior (MOI) were hardly surprising. In 1970–72, for example, a total of 1,542 complaints of bureaucratic corruption were filed with various government offices. Of these, more

than half were directed at MOI.[23] The powerful ministry was in charge of
local administration (which included appointing all provincial governors), the
police department, public works, immigration, the land department, water-
works, the electricity authority and rural development. The opportunities to
improve one's position at public expense were, and are, considerable. 'To a
large extent,' said one study by Thai academics, 'the police [force] still
operates along the principles of *gin muang* [literally, to 'eat the country'], the
system of remuneration of officials which prevailed in the traditional
bureaucracy.'[24]

Humane Deterrence

In 1976, Thailand's Ministry of Interior had published its first annual report
on Indochinese refugees with the prosaic title, *The Arrival of Displaced Persons
into Thailand from Cambodia, Laos and South Vietnam.* In 1977, the MOI report
pleaded poignantly, *Turn Not Your Eyes Away.* The following year, MOI
issued *A Call for Humanity.* By 1979, it was calling refugees *The Unfair Burden*:
1980 had become *Too Long to Wait.* By 1981, an air of grim reality seemed
to have set in. That year's report on Indochinese displaced persons, with its
cover of gun-metal grey, was called *An Instrument of Foreign Policy.*

The MOI report catalogued the contrary effects of the refugee presence,
ranging from economic and political factors to national security: the Indochinese were a financial burden to the government, they disrupted the local
economy, they damaged national resources, they promoted 'discontentment'
among the Thai people, they provoked 'hostile activity' between Thailand
and its neighbours, and they were a dangerous 'fifth column' for subversive
activities.[25] Harbouring them, the report suggested, may have promoted
Thailand's foreign policy interests but that did not mean they were welcome
on the home front.

MOI warned in 1981 that it was 'about to change some administrative
implementation [in order] to cease the new arrivals,' but added, 'This does
not mean that we will ignore the humanitarian attitude.'[26] It was no
coincidence that in March 1980, the same month that Thailand closed the
Cambodian border in earnest, it opened the Khmer holding centres to
resettlement. The next year, it would try the reverse with the Laotians and
Vietnamese. The policies that became known as 'humane deterrence' sought
to stem the flow of new arrivals by keeping the borders open while closing
the doors to resettlement and other UNHCR camp amenities.

International resettlement had moved large numbers of refugees out of
Thailand in 1980–1, and camp populations had begun to decline. More than
75,000 highland and lowland Lao refugees left Thailand for third countries
in 1980, along with 27,000 Cambodians and 25,000 Vietnamese. Though
these were offset by nearly 114,000 arrivals, for the first time since the
exodus into Thailand began, resettlement had outpaced the influx. The trend
continued into 1981, with 102,500 refugees leaving Thailand for resettlement

overseas, against 43,000 arrivals. Nevertheless, Thai officials remained concerned that the internationally serviced camps, combined with the ready opportunity of overseas resettlement for many, were creating too much of a lure. Much of the controversy centred on Nong Khai; its accessibility from Vientiane just up the river, according to one journalist, 'is almost laughable'.[27]

Opened in 1975 to accommodate Laotian refugees crossing from the capital city, Nong Khai had grown to nearly 40,000 people by early 1980. The Hmong by this time had been moved to Ban Vinai, making Nong Khai the exclusive preserve of ethnic Lao. One account by a relief worker said that the camp, which some were calling 'Vientiane II ... resembles a thriving city:

> Roadways are wide enough to permit numerous pedicab vehicles; restaurants abound, and the food is good enough and plentiful enough that even restaurant owners in town come out to purchase their food here. There is extraordinary freedom of movement between the refugee center and the town itself. Even though the Thai police charge 5 baht for each entrance or exit, there is a constant flow of people. Refugees are working in town [and] can spend the night in town at a hotel.[28]

Getting into Nong Khai, however, was by no means always a laughing matter. Guards were posted on both sides of the river and sometimes shot those trying to cross. 'If one has no money to pay the Thais,' said the relief official, 'refugees are often pushed back into the river or shot.' Inside the camp, many of the men were armed. 'Guerrilla fighters from camp go into Laos at night to fight.'[29]

As far as UNHCR was concerned, freedom fighters and fortune seekers alike had no business inside a refugee camp and, beginning in 1980, UNHCR officials in Thailand had begun reconsidering the possibility of establishing refugee status determination procedures for new arrivals. The July 1977 agreement between UNHCR and Thailand to establish such procedures was still legally valid although nothing much had come of it. In early 1981, a UNHCR official drafted a proposal for a joint Thai/UNHCR procedure to determine the refugee status of new lowland Lao arrivals. UNHCR, according to the draft proposal, 'has sufficient reason to seriously reconsider its position on the blanket acknowledgment of all lowland Lao arrivals, since a significant number of these people do not appear to fall within even the most liberal interpretation of a refugee'.[30]

But at a meeting on the subject in February 1981, Ivor Jackson, then deputy director of UNHCR's Division of International Protection, essentially rejected the idea. In an earlier analysis, he had written,

> It should be recalled that if a determination procedure were introduced in Thailand, the situation would be fundamentally different from that prevailing in various Western European countries where determination procedures exist. In these countries, persons whose applications for refugee status are rejected are nevertheless normally permitted to remain in the country pending their resettlement. In Thailand, this would presumably not be the case and the screening

procedure would almost certainly be used as a justification for forcible repatriation. For this reason alone, a considerable degree of caution and reflection is necessary.[31]

The basic proposal on the table, Jackson recalled later, 'was that those not considered to be refugees could be sent back. Those who were refugees could be resettled. "But what about local settlement?" I asked. "Don't talk about it," I was told, I felt in this case it was best to stick to the *prima facie* refugee status.... The definition is an elastic one, isn't it? To start fiddling around then didn't work.'[32]

Many UNHCR officials in Thailand and Laos tended to see no significant risk of reprisal at the hands of the socialist regime. Others shared Jackson's concern about forced return but felt that the introduction of screening might serve to reduce the influx, thus encouraging Thailand to consider some local settlement and persuading both countries (as well as the screened-out) to treat the option of voluntary return more seriously. In the end, Thailand also rejected the idea of screening, at least for the time being, opting instead for 'humane deterrence' measures to stem the flow.

In January 1981 Thailand opened a new camp for lowland Lao, Na Pho, in the province of Nakhon Phanom, and placed all new arrivals there, without access to resettlement. A more austere level of services was established, moreover, 'intended to maintain existing refugees at a living standard below that of Thai citizens'.[33] Refugees lived in block-style housing, five persons to a room, twenty rooms to a longhouse. Rations were 'survival-level', and international aid agencies, at least initially, were prohibited from entering camp.[34]

In May, the Thai Cabinet decided that the two Vietnamese boat people camps, Songkhla in the south and Laem Sing on the east coast, would be closed and their 7,000 residents moved to Panat Nikhom. Moreover, NW-9, the border camp for Vietnamese land refugees coming across Cambodia, would also be closed. Vietnamese arriving by boat, Thailand later clarified, would be sent to Sikhiu, an austere camp along the lines of Na Pho. The cut-off date of 15 August 1981 was set for resettlement of Vietnamese and Laotians. Arrivals after that date, announced a Supreme Command spokesman, would be sent to detention camps. 'The future of those in detention is not clear,' said Lieutenant Colonel Soonthorn Sophonsiri, 'but no resettlement opportunities will be offered, possibly for several years.'[35]

UNHCR had proposed some of these measures and the resettlement countries generally supported them, though not without misgivings from the United States.[36] In August 1981, a blue-ribbon panel of US citizens commissioned by the State Department and headed by Marshall Green filed its report on the Indochinese refugee programme:

> The prospect of an ongoing, substantial exodus strongly underlines the urgency for humane measures to deter the flow of increasing numbers of refugees whose reasons for fleeing derive more from normal migration motives than from fear of persecution. Certain deterrents, such as austere camps, sealing of borders, or

keeping people in holding centers or refugee camps for long periods of time, are not attractive prospects. Yet these and other measures … must be considered.[37]

By 1981 the US refugee programme in Southeast Asia was under close domestic scrutiny and significant pressure to scale back. More than 500,000 Indochinese had resettled in hundreds of communities across America, thousands more were arriving every month, and the resettlement system seemed strained to breaking. Refugee welfare dependency rates were at 77 per cent and rising, local service providers often were overwhelmed and local governments complained of being underfunded.

At the start of the new decade, the United States had passed a major new law, the Refugee Act of 1980, which had redefined refugee status to bring it in line with the worldwide standard as codified in the 1951 Convention. Gone were the old geographical and ideological restrictions that limited refugee status to someone fleeing a communist country or the Middle East. Gone, too, was the system of admission by *ad hoc* paroles. Instead, Congress and the administration were to consult each year on the number of refugees to be admitted. While the final authority for establishing annual admissions ceilings lay with the President, the consultations process sought to build consensus among the various federal agencies and branches of government involved in refugee resettlement. The new act also established an Office of Refugee Resettlement in the federal government and authorized reimbursement to states of up to 36 months of refugee resettlement costs.

During the spring and summer of 1980, in what has been called 'perhaps the most extraordinary event in the history of US refugee policy,' a flotilla of 130,000 Cubans poured out of Mariel harbour and onto the beaches of south Florida.[38] As if that were not enough, the arrival of the 'Marielitos' coincided with the exodus of thousands of Haitians fleeing an oppressive political regime and crushing poverty.

Up until 1980, it had been the policy of various US administrations to receive Cuban arrivals as political refugees while rejecting Haitians largely as economic migrants subject to deportation. But in July 1980, a federal judge, James Lawrence King, ordered the Immigration and Naturalization Service (INS) to halt Haitian deportations until their applications could be reviewed in a fair and individualized manner. In a decision on *Haitian Refugee Center vs. Civiletti*, a class action suit filed on behalf of 4,000 Haitian asylum seekers, King found that

> The plaintiffs are part of the first substantial flight of black refugees from a repressive regime to this country. All the plaintiffs are black. Prior to the most recent Cuban exodus all of the Cubans who sought political asylum … were granted asylum routinely. None of the over 4,000 Haitians processed during the INS program at issue in the lawsuit were granted asylum. No greater disparity can be imagined.[39]

Unprepared for this mass asylum crisis and unwilling either to carry out individual status determinations or to grant statutory refuge, the Carter administration came up with a new, provisional term for the new arrivals:

'entrants'. As such, Washington announced, the federal government would only pay 75 per cent of their resettlement costs, making Jimmy Carter a rather unpopular man in Florida. He would become more so.

'The first 55,000 Cubans went right off the boats into South Florida communities,' said Roger Winter, then director of the new Office of Refugee Resettlement. 'Then it started to become clear that there were some bad people in the mix, that Castro was emptying his prisons and mental institutions.... One psychiatrist who came out with the exodus pointed out some of his patients. There were some difficult and potentially violent people.'[40] The federal government's Cuban–Haitian Task Force began moving the Cubans to military bases around the country, both to relieve the burden on Florida and give the authorities a chance to run background checks. Two of the camps – Fort Chaffee, Arkansas and Indiantown Gap, Pennsylvania – had been used to process Vietnamese evacuees five years earlier. The mood this time around was rather more grim and outbreaks of violence and disorder in some of camps did nothing to improve public sentiments about this latest wave of boat people.

The sense of rationality and control that the Refugee Act of 1980 sought to bring to a previously *ad hoc* series of policy measures was undermined and, as Winter said, 'public support for refugees and immigrants dipped badly'. The Cuban/Haitian influx had three other significant effects according to Winter: 'One, it hurt the Carter campaign. He lost Florida,' a key southern state, and ultimately conceded the November 1980 elections to Republican candidate Ronald Reagan. Second, said Winter, 'it destroyed the state assumptions that the federal government would cover its share of resettlement costs'. State and local governments did not necessarily become anti-refugee after that, but, as the federal budget for refugee programmes continued to decline, the mood in Congress grew less and less enthusiastic about open-ended commitments for Indochinese. Third, the Cuban/Haitian influx 'set the stage for Reagan administration initiatives to stop the flow'.[41]

As Gil Loescher and John Scanlan write in *Calculated Kindness*, their 1986 study of American refugee policy,

> Domestic backlash and the negative perception of the Carter administration's response to the Cuban-Haitian influx, coming at the same time as a record flow from Indochina, cast new doubts on America's willingness to admit refugees. President Reagan capitalized on those doubts after he assumed office, employing them to justify an asylum policy which continued to ignore the persecution claims of those fleeing authoritarian regimes in this hemisphere and which treated such asylum seekers with unprecedented harshness.[42]

Among other things, the Reagan administration reinstated the policy of interdicting Haitian boats on the high seas and turning them away from US territorial waters. Although the United States continued to display an active concern for Indochinese, its arguments on behalf of temporary safety for asylum seekers in Southeast Asia were undercut by its own failure to offer the same assurances at home.

Not long after the Refugee Act of 1980 was passed, a debate arose as to whether the law required the government – specifically, INS – to conduct case-by-case determinations of refugee status or permitted it to continue what amounted to presumptive eligibility for certain nationalities and groups. The debate centred on the Indochinese programme and pitted INS, which favoured individual determinations, against the State Department, which supported the *status quo ante*.

The Green Report sought a middle ground in this debate. "It is imperative that the refugee, as defined, remain a distinctive category of person," the report said, though it stopped short of advocating case-by-case processing. The Vietnamese, it said, 'are entitled to refugee status. The same conclusion was reached as to the Hmong people of the Laotian highlands. The Panel was less certain of the validity of this conclusion as to Lao lowlanders and to many fleeing severe economic conditions in Cambodia.' Green and his colleagues, like some in UNHCR, seemed particularly doubtful of the Lao qualifications:

> The character of the Lao flow has changed over the past year. Some Lao continue to come for essentially political reasons: to escape persecution for close association with the past regime or oppression under the new system. The majority of people now fleeing, however, seem to be primarily motivated by a desire to improve their basic living conditions. Indeed, Nong Khai camp, housing about half of all Lao refugees … bustles with commercial activity and was considered by camp dwellers as a more attractive place to live than Vientiane.[43]

In 1980, the international community had resettled a total of 128,000 Indochinese refugees from Thailand, with the largest numbers going to the United States. The combined effect of 'humane deterrence' policies and declining overseas commitments reduced departures from Thailand to 102,500 in 1981 and 33,000 in 1982. Laotian resettlement dropped from over 75,000 in 1980 to about 9,000 two years later. This same period witnessed a swift and dramatic drop in Laotian arrivals in Thailand. Lowland Lao numbers dropped from 29,000 in 1980 to 16,300 in 1981 and then to 3,200 the following year. Hmong arrivals showed a corresponding decline from 14,800 in 1980 to just 1,800 in 1982.

Humane deterrence was not yet in place for the Hmong, and many already were showing a deeply ambivalent attitude toward resettlement, so the reasons for declining Hmong arrivals lay elsewhere – but for the ethnic Lao, the trend seemed clear: refuge without resettlement was not worth crossing the river for. Perhaps more accurately, far fewer Lao found it worth entering a refugee camp stripped of services where resettlement was only a remote prospect. There is no evidence to suggest that informal movements back and forth across the Mekong diminished to any extent.

As Laotian camp arrival rates fell, Thai authorities accelerated a process of consolidation and ethnic 'homogenization' begun in 1980. During 1982, three highland Lao camps – Chiang Khong, Chiang Kham and Sop Tuang – were closed and their populations moved to Ban Nam Yao. The lowland

Lao camps, Ubon and Nong Khai, were also closed, with the remaining numbers of Hmong moving to Ban Vinai and the Lao to Na Pho.

After 1981, the United States was increasingly alone in maintaining a significant interest in Laotian refugees.[44] Even though US numbers had dropped a long way from the beginning of the decade, America was not willing to write off Laotian resettlement entirely. By late 1981, the US Embassy was pressing Thailand for access to priority cases in Na Pho – former military officers and re-education camp prisoners as well as families that had been split by the new deterrence policies. A father might have reached Thailand in 1980 and been approved for resettlement, for example, but found himself separated from his wife and children, who had arrived later and were stuck in Na Pho.

In March 1983, the Ministry of Interior permitted resettlement interviews for several thousand such cases in Na Pho. In 1984, Lao arrivals in Thailand totalled 14,600, more than triple the previous year. Factors inside Laos contributing to this surge included the institution of a new tax and another round of military conscription. By the middle of 1985, Na Pho held 38,000 people, including 5,000 to 6,000 single men ranging in age from 15 to 25. To relieve the overcrowding in the camp and the larger numerical pressures on Thailand, Lao resettlement commitments rose from 4,800 in 1985 to 11,600 in 1986.

Hmong resettlement, on the other hand, languished at around 2,700 per year from 1981 to 1985, though it managed to keep pace with new arrivals. When the Thai authorities closed Ban Vinai to new arrivals in 1983 and re-opened Chiang Kham as a 'humane deterrence' camp, it was not so much to deter newcomers as to press the 35,000 residents of Ban Vinai either to pursue resettlement or go back to Laos. Thailand took a number of steps to make the 'Village of Discipline' more disciplined:

> From 1984 to 1985 some 3,000 undocumented residents – refugees who had sneaked into Ban Vinai to join relatives – were rounded up and sent to Chiang Kham. The post office, a vital link to relatives in the United States, was moved out of Ban Vinai, and a ban on the cutting of bamboo for construction was reissued, forcing the United Nations to use corrugated tin to build homes that became hotboxes in the intense heat.[45]

But even as it was making these changes inside the camps, the Thai government was adopting other means of discouraging new arrivals at the border.

Push-backs and Border Screening

'It has been understood all along,' a Thai legal officer for UNHCR wrote in a 1984 internal memorandum to the country representative, 'that the Royal Thai Government's official policy ... despite the repeated pledges to the international community that temporary asylum will be granted to Indochinese refugees, is that asylum will only be granted when it is unavoidable.'[46]

The memo quoted two Thai cabinet decisions, one in June 1975 and the other in August 1977, that outlined this ambivalent position:

> Preventive and retaliatory measures will be taken to drive any displaced persons out of the Kingdom in case of attempted entry. Should it be impossible to reject them, they will be detained in camps.
>
> Displaced persons entering Thailand must report to the authorities and be detained in camps. In case of failure to do so, they will be treated as illegal immigrants and legal proceedings will be instituted against them.

Once inside a camp, these decisions seemed to agree, asylum seekers would be free from 'preventive and retaliatory measures'. But those outside, whether they were avoiding the camps or seeking a way in, could find themselves in a hazardous no man's land, subject to detention, prosecution and forced return.

By 1984, UNHCR found that Thai 'screening committees' were operating in districts all along the Thai–Laotian border. Composed of representatives from the Immigration Department, the police, the military and district officials, these committees took it upon themselves to screen new arrivals and exclude those deemed not to be genuine refugees. Roving UNHCR field officers found that the provincial and district authorities had complete autonomy to carry out screening in any way they saw fit. In Nong Khai province, some districts conducted straightforward operations while others diverted new arrivals elsewhere. In Nakhon Phanom province, UNHCR found that in June 1984 officials had decided 'to cease all screening, disband the screening committees and prosecute all new arrivals. Fortunately, none of the prosecuted asylum-seekers have yet been returned to Laos. They are all in Na Pho camp, though still unauthorized'.[48]

From January to September 1984, UNHCR reported that more than 2,000 people had been prosecuted for illegal entry, more than 350 people had been detained in police stations for between eight and 14 weeks, and, of greatest concern, 209 people had been pushed back into Laos in eight separate incidents. In January and February 1985, UNHCR reported another 524 people had been pushed back, all of them Hmong. UNHCR officials who visited some of the group back in Laos said they had been approached by a member of the resistance in December 1984 who promised them 'a better life and a brighter future in Thailand'. Following a 22-day trek from their home villages in Xieng Khouang, they swam across the Mekong. During the crossing, the Hmong reported, eight people died and 13 others went missing. Once on the other side, Thai soldiers relieved them of their valuables – 69 silver bars, 744 silver coins, 5,000 kip, 22 knives and 10.4 kilograms of opium. They returned to Laos 'with no other property than the clothes they were wearing'.[49]

In June 1985 a non-profit organization, the US Committee for Refugees (USCR), visited a series of police stations and immigration offices along the border from Ubon to Loei. USCR director Roger Winter, who headed the investigation, found that although policies and practices varied widely from one district to the next, push-backs were a common occurrence and the principal victims were the Hmong. In Loei province, for example, where Ban Vinai was located, the provincial coordinator for refugee affairs told Winter that 'more people have arrived this year than last but most have been sent back. Almost all are Hmong.'[50]

In 1985, a total of 13,344 Lao entered camps in Thailand compared to 14,616 the previous year. Hmong arrivals in 1985 numbered only 943, down from 3,627 in 1984. USCR's assessment that several thousand Laotians, mostly Hmong, were pushed back in 1985 appears to have been accurate.

Under pressure from both UNHCR and the United States, the Thai government announced on 1 July 1985 that it would institute a more formal screening process on the border: Laotian new arrivals presenting themselves to screening committee offices in any of the nine border provinces would be interviewed by trained MOI officials. UNHCR legal officers were free to attend these interviews as observers. Those who were screened in were sent to Ban Vinai or Na Pho, depending on their ethnic background. If the case was rejected, UNHCR was given an opportunity to appeal before the screened-out were placed in detention pending repatriation to Laos.

According to MOI there were four criteria for determination of refugee status:

1   Former officials, military [and] police during the pre-LPDR era.

2   Persons who used to work with embassies, international agencies, foreign or private firms during the pre-LPDR era.

3   Persons who participated in political or social movements against the communist government.

4   Persons with close relatives in third countries.[51]

This last point originally had appeared on a list of MOI criteria for illegal immigrants, which also included 'persons who claim dissatisfaction with the new regime, owing to tax collection, forced labor or the draft' or persons who leave 'because of their dissatisfaction with the LPDR economic system'.[52] It was fortunate for the Laotians that MOI insisted on counting a third-country connection toward rather than against refugee status, and it certainly contributed to the generous approval rates. But the presence of relatives overseas, in fact, is irrelevant to refugee status and its inclusion in screening criteria only blurred the line between those in need of international protection and those in hope of international migration. There was overlap, to be sure, but they were not the same.

By the end of 1986, UNHCR reported that 7,021 Laotians had been screened, of whom 4,665 people had been approved and 1,822 rejected, while the rest were pending. Although the approval rate of at least 66 per cent exceeded many expectations, it was apparent that a problem was developing: hardly any Hmong were getting screened and push-backs, after a lull from mid-1985 to early 1986, were becoming more frequent. According to internal UNHCR documents, Thai authorities sent back 362 people in 1986, including a total of 254 Hmong in May alone.

Thailand denied that the push-backs were anything more than local aberrations, insisting instead that the Hmong were circumventing the screening programme deliberately and entering the country through organized smuggling rings. 'It's a vicious circle,' admitted a UNHCR legal officer in Bangkok, 'The Hmong are sneaking into Thailand because they feel they might be pushed back to Laos if they make their presence known. And because the Hmong are still sneaking in, pushbacks are more likely to take place.'[53]

The circle turned more vicious still in 1987. On 15 March Thai officials removed 38 Hmong from Ban Vinai and, charging them with illegal entry, turned them over to Lao authorities. Amnesty International later reported that some had been taken to a secluded detention centre away from the border. UNHCR's country representative, Gerald Walzer, protested the action, which was believed to be the first forced repatriation from a UNHCR-supported refugee camp in Thailand. The incident also drew a strong protest from the United States, which called it 'possibly the most serious instance of forced repatriation from Thailand since 1979'. Thai officials responded with equally strong language, saying, 'We don't want to be treated as a client state,' and called on the Americans to take half of the 50,000 Hmong then in Thailand.[54] 'We don't do it like the Americans do – get their boats and guns out to chase and shoot away Mexicans and Haitians trying to reach the American shore,' said Prasong Soonsiri, secretary-general to the prime minister's office and Thailand's top refugee official.[55]

Two days after the first incident in March 1987, 97 Hmong were caught trying to enter Ban Vinai without passing through screening and also were repatriated. In July, the head of Thailand's National Security Council, Suwit Suthanakun, confirmed that these were not isolated instances but official policy: 'Laotians caught trying to sneak into refugee camps', he announced, 'will be deported.'[56]

Push-backs continued throughout the year but the most shocking incident took place in November 1987 when a group of 33 Hmong paid smugglers to transport them across the Mekong and into Ban Vinai camp. Instead, they were met by Thai police who put them on boats and returned them to Laos. A short while later, they were intercepted by Pathet Lao soldiers who marched the Hmong into the forest. According to an eight-year-old survivor, Kia Lor,

> They took us to the top of a hill, putting a rope around the adults' necks, they made us sit in a line like we were going to dance. They told the women, 'Take your babies off your backs and hold them in front of you.' My mother told us, 'Now they will kill us. We don't talk.' Then the soldiers shot us with B-40 rockets and their guns.[57]

Kia Lor was hit by gunfire and passed out from loss of blood. When she woke up, everyone around her was dead. After several days, Thai fishermen found her on the banks of the Mekong and took her back across the river.

By early 1988, the Thai position toward the Hmong had eased somewhat, influenced by a US commitment to double annual resettlement numbers for Hmong from 4,000 to more than 8,000. At the end of 1987, Thai authorities agreed to admit a group of 1,700 Hmong stranded at the border for nearly one year. Around the same time, nearly 10,000 undocumented Hmong who had been living in Ban Vinai were permitted to register for refugee status, provided they moved to Chiang Kham camp and underwent screening.

From 1985 to 1989, Thai officials interviewed a total of 31,001 people, of whom they screened in 26,934 and screened out 3,101 for an approval rate of 90 per cent. UNHCR officials were able to overturn a few rejections on appeal and did not contest any positive decisions, even where they felt that the family connection overseas was the sole reason for approval by Thai immigration. At face value, the statistics were impressive. By the end of 1989, moreover, the number of Indochinese refugees in Thailand had dropped below 100,000 for the first time in more than a decade. Resettlement had removed 25,000 people from the camps, against 14,700 arrivals.

On the other hand, Hmong accounted for more than half of all refugees in the camps, their numbers holding at a discouraging constant for nearly 15 years. In 1986, Alan Wright, a public health nurse working in Ban Vinai, had noted an 'explosive' birth rate in the camp of 54 per thousand. For the previous five years, births alone had kept pace with the reductions through resettlement, death, or repatriation. Wright estimated that, in the absence of out-migrations, Ban Vinai would double its size in 15 years. Factoring in resettlement placed the principal Hmong camp in a 'steady state' said Wright. He titled his study of Ban Vinai 'A Never Ending Refugee Camp'.[58]

Repatriation or Resettlement?

Theoretically at least, Laotians could have returned home from the very beginning of the exodus. UNHCR had signed an aide-memoire on voluntary repatriation with the provisional government in September 1975 and, the following year, Laos reached agreement with the Thai government to accept the return of refugees.[59] Although the LPDR set up a number of reception centres along the border, most of the Lao who returned in the early years came back spontaneously, either because they never had entered refugee camps on the Thai side or they chose not to return through official channels.

Spontaneous repatriation to Laos was not insignificant, averaging an estimated two thousand people per year. But it was, by its nature, unmonitored and involved almost exclusively ethnic Lao. In early 1980, UNHCR and the LPDR renewed their agreement on voluntary repatriation and, for the first time, Laotians began returning from the camps under UNHCR auspices. In the first eight years of the programme, however, a total of only 3,403 people returned home, of whom nearly three quarters were Lao. The bulk of the highlanders returning in the 1980s, moreover, belonged to the Mien and Htin ethnic groups. The Hmong remained conspicuous by their absence from the repatriation lists. Hmong attitudes toward resettlement, by the same token, showed a deep ambiguity.

In 1990, in an attempt to gauge the preferences of Hmong for repatriation or resettlement, the Ford Foundation funded a survey in Ban Vinai camp. Of the more than 5,000 heads of family interviewed, 54 per cent said they preferred to repatriate to Laos and 46 per cent chose resettlement in another country. Neither choice, however, was without conditions. Four out of five families who preferred repatriation said they were unwilling to return to Laos 'unless significant political changes occur'. Similarly, 70 per cent of those choosing resettlement said they wanted to wait for at least three more years before making a final decision.[60] Their reasons for delay were revealing, as well over half had to do with issues of family unity.

The single most common reason for postponing resettlement was that the elders in the family didn't want to go abroad. 'Elderly Hmong generally wish to return to Laos,' the Ford study concluded, 'while their children, and in some cases, grandchildren, would like to resettle abroad.' The elders refused to let the younger members of the family leave on their own and, in keeping with the Hmong culture's strong family and clan traditions, the younger generation did not challenge them. While this strong desire to maintain family unity, even across several generations, often kept people pinned down in the camps while awaiting consensus from their elders, it contributed to one remarkable statistic about Hmong refugees: in more than twenty years, UNHCR records showed more than 12,000 Indochinese unaccompanied minors resettled in third countries. Not one was a Hmong.

Many others wishing to postpone resettlement said they were waiting for relatives still in Laos, or they were split from family members in Chiang Kham, or their relatives were living illegally in Ban Vinai and thus ineligible to apply for resettlement. Particularly since the border screening programme had been established in 1985, the study concluded, 'the road to family reunification from the hills of Laos is a long and winding one indeed'.[61] For still others, the problem was too many wives (polygamy is illegal in the United States) or no relatives abroad. Unlike the issue of polygamy, the lack of relatives overseas did not make the Hmong ineligible under US processing priorities. But the prospect of resettlement was disturbing enough to most Hmong. The lack of family members to ease the shock only made it more so.

Nearly one out of every ten families interested in resettlement also expressed concern about 'language problems'. It is possible that mentioning language served as a kind of shorthand answer for many of the adjustment problems Hmong were facing in America. By 1990, nearly 100,000 Hmong had made the United States their new home and, along with the remittances and appeals from friends and family to resettle, unnerving stories came back to the camps of unemployment, isolation and death that came – sudden and unexplained – in the middle of the night to seemingly healthy young men. Whole communities were living on welfare or picking up and moving by the busloads in search of farmland or better opportunities.

Large-scale resettlement in the United States was also discouraged by Vang Pao and the other resistance leaders, who worried that it would deplete both the supply and resolve of their fighters. Said one Hmong guerrilla commander, 'I stay [in Ban Vinai] I have power. In the US, I have free decision, independence, but no power.'[62]

Some of those who chose resettlement may have preferred repatriation. The Ford Foundation report suggested that many of those who chose to wait 'will eventually resettle unless drastic political changes occur in Laos in the next year or two. These respondents have essentially given up hope that this will happen, but choose to wait nevertheless.'[63]

Whether they preferred repatriation over resettlement or the other way around, most of the Hmong clearly wanted to 'wait and see'. Although it was not available as an official option, staying in the camps in Thailand had become for many a non-durable non-solution. Visitors to Ban Vinai often remarked that it looked more like a village than a refugee camp, its dusty roads lined with shops selling *pa ndau*, the brightly coloured, intricate Hmong embroidery. With its free food, education and health care, life in the camp compared favourably in many ways with that of poor Thai villagers in surrounding areas. But those who worked in Ban Vinai said the camp shared less with a country village than an urban slum:

> Like other poor urban communities, Ban Vinai has problems of inadequate health, overcrowding, welfare dependency, unemployment, substance abuse, prostitution, and anomie (suicide, abandonment, loneliness). Furthermore, like other rural migrants to the city, Ban Vinai refugees are adjusting to life in a densely populated area, and from the life of a cultivator to the schedule and complexity of an urban environment. As refugees, however, they face the additional stresses of living in at best a temporary haven. As much as they may want to remain in Ban Vinai, they must immigrate again.[64]

As the years passed and the fears of repatriation clashed with the fears of resettlement, many began to worry that Hmong might never get out of the camps. Said a Thai relief worker, 'I think in every refugee camp, something has changed, especially the Hmong because they are a hill tribe. Before they came here, they could move but now they stay here. I cannot say they can solve this.'[65]

Notes

1 'Report on UNHCR Activities in the LPDR in 1977', February 1978. The overall food deficit resulting from the 1977 drought later was estimated at 98,000 metric tons.
2 'Report on UNHCR Activities in the LPDR in 1978', February 1979.
3 See Amnesty International, 'Background paper on the Democratic People's Republic of Laos describing current Amnesty International concerns', April 1985, pp 1–3.
4 Author's communication with Werner Blatter, 18 April 1997.
5 Amnesty International, 'Background Paper', April 1985, pp. 4–6.
6 Author's interview with Vilay Chaleunrath, Washington, DC, 16 April 1996.
7 Author's interview with Doua Thao, Kilometer 52, Laos, 7 December 1995. Doua Thao was resettled in the United States where he works as a machine operator in St. Paul, Minnesota. His eldest daughter was now 17, but he and his wife have had ten more children since. Doua Thao has returned three times to Laos since 1993 to visit relatives in Kilo 52 outside of Vientiane. 'I do not tell people here what I did before,' he said. 'Some don't care but some still do.'
8 Bernard J. Van-es-Beeck, 'Refugees from Laos: 1975–1979', in Martin Stuart-Fox, ed., *Contemporary Laos: Studies in the Politics and Society of the Lao People's Democratic Republic* (St Lucia: University of Queensland Press, 1982), p. 327.
9 Joseph Zasloff, 'The Economy of the New Laos, Part II: Plans and Performance', *AUFS Reports* No. 45 (1981) p. 3.
10 UNHCR, 'Report on UNHCR assistance activities in 1978–1979 and Proposed Voluntary Funds Program and Budget for 1980', p. 165. UNHCR statistics showed a total of 67,405 arrivals in Thailand in 1978, of whom 3,137 were Cambodian, 8,216 were Vietnamese and 56,052 were Laotian. The Laotian figure includes 8,013 highland and 48,781 lowland Lao.
11 John O'Sullivan, *Thailand: Medical Care for Lao Refugees in Ubon Camp,1978–1979* (London: International Disaster Institute, 1981), pp. 2, 8.
12 Cited in a press release by the Thai Ministry of Foreign Affairs, 25 October 1975.
13 'Report on UNHCR Activities in the LPDR in 1979', February 1980.
14 Author's communication with Werner Blatter, 18 April 1997.
15 Nicholas Tapp, 'The Hmong of Thailand: opium people of the Golden Triangle', Anti-Slavery Society and Cultural Survival, Report No 4 (1986), pp. 9–10.
16 In Dia Cha and Jacquelyn Chagnon, *Farmer, War-wife, Refugee, Repatriate: A Needs Assessment of Women Repatriating to Laos* (Washington, DC: Asia Resource Center, 1993), p. 27.
17 See Lawyers Committee for Human Rights, *Forced Back and Forgotten: The Human Rights of Laotian Asylum Seekers in Thailand* (New York: 1989), p. 8. The report, which uses the estimate of 100,000 Hmong deaths, cites 'informed Laotian observers' as its source. As with estimates of Vietnamese deaths at sea, no rigorous assessment has been made of Hmong mortality rates. In February 1980, however, the ARC sponsored (but never published) a survey of 405 households (representing 2,654 individuals) in Ban Vinai. Among the questions asked was, 'How many people have died in your family since 1975?' The responses totalled 384 people, of whom 156 were five or younger. Averaged over a five-year period, this would give a crude death rate of 28.9 per thousand. Another question related to cause of death, of which 75 out of 260 reported deaths were attributed to 'war-related problems', the three most prevalent being 'gunshot', 'bombs', and 'smoke,

gas, or "rain"' (i.e., chemical toxins). Again, averaged over five years and assuming a constant total population, this would mean that out of 28.9 deaths per thousand, 8.3 deaths – roughly 29 per cent – were directly war-related. It is interesting that the survey's resultant crude death rate of 20.6 per thousand due to non-war-related events (disease, hunger, old age, accident and problems related to birth) correlates almost exactly with the UN figure of the crude death rate for Laos of 20.7 per thousand from 1975 to 1980. If one applied a crude death rate of 28.9 per thousand to a static population of 350,000 Hmong, one might project 50,575 deaths from 1975 to 1980, of which 14,525 could be directly attributed to war-related events. Missing, of course, from the ARC survey would be families that were wiped out entirely, which would increase the actual crude death rate by an unknown factor. The UN crude death rate for Laos, 1975–80, comes from United Nations, *World Population Prospects, The 1994 Revision* (New York: United Nations, 1995), p. 702. The author would like to thank Jerrold Huguet for assistance in analysing this data.

18 Robert Cooper, 'The Hmong of Laos: economic factors in refugee exodus and return', in Glenn L. Hendricks, Bruce T. Downing, and Amos S. Deinard, eds, *The Hmong in Transition* (New York: Center for Migration Studies, 1986), p. 23,

19 John and Jean Sibley, 'Report from Ban Vinai, No. 3', 5 December 1979. In May 1979, in the midst of this influx, Thai authorities decided to transfer into Ban Vinai about 11,000 Hmong who had been living in Nong Khai while moving about 3,000 Lao in the opposite direction.

20 *Ibid.*

21 From interview notes prepared by a Lao-speaking anthropologist, CCSDPT Files.

22 *Bangkok Post*, 3 September 1975.

23 Pasuk Phongpaichit and Sungsidh Piriyarangsan, *Corruption and Democracy in Thailand* (Bangkok: Chulalongkorn University, 1994), p. 26.

24 *Ibid.*, p. 100.

25 Thai Ministry of Interior, *An Instrument of Foreign Policy*, pp. 17–21.

26 *Ibid.*, p. 7.

27 Frances Starner, 'The Riddle of Nong Khai', *Asiaweek*, 26 December 1980–2 January 1981.

28 Memorandum from Pat Ferguson to Bill Sage, 26 January 1980, CCSDPT Files.

29 *Ibid.*

30 'Screening of lowland Lao', UNHCR internal memorandum, Bangkok, 23 February 1981.

31 Ivor Jackson, 'On the Proposal for the establishment of a procedure for the Determination of Refugee Status in Thailand', 7 August 1980.

32 Author's interview with Ivor Jackson, Geneva, 16 February 1996.

33 James A. Hafner, 'Lowland Lao and Hmong Refugees in Thailand: The Plight of Those Left Behind', *Disasters,* Vol. 9, No. 2 (1985), p. 83.

34 Marilyn Lacey, 'A case study in international refugee policy: lowland Lao refugees', *People in Upheaval* (New York: Center for Migration Studies, 1987), p.24.

35 *1981 Annual Conference on Displaced Persons in Thailand*, 23–24 July 1981, Bangkok, p. 72.

36 Dennis McNamara suggests that, following Geneva's rejection of the screening idea for lowland Lao, 'as an alternative, UNHCR officials in Bangkok suggested to the Thai authorities that the highly visible camp at Nong Khai should be closed to new arrivals, who as a deterrent should be held in a center away from the border where they would not be eligible for resettlement processing, at least

initially'. 'The politics of humanitarianism', Section III, p. 103.

37 *The Indochinese Refugee Situation: Report to the Secretary of State by the Special Refugee Advisory Committee, August 1981*, more commonly known as the 'Green Report', is included as an Appendix in US Congress, Senate, Committee on the Judiciary, Subcommittee on Immigration and Refugee Policy, *Refugee Problems in Southeast Asia, 1981: Staff Report*, 97th Congress, 2nd Session (Washington, DC: US Government Printing Office, 1982), pp. 43–79.

38 Loescher and Scanlan, *Calculated Kindness*, p. 170.

39 *Ibid.*, pp. 176–7.

40 Author's interview with Roger Winter, Washington, DC, 17 April 1996.

41 Both Roger Winter and Michael Myers, an aide to Senator Ted Kennedy, mentioned another result of the Mariel boatlift. As Myers put it, 'Some of the criminal component of the Cuba influx got out of prison and paraded down the streets of Fort Smith, Arkansas. It cost Governor Bill Clinton the election.' Author's interview with Michael Myers, Washington, DC, 18 April 1996.

42 Loescher and Scanlan, *Calculated Kindness*, p. 187.

43 Green Report, pp. 53, 55.

44 From 1975 to 1981, the United States took 50,962 out of the 58,581 highland Lao resettled worldwide, or nearly 87 per cent. For lowland Lao, during the same period, the US resettled 76,437 out of 121,555 or 63 per cent. From 1982 until 1995, the US resettled 73 per cent of all Lao and 96 per cent of all Hmong. Overall, from 1975 to 1995, the US resettled 77 per cent of all Laotians compared to 63 per cent of all Cambodians and 56 per cent of all Vietnamese.

45 Donald A. Renard, 'The Last Bus', *The Atlantic*, October 1987, p. 28.

46 'Push-backs and other measures against Lao asylum-seekers', UNHCR internal memorandum, Bangkok, 8 October 1984.

47 *Ibid.* The first quote is from the 1975 Cabinet decision and the second is from the 1977 decision which also authorized procedures for screening new arrivals.

48 *Ibid.*

49 'Hmong pushed back to Paksane', UNHCR internal memorandum, 1 March 1985.

50 Roger Winter, Field notes, 25 June 1985. See also Joseph Cerquone, *Refugees from Laos: In Harm's Way* (Washington, DC: US Committee for Refugees, 1986).

51 'Refugee seminar summary B.E. 2527 (1984)', Translation by UNHCR.

52 *Ibid.*

53 Jeff Crisp, 'Two-way traffic across the Mekong', *Refugees*, September 1987, p. 30.

54 *Washington Post*, 22 March 1987.

55 *Washington Times*, 30 March 1987.

56 *The Nation*, 8 July 1987.

57 Lawyers Committee, *Forced Back and Forgotten*, p. 17. Resettled in St. Paul, Minnesota, Kia Lor recounted her ordeal to the Lawyers Committee through her uncle.

58 Alan G. Wright, 'A Never Ending Refugee Camp? The Explosive Birth Rate in Ban Vinai', Bangkok: July 1986.

59 See Pranee Saipiroon, *ASEAN Government's Attitudes Toward Regional Security: 1975–1979* (Bangkok: Institute of Asian Studies, Chulalongkorn University, 1982), p. 64.

60 Thomas P. Conroy, *Highland Lao Refugees: Repatriation and Resettlement Preferences in Ban Vinai Camp, Thailand* (Bangkok: Ford Foundation, 1990). The survey covered 5,344 heads of family representing 28,992 refugees out of a population of 31,000.

61 *Ibid.*, p. 15.
62 David Moffat and Wendy Walker, 'I stay, I have power', *Boston Globe*, 17 March 1985.
63 Conroy, *Highland Lao Refugees*, p. 18.
64 Catholic Office for Emergency Relief and Refugees, *Report of Survey of Refugee Needs and Problems in Ban Vinai Refugee Camp, Thailand, 1985–1986* (Bangkok: COERR, Parasocial Services, 1986), p. 3.
65 Lynellyn D. Long, *Ban Vinai: The Refugee Camp* (New York: Columbia University Press, 1993), p. 107.

CHAPTER 6

Resettlement in the West

In April 1975, when the United States evacuated 130,000 Vietnamese refugees to Guam and thence to transit camps on the mainland, it did everything in its power to see that the resettlement burden was shared with other countries. The federal government's Interagency Task Force offered facilities in the camps to officials from the Canadian government and from UNHCR and assigned State Department personnel full time to the task of drumming up resettlement offers around the world. According to a contemporary account by Gail Paradise Kelly,

> Camp newspapers also encouraged the Vietnamese to think about resettling elsewhere. *Dat Lanh*, the bilingual daily at Fort Indiantown Gap, at one point ran a headline on its front page, 'And Why Not Malawi?' This article was accompanied by a map of Africa and a long description of how well suited Malawi, given its climate, was for Vietnamese.[1]

History does not record if any Vietnamese bought the idea of settlement in Malawi, although government figures do show ten people leaving the United States for the Ivory Coast by October 1975, along with 11 to Martinique, five to New Caledonia, and one to Bangladesh, warm climates all. But while the United States failed to attract little more than token offers of resettlement in 1975, over the next two decades more than two million Cambodians, Laotians and Vietnamese would find permanent new homes in some 50 countries around the world. They ended up in such far-flung places as Argentina, Iceland, French Guiana, Luxembourg, Senegal, and even Iran.

The majority of Indochinese refugees – more than 1.2 million in all, if one includes those who came via the Orderly Departure Programme – settled in the United States. An additional 500,000 went to Canada, Australia or France and a quarter of a million Vietnamese were locally settled in southern China. Thus 78 per cent of all Indochinese were accepted by just four Western countries with another 12 per cent going to China. But it was the remaining 10 per cent, while less significant in terms of sheer numbers, that gave the Indochinese resettlement programme its global reach.

It became one of UNHCR's main tasks in the first asylum camps to register new arrivals and try to match their needs and expectations with the particular interests of the resettlement countries. Cecilia Abrahams, a Malaysian national, worked for UNHCR in Malaysia from 1978, the opening of Pulau Bidong, until the closing of the programme. 'At first,' she said,

> the resettlement countries had no criteria. It was first come, first served. Later, everyone started to develop priorities, criteria, special populations. Norway took the heart patients. New Zealand took single women (under their 'women-at-risk' program), Holland took the blind, Switzerland took severely handicapped, France took the criminals and psychiatric cases, and the United States took all the farmers and fishermen.[2]

This is an impressionistic view, to be sure, but it captures the perspective of a field worker trying, day in and day out, to match refugees with a resettlement country.

At the height of the programme, the hardest work was simply keeping the processing pipeline primed with people. From July 1979 to July 1982, the United States and some 20 other countries combined to resettle more than 623,800 Indochinese refugees out of camps in Southeast Asia. This meant that roughly 600 people every single day were somewhere going through the stages of processing: case documentation, interviews, medical examinations, re-interviews, travel preparations and departure. Each country had its own procedures, and these changed with time, as Abraham suggests, so no single description captures the many parts that made up what some came to call the 'resettlement machine'. A look at the US procedures, *circa* 1980 when the machinery was operating at peak capacity, will necessarily stand for the whole, but it will reflect the realities faced by roughly half of the Indochinese refugees who sought resettlement in a third country.

1 *Joint Voluntary Agency (JVA) staff members, working under contract to the Department of State, screen the refugees through interviews in the camps.* The function of these interviews was to gather basic biographical information – including language capabilities, education and work experience – as well as information about relatives in the United States and other third countries. UNHCR staff members frequently performed these case documentation tasks for foreign embassies.

2 *JVA and US refugee officials verify the information presented by the refugee applicants.* This involved JVA cables to various organizations in the United States to verify relationships claimed with US residents, former employment with the US government, and to obtain security clearances for applicants over the age of 16. At this stage, US refugee officials known as Ethnic Affairs Officers (EAOs) also reviewed the accuracy of information presented by refugees claiming to have held positions in the pre-1975 Indochinese governments or armed forces, or to have had other close associations with US policies or programmes. In many cases, JVA staff members or

EAOs conducted additional interviews to ensure that the information contained in the refugee files was accurate and complete.

3 *Refugee cases are presented to INS officers for determination whether the refugees are admissible to the United States.* The INS officers conducted their own interviews with each principal applicant and then either approved or rejected their case. In addition to having to prove their eligibility as refugees under US law, applicants could be found inadmissible if INS determined they were communists, criminals, polygamists, mentally retarded or insane, suffering from a dangerous or contagious disease, or were guilty of fraud or misrepresentation in their application.

4 *Approved refugees are interviewed again by JVA staff members to obtain information required by US voluntary agencies to locate and confirm sponsors for the refugees.*

5 *Refugees receive medical examinations after sponsorship is assured.* These examinations were carried out by the Intergovernmental Committee for European Migration (ICEM), later renamed the International Organization for Migration. ICEM was under contract with the United States (and other resettlement countries) to identify refugees with excludable medical conditions, including mental disorders and certain dangerous contagious diseases such as venereal disease, active tuberculosis, and infectious leprosy. Although only about 4 to 5 per cent of applicants had medical problems, their whole families were either obliged or chose to remain in camp if any one member was on medical hold. Thus, as one US General Accounting Office report noted, to resettle 1,000 refugees, 1,400 had to be medically processed.

6 *Transportation is arranged and refugees depart for third countries.* Normally, onward transportation was arranged through ICEM, a task the organization had been performing since its establishment in 1952.[3]

As time passed, countries grew more and more selective as admissions numbers declined and suspicions rose about the motives of people leaving. The task fell to UNHCR, even while it shared some of those same suspicions, to be sure that foreign governments maintained their resettlement commitments, both in order to preserve asylum itself and to ensure that the especially vulnerable were not left behind in the camps. In the end, however, it was beyond UNHCR's scope to grant or deny permanent admission to another country. That authority lay with governments. Nor was it in UNHCR's power to ensure that resettlement was successful. That responsibility lay partly with governments; partly with the many voluntary agencies, sponsors, and service providers who got involved in resettlement; and most importantly with the refugees themselves. How then did the nearly two million Vietnamese, Laotians, and Cambodians manage once they arrived in the West? What sort of welcome greeted them and how have they fared in making a new life?

The United States

In May 1975, Robert De Vecchi was working in New York City but feeling, as he put it later, 'at loose ends'. He had been following news coverage of the evacuation from Vietnam and, one day, went to meet Carel Sternberg, then director of the International Rescue Committee (IRC), which was founded by Albert Einstein in 1933 to rescue victims of Nazi Germany, but had since involved itself with Hungarian exiles, Chinese refugees in Hong Kong, and, more recently, war refugees in Vietnam. Sternberg had only recently committed IRC to help resettle some of the estimated 130,000 Vietnamese who were then descending by the planeload into military camps around the United States.

'Carel Sternberg asked me if I wanted to go to Fort Smith, Arkansas,' De Vecchi recalled.

> I said, 'Yes, but I don't know where it is.' I went home, packed my bag and drove there that night. I had been watching the whole evacuation on television as a spectator. When I got to Fort Chaffee, I saw transport planes circling overhead, rows of white barracks, and thousands of people with black hair milling around. I thought, 'I've stepped through the looking glass. I've walked through the television set.'[4]

Ever since the Second World War, the US government had been turning to private voluntary agencies, or volags, to help refugees integrate into American society. Although volags historically had operated mainly with their own resources, an influx of more than 600,000 Cuban refugees in the 1960s and early 1970s persuaded the government to offer grants and contracts to the voluntary agencies in return for their services. In 1975, the government once again turned to the volags. As part of the new agreement, the State Department contracted with an initial nine voluntary agencies, paying them $500 for each refugee resettled.[5] Four of the nine volags were sectarian, including the US Catholic Conference (USCC), Church World Service (CWS), Lutheran Immigration and Refugee Service (LIRS), and the Hebrew Immigrant Aid Society (HIAS). The other five non-sectarian agencies included the Tolstoy Foundation, American Council for National-ities Service (ACNS), American Fund for Czechosolvak Refugees, Travellers Aid–International Social Services, and the IRC.[6]

In the chaotic days and weeks that followed in the transit camps, De Vecchi and other voluntary agency workers throughout the country tried to sort out exactly what their resettlement responsibilities would be and how to discharge them. The State Department grant was as basic as it was broad, tasking the voluntary agencies with the provision of 'reception and placement' services. This meant, obviously enough, meeting the refugees upon their arrival in the country and placing them with a sponsor. But beyond that, the specific roles and responsibilities of the sponsors and the agencies were not spelled out. The agreement only said that the grantee 'shall use its best efforts to assure successful resettlement of each assigned refugee into American life, leading towards economic self-sufficiency.'[7]

'It was quite confused at the beginning,' said De Vecchi. 'Nobody quite knew who was doing what. Most of what we were doing was matchmaking,' trying to match a refugee's needs and preferences with a sponsor somewhere in the country.

> There was a listing of the agencies in the camp. The refugees chose where they wanted to go. We felt we were competing with one another to get people out of there. We got $500 per refugee from the federal government and quickly the word spread in the camp that the refugees would be given all that money. In many ways, we have been fighting that battle ever since.

IRC had no field offices at that time, so refugees were given an initial $250 per person as a transitional allowance and sent on their way. 'If they had any needs, they were to contact us in New York,' De Vecchi said. 'I came back to New York and found a desk groaning with correspondence. They had housing problems. They had no winter clothing. They wanted to buy a car. We were sending out checks through the mail.'

A 1982 study of the resettlement agencies found that IRC was the largest user of the 'as needed' approach, though later it tended to provide goods and rental payments rather than cash outlays. The largest resettlement agency, USCC, offered a 'flat-rate' payment of $300 up front with other needs being met in kind rather than in cash. Still other agencies, such as the LIRS, avoided direct payments to refugees, relying instead on congregational sponsors to decide what forms of assistance would be most appropriate.[8]

Beyond the issue of cash payments, agency approaches to resettlement varied still further in terms of the sponsorship models they employed. Most of the sectarian agencies, not surprisingly, relied heavily on congregational sponsorships, in which individual churches and their members provided most of the direct assistance to the new refugee arrivals. Exceptions to this were USCC, which mainly used diocesan social service programmes, and the HIAS, which relied on professionally trained social workers and staff to do the bulk of the resettlement work. The non-sectarian agencies relied either on the agency sponsorship model or on individual sponsorships, where the refugee's sponsor could be anyone from a relative, to a friend, to a former business associate.

In their effort to get people out of the transit camps as quickly as possible, the agencies could not take the time to vet each and every sponsorship offer. Some, according to one volag official, were 'little more than requests for indentured servants, bed mates, or cheap labor'.[9] The huge majority, however, were sincere gestures from sympathetic Americans who wanted, somehow, to help, though they did not quite know what it would involve.

Early assessments of the resettlement programme found that the congregational model offered perhaps the most supportive relationship between sponsor and refugee, while the agency model offered the most structure.[10] Individual sponsorships, if they were not based on blood ties, could prove quite fragile. State Department official Thomas J. Barnes concluded in a 1977 study that 'Individual sponsorships tend to break down more easily than congregational ones, and occasionally there are shattering cross-cultural misunderstandings.' He went on to note, however, that

> There are nevertheless many encouraging cases. Mrs Ruth Champion, a Mexican-American woman of slender means near Tucson has successfully sponsored 20 refugees. Gordon Fasnacht, a blue collar employee of the Duval Mine lives with his wife, a refugee from Germany herself, in a trailer outside Sahuarita, Arizona. Sahuarita is a sort of fork in the desert between Green Valley and Tucson. The Fasnachts originally sponsored a family of eight Hmong who have since moved on to California, perhaps under the illusion there might be water there.[11]

It was not long before sponsors around the country began noticing the same phenomenon: refugees picking up and moving, looking not so much for water, but for warmth, for friends or family, for work or, sometimes, for welfare. In 1975, the federal government's newly formed Interagency Task Force (IATF) – aware that the Cuban refugees had tended to settle near their point of disembarkation – had decided to process the Indochinese through four widely scattered camps. The sites chosen were Camp Pendleton in California, Eglin Air Force Base in Florida, Indiantown Gap in Pennsylvania, and Fort Chaffee in Arkansas. Ironically though not unintentionally, the largest number of refugees in the 1975 wave were processed through Arkansas, a state with historically little appeal to immigrants. It was the clear aim of the Task Force, and it encouraged the voluntary agencies to do likewise, to scatter the Indochinese throughout the United States.[12]

That effort, according to a study of the first wave of Indochinese refugees by Reginald Baker and David North, succeeded in part. Five years later, the study found that 'Not only were the 1975 refugees scattered widely throughout the 50 states, they were sprinkled in fairly small groupings within those states.'[13] About 47 per cent of the refugees had been sent to the state of their choice, though of the half that had chosen California, only one-fifth had been sent there.

But a good bit of the IATF's attempt at social engineering was undone, or certainly rearranged, by the refugees' refusal to stay put. Baker and North noted that, between 1975 and 1980, about nine per cent of the US population moved across state lines. By contrast, by 1980, fully 45 per cent of Indochinese refugees lived in a different state from the one in which they had been settled in 1975. 'The overall direction of this secondary movement,' the two concluded, 'has been to the South and West'.[14] The most popular destination, it turned out, was California.

By January 1976, federal records showed that just over 30,000 Indochinese had been resettled in California, concentrating in and around Los Angeles and San Francisco. State officials, however, were citing a figure of 50,000 (20 years on, both those numbers had grown more than tenfold, in escalating disagreement). In his report, the State Department's Barnes commented that 'There has unquestionably been considerable refugee migration to California ... but just how much is debatable.'[15] Even more contentious than the numbers moving was the motive behind their move. Said Barnes, 'A phrase that has crept into the speech of many Vietnamese throughout the United States is: '*Di Cali an wel*' which comes out as 'Go to California and live off welfare'. He added in a prescient comment for 1977, 'The welfare rate could produce national disillusionment about the refugees.'[16]

By the end of 1975, the US camps were all closed and, said a former key member of the Interagency Task Force, Lionel Rosenblatt, 'by and large we thought the evacuation would be it. There wasn't ever a vision that this would be an ongoing refugee program.'[17] But Rosenblatt had begun to hear reports of Cambodian refugees living in squalid encampments on the Thai border and went to investigate. Following his trip to Thailand, Rosenblatt urged that the remaining 11,000 admissions numbers left over from the Vietnamese evacuation be used to resettle other Indochinese who had escaped into Thailand. From 1976 to 1978 – spurred by the persistence of Rosenblatt and a small group of State Department colleagues, the advocacy of such groups as the Citizens' Commission on Indochinese Refugees, and the dramatic, eyewitness reporting of *New York Times* correspondent Henry Kamm – the US government issued a series of temporary 'parole' authorizations to resettle Indochinese refugees from first-asylum countries.[18]

In July 1979, at the peak of the 'boat people' crisis in Southeast Asia, President Jimmy Carter authorized the admission of 168,000 Indochinese over the next year. Since the first major influx of 135,000 Vietnamese in 1975, US resettlement numbers had averaged less than 15,000 Indochinese annually. The new US commitment, though welcomed by the private agencies, meant that they were now to settle, each and every month, as many refugees as they had taken in the whole of the previous year. Beyond that, this second wave of refugees bore scant resemblance to the relatively homogenous, well-educated Vietnamese of the first wave. These were peasant Khmer fresh from the 'killing fields' of Cambodia; they were pre-literate Hmong from the highlands of Laos; they were ethnic Chinese and Vietnamese traumatized by perilous boat journeys, push-backs, and pirate attacks.

In 1980, the United States admitted 164,000 Indochinese for permanent resettlement and 207,000 refugees overall, still the highest single-year total in the history of US resettlement. The country had prepared itself somewhat for this massive influx by passing a comprehensive new law, the Refugee Act of 1980, which among other things codified a refugee definition consistent with international law, formalized refugee admissions procedures, and established an Office of Refugee Resettlement (ORR) in the Department of Health and Human Services as well as an Office of the Coordinator for Refugee Affairs, which came to be housed in the State Department. The Bureau for Refugee Programs in the State Department was responsible for setting admissions priorities and administering the reception and placement grants to the voluntary agencies.[19] ORR had primary responsibility for the domestic refugee assistance programme and funded a range of programmes

– mainly cash assistance, medical assistance, and social services – most of which were administered by state service agencies.

The new act also reiterated a point emphasized by the IATF at the very outset of the Indochinese programme: the goal was 'effective resettlement', or the achievement of economic self-sufficiency as rapidly as possible. In 1980, that meant within three years. The legislation provided for 100 per cent federal reimbursement of state costs for the first 36 months. Within just a year, however, that period had been reduced to 18 months (and was to drop still further) and some states and localities began to complain bitterly at the federal government's breach of promise. The Indochinese cause was not helped by skyrocketing inflation nor the Cuban–Haitian refugee crisis of 1980, which saw more than 150,000 asylum seekers wash ashore on Florida's beaches in the space of a few months.

But resettlement continued, albeit at lower levels. By 1985, five years after passage of the omnibus refugee act and ten years after the first wave of evacuees entered the United States, annual Indochinese admissions stood at 50,000 and the total number at over three quarters of a million. At what would prove to be the resettlement programme's halfway point, one might have said the glass was either half empty or half full. Refugees were doing well and they were not doing well. They were finding jobs and they were going on welfare. They were moving and they were staying put. They were a financial burden and they were a tax-paying asset. It all depended on one's perspective.

In 1985, the Refugee Policy Group (RPG) reported that 'Generally, the prospects for refugee economic self-sufficiency are promising in the long-term, but the immediate situation shows low labor force participation, high unemployment, large numbers living below the poverty line, and substantial reliance on public assistance programs.'[20] A study by the Department of Labor showed that, of the refugees who had arrived in 1975, labour force participation rates were 67 per cent, better than the overall US rate of 65 per cent, and unemployment was only 6 per cent. For new arrivals with less than three years in the country, between 30 and 40 per cent were in the labour force and similar percentages were unemployed.

At the end of 1975, according to federal government figures, just under 20 per cent of Indochinese refugees were using cash assistance. One year later, the number had risen to 30 per cent. By the end of 1980, the US government was spending more than one billion dollars per year on the domestic refugee resettlement programme, annual admissions were about 160,000 (including more than 130,000 Indochinese), and welfare rates for recent arrivals had climbed above 50 per cent. By 1985, both the admissions and the federal funding levels had fallen, but public assistance utilization rates were still above 50 per cent.[21]

From California's perspective, the numbers looked particularly discouraging. In that state, more than 85 per cent of refugees in the country for three years or less were using some form of public assistance. The state's refugee population, moreover, had grown to comprise about 40 per cent of all Indochinese in the country. By 1985, it appeared that one out of every three refugees had moved from his or her original place of resettlement. Of those who had chosen to become secondary migrants, nearly 63 per cent had moved to California.

In addition to the lure of family, community and climate, the Indochinese migration to California was spurred by two particular developments in the early 1980s. The first was a change in cash and medical assistance policies, which prompted thousands of families to move south from the neighbouring states of Washington and Oregon. The second and more dramatic factor was a decision by the Hmong leadership to establish a new community in California's Central Valley.[22]

Within a two-year period, from 1981 to 1983, more than 20,000 Hmong picked up and moved from their original settlement sites to the Central Valley towns of Fresno, Stockton, and Merced, creating what one observer called 'the largest peacetime concentration of Hmong in history.'[23] The move was prompted in part by a Hmong perception of limited prospects in their original communities, by the reductions in federal funding for cash and medical assistance, and by a desire for English classes and vocational training. But the motivating force for perhaps half of the Hmong secondary migrants was a 'dream of farming.'[24] The Central Valley was rumoured to have land enough for the Hmong to reclaim their agricultural traditions. But most found upon arrival that the investment costs and market risks were much too high to make a go of farming in the United States. One Hmong leader noted his people's long tradition of 'moving for betterment'. But in this case, the move left most of the community trapped in public housing and on welfare. The Central Valley, noted John Finck around that time, 'seems to be one of the least desirable sites in the country at present for employment and eventual self-sufficiency of large numbers of undereducated refugees'.[25]

The dismal prospects for the Hmong in Fresno prompted the Office of Refugee Resettlement to launch an initiative designed both to discourage further secondary migration to California and to support Hmong movements out of the state. Whether as a result of the ORR efforts or independent decisions in the Hmong community, or both, the percentage of the Hmong population in California changed only slightly from 51 per cent in 1983 to 52 per cent in 1990. New arrivals were coming into the state both from the camps overseas and from elsewhere in the United States, but a significant number also were moving out.[26]

Meanwhile, throughout the country, the Hmong were reconsolidating, moving out of areas where their numbers were small into larger communities where they hoped the whole might prove greater than the sum of its parts. By 1995, nearly 75 per cent of all Southeast Asian refugees in the United States were living in just ten states. California, of course, was first on the list with its estimated half a million Indochinese, followed by Texas and Washington state. But fourth in line, outranking the traditionally large immigration states of New York and Illinois, stood Minnesota. The largest Hmong numbers in America still are in California's Central Valley, but, having left the heartland once for the coast, the Hmong have been returning to Minnesota and Wisconsin. Fully 90 per cent of all Hmong now live in those three states.

Sceptics will say it is no coincidence that the three states are among the most generous in their welfare benefits, but advocates within and outside the community say the Hmong are seeking not public assistance but long-term economic betterment and an opportunity to 'preserve as much as feasible of their core customs and clan obligations'.[27] They are the first to admit they have a long way to go.

A recent study published by Hmong American Partnership, a local self-help group or mutual assistance association (MAA) in Minnesota, noted some of the myriad problems facing the Hmong community:

• 65 per cent of the community lives at or below the poverty line.

• 66 per cent of all Hmong households receive public assistance.

• 87 per cent of adults live in public housing or rental units.

• 48.8 per cent of Hmong adults speak little or no English.

• Single females head up 23.6 per cent of all Hmong households.

• Hmong households have an average of 5.3 children.

'In the 18 years since the Hmong first arrived in the United States,' the study concluded,

> families have deteriorated considerably. The role of the elders has been undermined by a language handicap while the younger generation have developed their own individual interests outside of the family. While the majority of the households remain typical nuclear families, many face new problems that once were nearly non-existent: discipline, drug use and divorce, for example. Though most families still hang on to the last vestiges of family unity, some have turned their backs on each other and some have completely ceased to function.[28]

But there are glimmers of hope, as well, and some of the brightest are to be found in the younger generation. Lee Pao Xiong, a dynamic young man of 30, helped found Hmong American Partnership and currently serves as director of the Minnesota Council on Asian–Pacific Islanders. When his family first came to America in 1975, Lee Pao Xiong recalled,

> We were resettled by a Mennonite church in Morganton, Indiana. We were placed on a farm on the top of a hill in the middle of nowhere. We stayed there for a while. I went to school and got in fights. Then we moved to another place equally deserted. My father started working as a janitor in an elementary school, making $1.75 per hour. Our sponsors gave us a beat-up Chevrolet car. We were mobile. At the time, the policy was to separate us all but that didn't work for the Hmong. We found each other and settled down together. In 1979, we came to Minnesota. My mother's parents lived here. They were the first Hmong to settle here, I believe.

When we came here, my father enrolled in a vocational school as a welder and my mother as a cook. But eventually he worked as an interpreter for the Department of Health and my mother in the public schools. There were lots of racial fights when we moved into McDonough public housing project. One Native American kid was always beating me up. We were the first Asian children to attend Cleveland Junior High School. (Right now, over 50 per cent are Hmong.) There was a black kid that was always beating me up. I used to get beat up in Laos, too, so I was getting used to it.[29]

Eventually, Lee Pao Xiong stopped fighting and began organizing efforts at cross-cultural bridge-building, both in high school and in college. Hmong American Partnership was formed in the same spirit, he says, because 'as Hmong, we must understand who we are as Americans just as we need to help Americans understand who we are as Hmong'. He is optimistic about the future of Hmong in America, pointing to the 64 Hmong who have received doctoral degrees in the United States since 1975, the 150 who have masters degrees and an estimated 2,000 college graduates.

I feel very positive for the community. We are a smart people, we are people who can adapt and still retain our cultural identity. The clan structure is still very strong. We help each other. There is a strong sense of community obligation. If I go to Wausau, Wisconsin and stay in a hotel, the Hmong there get very upset and say, 'Our homes are not good enough? Why would you stay in a hotel? Come stay with us.'

Overall, the trends for Vietnamese, Cambodians and Laotians in America seem hopeful. As with most other Asian immigrants, extended residence correlates positively to educational achievement, higher income levels, and stronger communities.[30] But there is also evidence of a bi-modal distribution within the Indochinese refugee populations. The ORR reports that labour force participation rates are twice as high for Vietnamese as for the other Southeast Asian refugee populations. Unemployment among Vietnamese in 1994 was only 4 per cent, against 42 per cent among other Indochinese groups. In terms of welfare, 58.1 per cent of Vietnamese were receiving some form of cash assistance, against 84.8 per cent for other Indochinese. For non-cash assistance like Medicaid, Food Stamps and public housing, Vietnamese utilization rates were substantially lower than other Indochinese refugee groups.[31]

The ORR data cover refugees for only their first three years in the United States. A more comprehensive picture comes from the 1990 census data. Vietnamese, who arrived in America sooner than the other groups and with higher levels of education, had 25 per cent of families receiving some sort of public assistance and 24 per cent below the poverty line. Interestingly, among Laotians (non-Hmong), only 20 per cent of families were on public assistance, lowest among all four Indochinese populations, but 32 per cent were below the poverty line. Cambodians, on the other hand, showed just the opposite trend, with 51 per cent on welfare but 42 per cent below the poverty line. Not unexpectedly, 67 per cent of Hmong families were receiving public assistance and 62 per cent were below the poverty line.[32]

For many Indochinese, the resettlement experience shows a pattern of gradual adjustment and increasing self-sufficiency but it is an experience marked by pockets of chronic poverty, isolation, juvenile delinquency and family dissolution. Walter Barnes, California's state refugee coordinator, concludes that 'There are some tremendous successes and some tremendous failures. In the middle is a bunch of people trying to do their best.'[33]

Canada

When the refugee ship, the Hai Hong, and its 2,450 passengers sat sweltering off the Malaysian coastline in November 1978, the Canadian government's offer of help was both dramatic and decisive in breaking the diplomatic deadlock. On 18 November, nine days after the overloaded freighter had first dropped anchor in Port Klang harbour with its cargo of Vietnamese and the Malaysian authorities had threatened to turn everyone back to sea, Canada's immigration minister, Bud Cullen, announced that his government would accept 600 of the boat people for resettlement. At the time, Canada was processing no more than 50 or 60 Indochinese cases per month, so the announcement came as a particular surprise to Ian Hamilton, one of only two immigration officers charged with interviewing refugees in seven Southeast Asian countries. 'All of a sudden, there were these planes coming down from Canada before the first refugees had even been selected,' Hamilton recalled later. 'It was unprecedented.'[34]

After three days of interviewing people from before dawn until after midnight, he and his colleagues filled four Canadian military transport planes with 604 Vietnamese, including the oldest person on board, an 82-year-old man, and two babies born on the ship. The Hai Hong affair not only established an important regional *quid pro quo* of permanent resettlement in exchange for temporary asylum – an open door for an open shore – but it was, as one observer commented, 'a milestone in the evolution of Canada's immigration policy'.[35] Before the year was out, the government announced a commitment to resettle 5,000 Southeast Asian refugees in 1979.

From 1947 to 1952, Canada admitted more than 186,000 Eastern European refugees, followed by 37,000 Hungarian refugees fleeing the Soviet invasion of their country in 1956. In the 1960s, Canada continued to respond to European victims of the Cold War by resettling 12,000 Czechoslovakian refugees while also taking steps to broaden its geographical and ideological reach. In 1967, Canada passed its first immigration act with 'an overt intention not to discriminate among immigrants (including refugees) on the basis of race, religion or national origin' and, in 1969, the government signed the 1951 Convention and 1967 Protocol on refugees.[36]

The 1970s bore witness to Canada's more egalitarian approach to refugee resettlement as several hundred Tibetans entered the country in 1970, followed by 7,000 Ugandan Asians in 1972–73, victims of expulsion at the hands of dictator Idi Amin. During 1973–79, Canada admitted more than 7,000 refugees from Latin America, principally Chileans fleeing the right-wing coup of General Augusto Pinochet. When the Canadian government agreed to accept 5,000 Vietnamese and Cambodian refugees in May 1975 (including about 1,800 from the evacuation camps in the United States), it was not motivated by token anti-communism so much as 'an obligation to demonstrate token solidarity with the United States'.[37]

In December 1978, Canada promulgated flexible new regulations that would have a profound impact on the Indochinese resettlement programme just gearing up for expansion. In addition to the admission of Convention refugees, the Immigration Act created a special 'designated class' of immigrants, which 'includes persons oppressed in their own country or displaced by emergency situations such as war or revolution'.[38] This meant that immigration officers no longer were required to make individual determinations of refugee status. Second, the act authorized the resettlement of refugees through either government or private sponsorships. Private sponsors were responsible for providing material assistance to the refugees for their first year in Canada, although the federal government provided transportation loans, temporary medical assistance, employment services, language lessons and occupational training. As Mike Molloy, the first coordinator for the government's Refugee Task Force put it, 'When the music began, we had our dancing clothes on.'[39]

By the middle of June 1979, Canada's annual quota for Indochinese resettlement had crept upwards from 5,000 to 8,000. Dramatic pictures of the boat people flashed across Western television screens, and began to galvanize a broader public response. Marion Dewar, then mayor of Ottawa, recalls watching the news while on vacation:

> I came back on Monday and said to some people in my office, 'We should do something.... Our government quota is 8,000. We can do half that. A city of 300,000 can take 4,000.' They said, 'A lot of people won't like it.' I said, 'We'll call a meeting at the Civic Center and ask people about it.' Well, nobody protested as far as I could see. They were too busy lining up for sponsorships.[40]

Project 4,000, as it came to be called, generated an outpouring of private commitments to help resettle the Indochinese. Said Pat Marshall, whose 20-year involvement with refugees began at that time,

> Project 4,000 brought a civic response to a refugee crisis. Bank tellers, nurses, bowling leagues, church groups, all kinds of people got together to sponsor families. Arrivals were featured regularly on the media. There was a complete absence of cynicism in those days. It was the high point of compassion. The public got involved and took ownership of the program.[41]

Farther south in Toronto, private citizens were also getting organized. Howard Adelman, a professor of philosophy at York University was just returning from a book-writing sabbatical when, he said,

> The news of the boat people hit me with a splash. I called together a Catholic

priest, an Anglican minister, some rabbis I knew. The idea was to write a collective letter to the Canadian government. It was on June 24, 1979, I think. Ron Atkey [then Minister of Employment and Immigration] had heard about the meeting and sent someone out. We talked about the problem and how we ought to do something. It was the government official who asked if we might be interested in private sponsorship. We thought that was a pretty good idea. We ended up deciding to sponsor 50 families. Dick Beddoes, a columnist for the Toronto *Globe and Mail*, picked up the idea and wrote an editorial. He named it Operation Lifeline and gave out my home phone number. I got a call early the next morning from Newfoundland. A woman asked, 'How can I help with Operation Lifeline?' I said, 'I don't know. What's Operation Lifeline?' The upshot was the phone never stopped ringing and by the end of the week we had 68 chapters around the country. We had our 50 families by the end of two weeks.[42]

In July 1979, just two days before the international conference on Indochinese refugees in Geneva, the Canadian government increased its admission quota to 50,000 refugees through the end of 1980. The additional numbers above 8,000, announced Ron Atkey, would be filled on a matching formula, with the government sponsoring one family for every one sponsored by the private sector. 'But the real incentive,' enthused an Operation Lifeline newsletter, 'is in the fact that the 50,000 figure … is NOT a ceiling. The competition is open-ended.'[43] While not every official agreed with that assessment, the government tried to make good on its initial matching pledge. But by October 1979 – just four months into an eighteen month programme – the private sector had already filled its 21,000 sponsorships and the government announced it could not keep pace. By the end of 1980, of the 60,000 refugees admitted, about 26,000 were government-assisted and 34,000 had been resettled by private sponsors or families.

What did private sponsorship involve in the Canadian context, how and why did it generate such support in the critical early days of the resettlement programme, and did it prove sucessful? The immigration regulations of 1978 permitted any group of five or more citizens or permanent residents of Canada to sponsor a refugee family, provided the group could demonstrate that it had sufficient resources and expertise to provide adequate lodging, food, clothing and other assistance during the first year of resettlement. Essentially private sponsors, either as *ad hoc* local groups or working through a constituent organization, agreed to to be legally responsible for the refugees during the first year. In all, more than 7,000 private sponsoring groups undertook such commitments in 1979–80.

Those refugees for whom no matching private sponsor could be found were resettled with government funding. This generally meant that the responsibilities assumed by the private sponsors were undertaken instead by local staff of the Canada Employment and Immigration Commission (CEIC), which was coordinated nationally by a government-appointed Refugee Task Force.

An evaluation of the sponsorship programme carried out in 1982 under CEIC auspices had the following findings:

• The most common form of private sponsorship was that by a group of church members of one congregation.

• The average size of family settled under private group sponsorship was five persons. Government-sponsored families tended to be smaller; indeed, government-assisted refugees were predominantly single young men, who were not a popular choice for private sponsors. 'The support provided by private sponsors was particularly important where large families were involved,' the evaluation concluded. 'Under government sponsorship, support is generally channelled to the head of household leaving non-working dependents to a large extent on their own. This can have negative consequences insofar as the adaptation of these persons is concerned. The private Group Sponsorship Program, on the other hand, greatly facilitates the involvement of non-working refugees in the larger community.'

• The single greatest problem cited by 21 per cent of sponsors was 'finding jobs for the refugees'. After 18 months in Canada, however, 89.4 per cent of working-age Indochinese were participating in the labour market. This exceeded the Canadian participation rate (63.7 per cent) especially among females refugees whose participation rate was 82.4 per cent against 50.9 per cent for all Canadians. Labour participation rates were about the same for privately sponsored and government-sponsored refugees but the privately sponsored averaged only 15.9 weeks before start of their first job against 19.9 for the government-sponsored.

• On average, Indochinese earned $211 per week against the Canadian national average of $315 in 1982. Seventy-seven per cent of Indochinese families earned less than $10,000 per year against 29.3 per cent for Canadians.

• In fiscal years 1979–80 and 1980–81, government expenditures averaged $3,416 *per capita* for a government-sponsored refugee, while private sponsorships cost the government an average of $2,663 *per capita*. This does not, however, include food, clothing, furniture and appliances purchased by group sponsors.

• About 50 per cent of refugees moved at least once and generally for employment-related reasons. Most movement was out of small communities to larger population centres and tended to be southward and/or westward, with Alberta and Ontario being the preferred provinces. Privately sponsored refugees appeared to be more mobile than government-sponsored refugees.

• Fifty-nine per cent of sponsors surveyed said they would do it again, although half of these gave conditions. For those who listed conditions, the most frequently listed item was: 'I would sponsor again if a real need can be demonstrated. I am not totally convinced that all the Indochinese admitted were refugees in the true sense.' The second most frequent answer was 'I would sponsor again if I were satisfied that, given world conditions, it is those refugees who are most in need of our help that are being admitted to Canada.'[44]

Overall, the evaluation concluded that private sponsorship had been a success: 'the voluntary sector, properly supported, can provide the needed services more adequately than the Government directly, and at considerably less cost.' The study noted, however, that 'the sponsorship wave of 1979–80 is not likely to be repeated in the foreseeable future for Indochinese or any other refugee group. The factors which made that phenomenon unique, it is agreed, were the sea drama itself, the intense media blitz, familiarity of Canadians with Vietnam, and the very novelty of sponsorship. These emotions have now played themselves out and sponsorship has become a much more considered and sober act.'[45]

As Howard Adelman noted, Operation Lifeline

> was a very spontaneous kind of thing … [but] it was not a populist movement. Polls showed that little over one-half of Canadians supported a quota of 5,000. When it went to 8,000, only 40 per cent were supportive. When it went to 50,000, opposition ran to nearly two-thirds. Canada is a nation of immigrants who hate immigrants. But there was strong middle-class support and the media was extremely supportive. Canadian politics is really small town politics. If you get the politicians, the mandarins, and the NGOs behind you, you don't have much opposition.[46]

In addition to the mainline Christian denominations, Adelman identified four sources of leadership for the private sponsorship movement that made it so effective, especially in its early days. The first were people like Ottawa's mayor, Marion Dewar, who helped to coalesce broad public support. Second were members of Canada's Jewish community who were 'affected by the association of the Indochinese refugee movement with the Holocaust' and the many unsuccessful attempts by Jewish refugees to find asylum. Third was the ethnic Chinese community and fourth were other ethnic groups, like the Hungarians and Ugandan Asians, who had arrived as refugees themselves. 'Thus the motivating factors were primarily refugee identification, ethnic identification, historical identification, or a tradition of social activism and Christian humanitarianism, but none of these motives excluded the others. In fact, it was probably a combination that led the leadership to devote the time and energy needed to develop the sponsorship movement.'[47]

In 1981, Indochinese admissions to Canada dropped to under 10,000. Of the 14,600 refugees resettled that year, only 4,400 were privately sponsored, one-fifth the number for 1980. But Indochinese refugees continued to come to Canada and private sponsors continued to open their homes to them and, in 1986, UNHCR awarded its Nansen Medal for the first time, not to an individual, a government, or an organization, but to an entire people. The award noted 'the remarkable achievements of individuals, families, voluntary agencies, community and religious organizations, as well as federal, provincial and municipal authorities in helping refugees to integrate successfully into Canadian society and regain human dignity'.

By ironic coincidence, the same year that the people of Canada were awarded a medal for their generous hospitality to refugees, the country's asylum policy was in turmoil, brought on by a dramatic increase in asylum seekers arriving on Canadian soil and laying claim to permanent status. By the middle of the year, a backlog of 25,000 refugee claims persuaded immigration authorities to institute procedural changes resulting in a 'fast-track' approach to processing and lower approval rates.

From 1981 to the middle of 1986, about 50,000 claims for asylum were lodged with the government. By the end of 1988, an additional 100,000 refugee claims were submitted. The Indochinese resettlement programme, the largest in Canada's history, geared itself up for one final push, resettling nearly 23,000 Vietnamese and Laotians under the terms of the Comprehensive Plan of Action from 1989 to 1995.[48] But, increasingly and not by choice, Canada was becoming more a country of asylum than a country of resettlement.

France

In the very early days of the Indochinese exodus, US State Department official Thomas Barnes visited France to compare their resettlement programme with that of the Americans, 'on the very feeble analogy that an understanding of English grammar can dawn only after exposure to Latin'. His conclusion in 1977 was that 'the French are handling it quite differently but that the results are more or less the same'.[49] Twenty years on, that assessment remains as positively ambiguous (or ambiguously positive) as when Barnes first made it.

It has been suggested that while the United States, Canada, and Australia are nations of immigrants – in these three countries immigration constitutes what Alexis de Tocqueville called a 'founding myth' of the nation – France is a country of immigration. In other words, 'immigration did not play a significant role in the historical process of building the French nation-state'. Thus, 'despite the long and continuous history of immigration in modern France, immigration has never achieved the legitimacy that it has enjoyed in the United States or Canada'.[50]

Since the early 1950s, annual levels of immigration to France have averaged around 100,000 per year, the right to asylum is written into the fore-word of the 1958 Constitution, and France has maintained one of the most generous naturalization policies in Europe.[51] Nevertheless, the movement of Indochinese began just as the French economy was hit by a major recession and the government began to talk seriously about *arrêt de l'immigration*, a total halt to immigration. Minister of Interior Charles Pasqua announced that France 'has been a country of immigration but it no longer wishes to be'.[52]

History, however, would have a say in the matter. France's colonial involvement in Indochina lasted from the early nineteenth century until its

1954 defeat by the Viet Minh at Dien Bien Phu.[53] Though the French government maintained an active interest in the affairs of Cambodia, Laos and Vietnam, it refused to support the American war effort. The fall of Vientiane, Phnom Penh and Saigon, observed Indochina scholar Serge Thion, 'were considered in France as expected results of a "wrong" policy of the Americans who never "understood" Indochina'.[54]

Thus, the initial exodus in April 1975 was considered largely a responsibility of the Americans, although the French government opened its doors to about 1,000 Indochinese per month and established the Comité National d'Entraide (CNE) to coordinate their resettlement. Responsibility for receiving the refugees in reception centres fell to France Terre d'Asile (FTA), a private organization founded in 1971 to provide reception services and legal aid for refugees and asylum seekers.

Père Parais, a Catholic missionary who had worked in Cambodia and Vietnam from 1956 to May 1975, joined FTA upon his return to France:

> Our job at first was to run the reception centres (*centre d'accueil*). Normally, people would spend about 6 months in the reception centres. In Limoges, the reception centre could hold more than 300 people. That was the largest in the country and almost a regional centre. The smallest held 20 people. The main function of the reception centres was board and lodging as well as medical follow-up and French lessons. Later, integration lessons were added. Cimade (le Service Ecumenique d'Entraide) gave each refugee 120 hours of French lessons. After a while, we called in other organizations to do technical training. In some centres, refugees got a total of 520 hours of training. Whichever organization was running the reception centre under the auspices of FTA would also have the responsibility of finding housing outside. During 1975–82 this was easier but it became harder later on.[55]

In part because of the difficulty of finding housing, one of the government's approaches, said Père Parais, 'was to try to spread the refugees across French territory'. Of 95 departments, 80 per cent had reception centres. About half of those settled in the departments, he said, ultimately gravitated toward Paris. Or as General Guy Simon, the first head of CNE, said, 'Half are in the Paris region where it is easier to find work than housing. The other half are in the provinces where it is just the reverse.'[56]

By June 1979, on the eve of the international conference in Geneva, France had resettled just over 50,000 Indochinese, second only to the US total. But the French contribution to the July meeting became contentious in two ways. First, while worldwide resettlement commitments ran to several hundred thousand, France offered to resettle only an additional 5,000 refugees, a pledge branded as parsimonious even at home. Said former prime minister, Pierre Mendès-France,

> Five thousand people is nothing. It even falls well short of the total offered by individuals and mayors. The least the government could have done was to offer the local authorities the number of refugees they had declared themselves ready to accept. If Valéry Giscard d'Estaing had announced 'France accepts 50,000 refugees,' he would have given our country an enormous moral advantage over

its allies and, what is most important, might have compelled them to make similar efforts.[57]

Still more controversial, however, was the lead role that France played in persuading Vietnam to impose a temporary halt to clandestine departures in July 1979. 'The moratorium is better than death at sea,' said French foreign minister, Jean François-Poncet. While most of the participant countries – and Secretary-General Kurt Waldheim himself – concurred in that assessment, the moratorium stirred deep concerns that a UN conference should endorse constraints on the right to freedom of movement. As long-time resident of France and *New York Times* journalist Henry Kamm put it, the moratorium 'made the Vietnamese police state more of a police state'.[58]

But Paris had no interest in using the 1979 Geneva Conference either to preach to or punish Hanoi. Unlike most of its Western allies, France had not severed normal diplomatic ties with Vietnam, either in 1975 or in 1979, when Vietnam invaded neighbouring Cambodia. The French were making it clear that, in responding to the Indochinese refugee crisis, they wished to draw closer to their former colonies rather than freeze them out.

In late 1979, UNHCR presented its Nansen Medal to President Valéry Giscard d'Estaing in recognition of the French Republic's traditional concern for the uprooted and the general policy of asylum extended to millions of refugees and displaced persons over the previous 50 years. UNHCR also noted the significant contribution France had made to the Indochinese refugee problem through its resettlement programmes. That year, for the first time, the Nansen Medal came with a monetary prize of $50,000. President Giscard d'Estaing announced that half would go towards building a school in a refugee camp in Botswana. The other half, he said, would help Kampucheans. The money did not go to the border, however, where refugees had begun to mass, but to finance a rural hospital inside the country.

But France, without much fanfare, continued to resettle Indochinese, most of whom received automatic refugee status from OFPRA (Office Français de Protection des Refugies et Apatrides) and were permitted to seek French citizenship soon after their arrival.[59] By 1985, the official resettlement figures showed more than 110,000 Indochinese in France, though estimates of clandestine arrivals pushed that number to 130,000 or more. Between 1983 and 1985, with Thailand imposing its 'humane deterrence' policies and international resettlement commitments in decline, somewhere between 20,000 and 30,000 Indochinese – many of them Sino-Vietnamese and Sino-Cambodians – bribed their way out of the camps, bought false identification papers, and travelled to France where they petitioned for asylum. OFPRA approved most of the claims but, over time, became more and more strict in applying the refugee definition.

By 1987, like most of the other resettlement countries, France had grown sceptical of the motives for leaving. As one French Red Cross official put it, 'The first ten years of resettlement up until 1987 we saw a certain class. After that, we started to see a different group: children of farmers, fishermen and microbusiness-people. They ceased to be entirely political refugees. There was an economic factor as well. Children would be put on boats in hopes they would be resettled.'[60]

French resettlement of Indochinese tapered off to no more than a few thousand per year, including family reunions directly from Vietnam. By the beginning of 1990, France had grown preoccupied with the influx of asylum seekers and the rise of an anti-immigrant political movement, the National Front, headed by Jean-Marie Le Pen. But the Indochinese, by and large, were not targets of the xenophobic backlash. As one State Secretary for Family and Migrant Worker Affairs said, 'Of all the waves of immigration, the one which comes from Southeast Asia is the best inserted into French society.'[61]

Former *New York Times* correspondent Henry Kamm echoed those sentiments:

> The Indochinese have done remarkably well in France. They are quiet and well-behaved. There are no anti-Indochinese sentiments nor are there invidious comparisons between the 'good' refugees from Vietnam and the 'bad' refugees from Morocco and Algeria. On the whole, you don't have ghettos or huge concentrations except in the 13th arrondissement. They provide lots of cheap restaurants and that's a boon. The dispersal policy, in that respect, has worked quite well. You find Vietnamese restaurants now in just about every town of note.

Père Parais continues to work with Asian immigrants, now with Centre France-Asie located in central Paris. Along with the family reunifications, he still sees 'a few hundred "irregular" Indochinese cases' per year. 'Most do not have strong claims to refugee status. The only ones who can afford to get out are children of cadres and rich businessmen. We work with the International Organization for Migration (IOM) to help them go back to Vietnam.'

Britain

Unlike its larger partners in resettlement – the United States, Canada, and Australia – Britain is not a nation of immigrants. Nor even, like France, is it a country of immigration. For the last three centuries, in fact, Britain has been a country of emigration, with millions of Britons settling the new territories in the United States, Canada, Australia, New Zealand, and South Africa. Britain's contemporary immigration policies might be said to have begun in the 1870s with the admission of Jewish refugees fleeing pogroms in the Russian Empire and Romania.[62] In the twentieth century, Britain absorbed a quarter of a million Poles and other East Europeans between 1935 and 1950, followed by 15,000 Hungarians in 1956 and about 5,000 Czechs in 1968. In the 1970s, somewhat paralleling Canada's response, Britain offered haven to 28,000 Ugandan Asians and roughly 3,000 Chileans.

In 1975, Margaret Thatcher was elected as leader of the Conservative Party. Though it would be four years before she became Prime Minister, the start of the Indochinese exodus also marked, in the words of one observer, the beginning of a 'strongly restrictionist period in Conservative immigration policy'.[63] Britain resettled only 32 Vietnamese refugees in 1975 (though it also brought 100 orphans directly from Vietnam in the *Daily Mail* airlift and permitted about 300 Vietnamese already in Britain to remain). In 1976 and 1977, scarcely more than 100 Vietnamese were resettled. Then, in October 1978, a British registered ship, the *Wellpark*, rescued over 380 boat people at sea, all of whom eventually were flown to the United Kingdom and resettled. But while the media coverage of this incident was overwhelmingly positive and the public welcome was warm, the *Wellpark* did not become Britain's *Hai Hong*. That is, the dramatic rescue did not seem to prompt a profound change but a rather more incremental shift in the government's (and the public's) response to the Vietnamese exodus.[64]

In early 1979, responding to appeals from UNHCR and the government of Hong Kong, which was seeing an upsurge in boat arrivals, Britain pledged to resettle 1,500 refugees from the Asian camps. Meanwhile, the government maintained its commitment to settle all boat people rescued by British vessels, bringing in more than 1,000 Vietnamese in the course of 1979. But as boats continued to pour into the crown colony of Hong Kong, Prime Minister Thatcher led the call for an international conference on the Indochinese refugee crisis.

At the Geneva meeting in July 1979, Thatcher's government agreed to take another 10,000 Vietnamese, mainly from Hong Kong. Critics noted that, at the time, that amounted to no more than one week's worth of arrivals in the region and less than the United States had offered to take in each month. Still, in terms of its domestic impact, the British pledge amounted to a ten-fold increase in arrivals and programmatic changes were in order.

In 1977, when the total incoming Vietnamese population numbered in the hundreds, resettlement was handled largely by a single voluntary agency, Ockenden Venture. By 1978, when annual admissions had climbed above 1,000, another private agency, British Council for Aid to Refugees (BCAR) got involved. When the admissions quota climbed again in 1979, the British Home Office called upon Save the Children Fund.[65] Although each agency functioned autonomously, in July 1979, the Joint Committee for Refugees from Vietnam was formed with representatives from each of the resettlement agencies and a secretariat seconded from the Home Office. The agencies divided the work into three geographical zones of responsibility: BCAR covered the south of England (including London), Ockenden Venture had Birmingham and the Midlands, and Save the Children Fund got Scotland and Northern Ireland.[66]

The broad aims of the Vietnamese reception and resettlement programme, according to a Home Office report, were

> to bring the refugees to the United Kingdom and, after an intial stay in a reception centre (originally to be for 3–4 months), to resettle the refugee families throughout the United Kindgdom. In reception, the refugees would be taught 'survival English' and learn something of the British way of life. Resettlement was to be governed by a policy of 'dispersed clusters,' the aim being to place as little burden

as possible on local authorities while trying to minimize isolation amongst the refugees. The dispersal policy was a result of several factors: the desire to avoid 'ghettoes'; the belief that dispersal would benefit the refugees in terms of eventual integration; and the need to obtain houses from local authorities, none of which received financial support from the central government for the resettled refugees.[67]

The 1982 Home Office report noted that 'a similar policy was employed in the resettlement of Ugandan Asians'. But as British refugee scholar Linda Hitchcox points out, although the Ugandan Asians

> were the first large group of refugees to arrive in the UK who were distinctly non-European in appearance, they represented an average demographic profile in health, age, and family composition.... The majority were white-collar workers without the depressing experience of refugee camps and many had relatives already living in Britain. It was therefore possible for a high proportion of this group (some accounts put it as high as 80 per cent) to seek out their own work and accommodation.[68]

The Vietnamese experience proved far different.

Instead of three or four months as expected, Indochinese refugees spent an average of six months in one of 46 government-funded reception centres throughout the United Kingdom. The centres – ranging in size from the former military barracks at Thorney Island, which accommodated over 700, to a country home at Ambleside, holding 18 – offered intensive English as a Second Language (ESL), medical screening, and basic orientation to British life. Once out of the reception centres, however, funding from the central government essentially ceased and any special help the refugees received beyond that was up to the voluntary agencies.

Most Vietnamese families went straight from the centres into locally funded council housing where they were eligible to receive social security grants as well as subsized medicine. Most tended to stay in council housing. By 1982, Indochinese refugees (all but a few hundred of them Vietnamese) numbered over 16,000 in the United Kingdom and government expenditures exceeded £20 million. Of the employable adults, only 16 per cent were working.[69] Of the men and women who had managed to find jobs, two-thirds were engaged in semi-skilled or unskilled manual labour. The difficulties faced by the early waves of refugees were immense:

> The Vietnamese had few transferable or immediately marketable skills. They were poorly educated even in their own language. Many were from North Vietnam and had very little contact with western civilization. Britain was often not their first choice of destination. There was no pre-existing community in the UK to which the new arrivals could turn for support. The Vietnamese are internally divided by race, religion and geographical origin, and they arrived in Britain at a time of recession and high unemployment.[70]

Lacking a pre-existing Vietnamese community and scattered to the ends of the United Kingdom, one of the first things the new immigrants began to do was look for each other. A Home Office survey of more than 1,500 households in 1982 found that nine per cent had moved from their initial settlement site.[71] That figure probably was low. In a 1989 study, geographer Vaughan Robinson noted that 'The speed with which secondary migration developed and the direction of that migration strongly suggest that forced dispersal was neither appropriate to the Vietnamese nor accepted by them. Over half of all households have now moved from their resettlement address and the overwhelming destinations for these migrants are those cities which have sizeable Vietnamese communities.'[72]

In 1983, Save the Children Fund scaled back on its refugee resettlement activities although some of its staff members helped to organize Refugee Action to fill the gap. According to Refugee Action's director, Sandy Buchan, 'We took a community development approach, finding out with refugees what their needs were, a grass roots approach.' The government's dispersal policy, he said 'meant that settlement was random. It was not refugee centred. What happened was that people were scattered all over the place and most of their initial efforts and energies were put into moving. From 1982–88, the same agencies who helped them settle were helping them all move again. We called it secondary resettlement.'[73] Out of an estimated 30,000 Indochinese in Britain, estimates are that London now has about 20,000 with another 2,000 in Birmingham and 1,500 in Manchester.

Nhung Bui's family, she said, had been refugees from the North in 1954 when the Geneva Accords divided the country:

> We lost a chance to flee in April 1975, although one part of my family got to the United States. I used to work for the old government. When the communists took over the country, I lost my job. My husband was not a soldier so he was not imprisoned but we were very worried about the future. We went to Cholon [Saigon's Chinatown] and I pretended to be Chinese. This was the 'half-official' period of April–June 1979. We had to pay $2,000 per person, ten ounces of gold. I borrowed money from my sister. She said it was like playing the lottery: you take a big risk, you might win, you might lose everything. My husband went to see a fortune teller and he said, 'It is good for you to go.' Many people in the South felt the same way. Many people lost their money. Some lost their lives.

Nhung Bui escaped with her husband and two sons in May 1979. They were nearly two weeks at sea and several people died in a storm before they were rescued by a British ship. In Britain, she continued,

> we stayed in the reception centres at least six months. They had ESL, women's groups, cooking, job training. It was basic information. At that time, everybody had to be in a reception centre. Everything was new to us. We felt very miserable. We had lots of professionals coming to talk with us but we were not confident in ourselves. We absorbed very little. After six months, they helped us with housing and resettlement. They scattered us in small towns and cities but not in London. Again, people were confused. My family was put in Essex, about ten miles outside of London. The Refugee Council worked hard but they did not know well what to do. We had language problems and communication problems.

I was asked to be an interpreter for 12 families in Essex. They put children in the schools but at the time the children had no English. My son sat in the class for one year. He didn't know anything. He didn't learn anything. He got bored, fed up. The same things happened for most of the first group.[74]

In 1983, Nhung Bui and other members of the Vietnamese community helped to set up Tower Hamlets Community Centre with some support from Refugee Action. Tower Hamlets, one of perhaps 50 Vietnamese community groups in London, organizes youth projects, employment training projects, counselling services, community activities, New Year's festivals, children's festivals, and luncheon clubs. But, she added, 'We have not had much success with employment... We have 65 per cent unemployment among the Vietnamese community in Tower Hamlets.' Nhung Bui said she was speaking only about the 'middle-aged generation', however. Among the younger generation, employment is at 85 per cent. 'The second generation is good,' she said, 'but the first generation is terrible. I think the Vietnamese in Canada and in America are doing better than the ones in Europe. It is paradise for the Vietnamese over there.'

In April 1985, Parliament's Select Committee on Refugee Resettlement and Immigration (SCORRI) published a report on refugees and asylum with a special focus on the Vietnamese. Among its findings and recommendations, the SCORRI report 'pointed to the value of involving refugees themselves in the planning and organization of resettlement at the earliest possible stages ... emphasized the undesirability of keeping refugees in reception centres any longer than is absolutely necessary' and observed that 'the policy of dispersal is now almost universally regarded as mistaken'. In its reply, the government acknowleged many of the programme's short-comings but, as to the continuing difficulties the Vietnamese faced in terms of employment, housing, and community services, the Home Office insisted that 'there must be a limit to what the central, or local, government can be expected to do'.[75]

From 1983 to 1988, a steady trickle of a few hundred Vietnamese entered the United Kingdom, some of them sea rescue cases, others family reunion cases coming out of the camps or directly from Vietnam via the Orderly Departure Programme. From 1989 to 1995, this steady but small flow of admissions was supplemented by the '2,000 Programme' which was established by the British government as part of its resettlement commitments to Hong Kong under the terms of the Comprehensive Plan of Action. In 1995, the British Home Office conducted a follow-up study of this later wave of Vietnamese arrivals. Their findings were not particularly encouraging:

• The majority of arrivals since 1982 could not speak English on arrival and still were coping with limited levels of English.

• 38 per cent of economicially active refugees were currently working in paid jobs.

• Only one-quarter of all households contained a wage-earner.

- 90 per cent were living in public housing.

- 10 per cent of the sample had been homeless at some time in the UK.

- 'In general, the refugees had little contact with the British population' although 'almost two-thirds said they felt part of a community and the majority felt safe and secure in Britain. However, half said they thought the people in Britain treated them differently.'

The report did not comment on the status of the pre-1982 arrivals although some of its findings suggested that the employment situation improved with time. Refugees who arrived between 1983 and 1988, for example, showed an employment rate of 53 per cent against 11 per cent for those who arrived later. The Home Office report also found a strong association between time spent in the Hong Kong camps and unemployment. The Vietnamese who had spent more than three years in Hong Kong had unemployment rates of 92 per cent against 46 per cent for those who had spent less than three years in the camps. 'Refugees who had spent time in the camps in Hong Kong were at a great disadvantage,' the report concluded, 'and the longer the refugees had spent in the camps the more disadvantaged they were.'[76]

Australia

Over a 20-year span from 1975 to 1995 Australia resettled more than 137,000 Indochinese refugees, a total second only to the United States and, on a *per capita* basis, more than any other country in the world. Nearly half of all migration to the country now comes from Asia, and Australia promotes itself as a multicultural society. Considering the nation's history, to have reached this point coming from the Eurocentric, even racist, policies of a few short decades ago constitutes, in the words of one scholar, 'something of a revolution'.[77]

Throughout the nineteenth and early twentieth centuries, migration to Australia came primarily from Britain, or at least from the British Empire. But the search for cheap labour in the form of Chinese, Indian and Pacific Island workers clashed with the Australian labour movement's desire for wages 'fit for white men' and, in 1901, one of the first acts of the new Federal Parliament was to promulgate a 'White Australia' policy.[78]

Shortly after the end of the Second World War, Australia launched an ambitious immigration programme designed to increase the population by an average of 1 per cent per year through net migration. Though it did not quite achieve this figure, in the next 30 years more than 2.5 million immigrants entered Australia. Along with their Australian-born children, immigrants accounted for 57 per cent of the nation's population growth during that period. Major migration waves included Britons and Irish, North Europeans (including 170,000 refugees from displaced persons camps in Germany), South Europeans and later Asians and Middle Easterners.[79]

In the 1950s and 1960s, policy makers began to take a few cautious steps toward greater heterogeneity, although in 1966 nearly 55 per cent of all immigrants still came from the United Kingdom and Ireland, with another 30 per cent from continental Europe, New Zealand or the United States. Then, in 1973, the Labour Party government rescinded the White Australia policy and established uniform rules that ended discrimination on the basis of race, nationality or colour.

In 1975, when Australia announced its first annual quota for refugees, Indochinese were nowhere on the list. In a somewhat token and piecemeal approach, officials of the Department of Labour and Immigration took 64 people from Guam in May 1975, 201 from Hong Kong in June, and 326 from staging camps in Singapore and Malaysia in July that same year. The press release from the Prime Minister described the latter group as people who 'ranged in age from infants to an 81 year old woman, and included a Cistercian monk, a former interpreter for an Australian civil affairs unit stationed in Phuoc Tuy province, a number of single parent families and a number of adolescents who had become separated from their families'. It added that 'Most of the refugees have no recognized skills or qualifications and under normal migration criteria would not be eligible for entry to Australia.'[80]

In 1976 and 1977 Australia resettled not many more than 1,000 Indochinese refugees per year. Though Australian forces had fought alongside the Americans in Vietnam and thus the country arguably had some historical responsibility for any human fall-out from the war, the Labour government of Prime Minister Whitlam had three reasons to wish to limit Indochinese resettlement: first, it felt that the main responsibility for the refugees lay with the United States. Second, it wanted 'normalization, not polarization' in Southeast Asia. Finally, it feared that resettlement of too many anti-communist Vietnamese would create 'division in Australia and a revival of the kind of cold war politics that had helped keep the Labor Party out of power for many years before 1972.'[81]

Then, from late 1977 to the middle of 1978, a total of 51 vessels carrying more than 2,000 Vietnamese boat people beached themselves on Australian shores, having stopped in Singapore, Malaysia, or Indonesia for food and water along the way. Reluctant enough to be a country of resettlement, Australia was panic-stricken to find it had become a country of first asylum. Or, as Bruce Grant wrote in *The Boat People: An 'Age' Investigation,* the aim of Australia's immigration policy,

> while not racially exclusive, was to increase the population without changing its dominantly European composition, or at least to change it slowly. The boat people were not part of the policy. They had not been processed thousands of kilometres away by skilful immigration officials. Reflecting population pressures and political turmoil near at hand, they simply turned up, uninvited, asking for refuge. For Australia, history and geography had merged, causing a shiver of apprehension.[82]

The news could not have been put more clearly: Australians, for the most part, may have come from Europe but they were living in Oceania, hard by Asia. Their neighbours' refugee crisis was their own as well. A new, collective approach was in order. Australia would take on larger resettlement commitments in return for which its ASEAN neighbours, particularly Malaysia and Indonesia, would bear the brunt of the first asylum responsibilities.

In May 1978 Australia's Minister for Immigration and Ethnic Affairs, Michael MacKellar, announced that his country would admit 9,000 additional Indochinese refugees in the next twelve months. He stressed that this action was intended to curb the influx of boat arrivals into Australia and to encourage refugees in the camps to wait for the opportunity for legal migration.[83]

Australia spearheaded the call for the first conference on Indochinese refugees in December 1978 (which proved ineffectual in generating new resettlement pledges) and was a primary actor in the far more successful conference in July 1979. The government established annual quotas to resettle 15,000 Indochinese refugees in 1979 and 1980. By 1982, more than 50,000 Indochinese – mostly Vietnamese boat people but including several thousand Cambodians and Laotians as well – had arrived to start new lives in Australia. They were not coming by boat, this time, but were culled from the first asylum camp populations by Australian immigration officials.

By 1978, Australia's immigration policy had established three main categories for admission: (1) family migration (mainly parents, children and, in some cases, siblings of migrants already in Australia); (2) refugees, and (3) special eligibility (primarily involving labour and skilled migration but also including retirees, business investors, etc.). To be admitted as a refugee, applicants first have to meet the definition of refugee status as set out in the 1951 Convention or meet the criteria the Special Humanitarian Programme. Until 1982, refugee status for Indochinese in first asylum countries was granted automatically. Refugees, furthermore, had to have a sponsor in Australia, either a family or an organization. Finally, refugees had to demonstrate a capacity to settle well in Australia, meaning they were in good health, employable, spoke some English, etc.[84] Sometimes, for humanitarian reasons, these last criteria were waived to admit some 'hard to settle' cases.

Given Australia's long history of receiving migrants, a network of migrant hostels already existed throughout the country, which were pressed into service for the Indochinese. New arrivals spent an average of 15 weeks in these hostels, where they had access to housing and employment counselling, dental and medical care, orientation classes, and intensive language instruction, all funded by the federal government.[85]

For a brief period in the early 1980s, the Australian government experimented with a scheme to disperse refugees more broadly across the country by sending them directly to sponsoring communities and thus bypassing the migrant hostels. But generally speaking, refugees entered the migrant hostels, which were located in the state capitals, and, upon leaving, were free to settle anywhere they wished. Not surprisingly, most refugees settled within ten kilometres of the migrant centres. Indeed, one study found that 96 per cent of all Vietnamese live in the eight state capital cities. Secondary migration has favoured the larger cities so that, by the early 1990s, 72 per cent of Indochinese migrants lived in Sydney and Melbourne alone.[86]

Social scientist Nancy Viviani has suggested that Indochinese refugees have had three preoccupations upon coming to Australia: family reunion, economic security and social mobility. In the context of special Indochinese programmes, family reunion was also a priority for the Australian government and was accomplished through ongoing resettlement from the camps and, in the case of the Vietnamese, through the Orderly Departure Programme. In terms of economic security, the 1981 census showed Vietnamese unemployment rates at 26 per cent, better than their Cambodian and Laotian counterparts but worse than the 8 per cent for the Australian population as a whole. Refugees, Viviani pointed out, 'are eligible for unemployment benefits, family allowances, and free health care as soon as they arrive and this puts a floor under their needs'. As for social mobility, she noted, the 'picture is fragmentary.... Broad economic growth and the maintenance of open economic opportunity are the keys to Indochinese movement into the middle class. And, over time, the willingness of Australians to accept Asian refugees depends on the working through of these broad social forces.'[87]

In 1978, the Australian government stated a clear commitment to the creation of a multicultural society. In a speech entitled 'Options for a Population Policy', Michael MacKellar, Minister for Immigration and Ethnic Affairs, said '[We] have now reached the situation where ethnic group cultures have become widely welcomed and appreciated by the Australian community as having made an important contribution to the richness and diversity of our own culture. This is wholly desirable.'[88]

Simply saying so, of course, did not make it so. One early arrival spoke of the difficulties both of interacting with the community at large and of establishing a community of one's own:

> The arrangements for social occasions in Vietnam were very easy to make; but in Australia we do not know the rules. We do not know the rules of sports, and we do not know the social conventions, so all the arrangements are far more difficult.... Therefore here in Australia, apart from buying some alcohol to take home and get drunk, we don't know what to do at all. Occasionally we get together and have a feast – but the foods here are plentiful so we grow tired of the joys of food quite quickly. Next, we may go to the pictures but there isn't much fun in that either. We know we need other sources of recreation, but these sources are hard to find. Back home we did simple things. We could while away half a day watching people go by. But here in Melbourne, the winter climate is too severe, there are no sidewalk cafes, and people don't even walk in the streets.[89]

By the early 1980s Australia's economy was in recession, the labour markets that had traditionally supplied jobs to migrants were in collapse, and policy makers were beginning to worry that their commitments to

Indochinese refugees had set off a growing and uncontrollable chain migration effect. In March 1982, following a visit to the Southeast Asian camps, then Minister of Immigration and Ethnic Affairs Sam McPhee announced the need for a new approach. 'A proportion of people now leaving their homelands', he said, 'were doing so to seek a better way of life rather than to escape from some form of persecution. In other words, their motivation is the same as over one million others who apply annually to migrate to Australia. To accept them as refugees would in effect condone queue-jumping as migrants.'[90] In July 1982 Australia eliminated group-basis determinations for Indochinese and shifted to case-by-case decisions. Said one official, 'We started rejecting people on the basis that they were not refugees. It was a new paradigm.'[91]

Through the remainder of the 1980s, Australia sought to apply this new paradigm regionally and internationally. *Bona fide* refugees continued to deserve resettlement, its officials argued, but economic migrants should be sent home. As early as 1985, Australian policy makers had produced what came to be known as the 'Canberra Paper', which outlined the idea of a regional screening programme, with third-country resettlement for those who were screened in and repatriation for the screened-out.

But by the beginning of the 1990s, as Indochinese refugee arrivals declined, the Australian immigration system was confronted with another wave of asylum seekers. Most did not come by boat but with visitor or student visas. Prior to 1989, on average only about 500 people sought asylum in Australia each year. By the end of 1991, there were 23,000 claims awaiting processing. About 70 per cent of these were students from the People's Republic of China who insisted that they could not return home in the wake of the killings at Tien An Men Square in 1989.

A small number of people, including about 300 Cambodians, reached Australia by boat between 1989 and 1991. They were detained for illegal entry, some for up to three years before their cases were adjudicated. Most of them ultimately were refused refugee status and were persuaded to return to Cambodia. Overall, Australia's Refugee Status Review Committee approves about 5 per cent of onshore claimants for refugee status. As the Indochinese programme wound down, Australia found itself where it was at the beginning: committed to Asian migration and resettlement of its fair share of refugees, but deeply reluctant to play the role of asylum country.

Notes

1 Gail Paradise Kelly, *From Vietnam to America: A Chronicle of the Vietnamese Immigration to the United States* (Boulder: Westview Press, 1977) p. 130.
2 Author's interview with Cecilia Abraham, Kuala Lumpur, 30 September 1995.
3 Adapted from US General Accounting Office, *Indochinese Refugees: Protection, Care and Processing Can Be Improved* (Washington, DC: GAO, 19 August 1980) pp. 15–16.
4 Author's interview with Robert De Vecchi, New York, 10 April 1996. For a

history of the International Rescue Committee see Mark Dawson, *Flight: Refugees and the Quest for Freedom. The History of the International Rescue Committee, 1933–1993* (New York: IRC, 1993).

5 US General Accounting Office, *Domestic Resettlement of Indochinese – Struggle for Self-Reliance*. Report to the Congress/ HRD-77-35. (Washington, DC: GAO, 10 May 1977).

6 By 1979, other voluntary resettlement agencies included World Relief Refugee Service, the YMCA, Buddhist Council for Refugee Rescue and Resettlement, the Rav Tov Committee to Aid New Immigrants, and the Polish American Immigration and Refugee Committee. Several states, notably Iowa and Idaho, formed resettlement agencies to coordinate efforts in their jurisdictions.

7 In David S. North, Lawrence S. Lewin, and Jennifer R. Wagner, 'Kaleidoscope: the resettlement of refugees in the United States by the voluntary agencies', Report prepared for the Bureau for Refugee Programs, US Department of State, February 1982, p. 42.

8 *Ibid.*, p. 72.

9 In Kelly, *From Vietnam to America*, p. 133.

10 A 1976 study by the Health, Education, and Welfare (HEW) Task Force concluded that 'sponsorships by church and civic organizations had been more successful than those of individuals, that urban areas were better able to provide the educational and employment aid which refugees needed, that most refugees needed additional language training and that except for dental problems, refugees' health generally was good'. *HEW Report to Congress*, 15 June 1976, p. 5.

11 Thomas J. Barnes, *Of All the 36 Alternatives: Indochinese Resettlement in America* (Washington: Department of State, Senior Seminar in Foreign Policy, April 1977), p. 15.

12 Baker and North, *The 1975 Refugees*, pp. 52–53.

13 *Ibid.*, p. 57.

14 *Ibid.*, p. 59.

15 Barnes, *Of All the 36 Alternatives*, p. 16.

16 *Ibid.*, p. 51.

17 Author's interview with Lionel Rosenblatt, Bangkok, 19 January 1996.

18 See Loescher and Scanlan, *Calculated Kindness*, pp. 120–46. In 1978, Henry Kamm was awarded the Pulitzer Prize for his writing on Indochinese refugees. In a letter to the Advisory Board on the Pulitzer Prizes at Columbia University, Frank Sieverts, then Deputy Assistant Secretary for Human Rights and Humanitarian Affairs, wrote that the effect of Kamm's articles on US policy was 'most striking... His stories helped pave the way for new consultations with the Congress which led in August 1977 to the parole of an additional 15,000 refugees from Indochina. A further 7,000 were authorized for parole into the US in January 1978.'

19 The Refugee Act of 1980 spelled out a process of consultations between Congress and the Administration to establish the number of refugees to be admitted in a given year. Authority for determining who was or was not deserving of refugee status rested with the INS in the Department of Justice.

20 Susan S. Forbes, *Adaptation and Integration of Recent Refugees to the United States* (Washington, DC: Refugee Policy Group, August 1985), pp. 4–5.

21 *Ibid.*, p. 15.

22 *Ibid.*, p. 25.

23 John Finck, 'Secondary migration to California's Central Valley,' in Hendricks, Downing, and Deinard, *The Hmong in Transition*, p. 184.

24 *Ibid.*, p. 186.

25 *Ibid.*, p. 185.

26 Jack D. Bulk, 'American Hmong on the move', in *Hmong Forum*, January 1996. p. 12.

27 *Ibid.*, p. 16.

28 Pai Yang and Nora Murphy, *Hmong in the 90s: Stepping Towards the Future* (St. Paul: Hmong American Partnership, 1993), p. 16.

29 Author's interview with Lee Pao Xiong, St. Paul, 29 April 1996.

30 Leif Jensen, 'Secondary earner strategies and family poverty: immigrant–native differentials, 1960–1980', *International Migration Review*, Vol. 25 (Spring 1991) (New York: Center for Migration Studies). Using data from the 1960, 1970 and 1980 US Census Public Use Samples, Jensen found that among Asian immigrant families in the United States for less than five years, absolute poverty rates stood at 26.1 per cent. For those resident for more than five years, the absolute poverty rate was 5.2 per cent.

31 Office of Refugee Resettlement, *Report to the Congress: FY 1994 Refugee Resettlement Program* (Washington, DC: US Department of Health and Human Services, 1995), pp. 60, 64.

32 Jeremy Hein, *From Vietnam, Laos and Cambodia: A Refugee Experience in the United States* (New York: Twayne Publishers, 1995), p. 158. Other studies of Indochinese adaptation include John Tenhula, *Voices from Southeast Asia: The Refugee Experience in the United States* (New York: Holmes and Meier, 1991), Nathan Caplan, John K. Whitmore and Marcella H. Choy, *The Boat People in America: A Study of Family Life, Hard Work, and Cultural Values* (Ann Arbor: University of Michigan Press, 1989), James M. Freeman, *Hearts of Sorrow: Vietnamese-American Lives* (Stanford: Stanford University Press, 1989), Paul Strand and Woodrow Jones, Jr., *Indochinese Refugees in America: Problems of Adaptation and Assimilation* (Durham, North Carolina: Duke University Press, 1985), and David W. Haines, ed., *Refugees in the United States: A Reference Handbook* (Westport, Connecticut: Greenwood Press, 1985).

33 In Stanley Karnow, 'In Orange County's Little Saigon, Vietnamese try to bridge two worlds', *Smithsonian*, Vol. 23, No. 5 (August 1992), p. 32.

34 Maxwell Brem, 'Mission of mercy,' *The Weekend Observer*, 26 November 1988.

35 *Ibid.*

36 Howard Adelman, 'Canadian refugee policy in the postwar period: an analysis,' in Howard Adelman, ed., *Refugee Policy: Canada and the United States* (Toronto: York Lanes Press, 1991), p. 193.

37 *Ibid.*, p. 198.

38 Employment and Immigration Canada, *Sponsoring Refugees: Facts for Canadian Groups and Organizations* (1986), p. 4

39 Author's interview with Mike Molloy, Toronto, 26 April 1996.

40 Author's interview with Marion Dewar, Ottawa, 22 April 1996.

41 Author's interview with Pat Marshall, Ottawa, 22 April 1996.

42 Author's interview with Howard Adelman, Toronto, 26 April 1996. For a detailed history of Operation Lifeline, see Howard Adelman, *Canada and the Indochinese Refugees* (Regina: L.A. Weigl Educational Associates, 1982), pp. 89–106.

43 Operation Lifeline Newsletter, No. 2, 30 July 1979.

44 Employment and Immigration Canada, Program Evaluation Branch, *Evaluation of the 1979–80 Indochinese Refugee Program*, April 1982. Another survey conducted around the same time found that 92 per cent of private sponsors said the sponsoring relationship was good and ongoing but only 42 per cent said they

would do it again. See San Duy Nguyen, Terence Cooke and Tran Q. Phung, 'Refugee needs asssessment', Ottawa–Carleton SEA Refugee Project, March 1983.

45 DPA Consulting Ltd, *Evaluation of the Indochinese Refugee Group Sponsorship Program, Prepared for Employment and Immigration Canada*, February 1982, pp. 5, 59.

46 Author's interview with Howard Adelman, Toronto, 26 April 1996.

47 Adelman, *Canada and the Indochinese Refugees*, p. 89.

48 In all, in 1975–95, Canada resettled 99,935 Vietnamese boat people, 3,118 Viet land people, 16,301 lowland Lao, 973 highland Lao, and 16,818 Cambodians for a total of 137,145 refugees. In addition, Canada resettled 57,780 Vietnamese and 4,637 Cambodians via the Orderly Departure Program (what Canada called the Family Reunification Program).

49 Barnes, *Of All the 36 Alternatives*, pp. 44–45.

50 James F. Hollifield, 'Immigration and republicanism in France: the hidden consensus,' in Wayne A. Cornelius, Philip L. Martin, and James F. Hollifield, eds, *Controlling Immigration: A Global Perspective* (Stanford: Stanford University Press, 1994), p. 144.

51 *Ibid.*, p. 143

52 *Ibid.*, p. 171.

53 See Bernard B. Fall, *Hell in a Very Small Place: The Siege of Dien Bien Phu* (Philadelphia: J.B. Lippincott, 1967).

54 Serge Thion, 'Indochinese refugees in France: solidarity and its limits,' in Supang Chantavanich and Bruce Reynolds, eds, *Indochinese Refugees: Asylum and Resettlement* (Bangkok: Chulalongkorn University, 1988) pp. 293–4.

55 Author's interview with Père Parais, Paris, 27 February 1996.

56 Author's interview with General Guy Simon, Paris, 26 February 1996. The full name of the CNE was Le Comité National D'Entraide Franco-Vietnamien, Franco-Cambodgien, Franco-Laotien. As the name implies, said the general, 'The French took people who had family in France or who had served in the French army. It was a more selective process. The Americans took large numbers indiscriminately. It was also a generational thing. The older generation were quite happy to come to France. The younger generation wanted to go to America.'

57 In Grant, *The Boat People*, p. 170.

58 Author's telephone interview with Henry Kamm, Paris, 28 February 1996.

59 Thion, 'Indochinese Refugees in France', p. 295.

60 Author's interview with M. Wihm, Paris, 27 February 1996.

61 In Thion, 'Indochinese Refugees in France', p. 305.

62 Zig Layton-Henry, 'Britain: The would-be zero-immigration country,' in Wayne A. Cornelius, Philip L. Martin, and James F. Hollifield, eds, *Controlling Immigration: A Global Perspective* (Stanford: Stanford University Press, 1994).

63 *Ibid.*, p. 286.

64 See Peter R. Jones, *Vietnamese Refugees: A Study of Their Reception and Resettlement in the United Kingdom* (London: Home Office, 1982), p. 2.

65 Author's interview with Rosalind Finlay, London, 22 February 1996.

66 Author's interview with Margaret Kemp, London, 22 February 1996.

67 Jones, *Vietnamese Refugees*, p. 4.

68 Linda Hitchcox, 'Britain and the Vietnamese refugees', in Chantavanich and Reynolds, eds, *Indochinese Refugees: Asylum and Resettlement*, p. 316.

69 Jones, *Vietnamese Refugees*, p. 27.

70 Samantha Hale, 'The reception and resettlement of Vietnamese refugees in Britain', in Vaughan Robinson, ed., *The International Refugee Crisis: British and*

Canadian Responses (London: Macmillan Press, 1993), p. 279. In fact, more than 62 per cent of the refugees resettled in Britain as of 1982 were from North Vietnam and more than 70 per cent were ethnic Chinese, a reflection of the demographics in the Hong Kong camps in 1979–80. By contrast, of the Vietnamese who settled in Britain between 1975 and 1978, the majority were from the South and only about 18 per cent were ethnic Chinese.

71 Jones, *Vietnamese Refugees*, p. 18.

72 Vaughan Robinson, 'Up the creek without a paddle? Britain's boat people ten years on', *Geography,* Vol. 74, No. 325 (October 1989), p. 338.

73 Author's interview with Sandy Buchan, London, 21 February 1996.

74 Author's interview with Nhung Bui, London, 22 February 1996.

75 From The Government Reply to the Third Report from the Home Affairs Committee Session 1984–85 HC 72-I, *Refugees and Asylum, with Special Reference to the Vietnamese* (London: Her Majesty's Stationery Office, 1985), pp. 10, 16.

76 Karen Duke and Tony Marshall, *Vietnamese Refugees Since 1982* (London: HMSO Books, 1995).

77 Nancy Viviani, 'Indochinese refugees and Australia', in Chantavanich and Reynolds, *Indochinese Refugees: Asylum and Resettlement*, p. 171.

78 Stephen Castles and Mark J. Miller, *The Age of Migration: International Population Movements in the Modern World* (New York: The Guilford Press, 1993), p. 53.

79 Jerry Zubrzycki, 'International Migration in Australasia and the South Pacific,' in Mary M. Kritz, Charles B. Keely, and Silvano M. Tomasi, eds, *Global Trends in Migration: Theory and Research on International Population Movements* (New York: Center for Migration Studies, 1981), p. 160.

80 Frank Lewins and Judith Ly, *The First Wave: The Settlement of Australia's First Vietnamese Refugees* (Sydney: George Allen & Unwin, 1985), pp. 14–15.

81 Viviani, 'Indochinese refugees and Australia', p. 174.

82 Grant, *The Boat People*, p. 179.

83 Lester A. Sobel, ed., *Refugees: A World Report* (New York: Facts on File, 1979), p. 27.

84 Viviani, 'Indochinese refugees and Australia', p. 180.

85 Vaughan Robinson, 'North and South: resettling Vietnamese refugees in Australia and the UK', in Richard Black and Vaughan Robinson, *Geography and Refugees: Patterns and Processes of Change* (London and New York: Bellhaven Press, 1993). p. 141.

86 *Ibid*, p. 144.

87 Viviani, 'Indochinese refugees and Australia', pp. 183, 187, 189.

88 Zubrzycki, 'International migration in Australasia and the South Pacific', p. 177.

89 In Hawthorne, ed., *Refugee: The Vietnamese Experience*, pp. 307–8.

90 In Stephen B. Young, 'Who is a refugee? A theory of persecution', in Lydio F. Tomasi, ed., *In Defense of the Alien, Volume V, Refugees and Territorial Asylum* (New York: Center for Migration Studies, 1983), p. 38.

91 Author's interview with Evan Arthur, Canberra, 25 July 1996.

CHAPTER 7

Things Fall Apart

At a 1983 conference on the ethical and religious dimensions of US refugee policy, scholar Michael Teitelbaum noted four 'tragic choices' in refugee policy, all of which were born, directly or indirectly, out of the crisis in Southeast Asia. The first was one of definition. The 1951 Refugee Convention, Teitelbaum said, designated as refugees

> only those who have left their country owing to a well-founded fear of persecution for reasons of race, religion, nationality, membership in a particular group, or political opinion [and] … excludes tens of millions of equally desperate people fleeing the random and general violence of a civil war or an international war; people starving in a desperately poor country; or people fleeing the aftermath of a natural disaster such as an earthquake or drought.

Second was the question of who would benefit from a grant of permanent refuge. America's Refugee Act of 1980 had contemplated a 'normal flow' of 50,000. Tragic choice number two, Teitelbaum suggested, was 'how to allocate 50,000 – or even 200,000 or 500,000 – slots among 8 million deserving people'. Third was the matter of resources and the choices 'posed by a limited supply of resettlement slots and other resources in the context of virtually unlimited demand'. In 1982, the United States had spent more than $2.3 billion on various forms of assistance to refugees, more than three-quarters of which was spent on domestic resettlement of several hundred thousand refugees while the remainder helped to sustain millions in camps around the world.

The last choice involved what Teitelbaum called a 'moral hazard', borrowing a term from the banking industry. Insurance is necessary to cover risk but the availability of insurance then encourages risk-taking, some of which may be ill-advised and unhealthy. In a refugee context, to build a camp and offer food and medical care to a desperate population may encourage others to leave their homes in search of the same securities. More specifically, Teitelbaum applied the term to 'the apparent reality that explicit or implicit promise of admission as refugees stimulates its own refugee flows'. Or, as he put it in a comment that could have applied equally to

Vietnamese, Cubans or even Haitians, 'To guarantee admission to a high-wage economy to successful boat people is an invitation to them to risk their lives in boats.'[1]

In Southeast Asia, if it was flight itself that made one a refugee, and successful flight that virtually guaranteed admission overseas, especially in the case of the Vietnamese, then all one needed to be resettled from a first-asylum country, as one observer put it, was 'to be Vietnamese and alive'.[2] Those who said that the dangers of the journey were such that only a genuine refugee would face them were only restating the tautology. If to be a refugee was to flee one's country then to flee was to be a refugee.

From mid-1979 to mid-1982, a broad international consensus enabled the resettlement of more than 600,000 Indochinese refugees, half of those coming from camps in Thailand. In 1981, for the first time since the beginning of the refugee problem in Thailand, the number of refugees decreased by more than 70,000. By the end of the year, an estimated 200,000 border Cambodians had returned to their villages. Six refugee camps in Thailand closed. As the sense of emergency receded, however, the debate sharpened considerably as to the question of definition, numerical allocations and the level of resources committed to Indochinese resettlement. The sharpest divide of all pitted those who saw large-scale resettlement as a hazard and those who defended its moral imperative.

In July 1981 the influential *Far Eastern Economic Review* published a cover story which stated, 'The high resettlement quotas and the ease with which [Indochinese] refugees pass through the pipeline are blamed as the principal pull factors encouraging and perpetuating the exodus.' One UNHCR official was quoted as saying that 'This is no longer a refugee program. It now more closely resembles an immigration service.' Backing up its claim that 'there is a growing conviction among refugee agency officials that the majority of those now leaving Indochina are not political refugees but economic migrants', the article cited a confidential report from a refugee agency in Hong Kong and a survey conducted by the US consulate in Songkhla, both of which found that a majority of people had left Vietnam for economic reasons.[3]

The authors of the *Review* article went still further, suggesting that 'cynical strategists' in Washington 'are not only manipulating the US public but also exploiting the refugees'. US officials, wrote Patrick Smith and Derek Davies, were encouraging the exodus 'partly to leech able-bodied people away from the task of reconstructing Vietnam but mostly to provide living evidence of the hatefulness of the oppressive Hanoi regime'.[4]

The article struck a raw nerve in the refugee community. The following week, departing US Ambassador to Thailand, Morton Abramowitz, fired back, saying that 'the notion that the United States has sought to bring out refugees to destabilize Vietnam is nonsense. Sheer nonsense.... In fact, people could argue we are helping to stabilize those regimes by taking away the people who are flowing. If you kept those people in those countries, they would perhaps be a source of dissidence.' As to the question of why people continued to leave, Abramowitz told a Thai newspaper

> This is a problem that has bothered me for a year ... because many people asserted that there are many people coming out for economic reasons.... Getting at the notion of motivation in countries like Vietnam is exceedingly difficult ... I mean, for example, a person whose father was in the South Vietnamese Army and is dead and the son can't find a good job because he has a bad class background and he leaves Vietnam, is he leaving for economic reasons or for political reasons? A person who avoids the draft trying to avoid Cambodia, does he leave for economic purposes or for political purposes? Everybody knows that the Vietnamese Army gives favoritism to northerners rather than southerners. Is that a political reason? Economic reason? I'm not saying there isn't a problem. I think there may very well be a problem. But the point I'm making is that it's very difficult to get at this.[5]

The problem was, indeed, difficult to get at. The definitional questions were knotty enough but, even assuming a clear distinction could be made between a *bona fide* refugee and an economic migrant, it was not at all clear whether safe and humane solutions could be found for both groups, or what the consequences would be of trying to do so. A British journalist, Alan Dawson, offered a solution for ending the boat flow, though he admitted it would be 'heart-rending at the beginnning':

> Since most boat people get their technical information from the Voice of America and the BBC, these media would have to be counted on to spread the word that effective immediately, no more boat people would be accepted for immigration abroad. The US 7th Fleet would have to be pulled away from the boat people routes. And it is possible – no, likely – that some boat people would have to be sent back quickly to Vietnam, after officials had examined arrivals to ensure there were no special-case political refugees. True immigration and family reunion cases could then be decided as they are for any nationality, instead of awarding Indochinese special status.... But in fairly short order, the flow of boat people would virtually halt.[6]

The boat flow might well have ended if resettlement had been categorically denied to the Vietnamese boat people but, given the years of virtually automatic status and resettlement, it may not have halted all that quickly. Dawson's proposal, moreover, overlooked several critical issues. First, if resettlement truly were ended, it would strand all *bona fide* refugees in the camps with nowhere to go. If resettlement were resumed for 'special case political refugees,' then the boat flow probably would have resumed as well. Second, the return of Vietnamese migrants would have required both the consent of the Vietnamese government and the acquiescence of the United States, both of which were highly unlikely prospects at the time. Third, and most important, the ASEAN countries' grant of first asylum was conditional upon expeditious resettlement of the refugees. Would they have granted time to seek alternative solutions or would abandonment of resettlement pledges have been answered with more push-backs?

Vietnam was insisting that none who left were refugees but none were welcome back; the first asylum countries were saying that most were not refugees but should be resettled nonetheless, while the resettlement countries could find no consensus amongst themselves, or even internally, as to how to respond to the continuing exodus. Their solution was to cut back admissions numbers, tighten criteria, lengthen the waiting period in camps and hope that these measures, in conjunction with the 'humane deterrence' policies being enacted in the region, gradually would reduce the outflow, particularly of boat people from Vietnam.

That certainly was the plan of some within the US government, most notably the State Department. As Shepard Lowman told a Congressional committee in October 1981,

> the central goal in the implementation and management of the US program will be to utilize only that admission authority required to maintain first asylum and to use the forthcoming months to develop a system of humane deterrence which could act to bring down the overall requirements of the Indochinese refugee program over time to much more manageable levels.[7]

This line of reasoning appeared to accept the idea that levels of resettlement, to some degree, were linked to the level of outflows and, if properly modulated, resettlement commitments could be just sufficient to preserve first asylum but not so generous as to spur new arrivals. What the State Department plan did not countenance, however, was the notion that resettlement should be reduced because the percentage of real refugees was falling. Lowman stated that 'There is, of course, some substance underlying the complaints about refugee motivations. No refugee flow is purely political [and] the Indochinese situation is no exception.' But he went on to note the 'inextricable linkages between political status and economic deprivation in a country undergoing communist revolution such as those in Vietnam, Laos, and Kampuchea – in short the commonplace of political persecution through economic means'.

The great majority of the Indochinese arrivals, then, were still of concern to the State Department and even if they were not in high priority categories, their alternatives to resettlement were slim and unappealing. Expectations of voluntary return to Vietnam, according to Lowman were 'minuscule' and as for local settlement,

> the problem with the Indochinese refugee flow is that most of these refugees are viewed as totally unacceptable for local settlement by the countries of first asylum. Those countries feel sufficiently strongly that they have been prepared to engage in sometimes brutal acts of forcible repatriation or to push off unseaworthy boats back out to sea.[8]

If the State Department saw no alternative but to continue resettlement, albeit at reduced levels, the INS saw things quite differently. In their view, the ongoing, automatic admission of Indochinese was not only short-sighted but essentially illegal, contravening the terms of the new Refugee

Act of 1980. By late 1980, senior INS officials were insisting that the new refugee legislation required them to carry out case-by-case determinations of eligibility. It was time, INS felt, to assert their role in the admissions process.

In early 1981, for the first time, INS interviewers in the region began to deny refugee status to significant numbers of Indochinese applicants. The State Department and the Joint Voluntary Agencies, private organizations working under contract to the State Department to do refugee case documentation, protested publicly. INS backed off slightly, calling the non-approvals 'deferrals' rather than outright rejections but the problem continued. As Jerry Tinker, a long-time aide to Senator Edward Kennedy, noted, 'the issue was allowed to roll out of control, to tie up the bureaucracy for months, to cripple the functioning of the refugee program, and to confuse all concerned in the field'. What he called the 'petty squabbling' between State Department officials and the INS had reached a point that they 'now act as if they were not working for the same government, much less under the same program'.[9]

The problem was resolved temporarily in July 1981 when US Secretary of State Al Haig and Attorney-General William French-Smith of the Justice Department signed a joint letter restoring the *status quo* for Indochinese. Seizing the opportunity, the US resettlement machinery processed 40,000 Indochinese in three months before the fiscal year came to an end in September 1981. But INS was not willing to concede defeat. 'Their attitude toward State', according to Dennis Grace, former JVA representative in Thailand was, 'You've won a battle but not the war.'[10]

For the next few months, Grace said, 'Everyone was expecting a fight but there was no fight. The number of denials [was] smaller for Vietnamese. INS was trying to decide where to take a stand. Ironically, the issue did not turn on the Vietnamese. It turned on the Cambodians.' In March 1982, INS interviewers suddenly began taking two to three hours per interview in the predominantly Hmong camp of Chiang Khong, rather than the more typical 20 to 30 minutes. Processing slowed to a trickle. 'The US', suggested Grace, 'was making a statement that it would not take all these Indochinese. The talk worldwide had been of the boat people. The first signs of trouble showed with the Hmong. But when the hammer fell, it fell on the Cambodians.'

In May 1982, authorization had come through to process some 23,000 Cambodians remaining in Kamput. As Grace recollected, 'State Department was thinking, "We've got 23,000 people to push through the pipeline." But INS was saying, "No, we've got a new way of going about this. Here is where we are going to draw the line in the sand."' At the beginning of 1982, INS approval rates had been near 100 per cent for Cambodian applicants. From May to August, however, they fluctuated from a low of 30 to a high of only 60 per cent. When State Department officials protested, INS responded with more slowdowns and higher denial rates. State and Justice once more were locked in a bitter fight for control of the Indochinese admissions programme.

Grace gives much of the credit to Senator Mark Hatfield from Oregon for turning the tide and resolving the crisis. A liberal Republican in a conservative era, Hatfield did not carry great influence in the White House but he happened to be chairman of the Senate Appropriations Committee, which exercised control over the federal purse-strings. Hatfield wrote to President Ronald Reagan and to Attorney-General French-Smith, urging them to redress the problem. The Attorney-General visited Thailand in November 1982 and personally interviewed several of the cases. 'Before French-Smith left Bangkok,' said Grace, 'the decision was made to replace the whole INS team. Immediately, it was over. Approvals went up. Everyone was gone within two months. As a trade-off, two senior State Department officials were replaced within six months.'[11]

In October and November 1982, INS issued the 'Kamput cables', which were essentially processing guidelines for the Thailand team. The State Department later reinforced its position in favour of presumptive eligibility for Indochinese by securing a Presidential directive in May 1993, which called upon the Attorney-General

> to determine whether there are categories of persons who, under the Refugee Act of 1980, share common characteristics that identify them as targets of persecution in a particular country. This review should focus initially on the following categories for Indochinese refugees: those who fled Pol Pot because of occurrences during the Pol Pot regime, former members of the military, those with close relatives in the United States, and persons who refuse to work with the new regime in Cambodia.[12]

In August 1983, INS issued 'Worldwide Guidelines for Overseas Refugee Processing' which identified category groups as targets of persecution in Vietnam, Laos, and Cambodia. Among these were former officials of the pre-1975, non-communist governments, former members of the military, ethnic Chinese, Catholics, Buddhist monks, Hmong, re-education camp prisoners, and persons with close relatives in the United States.

The years 1981–83, noted Dennis Grace, 'was a crucial period for the US programme. It resolved the Kamput crisis, issued the Worldwide Guidelines, and put the programme in good stead for having reasonable generosity.' But it also marked what he called the 'first break point, the first hint that this was not going to be an open-ended programme.'

In September 1981, the United States resettled more than 20,000 Indochinese in a single month, the highest figure in the history of the programme. Worldwide resettlement of Indochinese exceeded 25,000 for the month but then dropped to half that amount in October. Throughout 1982, resettlement from Southeast Asia totalled under 75,000, less than half of the previous year's totals. As one observer noted at the time, 'The traditional refugee resettlement countries – such as the United States, France, Canada, and Australia – are nearing the end of an extraordinary period of resettlement.'[13] But was resettlement declining because the boat arrivals were dropping or was it the other way around?

Thailand, for one, could not be sure, but it watched with what must have been satisfaction as Vietnamese arrivals dropped from 18,000 in 1981 to one-third that amount the next year. Thai humane deterrence policies, according to Dennis Grace, 'broke the link between arrivals and the automatic shift to Panat Nikhom [processing centre] for resettlement. Obviously, the word got back to Vietnam immediately that Thailand was not taking people, so they went south to Malaysia.'[14]

There were other factors at work as well in the drop in Vietnamese arrivals in Thailand, besides the moratorium on resettlement. Piracy was still rampant in the Gulf of Siam and word was also getting back to Vietnam about the risk of killings, beatings, rammings, and rape at the hands of sea-going marauders. And, at least on a selective basis, Thai authorities had reinstated push-offs. One confidential UNHCR report in February 1982 noted that 'The vast majority of Vietnamese boat refugees have been allowed to land in Thailand. In the period May 1981 to January 1982, however, sixteen boats were pushed off. Of these, thirteen re-landed either in Thailand or Malaysia and obtained asylum. Three, with a total of 159 persons on board, are still missing. Their occupants are now presumed dead.'

Anti-Piracy

Piracy in the waters of the South China Sea, wrote D.G.E. Hall in his *History of Southeast Asia*, 'was an evil so old, so widespread, and with so many facets that it baffled efforts [to suppress it] for many years, for it was an honorable profession which was connived at, promoted, or even directly engaged in by the highest potentates.... And nowhere else in the world is geography so conducive to piracy.'[15]

Despite the heroics of individuals like UNHCR's Ted Schweitzer, attacks on Vietnamese boat people had continued undiminished. In 1981, the first year that it kept statistics, UNHCR reported a total of 1,122 pirate attacks on 349 out of 452 Vietnamese boats arriving in Thailand that year. Each boat had been attacked an average of 3.2 times and 77 per cent of all arriving boats had been attacked at least once. A total of 881 people were listed as dead or missing, 578 women had been raped and 228 people (virtually all of them women and girls) had been abducted.

Typically, pirates were fishermen from southern Thailand who turned renegade upon occasion, sometimes committing 'only' robbery, sometimes much worse. It was not an honorable profession, perhaps, but it was practised by enough people within the fishing industry – one estimate in 1982 was that two per cent of the Thai fishing fleet engaged regularly in piracy – that the perpetrators were well protected by their peers.[16] It was felt by some that Thai authorities also were turning a blind eye to the outrages in so far as the pirate attacks served to deter at least some boats from coming to Thailand.

In May 1980, UNHCR donated an unarmed speedboat to the Thai government in a token effort to bolster sea patrolling. Meanwhile, some of the international mercy ships that had been serving the island camps in Malaysia and Indonesia began to redeploy themselves from resupply operations to rescue missions. Most prominent among these were the West German vessel, *Cap Anamur* and the *Ile de Lumière*, supported by Médicins sans Frontières, which together rescued hundreds of boat people in their years of operation. One former Vietnam veteran, Colonel Jack Bailey, launched Operation Rescue, whose entire fleet consisted of one retrofitted Second World War-vintage hulk, dubbed the *Sri Akuna*. These private efforts lacked nothing for zeal but they were piecemeal, unsophisticated operations and could not begin to cover the 18,000 square miles of high seas where the pirates ranged.

Responding to mounting international outrage and a demand for action, in February 1981 the US government funded a $2 million bilateral anti-piracy effort, under which the Royal Thai Navy carried out air–sea surveillance, using two twin-engined O-2 spotter aircraft and a Thai coastguard cutter. Within eight months, however, the programme was out of money and under fire for its over-commitment to air surveillance. Stephen Solarz, then head of the Asia subcommittee for the House Committee on Foreign Affairs and a leader in promoting anti-piracy efforts, said, 'I went up in one of those spotter planes and immediately I saw the idea was ludicrous. It was like looking for a needle in a haystack. Even if one happened to spot an attack taking place, there would have been no way to stop it.'[17]

The initial programme was not altogether a failure. As a result of sea- and land-based initiatives, Thai authorities were able to arrest 25 fishermen on charges of piracy, seize five vessels, and assist in the rescue of 180 boat people under attack. But, clearly, much more needed to be done. In August 1981, ICRC convened a meeting of some twenty potential donor states in Geneva and, by the end of the year, UNHCR had launched an international appeal for a $3.67 million anti-piracy programme.

More delays followed, as UNHCR and foreign governments sought to persuade Squadron Leader Prasong Soonsiri, then head of Thailand's National Security Council, to accept less than an all-or-nothing demand for $33 million. It was not until 23 June 1982 that the Anti-Piracy Arrangement (APA) was officially begun with $3.6 million in funding from 12 countries. This enabled the Thai Navy to purchase two additional fast patrol craft, while one boat was given to the Marine Police along with three converted fishing trawlers to serve as decoy boats. The Harbour Department also received a boat and a computer to begin the arduous task of registering the 13,000 boats in Thailand's fishing fleet. The Thai Navy, which headed the operations from its Anti-Piracy Unit in Songkhla, continued to fly the two spotter planes.

UNHCR, which had begun keeping statistics on piracy incidents since February 1981, noted that the percentage of boats arriving in Thailand that had been attacked in 1982 had dropped from 77 per cent the previous year to 64 per cent. The percentage of people dead or missing as a result of these attacks, however, had climbed from 5.7 per cent in 1981 to 7.2 per cent in 1982. The following year showed similar trends. A 1983 assessment conducted for UNHCR by three international maritime experts concluded that the programme

> has not produced spectacular results for the Navy. It is difficult to measure the value of the deterrence factor, which may be significant, as in spite of some statistical uncertainties, there seems to be a downward trend in the percentage of refugee boats reputedly attacked. But so far the unit can only claim two qualified successes. A patrol aircraft successfully foiled a piracy (although later on the same day the same refugee boat was pirated) and on one occasion as a result of the decoy boat ploy, arrests were made but the charges were dismissed at the subsequent hearings.[18]

The team recommended doing away with the decoy efforts. It concluded that the spotter aircraft, however, were making a 'significant contribution' in terms of deterrence though they needed to be coordinated with the movements of the patrol craft on the water. 'Suppression of piracy', the team's report also noted, 'requires deterrence on land as well as deterrence at sea. Essential elements of deterrence on land are police investigations and court actions leading to convictions.'

In the case of claims involving Vietnamese refugees, the team assessment acknowledged that police work was hampered by a 'host of reasons, including language difficulties, access to witnesses (who might be in Malaysia), reluctance of witnesses to testify, insufficient police resources … and difficulties with the Thai script and boat recognition.'[19] Both despite and because of these special problems, the team recommended an increase in the allocations for the police and for the Harbour Department's registration activities. 'Pirates are rarely if ever going to be caught in the act in the Gulf of Thailand,' the team concluded, 'they are going to be caught ashore.'

In April 1982, several months before the UNHCR programme got under way, Congressman Solarz held a hearing on the anti-piracy problem, at which several private witnesses both vented their frustrations at the slow pace of the international response and proposed their own, sometimes radical, solutions. The Citizens Commission on Indochinese Refugees, sponsored by the IRC, wanted the United States to resume its own surveillance flights and called for the formation of an international task force of ships to patrol sea lanes in the Gulf of Thailand. Colonel Jack Bailey's Operation Rescue proposed stationing the *Sri Akuna* in the centre of the Thai fishing fleet and supplying 2-way radios to 1,000 selected fishing trawlers. Ted Schweitzer, who had left UNHCR and founded the SEA Rescue Foundation, sought $8 million to deploy twenty wooden-hulled fishing boats and two large steel-hulled ships to create a 'piracy-free zone' stretching from the limits of Vietnamese territorial waters to the shores of the first asylum countries.[20]

All of the private witnesses assured Congress that their proposals, even if they proved fully effective in combating piracy, would not add significantly to the numbers of people leaving Vietnam. The US State Department, for one, was sceptical. Richard Vine, then director of the Bureau for Refugee Programs, noted 'the irony that a solution to piracy which tended in any way to encourage or permit a larger boat exodus could present the Thai, the other countries of first asylum, and other resettlement nations with quite difficult technical problems and quite difficult political problems.'[21] The Reagan Administration was prepared to support the UNHCR anti-piracy programme but it was cool to the grander schemes of international flotillas and 'piracy-free zones', preferring instead to support an expansion of the Orderly Departure Programme as an alternative to clandestine flight.

The US Congress authorized an additional $10 million for anti-piracy efforts in 1984 and 1985 over and above the US contributions already allocated to UNHCR. Most of the money, however, eventually was channelled through UNHCR, with significant amounts going to a fund to reimburse ship owners for the cost of rescuing boat refugees. At one point, Solarz presented Prasong with an idea to equip to all Thai fishing boats with 2-way radios. 'If they phoned in the location of a Vietnamese boat and it reached shore safely,' Solarz later recalled, 'they would get a bounty. Prasong said, "Then everyone would come to Thailand." Essentially what he was saying is, "We want to deter these boats."'[22]

New York Times journalist Henry Kamm had won a Pulitzer Prize in 1978 for his graphic and incisive reporting on the push-backs, piracy and the Indochinese refugee crisis. On 4 July 1984, the *New York Times* carried his story 'Vietnam's refugees sail into heart of darkness', which noted that 'although the number of refugee boats, and thus the number of attacks, is in general declining … [it] is certain that piracy against the Vietnamese "boat people" has never been more savage than now.'[23] Of the UNHCR officials whom Kamm interviewed, only one agreed to be mentioned by name, that being the High Commissioner for Refugees himself, Poul Hartling, who was quoted as saying 'Even if the quantity has gone down, the quality of the attacks, if you can say that, is going up…. What we hear is even more horrifying than in the past.' The reports, Hartling said, 'tell of cruelty, brutality and inhumanity that go beyond my imagination. The refugees are attacked with knives and clubs. There is murder, robbery and rape, everything in this world.'

Kamm also quoted Hartling as saying that 'some people in Thailand have a clear position that refugees should not be there and should be kept away'. He named the former Deputy Prime Minister and Foreign Minister, Thanat Khoman, whose opposition to asylum was a matter of record. 'It is clear the Thais are very touchy,' said Hartling, 'If you say bad things, they react very badly.' Thanat Khoman did react, writing a letter to the editor to the effect that 'this shameless press campaign is nothing but a blackmail'. Hartling, he said, 'should realize that he has committed a serious breach of his obligations as an international official and, as such, has debased the Organization'.[24] If subsequent Thai press accounts are correct, Hartling issued a denial that he had made such statements, prompting the secretary-general of the National Security Council, Prasong Soonsiri, to blast Henry Kamm for 'irresponsible journalism'.[25]

From 1984 onward, the UNHCR anti-piracy programme began to shift increasingly toward land-based operations with Thai police units and harbour officials registering fishing boats, photographing crews, and conducting public awareness campaigns on the penalties for piracy. UNHCR played a key role in linking piracy victims with police and, ultimately, prosecutors. UNHCR officials developed standard forms for reporting attacks regionwide, monitored court trials, arranged witness transfers from abroad, and provided interpretation services through the course of investigation, arrest, and trial.

From 1984 to the end of 1991, Thai officials arrested and charged 161 suspects for piracy offences. A total of 106 defendants were found guilty of one or more charges and given sentences ranging from probation to life imprisonment. As an added deterrent measure, the Thai navy and marine police targeted sea and air patrols in areas of frequent attacks in the southern Gulf of Thailand and maintained an observation post at Koh Kra, the island that was once a notorious pirate lair.

According to Henry Domzalski, UNHCR's first anti-piracy coordinator in Thailand from 1981 to 1984, the 'reduction in carnage took several years'. The number of attacks did decrease, from 349 in 1981 to 66 in 1984. The percentage of boats attacked likewise declined, from 77 per cent in 1981 to 36 per cent in 1984. Upon further analysis, however, this latter statistic revealed a more troubling reality. Attacks along Thailand's eastern coastline had indeed dropped from 65 to 14 per cent in four years. But in the south, where attacks were both more frequent and more vicious, the percentage of boats attacked dropped from 80 to 64 per cent by 1984. 'There were some arrests,' said Domzalski, 'but it was still a horror show out there – wanton killings, rape, abductions. We had people with gold fillings torn out of their mouths; infants thrown in the water in front of their mothers; people dipped in fishing nets into the sea until they drowned; people attacked with harpoons and ice picks. The tales of rapes – they passed girls around like bees finding a field full of flowers.'[26]

In 1988, even as the numbers continued to fall, the level of violence of the attacks began to rise alarmingly, with more than 500 people reported dead or missing, against 95 the previous year. In 1989, the number of dead or missing climbed above 750. Rapes and abductions spiralled upward as well. In August 1989, Vietnamese survivors of one attack told how Thai pirates had seized and plundered their boat. According to a UNHCR official who debriefed the survivors, the pirates 'brought up men singly from the hold, clubbed them and then killed them with axes.... Ramming, sinking and killing of Vietnamese in the water followed.' In all, 71 people perished, including 15 women and 11 children.[27]

Why the horrifying rise in violence? Although boat flows had been steadily increasing for several years in the region since 1987, attack rates had continued to fall. In part, it seemed that the very success of the anti-piracy effort was to blame. Anti-piracy experts suggested that with the growing sophistication of investigative techniques, coupled with higher rates of arrests and convictions, two things were happening. First, most of the occasional opportunists had been scared off, leaving behind a hard core of professional criminals. Second, these sea marauders were taking greater pains to leave no witnesses.

But the governments of Thailand and Malaysia, for all the credit they deserved in combating piracy, had also helped to contribute to the surge of violence in the gulf. First Thailand in 1988, followed by Malaysia in 1989, reintroduced systematic boat push-backs as an instrument of state policy. One Thai Marine Police official, whose salary at the time was covered by the anti-piracy programme, admitted that he had assisted in several push-backs while out on patrol.[28] In such a climate, it was not surprising that criminal violence would flourish anew.

The Breakdown of the Orderly Departure Programme

The seven-point Memorandum of Understanding that was signed on 30 May 1979 between UNHCR and Vietnam established two fundamental guidelines for what came to be known as the Orderly Departure Programme (ODP): the programme would be for 'family reunion and other humanitarian cases', and selection would be made 'on the basis of lists prepared by the Vietnamese government and ... the receiving countries'. Within these two brief clauses, however, lay worlds of ambiguity and potential discord. Was the priority of ODP to reunite families or to offer migration opportunities to humanitarian cases, especially those who had faced persecution or discrimination in Vietnam? As for the lists, all was well if they matched, but what if they did not? How would the parties find room for compromise?

France, like most of the European countries, regarded ODP as a refugee programme, meaning the admissions numbers counted against annual refugee quotas, although most of the people were resettled on the basis of family links. Canada, Australia and New Zealand regarded ODP strictly as an immigration programme, with priority going to cases of immediate family reunion. Though the high hopes and expectations with which the Orderly Departure Programme began soon gave way to long and painstaking negotiations on processing guidelines, most of these countries had the benefit of clear programmatic guidelines and a consular presence in Vietnam. Alone among the forty countries that came to participate in the ODP programme, the United States lacked consular relations with Vietnam; although its programme grew to become the largest, its procedures were ever the most labyrinthine.

In late 1979, the United States and Vietnam exchanged their first lists. The US list contained 4,000 names, mostly people with family links or pre-1975 employees of the US government. The Vietnamese list had 21,000 names, most of them ethnic Chinese, leading some officials to dub it the 'Cholon phone book', after Saigon's Chinatown. The overlap was fewer than one dozen names at first and it took nearly eighteen months of wrangling and delays to clear a total of 1,700 people for departure.[29]

Lack of diplomatic ties between the two countries prevented US government staff from living and working in Vietnam, so work had to be carried out by a private voluntary agency official under secondment to UNHCR. The first such person was Michael Myers from CWS, whose parents had been missionaries in Vietnam. Myers, who spoke fluent Vietnamese and had been working with boat people in Malaysia, spent a year in Hanoi hammering out details for a US–Vietnam program. The result was an October 1980 *aide memoire* which elaborated on the original seven-point agreement. 'Most signficant,' according to one study, 'was the initial premise ... that the US would accept for movement to the US essentially all persons whose names appeared on both the US and the SRV lists.'[30] US officials spoke positively of soon reaching more than 1,000 departures per month.

Myers and CWS pulled out of ODP in October to be replaced by Tom Malia and the USCC (who later transferred JVA responsibilities to the International Catholic Migration Commission). Malia actually began exit interviews of the first batch of people whose names were on the 'joint working list' in November 1980. Under ODP guidelines, the United States was prepared to admit, as immigrants, anyone with an approved immigration petition so long as they were not otherwise excludable. The refugee component of the programme established three basic categories for admission. Category I included family members of persons in the United States who were not currently eligible for immigrant visas. Category II comprised former employees of the US government and Category III included other persons closely associated with the US presence prior to 1975. This third category later was expanded to include Amerasians and their close family members.[31]

'At first there was no agreement on who would be eligible,' Tom Malia said. 'We made lists of family reunion and former employees and the Vietnamese made lists of ethnic Chinese and people with medical problems. We didn't accept their medical cases and they didn't accept our former employees. There was a lot of posturing on each side. Nobody left at all for the United States until December 1980.' Although the State Department was not particularly happy about it, the US programme remained 'heavily Chinese for a long time', Malia said. 'The "Cholon phone book" was people who had paid their departure fees but got stuck when the moratorium on [quasi-legal] departures was signed. Some people literally were sitting on boats. Gradually, they began to impose sanctions on leaving.'[32]

But as clandestine departures dropped, orderly departures gradually rose. In 1980, the first full year of ODP operations, more than 71,400 Vietnamese boat people arrived in first asylum countries while only 4,700 left safely and legally. By 1982, boat arrivals had slipped to 43,800 while ODP departures exceeded 10,000 for the year. In 1984, for the first time, total ODP movements (29,100) actually exceeded regional boat arrivals (24,865) and US processing finally achieved the magic number of 1,000 per month. Five years of international cooperation, concluded a study by the USCC, 'have proved the sceptics wrong. Seemingly insurmountable operational obstacles have been removed, and more Vietnamese emigrate to other countries via ODP than by any other means, including illegal ones'. Although the effect of the programme as a direct deterrent to clandestine departure was hard to gauge, the study concluded that 'it is clear that the UNHCR program for orderly departures has supplanted illegal boat escape as the predominant means of exit from Vietnam.'[33] By the middle of 1986, more than 115,000 Vietnamese had travelled safely and legally to receiving countries, including more than 50,000 to the United States.

But despite the programme's successes, many issues remained unresolved. For the US government, these could be summed up in one word: reciprocity. By late 1982, US ODP officials had come to feel that submitting a single massive list of tens of thousands of names to the Vietnamese authorities was increasingly unworkable. Beginning in October of that year, US officials began to supplement the main list – known in official parlance as the Visa Entry Working List – with a much smaller one, which became known as the Short Priority List. This rarely encompassed more than a few hundred names and represented groups of particular priority to the US programme: American citizens, current and former re-education camp prisoners, Amerasian children, etc.

The Vietnamese gradually grew more responsive to these short lists but not enough to satisfy some American policy makers and opinion shapers. Criticisms were heard from various quarters – Congress, the media, and the State Department – that the United States was taking too many of 'their cases' and not enough of 'our cases'. Roughly speaking, this meant too many extended family reunion cases and not enough high-priority groups. Pressed to define reciprocity at a Congressional hearing in 1986, then director of the Bureau for Refugee Programmes, James Purcell, said

> I say that our 50 per cent or whatever share should include family reunification through immigrant visas; it should include fiancees of American citizens; it should include former US government employees; it should include others of concern to the United States which include employees of the pre-1975 government in South Vietnam, employees of US firms, Vietnamese who studied in the US, or others with close ties. It should include Amerasians and families, and political prisoners and their families.[34]

In other words, the US government wanted more people who were clearly immigrants, and thus could enter without charge to the refugee admissions quotas or budget, and more who were clearly refugees, particularly those who had identified themselves with US interests prior to 1975. What it was getting too many of, Purcell suggested, were family reunion cases in the lower preference categories for immigration: married children, siblings, grandparents and the like. ODP guidelines had always permitted those whose visa petitions were not current to avoid the long delays and enter the United States immediately as refugees, although they may have lacked any compelling claim as victims of persecution.

In the middle of the 1980s, then, the glass seemed both half empty and half full. Roughly the same number of people were leaving Vietnam via the ODP as were doing so by boat. ODP numbers were going up and the boat flows were going down but, from the perspective of many governments and many in UNHCR as well, the mix of people in the resettlement stream was troubling. There was a place in the system for immigrants and a place for refugees, but what to do with the immigrants being counted as refugees?

As the US debated the issues of priority and reciprocity, it began to defer final decisions on a growing number of ODP applicants. Previously, once an interview was completed in Vietnam, would-be emigrants were given exit clearances and could look forward to a fairly prompt approval and departure. By early 1985, however, the Vietnamese authorities had begun to voice concern over a growing backlog of people who had been interviewed by US officials but not yet approved or rejected. In April, the Ministry of Foreign Affairs sent a letter to the UNHCR delegation in Hanoi, noting that 'there are about 17,000 pending persons ... already interviewed by the US side but to whom entry visas have not been granted yet.' The letter called on the United States to accept 1,200 to 1,300 people per month from among those already interviewed.[35] Later in the year, France, Canada and Australia likewise were chided for growing backlogs in their own caseloads.

In December 1985, with the US backlog grown to 22,000, Vietnam announced a moratorium on new interviewing until the problem was resolved. In January 1986, the last two US interviewers in Ho Chi Minh City were asked to leave the country. That same month, the United States imposed what amounted to a virtual embargo on the movement of refugee family reunification cases. Some State Department officials complained bitterly of Vietnam's unilateral and unfriendly act but, as Malia put it, 'It was our fault. The Vietnamese were not being unreasonable.'[36] Wherever the fault lay, it was clear that the ODP was in a state of unpredictable flux. But no one could be sure whether it was stalling out or just shifting gears.

Throughout the remainder of 1986 and most of the following year, as technical talks dragged on, the United States and other countries whittled away at their backlogs. ODP movements continued but, after a steady increase since the beginning of the programme, the numbers began falling, from nearly 30,000 in 1985, to 18,000 in 1986, to under 13,000 in 1987. By late in the second year of the ODP moratorium, refugee watchers in

Southeast Asia were tracking a troubling new development: after a seven-year decline, Vietnamese boat arrivals were on the rise.

The Build-up to the Comprehensive Plan of Action

In the spring of 1983, Eugene Douglas, the US Coordinator for Refugee Affairs and the Reagan Administration's senior refugee official, issued an invitation to a select group of industrialized nations to attend a meeting in Hawaii. The structure was informal and the topic was Indochinese resettlement. Australia, Canada and Japan accepted the invitation to what became the first meeting of the Informal Consultative Group (ICG).[37] France and Great Britain, at least for the time being, declined.

The US delegation wanted to limit the discussion to the question of resettlement. In April 1982, the United States had decided to stop interviewing any refugee applicants who lacked a tie – be it family, professional or political – to the country. In July that year, Australia had eliminated group-basis determination of refugee status and shifted to case-by-case determinations. As these were the two largest resettlement programmes at the time, the result had been a steady build-up of people in the camps who either had been rejected outright or simply were not getting interviewed.[38]

But if Douglas wanted to talk about resettlement and sharing the burden, the Australian and Canadian delegations had a much broader agenda in mind. According to one participant, 'By 1983, many governments were asking, "When is this going to end?" Australia and Canada were saying it was time to seek alternatives to open-ended resettlement while preserving asylum.'[39] But what were the alternatives? The asylum countries were not offering local settlement, Vietnam was not willing to take people back (assuming any were willing to go) and the United States would not countenance involuntary returns.

The Honolulu meeting produced no agreements. Indeed, commented Ian Simington, who attended as a UNHCR observer but had formerly served as a senior immigration official for Australia, 'We all came away from Hawaii fairly confused. The only concrete result was that Japan committed large sums of money to the Indochinese programme.'[40] But the participants agreed to keep meeting informally to engage in discussions and consensus building even if they reached no decisions. 'For several years,' said one observer, 'this is the way the meetings went: Australia would say, "These are not refugees. Something must be done." Canada would agree completely and do nothing about it. The US would agree at some level but also do nothing.'[41] Gradually, the debate grew more focused as the sense of urgency mounted. In 1985, at a meeting in Canberra, the Australian delegation produced a paper that sketched out the concept of a regional screening programme linked to repatriation for the screened-out. The Canadians endorsed it but the Americans were opposed.

UNHCR attended the ICG meetings as an observer while engaged in its own search for solutions. In May 1985, UNHCR's Director of International Protection, Michel Moussali, asked the General Legal Section and the Bureau for Asia to conduct an assessment of recent boat arrivals with a threefold objective – to determine who was leaving Vietnam, what were their reasons, and what were the 'refugee characteristics' of this movement.[42] Over a two-month period, UNHCR protection officers interviewed 466 heads of family of newly arriving Vietnamese boat people in the five principal countries of first asylum – Hong Kong, Indonesia, Malaysia, Philippines and Thailand. During the first six months of 1985, a total of 12,787 Vietnamese asylum seekers arrived in these countries, so the 917 people covered by the UNHCR interviews made up 7 per cent of arrivals during that period. The confidential report, drafted by Anders B. Johnsson, reached the following conclusions about the composition of the flow:

• By far the 'largest single identifiable group' (comprising 51 per cent of the cases and 33 per cent of all individuals) were a group the report called 'students'. These were 'unmarried persons who in 1975 were below 15 years. They have not started a family of their own and have left the country on their own, i.e., not accompanied by their parents.'

• The second group (representing 10 per cent of all cases and 10 per cent of all individuals) was 'persons closely linked to the previous regime', that is, 'high level military, police and civilians who were connected with the former Republic of South Vietnam. Many of these persons, but not all, have been in re-education camps.'

• Fishermen and others involved in the fishing industry made up 12 per cent of all cases interviewed but, because the families tended to be larger, comprised 22 per cent of all individuals. Similarly, farmers represented 9 per cent of the cases and 14 per cent of all individuals.

• Professionals – teachers, architects, doctors, nurses and administrators – accounted for only 3 per cent of all cases and individuals, while those in non-professional occupations – drivers, carpenters, mechanics, bicycle repairmen, welders, bricklayers, etc – and traders represented 16 per cent of all cases and 18 per cent of individuals. 'The persons involved in the non-professional occupations', the report noted, 'very often ... were people who, being young and having no particular profession, were drafted into the army of the Republic of South Vietnam and who were later demobilized in 1975 in the main cities of the south. In an effort to remain in those cities they took to any profession that could provide an earning for them and their families.'[43]

The great majority of Vietnamese boat people – 84 per cent in all – originated from the Saigon area and other southern locations, Johnsson's report found. They travelled mainly to Malaysia and Indonesia and, to a lesser extent, Thailand. The remaining 16 per cent of the boat people came from Central Vietnam and their two primary destinations were Hong Kong and the Philippines.

The profiles of the caseloads arriving in Malaysia, Indonesia and Thailand were fairly similar to one another, but the report noted (though it did not explain) a significant difference between the Hong Kong and Philippines caseloads. Though both originated in Central Vietnam, fully 75 per cent of all cases interviewed in Hong Kong were fishermen. Together with accompanying family members, they comprised 85 per cent of all individuals. The remainder were students. In the Philippines, on the other hand, fishermen made up only 20 per cent of the cases and 32 per cent of individuals. Another 20 per cent were persons closely linked to the previous regime, the highest percentage of any country in the region. The report recorded no arrivals anywhere from North Vietnam.[44]

As to motives people gave for leaving, the UNHCR study noted that generally a number of factors came into play. For the 15 per cent of the cases who were ethnic Chinese, many cited ethnic discrimination as a reason for leaving. Going through the interviews, however, Johnsson concluded that

> The repressive measures against rich Chinese businessmen and traders earlier reported on in the international media appear to have given way to more subtle and milder forms of discrimination.... By and large, they appear to have difficulties in obtaining officially sanctioned jobs as well as obtaining access to higher education. The interviewed cases however also include persons who had obtained and held such jobs and others who had entered institutes of higher learning.

Johnsson recommended that the refugee characteristics of ethnic Chinese should be examined on a case-by-case basis.

Catholics also represented 15 per cent of the caseload interviewed for the 1985 UNHCR assessment; here, too, Johnsson noted 'some very clear cases of severe discrimination amounting to persecution on grounds of religion', particularly in Central Vietnam, while noting that 'elsewhere in the country, there appears to be a relative freedom to practice one's religion'. He concluded that Catholics were not systematically persecuted and, thus, 'a careful examination would have to be made of each case'.

For those who spent more than several years in re-education camps, Johnsson said that 'Their claim to refugee status is possibly the easiest to determine positively.' More difficult to assess were the claims of those who had spent time in the New Economic Zones. Here, Johnsson distinguished not only between those who had been forced to go and those who went of their own free will, but between those who escaped from the zones (or refused to go at all), and suffered severe consequences, and those who did not.

As for the students – the 'unmarried and unaccompanied youngsters' – the UNHCR study found they gave two principal reasons for leaving: they were evading military service or they had been sent abroad by their parents. 'In some cases,' it noted, 'the children concerned received specific instructions to arrange for their parents' travel at a later stage – either by sending funds to finance an illegal departure or as sponsors under the ODP.' The most frequently cited reason for leaving, mentioned by 42 per cent of those interviewed, was to join family members in third countries.[45]

For the UNHCR study, two protection officers separately examined the interview files in order to assess the refugee characteristics involved. In 8 per cent of the cases, both officers agreed that the case clearly merited refugee status. These were labelled Category A. In an additional 31 per cent of the cases, only one officer concluded that the individual deserved refugee status. These were called Category B. 'By adding the two categories together,' wrote Johnsson, 'one therefore arrives at the most liberal interpretation of the refugee characteristics of current arrivals from Vietnam. It would appear that somewhat less than two thirds have no claim to refugee status.'[46]

Needless to say, the UNHCR study did not meet with unanimous agreement in the government houses of the Western resettlement countries, still less so among the refugee communities in diaspora. But it offered a carefully considered though provocative challenge to many of the long-held assumptions upon which the Indochinese refugee programme had been based since 1979, the most important being presumptive eligibility of refugee status for all Vietnamese asylum seekers. Although the resettlement countries gradually had introduced tighter admissions criteria and tougher interview protocols, up until 1987 most Vietnamese had been moving through the asylum countries in less than one year. Those who did not qualify for resettlement under one country's criteria were shopped to other countries until they secured admission. And even those who were rejected for resettlement by every country, though it was cold comfort to them, continued to enjoy presumptive refugee status under UNHCR protection.

The conclusions of the new UNHCR study, then, were at once quite radical and old hat. As Johnsson saw it, most of the Vietnamese were not refugees at all. They not only did not need resettlement but they had no claim to international protection and could be sent back to their home country. The refugee advocacy groups and the Vietnamese overseas communities, by and large, rejected that assessment, holding to the view that persecution still was systematic in Vietnam and that those few who may not have merited concern prior to departure had earned their status from the dangers they had survived on the journey out. Resettlement countries like the United States and Canada hoped simply to 'manage down' the flow until it stopped, without having to deal with knotty issues like repatriation.

Then, in 1987, following a five-year decline, Vietnamese refugee arrivals surged again. With the relaxation of many internal travel restrictions, thousands had discovered a new route, which took them overland through Cambodia as far as the port of Kompong Som and then, via a boat ride of just a few hours, to Thailand's east coast. This route managed to avoid both the dangers of the Cambodian border and the perils of the open-sea journey. By year's end, Vietnamese arrivals totalled almost 12,000, three times the number for 1986. Worse yet, the numbers were going up even as the resettlement qualifications of the boat people appeared to be weakening.

According to a study conducted for the Ford Foundation, up until 1986, about 80 per cent of boat arrivals in Thailand qualified for US resettlement interviews. The majority subsequently were approved for US resettlement while the rest were admitted to other countries like Australia, Canada and France. By 1987, however, fewer than 50 per cent of Vietnamese arriving in Thailand were qualifying for resettlement interviews with the United States. Regionwide, rough estimates suggested that 60 per cent of newly arriving Vietnamese would be ineligible for resettlement anywhere and thus would join the growing ranks of 'long-stayers' in the camps.[47]

The surge was happening at a particularly vulnerable time for refugee resettlement. Several of the major Western economies were in recession, the *per capita* costs of resettlement remained high and, perhaps most significantly, Europe and North America had begun to experience an exponential increase in the number of asylum seekers arriving at their borders. In 1981, a total of 116,000 new asylum seekers registered themselves in European countries. Within ten years, that number had increased nearly five-fold to 541,000.[48] The Immigration Reform and Control Act of 1986 in the United States and the 1985 Schengen Agreement in Europe were expressions of a common political sentiment to 'regain control of the borders', a feeling that only grew stronger as the decade drew to a close.

According to an editorial in *Le Monde* in late 1986, commenting on a campaign by 170 NGOs to preserve the right of asylum:

> It would be difficult to choose a worse time to defend the refugees. In this period of unemployment, would they not look like hidden job seekers?.... They are often seen as dangerous people, potential terrorists, able to bring in their luggage some of the violence they are escaping from. If the refugees in France have always been perceived in a more positive manner than migrant workers, their image has been eroding in the past years. Today, individual victims seem to look more and more like a troop of unwanted persons. There is less talk about the quality of reception than about the size of the invasion.[49]

From the perspective of many governments, particularly the asylum countries in Southeast Asia, the Vietnamese were looking more and more like a troop of unwanted persons. Some voiced growing impatience at the size of the continuing exodus; a few made noises about ending asylum altogether. But no one could help but be struck by the sheer tenacity of the Vietnamese exodus.

Among its other findings, the 1985 UNHCR study reported that fully two-thirds of the boat people had tried to leave Vietnam at least once before. Many had failed several times before they succeeded, including one man who claimed to have made 17 previous attempts. Of the failed attempts, 61 per cent were unsuccessful due to reasons such as unscrupulous organizers, bad weather, or poor coordination, while 38 per cent were stopped by the authorities. By that time, Vietnamese law stipulated that illegal departure was a crime punishable by up to three years in prison and up to six years for those who organized such departures. 'The practice', suggested Johnsson, 'shows a more nuanced picture.' Of the 249 attempts stopped by the authorities, only 65 per cent resulted in detention for the would-be refugees and, of these, 86 per cent were held for less than one year and 30 per cent for less than one month.

Another UNHCR survey conducted in early 1989 showed more than 72 per cent of all boat people arriving in Malaysia had tried to leave at least once before. Over one quarter of all new arrivals had made more than four unsuccessful attempts. Planning and organizing the trip took anywhere from one month to more than one year. Payment for the trip could be made a number of ways. In about one third of the cases, departees made their full payments up front in Vietnam. Some paid nothing as they were either boat leaders, crew members, or relatives of one or the other. But a majority of people (about 54 per cent), made a partial payment in Vietnam with the balance to be paid, often by a relative in a third country, once they had reached a country of asylum or resettlement.[50]

If the motives to leave were mixed and the modes of departure were many, one common feature united virtually all of those who were setting out from Vietnam by boat. As Mary Pack, the author of the Ford Foundation study on Vietnamese refugees put it,

> Interview after interview, not only with new arrivals but also with long-stayers, pointed to a common link shared by those who had suffered long years of re-education as well as those who had joined the flow for reasons less obvious: high expectations.... The three expectations most frequently recorded were:
>
> • Firstly, most people leave Vietnam with the belief that they will be resettled relatively quickly, at least within six months to a year.
>
> • Secondly, most expect to be resettled in the United States, Canada or Australia.
>
> • Thirdly, most feel that they are entitled to choose their country of resettlement and even fail to pursue offers which they feel are unacceptable.[51]

Pack, who worked at the time for JVA/Thailand processing refugees for US resettlement, insists that her discussion 'in no way intends to suggest that a person with misguided expectations is not a refugee with a well-founded fear of persecution' though many were happy to draw that conclusion just the same.[53] But whatever one's views on conditions in Vietnam, by 1988 it was impossible to deny that the prospect of quick resettlement in an affluent Western country was a strong motive to depart. In 1979, massive third-country resettlement had been the solution to the problems of asylum in Southeast Asia. A decade later, resettlement itself had become part of the problem. Those who would have solved this problem by ending resettle-ment, however, faced another conundrum: The pull factor not only seemed to be perpetuating the outflow but aggravating the factors of push.

The desire to leave Vietnam – spurred by the prospect of a new life in the West – was fuelling an industry of departure which was leading to further arrests, detentions, confiscations of property and restrictions on work and educational opportunities. Disenfranchisement further stimulated the desire to leave, which perpetuated the boat flows and the need for asylum and resettlement. At some point, it had ceased to be a matter of simple cause and effect, push or pull, and had become its own self-generating dynamo. Incremental change – in Vietnam, in the region, or in the West – would have only incremental effect on the outflows. Only a radical break with the past – an end to class struggle and hardship in Vietnam or an end to asylum – would stop the boats for good. Journalist Nayan Chanda had said of the earlier ethnic Chinese migrations: 'Although Hanoi and Peking pushed and pulled the Chinese residents, the exodus soon developed a momentum of its own and assumed proportions that served neither.'[53] Much the same now could be said of the Vietnamese exodus: while Hanoi once was pleased to have its malcontents pay to leave the country and Washington was keen to take them in, the benefits that either side may have hoped to derive had long since lost their appeal.

The exodus had taken on a momentum all its own. The question was how to stop it. The answers seemed, at best, bafflingly complex, or, at worst, brutally simple. Anders Johnsson offered his own suggestion:

> A 'solution' to the Vietnamese problem cannot, and should not, be achieved through pressures on the authorities to stop illegal departures. Instead a global approach is required involving Vietnam, receiving countries in the region, resettlement countries, other interested states … and UNHCR. Such a holistic approach must be designed to attain solutions to the causes of departures through respect for human rights, the non-use of force, the peaceful settlement of disputes and economic and social development. An integral part of such an approach should also ultimately include a screening procedure, deportation arrangements for non-refugees and a strengthening of the Orderly Departure Program.[54]

Although Johnsson did not give a name to it, he had just sketched one of the earliest outlines of the Comprehensive Plan of Action. But several chaotic and violent years lay ahead before that plan would come into being.

Thailand Pushes Back

Looking back, the warning signs were clear. In the span of one year, Vietnamese boat arrivals in Thailand had more than tripled, with most of the new arrivals coming by way of a relatively safe route to the east coast. Particularly disturbing to Thai officials was the fact that well-organized smuggling operations were dropping the Vietnamese on the beaches for fees averaging $1,500 per person. Said one diplomat at the time, 'Thailand is feeling besieged on all of its borders,' pointing to Muslim separatists and communist insurgents on the Malaysian border, hilltribe refugee groups on the Burmese border, a bloody two-month border dispute with Laos, and the presence of 280,000 displaced persons on the Cambodian border. 'Xenophobia,' he said, 'is increasing.'[55]

The fuse was lit when Thailand's Minister of Interior visited Panat Nikhom refugee processing centre at the end of December 1987 and found the camp crowded with more than 15,000 Vietnamese. Reports on the smuggling networks appeared to implicate some local officials in the eastern province of Trat. The scope of the MOI investigation broadened with visits to Ban Vinai, then home to more than 40,000 Hmong. In early January 1988, the secretary-general of the National Security Council (NSC), Suwit Suthanakun, announced that smuggling of Vietnamese and Laotians had become a major security problem. 'It is therefore necessary,' he said, 'for Thailand to arrest these illegal immigrants and send them back to their homeland, the same way the United States is doing with Mexicans.'[56]

On 27 January 1988, Thai marine police forced a boatload of 40 Vietnamese asylum seekers back into international waters. The next day, the MOI announced that all Vietnamese boats seeking to reach Thailand would be turned away. Within six weeks, more than 1,500 boat arrivals had been pushed back and, according to a confidential UNHCR report, 'some 170 refugees have lost their lives directly as a result'. The Thai push-backs, noted the report, 'amount to the gravest infringement of refugee rights in the region since the mass expulsions of Kampucheans and Vietnamese in 1979'.[57]

The Thai government acknowledged that deaths did occur, although as one official insisted, 'the loss of life was not the direct consequence of deterrence measures instituted by the Government and ... the numbers have been greatly exaggerated'. But faced with the prospect of 'an unending migratory influx of enormous numbers', the official said, 'the Royal Thai Government had to take corrective measures.'[58]

In February, NSC chief Suwit announced that Vietnamese boat people who arrived in Thailand after 1 January would be transferred to Site 2. Since most had come by way of Cambodia, Thai officials argued, they would be treated as 'land Vietnamese' with no automatic eligibility to seek resettlement.[59] The Thai announcement came just two days after US Ambassador to Thailand, William A. Brown, had written a letter to Foreign Minister Siddhi, outlining a six-point plan for resolving the Vietnamese refugee crisis. According to a US refugee official, the main three points were '(1) stop all boat push-backs; (2) close Panat Nikhom to new boat arrivals with newcomers going instead to a UNHCR holding centre; and (3) establish a screening programme at the holding centre to identify people of special concern. There would be no more generalized resettlement.'[60]

Several months later, Thailand reversed its push-back policy and restored first asylum to Vietnamese boat people but its actions had catalysed thinking in the region and around the world. Suddenly, it seemed that everyone was drafting papers, in Geneva, Washington, Canberra, Ottawa, Kuala Lumpur and Bangkok. Even London, which had declined participation in the ICG meetings for many years, now wanted in on the act. Vietnamese arrivals in Hong Kong also had climbed dramatically, from 3,400 in 1987 to over 18,000 in 1988. Even more disturbing to the Home Office was the fact that more than 70 per cent of the new arrivals were from North Vietnam, by far the highest percentage Hong Kong had ever seen and by far the most difficult group to resettle.

If Thailand had ignited the crisis, it also took an important step in turning danger into opportunity by hosting a regional meeting at the beach resort of Cha-am in May 1988, which UNHCR attended as an observer. The ICG sessions had given the resettlement and donor countries a venue to meet informally and brainstorm. The Cha-am meeting did the same for the countries of first asylum even as it gave them a chance to interact with their Western counterparts. Gervais Appave, then refugee counsellor at the Australian Embassy in Thailand, said, 'The countries had begun coming together saying, "We need a new framework," but Cha-am really got it going. That was the beginning of the road.'[61]

At Cha-am, the participants recommended, among other things, that 'mechanisms should be developed to determine the claims of new arrivals to refugee status on a regional basis'. The participants also agreed on the need for a new international conference on Indochinese refugees, a call that was reaffirmed at the ASEAN Foreign Ministers meeting two months later. The High Commissioner for Refugees, Jean Pierre Hocke, attended the ICG meeting in Tokyo in November 1988, along with Sergio Vieira de Mello, who had become UNHCR's point man for Southeast Asia. It was de Mello who took the lead in negotiations with Vietnam which culminated in the signing of a Memorandum of Understanding in December 1988. Significant in this agreement was Vietnam's commitment to allow voluntary repatriation of its citizens, to expand and accelerate the Orderly Departure Programme, and to permit UNHCR access to the returnees.

Not all of the countries involved in the new Vietnamese refugee crisis were prepared to wait until a new international consensus could be reached. Following Hong Kong's first crisis with the boat people in 1979, when nearly 70,000 arrived in the British colony, Vietnamese arrivals had averaged 7,700 annually for the next three years. In July 1982, despite pleas from UNHCR, Hong Kong instituted a closed camp policy, reducing services and restricting opportunities for outside employment. Arrivals dropped to about 2,500 per year through 1987. When boat flows jumped again in 1988, the Hong Kong government unilaterally announced that any Vietnamese boat people entering the territory after 16 June 1988 would be placed in a detention center subject to screening.

In early March 1989, a preparatory meeting was held in Kuala Lumpur to draft a comprehensive plan of action for the upcoming international conference scheduled for June. As boat arrivals continued to increase, Thailand, Malaysia, Indonesia and the Philippines announced their own cut-off dates in mid-March, after which new arrivals would be subject to screening. But the numbers only rose higher. By April 1989, the total number of Vietnamese in first asylum camps had climbed above 100,000 for the first time in ten years.

Notes

1 Michael S. Teitelbaum, 'Tragic Choices in Refugee Policy,' in J.M. Kitagawa, ed., *American Refugee Policy* (Minneapolis: Winston Press, 1983), pp. 32–4.
2 Author's interview with Andrew Shacknove, Oxford, 20 February 1996.
3 *Far Eastern Economic Review*, 17 July 1981.
4 *Ibid.*
5 *The Nation*, 25 July 1981.
6 *Bangkok Post*, 17 June 1981.
7 Unclassified State Department Cable 297379, November 1981.
8 *Ibid.*
9 US Congress, Senate, Committee on the Judiciary, *Refugee Problems in Asia: 1981*, p. 39.
10 Author's interview with Dennis Grace, Bangkok, 18 September 1995.
11 *Ibid.* 'I don't think this would have happened with the Vietnamese boat people,' Grace offered. 'INS' major tactical error was to take on the Cambodians. It was the wrong time to do that in the United States. There was a lot of emotion about what had happened under Pol Pot. Intellectually, maybe some people understood there had been a change in government but it was communist too. The Cambodians had suffered enough. They deserved resettlement.'
12 National Security Decision Directive Number 93, 'Refugee policy and processing refugees from Indochina'.
13 Barry Stein, 'The commitment to refugee resettlement', *The Annals of the American Academy of Political and Social Science*, Vol. 467, May 1983, p. 188.
14 Author's interview with Dennis Grace.
15 Cited in US Committee for Refugees, *Vietnamese Boat People: Pirates' Vulnerable Prey*, p. 3.
16 The figure of two per cent was cited by Col. Jack Bailey, president of Operation Rescue, in April 1982 testimony before the House Subcommittee Asian and Pacific Affairs. See US Congress, House Committee on Foreign Affairs, *Piracy in the Gulf of Thailand: A Crisis for the International Community* (Washington, DC: Government Printing Office, 29 April 1982), p. 59.
17 Author's interview with Stephen Solarz, Washington, DC, 18 April 1996.
18 'Anti-Piracy Assessment Team Report', July 1983, p. 11.
19 *Ibid.*, pp. 14–15.
20 See US Congress, House Committee on Foreign Affairs, *Piracy in the Gulf of Thailand: A Crisis for the International Community*.
21 *Ibid.*, p. 5.
22 Author's interview with Stephen Solarz.
23 Henry Kamm, 'Vietnam's refugees sail into heart of darkness', *New York Times*, 4 July 1984. The article ran the following day in the *International Herald Tribune* under the headline, 'Cruelty stalks the boat people.'
24 Thanat Khoman, Letter to the Editor, *International Herald Tribune*, 9 July 1984. Mimeograph.
25 *Bangkok Post*, 13 July 1984.
26 Author's interview with Henry Domzalski, Geneva, 20 February 1996.
27 See Court Robinson, 'Pirate Attacks on Vietnamese Refugees Grow More Vicious', *World Refugee Survey–1989 in Review* (Washington, DC: US Committee for Refugees, 1990).
28 Author's interview with Carl Harris, Bangkok, 18 January 1996. Harris, a former

State Department official, was seconded to UNHCR for several years to work in the anti-piracy programme. Domzalski also said that in 1983, 'one of the boats we had clearly identified as a naval vessel was involved in a pushback.... I felt bad that people were getting our anti-piracy money and here they were killing people.'

29 See US Catholic Conference, *The Orderly Departure Program: The Need for Reassessment* (Washington, DC: November 1986), p. 4. See also Judith Kumin, 'Orderly departure from Vietnam: a humanitarian alternative?', PhD Thesis for the Fletcher School of Law and Diplomacy, June 1987. See also Janina Wiktoria Dacyl, *Between Compassion and Realpolitik: In Search of a General Model of the Responses of Recipient Countries to Large-Scale Refugee Flows with Reference to the South-East Asian Refugee Crisis* (Stockholm: University of Stockholm, 1992), p. 198.

30 USCC, *The Orderly Departure Program*, p. 5.

31 *Ibid.*, p. 11.

32 Author's interview with Tom Malia, Bangkok, 20 December 1995.

33 USCC, *The Orderly Departure Program*, p. 16–17.

34 *Ibid*, p. 27.

35 *Ibid*, Annex VI, p. 1.

36 Author's interview with Tom Malia, Bangkok, 20 December 1995.

37 The process was so informal, in fact, that participants cannot seem to agree on what the meeting was called. The Canadians and Americans called it the ICG while the Australians referred to it as the 'Inter-governmental Consultation', or IGC.

38 See Nancy Viviani, 'Indochinese Refugees and Australia', in Supang and Reynolds, eds., *Indochinese Refugees: Asylum and Resettlement.*

39 Author's interview with Scott Heatherington, Ottawa, 23 April 1996.

40 Author's interview with Ian Simington, Canberra, 25 July 1996. Simington had taken over from Zia Rizvi as UNHCR's Senior Regional Coordinator for Southeast Asia.

41 Author's interview with Evan Arthur, Canberra, 26 July 1996.

42 The confidential UNHCR study was drafted by Anders B. Johnsson in August 1985. Hereinafter referred to as 'Johnsson 1985.'

43 *Ibid.*, pp. 3-5.

44 There is an apparent discrepancy between the Johnsson report and statistics from the Hong Kong government, which record 37 per cent of the 1,112 arrivals in 1985 as coming from North Vietnam. Hong Kong statistics, however, bifurcate the country between north and south with no reference to the central regions, so it is possible that the same people Johnsson recorded as hailing from north-central provinces like Hue and Quang Ninh, Hong Kong recorded as coming from North Vietnam.

45 The quotations regarding motives for leaving are from 'Johnsson 1985', pp. 9–16.

46 *Ibid.*, p. 20.

47 Mary E. Pack, *The Human Dimension of Longterm Encampment: Vietnamese Boat Refugees in First Asylum Camps* (Bangkok: Ford Foundation, 1988), pp. 1–2.

48 Castles and Miller, *The Age of Migration* p. 84.

49 In Thion, 'Indochinese refugees in France: solidarity and its limits', Supang and Reynolds, *Indochinese Refugees: Asylum and Resettlement*, p. 308.

50 UNHCR Malaysia, 'Survey V: VBP [Vietnamese Boat People] New Arrivals', April 1989.

51 Pack, *The Human Dimension of Longterm Encampment*, p. 5.

52 *Ibid.*

53 Chanda, *Brother Enemy*, p. 243.

54 'Johnsson 1985', p. 24.

55 See Court Robinson, 'Vietnamese refugees in Thailand face first asylum crisis', *Refugee Reports*, Vol. 9, No. 2 (26 February 1988), p. 2.

56 *Ibid.*

57 Memorandum from Dennis McNamara, Deputy Director, Division of Refugee Law and Doctrine, to G. Arnaout, Director, Division of Refugee Law and Doctrine, 11 March 1988.

58 Kopsak Chutikul, 'Thai perspectives on the influx of Vietnamese boat people', Ministry of Foreign Affairs, April 1988.

59 In Court Robinson, 'The Vietnamese refugee crisis in Thailand continues to elude solutions', *Refugee Reports*, Vol. 9, No. 3 (18 March 1988), p. 3.

60 Author's interview with Allan Jury, Bangkok, February 1988.

61 Author's interview with Gervais Appave, Canberra, 26 July 1996.

CHAPTER 8

The Comprehensive Plan of Action

Nguyen Thi Anh's boat scarcely had set out from Vietnam near midnight on 5 March 1989 when trouble struck. 'We had barely reached the mouth of the Bai Hap river,' she later recalled, 'when the engine died. It was an old boat and the water was coming in. We all had to start bailing. The pilot was very nervous. We were afraid of the authorities discovering us.'[1] The boat drifted for several hours before the pilot could get the reserve engine running. From the southernmost province of Minh Hai, the boatload of 31 refugees then set a course towards Malaysia.

Aided by calm seas and a favourable wind, Anh and her companions could have reached Malaysia easily within a week. But the second engine sputtered into silence three days out and the boat went drifting again. 'Even the smallest of storms would have sunk us,' said Anh. But when dawn broke on 15 March the Malaysian coastline rose in the distance. Some fishermen who happened past towed the group to the island refugee camp of Pulau Bidong and, at six o'clock that evening, the Vietnamese boat people stepped out again on dry land.

The passengers on Boat MC327 did not realize that they had disembarked on uncharted territory. Had they arrived just one day earlier, they would have been registered as refugees like more than 240,000 compatriots who had arrived in Malaysia before them (and nearly 700,000 boat people regionwide) and eventually they would have been resettled overseas, most likely in the United States, Canada, France or Australia. But the Malaysian government had set 14 March as the cut-off date – neighbouring asylum countries had established similar deadlines – after which all new Vietnamese boat arrivals were required to undergo a screening interview.[2] Those who met the test for refugee status would continue on for resettlement while those who were screened out would have to return home.

Scarcely a week before boat MC327's arrival in Malaysia, delegates from 36 countries along with a number of intergovernmental and non-governmental agencies had assembled in Kuala Lumpur to lay out a new approach to the problem of the continuing Vietnamese boat exodus. At the March preparatory meeting, the participants approved by consensus a draft document which more than 70 countries would come to endorse on 13–14 June 1989 at a second international conference on Indochinese refugees in Geneva. The first international conference ten years earlier, as High Commissioner for Refugees Sadako Ogata remarked in a 1995 speech,

> recognized the principle of admission and refuge in the region but on a temporary basis only: it was coupled with the commitment to resettle the refugees in third countries. This compromise, which was essentially a burden-sharing arrangement, was to survive for a decade, providing temporary refuge as well as resettlement to over a million refugees…. [But] by concentrating on the obligations of the regional countries of refuge and the international community, the 1979 arrangement ignored the responsibilities of countries of origin towards their own citizens. It failed to recognize the right of people to return, far less the right of people to remain in their own homes in safety and security.[3]

The 1979 agreements had collapsed in Thailand and were soon to do so in Malaysia. Hong Kong had chosen to set its own course with local screening. Renewed commitments of resettlement, even assuming they could be elicited from the dwindling number of interested countries, seemed little likely to turn the tide and restore asylum all by themselves. The old formula of an open door for an open shore had fallen victim, in some respects, to its own success. The asylum countries were no longer willing to offer open-ended asylum, just as the resettlement countries were unwilling to maintain open-ended resettlement. Each seemed to be perpetuating a need for the other. The 1989 conference decoupled the automatic link between asylum and resettlement and introduced a volatile new factor into the equation: screening and all that followed it.

The agreement reached at the 1989 conference on Indochinese refugees, which came to be known as the Comprehensive Plan of Action (CPA), had five main objectives:

- to maintain guarantees of temporary refuge for asylum seekers;

- to discourage organized clandestine flight and promote regular departures and migration programmes;

- to establish 'a consistent regionwide refugee status determination process … in accordance with national legislation and internationally accepted practice';

- to continue resettlement of Vietnamese refugees, both long-stayers who had arrived in the camps prior to the cut-off dates and those determined to be refugees under the new screening procedures; and

- to return persons determined not to be refugees to their country of origin. The agreement stated that, 'In the first instance, every effort will be made to encourage the voluntary return of such persons…. If, after the passage of reasonable time, it becomes clear that voluntary repatriation is not making sufficient progress towards the desired objective, alternatives recognized as being acceptable under international practices would be examined.'⁴

Though the implementation of any one of these points generated its own share of crises and confrontations, pride of place for controversy certainly went to the final objective, repatriation of the screened-out. Though the language of the CPA was deliberately vague, it was perfectly clear to all concerned that the 'alternatives' to voluntary return could only mean one thing: *involuntary* return. In his statement at the June 1989 conference, the head of the US delegation, Deputy Secretary of State Lawrence Eagleburger, had stated the US position unequivocally: 'the United States will remain unalterably opposed to the forced repatriation of Vietnamese asylum-seekers. We will not consider forced repatriation as falling within the rubric of "acceptable under international practices." '⁵ The lone support for this position among all the assembled governmental delegates came, ironically enough, from the Socialist Republic of Vietnam.

In one respect, by severing the link between arrival in a UNHCR camp and presumptive refugee status, the CPA marked a fundamental break with the Indochinese programme of the previous fourteen years. In another respect, the CPA simply confirmed what many had known for some years already: there was no such thing as an Indochinese refugee programme but three ever more distinct programmes, one for Cambodians, one for Laotians, and one for Vietnamese. Refugee status and third-country resettlement was never a prospect for border Cambodians outside the UNHCR holding centres, and Laotians had been getting screened in Thailand since 1985.

At the end of 1989, when the CPA became operational, there were about 200,000 Indochinese refugees in UNHCR camps throughout Southeast Asia. This included 17,000 Cambodians in the UNHCR holding centre, Khao I Dang, and excluded another 270,000 'displaced persons' on the Thai–Cambodian border who were assisted by the UNBRO. But the CPA made no provisions for Cambodians, either refugees or displaced persons. It made parenthetical reference to Laotian asylum seekers, who then numbered about 70,000 in Thailand. The focus of the CPA, whose costs would run in excess of $500 million over the next eight years, was some 100,000 Vietnamese boat people spread out over five Southeast Asian countries and the territory of Hong Kong.

Asylum

In 1978, when Malaysia was struggling to find temporary shelter for 63,000 boat arrivals, Indonesia received scarcely 3,000. In 1979, however, the levels equalized quite dramatically as each country took in about 50,000 more boat people. As it turned out, Malaysia had been engaged in a brutal sort of burden sharing, sending toward its neighbour roughly half the boats that were turning up first in Malaysian waters. For fully a decade after it had stopped turning boat people back to sea in 1979, however, Malaysia had maintained a creditable record of generosity, granting temporary asylum to more than 250,000 Vietnamese.

After a six-year decline, boat arrivals increased modestly in 1987 and then more dramatically in 1988, as Malaysia began to receive the push-backs from Thailand. The March 1989 cut-off date, intended as a deterrent, seemed only to spur on the exodus, triggering what one UNHCR official called a 'last-chance mentality'.[6] By April 1989, the refugee caseload in Malaysia had climbed past 20,000 for the first time in ten years.

Although it was not reported in the Western press, Malaysian policy on Vietnamese arrivals had shifted more radically than the imposition of a cut-off date. On 18 March 1989 Deputy Prime Minister Abdul Ghafar Baba had told the *New Straits Times* that 'The government's stand is that Vietnamese refugees who arrive here from March 14 are considered illegal immigrants. As such we will deport them.' Asked to elaborate, Ghafar said that 'on humanitarian grounds', the navy and marine police would allow boats to land and reprovision with supplies and fuel before towing them back to sea.[7]

In late May, Malaysian authorities began turning away Vietnamese boats. In June, Malaysia's foreign minister, Abu Hassan Omar, chaired the second international conference on Indochinese refugees in Geneva, at which all participants pledged that 'temporary refuge will be given to all asylum seekers', even as his government was pushing scores of people back out to sea. One UNHCR official (who declined to be identified) saw a direct link between the push-backs and the cut-off date. In the negotiations over the CPA, Malaysia and some of the other asylum countries had supported the idea of a June 1989 cut-off date, synchronized with the international conference in Geneva. This, of course, would have made all arrivals up to that point the responsibility of the international community to resettle. Australia, on the other hand, and the other resettlement countries pushed strongly for the earliest possible cut-off date, especially in the light of the escalating arrivals. 'If you fix the cut-off date at the height of the arrival season,' suggested the official, 'you know who wins and who loses.' The resettlement countries ultimately prevailed and an embittered Malaysia took steps to cut its losses.

On 20 October 1989, a Greek ship rescued a boatload of Vietnamese 75 miles off the coast of Borneo and took them to Singapore. The group told refugee officials there that about one week earlier, a Malaysian vessel had provided them with food and water but then towed them for 19 hours back out to sea before cutting the boat adrift. In all, four people died of dehydration, starvation and exposure. By the end of 1989, Malaysia had pushed back at least 3,200 people, most of whom had been 'redirected' to neighbouring Indonesia.

On 26 October the UNHCR representative in Malaysia, Eric Morris, issued a statement accusing Malaysia of violating its commitments under the CPA. 'It sets an extremely unfortunate precedent when an agreement is entered into one moment and repudiated at the next moment,' said Morris.

'Malaysia was elected to the presidency of the international conference. International recognition must surely entail a commitment to fulfill international responsibilities.'[8]

In 1990, Malaysian arrival figures dropped to 1,300 for the year even as Indonesia's soared to ten times that number. In April of that year, Prime Minister Mahathir refuted foreign news reports that push-backs were taking place. 'If you do not believe me,' he said, 'you can go to Pulau Bidong and see for yourself the large number of refugees staying there.' Following public protests from UNHCR and the US government, however, Deputy Prime Minister Abdul Ghafar Baba tried another tack. 'Actually, the boat people do not want to stay in Malaysia,' he said. 'So they make a short stop in our waters to seek assistance such as food and medicine, which we help them with…. They leave of their own choice.'[9]

'That simply is not true,' said Lionel Rosenblatt, executive director of Refugees International, who investigated the push-backs from Malaysia. 'Based on interviews with boat people on Pulau Bidong and UNHCR reports from Indonesia, we know that boats are not necessarily reprovisioned or repaired. Boats laden with men, women, and children are towed out to sea at high speed, which is extremely alarming and dangerous, and left to fend for themselves.'

One push-back victim interviewed on Pulau Bidong said that his group of 51 asylum seekers had arrived in Sarawak in east Malaysia on 25 June 1989. Malaysian marine police told them they would be transferred to Pulau Bidong. Instead, they were towed out to sea for 12 hours, their compass and sea charts were confiscated, and they were pointed toward an island and told it was Pulau Bidong.

In fact, Pulau Bidong was still far away. The Vietnamese were attacked and robbed by local fishermen. They made their way back to the Malaysian coastline, where they were detained for two months in a deserted area. On 21 September the group was put on what one called 'a very old Vietnamese escape boat' and again towed back out to sea. 'But the boat was in bad condition, leaking a lot,' the man said. 'We were very frightened and begged for help and told them to stop. Finally, they brought us back to land.' Through the help of two local people, the Vietnamese were able to get a letter to the Malaysian Red Crescent Sociey in Kuala Lumpur who intervened on their behalf and brought them to Pulau Bidong, four months after they had first set out.[10]

It could be argued that the CPA restored asylum in Thailand – there were no reports of push-backs after 1989 – and the rest of the region by and large held to the CPA commitments. Malaysia, however, never restored asylum after 1989. The Vietnamese simply stopped coming. From 1991 to 1996, only one Vietnamese arrival was recorded in Malaysia. Although some of the neighbouring countries, especially Indonesia, privately grumbled at Malaysia's push-back policy, in public the countries of first asylum showed a united front. At a CPA steering committee meeting in Manila in May 1990, they issued a statement saying that 'The viability of the CPA ... has been undermined by selective implementation of its provisions. While countries of temporary refuge have been urged to continue to provide first asylum, crucial elements of the CPA have either not been given due focus or totally ignored.' Failure to agree on the involuntary repatriation of the screened-out or any alternative solutions, the statement said, gave the countries of asylum 'the right to take such unilateral action as they deem necessary to safeguard their national interests, including the abandonment of temporary refuge'.[11]

In April 1990, even as Malaysian push-backs were choking off Vietnamese boat arrivals, High Commissioner Thorvald Stoltenberg was in Geneva bestowing an award on the Danish shipping company, Maersk Line, for its exemplary performance in coming to the aid of Vietnamese asylum seekers at sea. Of the 67,000 Vietnamese who had been rescued at sea by merchant ships, naval vessels and fishing boats since 1975, Maersk Line alone had been responsible for the rescue of some 7,000 boat people in distress.[12]

Since 1979, UNHCR had administered the Disembarkation Resettlement Offers (Disero) programme under which the United States, Canada, Australia, New Zealand and four European countries (France, Germany, Sweden and Switzerland) guaranteed that any Vietnamese rescued at sea would be resettled within 90 days.[13] The programme encouraged merchant ships to rescue boat people in distress by guaranteeing prompt disembarkation at the next port of call and promoted disembarkation by guaranteeing prompt resettlement. Under the Disero programme, by late 1990 more than 68,000 people had been rescued and resettled in Western countries.[14]

But a guarantee of automatic resettlement, even for those rescued at sea, was inconsistent with the CPA's terms of understanding, which required that all new arrivals must undergo screening. Disero and its companion programme, Rescue at Sea Resettlement Offers (RASRO), essentially collapsed as countries in the region proved unwilling to disembark rescued boat people. In late August 1990, the *General Jacinto*, a Norwegian-owned, Panamanian-registered vessel, rescued 14 Vietnamese. One month later, the asylum seekers were still on the ship as, in succession, China, Hong Kong, Indonesia, and the Philippines spurned requests to disembark. Finally, on 27 September, following interventions by UNHCR, the Vietnamese stepped off on dry land in Papua New Guinea.

As disembarkation difficulties mounted, rescue attempts dwindled. From July to September 1989, for example, merchant and navy ships had carried out 37 successful rescue operations, involving 2,127 Vietnamese boat people. During that same period in 1990, by comparison, only 179 Vietnamese in 7 boats were rescued. With no place to drop people off, ships had little incentive to pick them up, particularly when delays could cost commercial vessels anywhere from $10,000 to $90,000 per day.

In the end, only a patchwork solution could be found. The Philippines proved most flexible in accommodating disembarked Vietnamese. Singapore, on the other hand, never accepted the new measures. For many years it had refused asylum to any Vietnamese seeking to land directly. Rescue cases were only accepted with guarantees of resettlement within 90 days and the Singapore government never budged from that position throughout the tenure of the CPA.

Resettlement

If the principal aim of the CPA was to preserve asylum, as US officials are wont to say, then the agreement proved effective in four out of six participating states (though the *quality* of asylum proved another matter). Most would agree that the CPA, first and foremost, was an effort to control migration. Lest anyone doubt that, it is worth noting that the very first point of action endorsed by the plan was the 'Continuation of official [Vietnamese] measures directed against those organizing clandestine departures'.[15] The planners wanted this done humanely through the use of mass media activities and through the expansion of orderly departure procedures, but they wanted the boats to stop. If official measures encompassed interdiction of boats and arrest of organizers – and they did – then the plan encompassed these measures and, albeit tacitly, sanctioned them.

There is no doubt that the CPA brought an end to the flow of asylum seekers from Vietnam (and from Laos). In 1989, roughly 70,000 Vietnamese sought asylum in Southeast Asia along with 3,300 Laotians. By 1992, only 41 Vietnamese and 10 Laotians asylum seekers had arrived in Southeast Asian camps and the numbers have remained negligible ever since. How much of this was due to mass information campaigns as opposed to coastal crackdowns? How much credit should go to improved opportunities in Vietnam and how much blame rests with the more onerous conditions in the first asylum camps, particularly in Hong Kong? The evidence does not exist to answer these questions with anything more than impressions or anecdotes. All that can be said reliably, perhaps, is that under the CPA the costs of leaving Vietnam by boat finally outweighed the potential benefits.

But although the CPA was about controlling migration, its overall effect was not to halt so much as to redirect the outflow. Indeed, as one veteran refugee official noted in 1995, more people were resettled during the first six years of the CPA than in the six years prior to it.[16] During the period 1984–89, a total of 442,168 Indochinese refugees and immigrants moved on to new lives. During 1990–95, a total of 507,549 did so, including a great many high-priority cases like former re-education camp prisoners, Amerasians, and others. For the Vietnamese, there were two ways of getting resettled: as refugees out of the first asylum camps and as refugees or special immigrants moving via the Orderly Departure Programme.

Refugee Resettlement

When the CPA was endorsed formally in June 1989, a total of 50,670 Vietnamese were identified as having arrived in first asylum camps before the various cut-off dates were imposed. It was one of the central, inter-locking agreements of the CPA that all refugees arriving before the cut-off date would be resettled, despite the fact that nearly a quarter of them already had been rejected for failing to meet resettlement criteria of at least one country. Some had been turned down many times over. Among those with the highest rejection rates were single young men (45 per cent) and people without family or other links in third countries (33 per cent).[17]

Shortly after the preparatory meeting was concluded in March 1989, UNHCR issued written appeals to more than 30 countries, appealing for their help in resettling Vietnamese arriving before the cut-off dates and, in many cases, even suggesting an admissions level. For the United States, UNHCR proposed a figure of 22,000. Australia and Canada were encouraged to take 10,000 each, followed by 4,400 for France, 2,000 for the United Kingdom, and smaller numbers to be scattered throughout Europe and South America.

At the international conference in July 1979, the Philippine government had offered to establish a site for the temporary accommodation of 50,000 Indochinese refugees, in order to relieve the burden of the other first asylum countries in Southeast Asia. Four months later, on 12 November 1979, the government of the Philippines and UNHCR signed an agreement for the construction and operation of the Philippine Refugee Processing Centre (PRPC) at Morong, Bataan. By the time the PRPC closed 15 years later, the centre had served as a way station for more than 350,000 Indochinese coming from other first asylum countries or directly from Vietnam under the ODP.

Following the CPA conference in 1989, the Philippines once again offered a helping hand to the region. With funding from the British government, a Regional Resettlement Transit Centre (RRTC) was constructed to relieve congestion in the camps in Hong Kong and to facilitate third-country resettlement of refugees. The Philippines also continued to permit more than 2,300 at-sea rescue cases to be disembarked for screening, when other countries in the region had shut their doors.

By the end of 1992 most of the Vietnamese who had arrived before the cut-off dates had been resettled overseas. In addition, a total of more than 32,000 Vietnamese were screened in as refugees under the CPA status determination procedures, along with nearly 5,000 Laotians. As of early 1997, most of these had been resettled as well. All told, in the seven full years of the CPA, nearly 125,000 refugees were resettled out of the first asylum camps, including more than 80,000 Vietnamese and 44,000 Laotians.

Orderly Departure Programme

When the Vietnamese authorities suspended processing of new ODP cases in January 1986, protesting a backlog of 25,000 applicants in the US pipeline, the moratorium prompted what two observers called 'some rethinking among US policymakers' about how the ODP might best be run.[18] Until that time, the State Department had bent over backwards to avoid any semblance of bilateralism in its relations with Vietnam over ODP. Because US officials were prohibited from setting foot on Vietnamese soil, for example, all interviews were carried out by private voluntary agency staff seconded to UNHCR; the files were then carried to the US Embassy in Bangkok where consular and immigration officials made the final decisions on cases.

Likewise, overtures by the Vietnamese in 1983 and 1984 to establish a special, bilateral programme for Amerasian migration were rebuffed as 'grossly inappropriate' by the Reagan Administration.[19] Washington had no interest in giving Hanoi any means to capitalize politically on what both sides insisted was a strictly humanitarian programme. Among the most compelling and visible legacies of the Vietnam War were an estimated eight to twelve thousand Amerasian children, many of them living on the streets of Ho Chi Minh City or in otherwise marginal circumstances. Mounting public interest in the Amerasians had helped persuade the State Department to announce, in September 1984, the establishment of an Amerasian 'sub-programme' within ODP but only a trickle of children and their accompanying family members found their way through the red tape and long delays that plagued the programme on both sides.

Then, in late 1986, the United States agreed to meet with Vietnam to discuss Amerasians on a bilateral basis. It took over a year for talks to bear fruit, but on 11 September 1987 the two governments announced an 'agreement in principle' to expand Amerasian processing. At the same time, Vietnam lifted the 21-month moratorium, allowing ODP interviewing to resume, and also agreed to permit US officials to carry out interviews and adjudications directly in Ho Chi Minh City. In 1988 the number of orderly departures from Vietnam, which had suffered a four-year decline, reversed direction and began to climb. ODP was back on track and, thanks to US legislation passed in December 1987 – the Amerasian Homecoming Act – Amerasians and their families had a numerical target for admissions and funding for their special resettlement needs. But still eluding the two countries was an agreement on the most sensitive population of all: the re-education camp prisoners.

By the government's own admission, Vietnam had sent one million people through a course of political re-education following the communist victory in 1975. For most, this had involved three days of lectures and sessions but no more. The estimates of those detained for longer periods, however, ranged from 100,000 to 300,000 according to international human rights observers and 40,000 by official accounts. At the end of 1979, Vietnamese authorities told a visiting Amnesty International delegation that 14,000 long-term prisoners had been released since 1975 and 26,000 remained in detention. The total, by the official reckoning, included '29,000 puppet military personnel, 7,000 civilian officials, 3,000 policemen and security officials, and 900 members of reactionary parties or organizations'.[20]

Diem Ngoc Nguyen, a career foreign service officer, was director of

European Affairs at the Foreign Ministry in Saigon in 1975. 'One day after the collapse', he recalled many years later, 'they asked everyone to report:'

> We were asked to jot down our name and address and then we went home. But we knew that they knew everything. Anyone who was above the rank of assistant director or deputy director in the Foreign Ministry was placed in re-education. I was also a military officer. They thought that the military ran the department which, of course, was how it worked in the north. They had checked everything.
>
> We spent one month free and then we reported again and went to re-education in mid-June 1975. I was sent to Long Thanh camp, formerly an orphanage. There were about 2,000 of us. They reorganized it for government officials, members of various parties and civilians working for intelligence agencies. We were in the administration block. There was a block for party officials and a block for intelligence officers. The military went to other camps. We were told that we would stay there for one month but we knew it was not true. We knew that we would be sent to the north. Conditions were not too bad in Long Thanh. I had a thin blanket. We slept on the floor but they gave us mosquito nets. We were not required to do labour. There was some manual work but it was not too heavy. Food was not sufficient. We had our first suicide there.
>
> I think they didn't have much of a plan. Most of the time was spent in political lessons. One of the things we had to do was write our biography – our studies, our religion, our occupation, our title, and most of all we had to write what they called our 'crimes'. As a teacher, for example, I had taught decadent literature, French poetry, that had poisoned the minds of my pupils. As a diplomat I had defended the southern regime. While I was in Vientiane, our Embassy gave scholarships to poor children. We had thus attracted their parents to our cause. I had strengthened cultural ties. In Manila, I issued visas to Filipinos and Americans coming to Vietnam to do harm against the communists. When we went north, we had to repeat this biography each year. We always had to say the same thing so it was important to memorize. These were our self-confessions. They proved we were criminals which justified the lack of trials.[21]

In 1976, Diem Ngoc Nguyen was put in the hold of a large boat and transferred to the north. He was in Phu Son camp near the Chinese border until 1978 and then in Thanh Phong for one year. 'They had to close this camp because the mortality rates were so high,' he said. 'When you got sick, you died. There was no medical treatment. We ate only rice and some vegetables we picked from the jungle. The cadres there were very fierce, very cruel because they considered themselves exiled too. For them it was the end of the world. They were desperate. Their food was little better than ours.'

After one year in Thanh Phong, Diem Ngoc Nguyen was moved to Nam Ha camp in Ha Nam Ninh province. It would be another eight years before he could leave. 'The cruellest thing they did', he said,

> was to try to take away our human dignity. Our punishment was not simply deprivation of our liberty but intentional debasement. For three years, we were cut off from all contact with our families. Every month, we got 15 kilograms of rice with salt and vegetables. A thin man like me can hardly survive. A bigger man would have even more intense hunger. When you are hungry, you always

think of food. I remember inmates who copied recipes just to cheat their hunger.... I think they kept us hungry deliberately and for our intellectual and spiritual hunger we got only *Nhan Dan* [the party newspaper].

In 1982 and again in 1984, the Vietnamese government offered to release the remaining re-education camp prisoners if the United States agreed to take them all for resettlement. Several months after the second offer, the Reagan Administration finally pledged to accept 10,000 detainees but the Vietnamese quickly backpedalled. Just as with the Amerasians, Hanoi wanted a bilateral agreement and Washington wanted to move the former prisoners as refugees under ODP.

In February 1988, Diem Ngoc Nguyen was released from Nam Ha along with more than 1,000 other military and intelligence officers, politicians and priests. 'I served twelve years,' he said. 'When I was released, I looked like a monkey, perhaps less presentable.' Another 2,000 political prisoners were released in September 1988 to celebrate Vietnam's national day.[22] By July 1988, the two countries had agreed in principle to move 50,000 people (10,000 former prisoners and 40,000 accompanying family members) but both sides insisted that more meetings were needed to work out the details. According to one senior State Department official, 'We had made it part of our agreement to participate in the CPA that we must have cooperation on the re-ed prisoners. The CPA was absolutely critical in getting Vietnam to negotiate.'[23]

Finally, on 30 July 1989, Senior Deputy Assistant Secretary of State Robert Funseth and Vietnam's Director of Immigration Nguyen Can issued a joint statement following meetings in Hanoi that the two countries would 'allow those released reeducation center detainees who were closely associated with the United States or its allies and who wish to do so, to emigrate, together with their close relatives, to the United States'.[24] The two sides further agreed that this initiative would be in addition to the existing Amerasian and regular ODP and expressed hope that the first group of 3,000 would leave Vietnam before the end of the year.

It was not until January 1990 that the first group of 190 former re-education camp prisoners touched down at San Francisco airport. One early arrival, Vinh Duc Do, a former captain in the South Vietnamese army, was reluctant to talk about his six years in prison for fear of jeopardizing the migration agreements, saying only that, 'When we got out of the camp, there was a bias against the people who worked for the former regime. It's hard to find a job and if there's anything, it's got to be heavy labour.' He said he was looking forward to doing 'anything that would give me independence'.[25]

Diem Ngoc Nguyen rejoined his family in St Paul, Minnesota and works as a medical interpreter for the St Paul-Ramsey Medical Center. Even in America, he suggested, independence is still an elusive thing.

Many of the former political prisoners resettled in the United States are experiencing a crisis of authority. English is a sign of knowledge. They have no English. Employment is a sign of independence. They have no job. In the eyes of their children, their image is diminished. Your children look at you in a different way; your wife. Society here is very materialistic. Here children respect money. They do not respect their father. We are old already. We look at those who came in 1975 and so many are successful. But those who stayed and paid the full price of staying, we feel we have lost twice. We were cast aside by the new society in Vietnam and we have no place in the new Vietnamese society in America.[26]

Whatever their doubts and misgivings about starting over after losing so much, the former prisoners and their families poured out of Vietnam. In 1991, the ODP reached a high water mark of 86,451 departures worldwide, including 21,500 re-education camp detainees and family members and nearly 18,000 Amerasians. From 1991 to 1995, orderly departures averaged more than 66,000 people per year before finally tailing off to one-third that number in 1996.

In all, over the course of the CPA, a total of more than 400,000 people left Vietnam safely and legally, twice the number that had done so in the first ten years of the ODP. The huge majority of this number went to the United States, including 140,000 former re-education camp prisoners and their families and 40,000 Amerasians. Overall, the shift from dangerous, clandestine departure routes to legal migration channels for Vietnamese may be the CPA's most significant and durable accomplishment.

Status Determination

In late 1974 Hong Kong's lawmaking body, the Legislative Council, decreed that illegal immigrants caught trying to enter the territory from mainland China would be returned summarily. From 1975 to 1977, only about 4,000 Chinese were arrested and deported but the number of deportations grew to 8,000 in 1978 and then simply exploded to 89,000 in 1979. It is both curious, and highly significant in terms of understanding Hong Kong's response to the boat people, that during the same five-year period the pattern of Vietnamese arrivals almost exactly matched that of Chinese deportations.

Many of the predominantly Chinese residents of Hong Kong came to voice strong frustrations at this double standard: no matter how onerous the asylum conditions for the boat people may have become, none of the 185,000 Vietnamese asylum seekers who reached Hong Kong were turned away, most were resettled as refugees in Western countries and all were granted an internationally monitored determination of their status, while virtually all Chinese citizens apprehended at the frontier by Hong Kong police in the last two decades have faced swift and certain deportation.[27]

Following Hong Kong's first crisis with the boat people in 1979, when nearly 70,000 arrived in the British colony, Vietnamese arrivals averaged about 7,700 annually for the next three years. In July 1982, despite UNHCR expressions of concern, Hong Kong instituted a closed camp policy, reducing services and restricting opportunities for outside employment.

Arrivals dropped still further to about 2,500 per year through 1987.

When boat arrivals jumped again in 1988, the Hong Kong government unilaterally announced that any Vietnamese boat people entering the territory after 16 June 1988 would be placed in a detention centre and subject to screening. This time, the numbers only climbed higher, to 34,000 in 1989. As with the large influx in 1979, most of the new wave were from North Vietnam, only this time the vast majority were Vietnamese, not ethnic Chinese. Much of the flow, ironically, stemmed not from new repression but a relaxation of internal travel restrictions and, perhaps most importantly, a dismantling of state industries that left tens of thousands unemployed and deeply uncertain about their future. One UNHCR repatriation officer described the changes that *doi moi*, or renovation, brought to the country beginning in 1986:

> Before, if you lived in Hanoi and had a brother in Haiphong and wanted to visit him, you had to go to your boss and get permission. Based on his judgment you brought it to the political committee of your work unit then to the local police and then maybe it was permitted for a certain period of time specified in the permit. When you reached Haiphong you had to go with your brother and announce your arrival to the local police and leave your ID card to be retrieved on your departure. Then you had to report back to the Hanoi police for your work unit. If you had carried two eggs in your pocket from Hanoi to Haiphong or back that would have been illegal trade. In 1987, road barriers to Haiphong were lifted. Suddenly, you didn't need to work for the state anymore. In fact, the state wanted to lay off 25 per cent of its workers. Cooperatives were going bankrupt. A lot of things happened very quickly. People were very insecure and unsure about what to do. The rumours about screening in Hong Kong were very unspecific. People could actually go to the coast and they could leave. Before, they had protected the coastline; they were shooting people.

When Hong Kong unilaterally instituted its new screening policy in June 1988, more than 5,000 people had arrived in the first five months of the year. Said Mike Hanson, who became the territory's refugee coordinator several months later, 'The priority was to stop the exodus. The problem was we had made no contingencies for extra accommodations. We had only one factory building in San Yick. The announcement of screening was intended to stop the influx but instead they were rolling in in very large numbers.' By the end of 1988, more than 18,000 Vietnamese had arrived in Hong Kong, the highest total for any country in the region. 'We found ourselves sideways to a storm,' said Hanson. 'We had a community clamouring for an end to asylum and a Legislative Council that was unwilling to fund it.'[28]

The government's first priority, according to Hanson, was to establish new accommodations. Acknowledging widespread criticism of conditions in some of the detention centres, Hanson said, 'San Yick was a disgrace. There was no light, no air, no place for recreation, no adequate sewage system. It was a real blot on the government's reputation.' The authorities opened a military base, Erskine Barracks, on the outer islands and built another site called Whitehead. 'It was awful,' said Hanson, 'but better than San Yick and better than leaving people on boats in the harbour.'

The second priority, according to Hanson, was to get the social service agencies back in the camps. The government's original thought had been to restrict the work of the private voluntary agencies in the detention centres. 'But half the population was children,' he said. 'You couldn't hold them in detention camps without services.'

The third priority of the government, Hanson said, 'was to rebuild relations with UNHCR', which had been vocal in its complaints about conditions in the closed camps and likewise was critical of the new screening policy. The Hong Kong government and UNHCR, moreover, had begun to dispute the issue of who would pay for the boat people in the detention centres. In a June 1988 confidential memorandum to UNHCR headquarters in Geneva, the UNHCR branch office in Hong Kong had laid out its concerns and questions:

> • the UK/HK governments' speaking note states that 'new policy will involve the screening of arrivals under UNHCR guidelines. UNHCR will be invited to view the screening procedures in action and will be invited to appeal if they wish.' We need to clarify the criteria for screening (strict Convention definition or wider definition) and UNHCR's participation/role in screening and appeals procedures.

> • We also need to clarify our position re treatment of those who are screened out, conditions under which they are to be held in Hong Kong and conditions under which their eventual repatriation will be acceptable to UNHCR. Will ineligible asylum seekers still remain persons of concern to the High Commissioner? Is it proper to treat them as 'illegal immigrants'?

> • re Hong Kong government's request to discuss new funding arrangements ... we should maintain our current commitments for those who are accepted as refugees but all expenses for looking after screened out should be borne by the government.[29]

For different reasons, both UNHCR Geneva and the Hong Kong government wanted the UNHCR branch office, despite its initial misgivings, to play an active role in the screening and follow-up care of the new arrivals. Geneva saw that screening was inevitable in Hong Kong and did not wish to be sidelined in what showed every prospect of becoming a regionwide undertaking. The government, said Hanson, needed UNHCR's 'help in running the camps and getting agencies back in. We needed a credible screening programme'.

In September, the two parties signed a Memorandum of Understanding in which UNHCR affirmed 'its readiness to assist in the care of all asylum seekers in Hong Kong and to participate by monitoring the procedures (including the appeals procedures) for the determination of refugee status, in order to advise the Hong Kong government on measures necessary to abide by established and accepted international measures'.[30] Hong Kong, for its part, agreed to permit all asylum seekers – screened in, screened out, or status pending – access not only to UNHCR officials but to a 'legal advisor'.

Screening criteria, the government promised, would follow the UNHCR *Handbook on Procedures and Criteria for Determining Refugee Status under the 1951 Convention and the 1967 Protocol relating to the Status of Refugees*, the slim yellow volume with a ponderous name that had become every legal officer's bible since it was issued in September 1979. More than that, however, screening criteria were to 'take into account the special situation of asylum seekers from Vietnam', though the understanding never spelled out in what way they were special or just how this would be taken into account.

In terms of camp conditions, the government agreed to open all of the camps that had been closed since 1982 and to relocate the residents of the infamous San Yick factory to more acceptable facilities. Finally, Hong Kong gave its assurances that all refugee children would be offered primary and secondary education through programmes run by the operational partners of UNHCR.

All in all, everyone seemed to emerge better off under the new agreement. UNHCR secured the improvements in camp conditions and permission to monitor and advise in the screening and appeals procedures. Asylum seekers, whatever their ultimate status, remained of concern to UNHCR in internationally monitored camps. And the Hong Kong government got what it most wanted: as Mike Hanson put it, 'the establishment of camps under UNHCR standards and screening under UNHCR guidelines. We wanted to be able to say that no one we called a non-refugee was challenged by UNHCR. We needed their endorsement.'[31] In short, the government had found someone else to take the heat. If camp conditions were deficient or screening decisions were disputed, the buck now seemed to stop with UNHCR.

In 1989, Vietnamese boat arrivals in Hong Kong totalled 34,000 people and camp populations soared to a record high of 55,000. The government, at one point, resorted to towing 7,000 asylum seekers to the Soko Islands where, according to one report, 'they were kept under the guard of the Royal Hong Kong Police without shelter or sanitation facilities, and on dry rations.... The primitive conditions on the island forced many Vietnamese to eat leaves and grass and drew criticism from the UNHCR and medical workers.'[32]

Meanwhile, by April 1989, the Hong Kong authorities had screened more than 1,300 Vietnamese cases but approved only three, and these for reasons of family reunification, not their refugee qualifications.[33] Even as the Southeast Asian nations prepared to institute screening on a regionwide basis by June 1989, Hong Kong found itself under growing international pressure to review and reform its status determination procedures.[34] By the middle of the year, Hong Kong had put in place a new, three-tiered system, which was described by the human rights group, Asia Watch, in a 1991 report:

> Immediately upon interception in the colony's waters, Vietnamese are taken to a reception center and interviewed as to biographical information and place of origin. The asylum seeker is then detained in one of Hong Kong's camps and awaits an interview with an Immigration Officer on the question of refugee status.

The wait for this initial interview is now between two and three years.

In the case of rejection, the asylum seeker has 28 days from notice of rejection in which to file all materials for an appeal to the Refugee Status Review Board, four panels of two non-lawyers, headed by a former judge. The asylum seeker is not given any reasons for an initial rejection; however, a copy of his or her file is given to the UNHCR and lawyers from the Agency for Volunteer Service (AVS), a group under contract with the UNHCR. AVS lawyers review the file and help those asylum seekers they feel have the strongest cases to file an appeal. The vast majority of asylum seekers are left to prepare and submit their appeal on their own, without access to their Immigration file. Over 90 per cent of appeals are rejected. The rejection of an appeal is the end of the road for most asylum seekers. However, AVS lawyers may select some of those cases which they have rated most highly and submit them for review by the UNHCR as to whether these persons fall within its mandate for protection. The Hong Kong government has agreed to accept such 'mandate' refugees as eligible for resettlement.[35]

The CPA had spelled out a number of critical roles for UNHCR in regard to the regional status determination procedures:

• UNHCR was to participate in 'an observer and advisory capacity' in the status determination process, which was to be carried out by a 'qualified and competent national authority body in accordance with established refugee criteria and procedures'.

• UNHCR was to 'advise in writing each individual of the nature of the procedure, of the implications for rejected cases and of the right to appeal the first-level determination'.

• UNHCR was to help in the development of a uniform questionnaire which was to serve as the basis for the interviews and was to reflect the elements of the 1951 Convention and 1967 Protocol 'and other relevant international instruments concerning refugees'.

• UNHCR was to institute, in cooperation with the governments concerned, a comprehensive regional training programme for officials involved in the screening process 'with a view to ensuring the proper and consistent functioning of the procedures and application of the criteria, taking full advantage of the experience gained in Hong Kong'.[36]

In 1989, of course, the principal advantage to be gained from the Hong Kong experience was as a case-study in how *not* to do screening. By 1991, all of the countries in the region had implemented their screening programmes. Sceptics of the CPA noted the generally low approval rates at first instance as a sign of Hong Kong's pioneering influence. Those of a more optimistic mindset noted the explicit assurance given by the Hong Kong government to recognize UNHCR's mandate and hoped it would be granted similar weight throughout the region. As the months wore on, however, the most fundamental consistency across the region proved to be that each country did things differently, some better than others and none perfectly. With this realization, more and more people both within and outside the camps began to insist that UNHCR should be more than just observer and adviser to the status determination process but an active participant, advocate and, if necessary, final arbiter.

In March 1992, three years after the regional cut-off dates were put in place, UNHCR convened a meeting in Manila of senior government officials from around the Southeast Asia region. The subject, not surprisingly, was screening. Though the Vietnamese camp populations still exceeded 100,000 (with 57,000 in Hong Kong alone), new arrivals had dwindled to trifling numbers. The countries of asylum were eager to work through the caseloads in the camps and get people on to their final destinations, be it onward or return passage. Acceptance rates at the first instance (prior to appeal) ranged from a high of 32 per cent in Malaysia to a low of 3 per cent in neighbouring Indonesia. Hong Kong authorities had screened 24,000 people, of whom 7 per cent had been approved for refugee status. All told, more than 22,000 people had returned to Vietnam.

One of three outside experts invited to comment on refugee status determination and conditions in Vietnam, noted human rights lawyer Arthur Helton of the Lawyers Committee for Human Rights, urged that asylum applicants should be given the benefit of the doubt, this being the standard in customary international law. The concept of persecution, Helton said, was problematic. It must imply serious harm to the person concerned, it must be unjustified, it must be propagated by the State or an 'agent of persecution,' and it must be attributed to one of the five reasons articulated in the 1951 Refugee Convention: race, religion, nationality, membership of a particular social group or political opinion. But given all this, he suggested, 'the refugee definition is very flexible, as are the persecutors.'[37]

As an exercise, the assembled delegates went through a series of case studies, one from each country of asylum, to review determination procedures and criteria. A case from Hong Kong based on a short punishment for organizing a strike was rejected by consensus. A case from Indonesia involving the son of a South Vietnamese army officer subjected to prolonged re-education was accepted on the basis of benefit of the doubt. From the Philippines came a case involving a man relocated to a New Economic Zone who escaped in order to avoid the draft and subsequently lived a clandestine life on the run from the authorities. The case had been rejected but the meeting participants could not agree if that was the correct decision.

Nguyen Thi Anh left Vietnam, she said, because 'it was very difficult for me to find work'. On first glance, that appears to fit the profile of an economic migrant more than a refugee. There is more to Anh's story, however. Her father was a Catholic from North Vietnam, who brought the family south when the country was partitioned following the 1954 Geneva Accords. Her older brother served in the South Vietnamese army and her father worked for two years as a carpenter on a US military base. 'Because of this,' she said, 'we got a black mark from the authorities. We were *ly lich xâu.*' This term literally means 'wicked family background' but often is translated as 'black-listed family'. According to a study by Anne Wagley Gow, a former UNHCR field officer in Hong Kong, a black-listed family

> is generally one which has direct, parental or grandparental relationship with the French, the South, or is from a landowning/capitalist class. The relative with direct connections typically was imprisoned in re-education camp, experienced forced labour, had properties confiscated. Commencing in the late 1970s, Black-listed Families were also forced to New Economic Zones (NEZ). Confiscation of property, forced movement to NEZ, forced labor, denial of citizenship rights may also affect the immediate family and succeeding generations.[38]

Neither Anh's brother nor her father were placed in re-education camps but, between 1978 and 1985, the authorities sent her brother to work one month out of each year in a NEZ. During the same period, she was forced to work 15 days every six months digging irrigation canals. Anh said she had tried to escape six times before. Once, she was detained at a police station for two weeks but was freed by a bribe from a family member.

After reading these facts, her Malaysian interviewers and the UNHCR legal observer all agreed Nguyen Thi Anh's story was credible but chose to reject her case. She was not alone. Based on interviews with asylum seekers during her term as a UNHCR field officer in the Hong Kong camps, Gow concluded that black-listed families constituted about 40 per cent of the Vietnamese camp population. This figure was corroborated by a survey commissioned by UNHCR in early 1990 of more than 500 cases in three Vietnamese camps in the region: Whitehead in Hong Kong, Panat Nikhom in Thailand, and Pulau Bidong in Malaysia. The study found that about 37 per cent of the respondents in Whitehead camp reported themselves as having 'bad family status'. The majority of respondents to the survey who identified themselves as a member of a black-listed family were 'enlisted soldiers, officers, employees of, or attached to, the occupying forces'. [39]

In a 1990 memorandum to UNHCR's chief of mission in Hong Kong, Robert Van Leeuwen, Gow urged that the agency give 'full and due consideration' to the issue of black-listed families and their prejudiced position in Vietnam. She warned,

> UNHCR is in a very dangerous position right now of losing all credibility with the Vietnamese asylum seekers. UNHCR staff who are in close contact with the Vietnamese and who understand their concerns are so over-worked that they are unable to provide needed assistance in terms of counseling.... Most unfortunately, those UNHCR staff who are in a position to press for changes on the screening policy and mandate people in, do not understand and/or do not accept the Vietnamese perception of who is a 'refugee.'... If we do not listen to what they are saying, we can only expect an increasing level of tension and anger in the camps, which will eventually be directed at us, and we will eventually have to withdraw from contact with the asylum-seeker community and thus fail in our role of protector.[40]

Data on screening decisions do not indicate reasons either for approval or denial so it is not possible to say what percentage of black-listed families ultimately were screened-in or screened-out. But it is probably fair to say that most UNHCR staff did not accept the Vietnamese asylum seekers' perceptions, nor Gow's either, of who was a refugee.

As UNHCR's representative in Malaysia and regional coordinator of status determination, Erika Feller looked at thousands of files of Vietnamese asylum seekers. 'These are stories I would not like to have for my children,' she said 'but these are not refugee stories. People have good humanitarian reasons to leave, their expectations have been frustrated. But increasingly, the stories are derivative stories, derivative fears. Fathers, grandfathers, older family members have experienced problems and the younger ones are citing fears.'[41]

In its regional guidelines on refugee status determination for Vietnamese boat people, UNHCR acknowledged that 'family discrimination ... is said to be prevalent in Vietnamese society.... Moreover, Vietnamese tradition and concurrent practices under the present regime are said to consider families as collectively responsible for a member's conduct.'[42] The fact that an applicant came from a black-listed family, however, was not in and of itself grounds for approval. Interviewers were urged instead to look for 'cumulative elements' of severe discrimination or evidence of past persecution. If the effect of these events in the past 'would still be such as to render life intolerable upon return, refugee status should be applicable.' But the guidelines went on to state that 'many Vietnamese claims based on future persecution to follow from past events can no longer be entertained in view of the ongoing reforms in the country which render the need for international protection redundant'.[43]

If members of black-listed families, or anyone else for that matter, were screened out under these criteria, UNHCR argued, it was likely for one of three reasons: (1) either their case was not deemed credible; or (2) cumulative elements of discrimination failed to add up to persecution; or (3) past persecution was not judged sufficiently severe or recent as to render life intolerable upon return.

The 1992 guidelines on screening were intended to 'contribute to a harmonization in the region' but if approval and denial rates are any measure, that did not occur. Despite efforts by UNHCR to coordinate screening procedures and standardize guidelines across the region, both the national procedures and the results varied widely from one country to the next. Hong Kong, which screened the most people (60,275), also had the lowest approval rate (11.6 per cent at the first instance and 18.8 per cent overall). The Philippines, which screened the fewest people (7,272) had the highest percentage of screened-in (46.6 per cent after the first interview and 53.4 per cent following appeals). Overall, about 28 per cent of Vietnamese asylum seekers who applied for refugee status under CPA procedures were successful (see Table 8.1).

Table 8.1 Status Determination Decisions for Vietnamese Boat People

	First instance			Appeal			UNHCR Mandated		Total Persons		
	Screened in	Screened out	%	Screened in	Screened out	%	Persons	%	Screened in	Screened out	%
Hong Kong	6974	55301	11.6	2821	46078	5.8	1553	3.1	11348	48927	18.8
Indonesia	5083	13048	28	2759	4411	38.5	-	-	7842	10289	43.3
Malaysia	4088	11400	26.4	1892	8138	18.9	55	0.6	6035	9453	39
Philippines	3392	3880	46.6	471	3110	13.2	19	0.6	3882	3390	53.4
Thailand	2823	10666	21	210	7378	2.8	-	-	3048	10456	22.5
Japan	141	894	13.6	4	131	2.9	14	10.7	159	876	15.4
TOTAL	22516	93189	19.5	8157	69246	10.5	1641		32314	83391	27.9

Some have argued that the low rates in Hong Kong are at least partly due to the former British colony's high percentage of Vietnamese from the north, whose claim to refugee status was not as well established as that of their counterparts in the south. But how then to explain the substantial variance in the approval rates of Indonesia, Malaysia and Thailand when all three countries received a largely southern caseload? The difference lies less in the factual backgrounds than in their interpretation.

'It should be remembered that most officials had virtually no experience with refugee status determination' prior to the start of the CPA, said Erika Feller. 'With the years, people gained a lot more expertise, standardized interpretation of criteria, harmonization of decision making, a database on country of origin information…. Still there were regional differences: Indonesia and the Philippines felt that it was better to screen in and get people resettled. Malaysia was fairly balanced. Thailand was fairly tough.'[44]

In August 1994, a group called the New South Wales Refugee Fund Committee issued a slim report with an explosive charge: the screening process in Indonesia was 'severely rigged by widespread corruption, including bribery and sexual favour'.[45] Screening officials, Indonesian military officers and even UNHCR legal consultants, the report alleged, were involved in corruption rings in which asylum seekers were asked to pay bribes or offer sexual favours in exchange for positive decisions. 'As a consequence of widespread corruption', the report charged, 'criminal elements, collaborators, middlemen and those with cash were regularly screened in. On the other hand, cases with strong refugee claims but without money to pay, or wives and daughters to offer, were often denied refugee status.'

Under increasing pressure from refugee advocacy groups and the US Congress to investigate the corruption charges, UNHCR launched a series of reviews of the screening process in Indonesia. The review was internal and did not involve any re-interviewing of asylum seekers, nor did it investigate the corruption charges as such. Instead, UNHCR seemed principally concerned with whether any deserving case might have been screened out unfairly. Senior UNHCR officials examined 486 selected 'high visibility' cases. Their conclusions never were released publicly but, according a report by the US General Accounting Office (GAO), the UNHCR review upheld the screening decisions in 481 of the 486 cases. The remaining five were given mandate status. According to the GAO report

> The [UNHCR] reviews concluded that, overall, Indonesia's screening procedures properly identified and screened in cases with serious protection concerns, but that a small number of borderline cases could possibly have benefited from more sympathetic application of the screening criteria. The reviews found that corruption was a factor that impinged on screening procedures but was rarely, of ever, substantiated in the case files and that the chief effect was to inflate the number of positive decisions by also screening in weak cases. The reviews did not support the assertion that strong cases failed because they could not pay corruption demands.[46]

The GAO report went on to say that 'the reviews also concluded that UNHCR did not take adequate steps to detect or prevent corruption in the screening process, allowing corruption to undermine the integrity of the process'. Although the two legal consultants were dismissed from UNHCR in 1994, no further actions were taken against them.

In the end, UNHCR declared itself satisfied that

> while the [status determination] procedures were far from perfect, there were safeguards built in to ensure that those with a valid claim to refugee status were 'screened in'. UNHCR is satisfied that it was given adequate access by the authorities concerned to monitor the screening procedure and application of criteria, and assess the merits of the cases. UNHCR is also satisfied that its views on a case, particularly those which favored the screening-in of a case, were generally accepted by the authorities, or failing that, UNHCR was able to exercise its mandate, which it used on behalf of about 1,600 people.[47]

But how satisfied were the other participants? Assuming that they did not find the screening process perfect, just how far from perfection did it fall? The governments involved – donor countries, countries of asylum and countries of origin – carped from time to time but ultimately expressed satisfaction with the results. The reactions of human rights organizations and refugee advocacy groups, particularly those drawn from overseas Vietnamese, ranged from mild concern to total outrage. Nguyen Dinh Thang, director of the Boat People SOS Committee in Washington, DC had this to say:

> Corruption was only part of the problem. There was also an acute lack of competent interpreters, lack of adequate training for UNHCR legal consultants, incompetent screening officials, inadequate understanding of Vietnamese country conditions, overly brief interviews – the average was 20 minutes – relying extensively on yes–no questions, no legal representation or assistance in the appeals stage, no reason for denial given except in the Philippines, no access to one's own records to review or correct possible errors. All of these procedural flaws compounded the problems of corruption. UNHCR was not in control of these procedures and it was unwilling to exercise its mandate sufficiently to correct the flaws. The Vietnamese called this 'xo', a lottery.[48]

As for the asylum seekers themselves, it is hard to find anyone, screened-in or screened-out, happy with the status determination process. The screened-in clearly were happier with the results than those who were rejected but many found the procedures arcane and arbitrary. When one young man got his rejection after the first interview, he said

> It caused me real shock. After the decision, everyone was allowed to make an appeal within 21 days. But without guidelines, I did not know on what grounds to make my appeal. I was struggling like Don Quixote, you see. Somehow, I had to comply with the system but I didn't understand the system.... Our cases were decided seemingly not based on any specific criteria and people did not know how to fight for their cases. The fight was unfair in the minds of the people. We

were fighting with no weapons. Now everyone is required by law to leave but our fate was decided with no specific law.[49]

One impartial and fairly thorough assessment of the process comes from the US General Accounting Office, which conducted a review of the implementation of the CPA at the behest of Congressman Christopher Smith, Chairman of the Subcommittee on International Operations and Human Rights in the House of Representatives, and an outspoken critic of the screening procedures. Looking specifically at Hong Kong and Indonesia, the focus of the strongest complaints about the screening process, the GAO concluded that 'both programmes met the CPA's basic structural requirements for refugee adjudication criteria and screening procedures ... and both countries' procedures met minimal procedural requirements endorsed by the Executive Committee of UNHCR'.[50]

In the case of Hong Kong, the report found that 'the process contained sufficient checks and balances to provide reasonable assurances that asylum seekers' cases could be heard and errors could be identified and corrected'. As for Indonesia, GAO officials concluded that 'corruption in the process was likely' but 'it is unlikely that strong cases were denied refugee status due to unmet corruption demands'.

As a 'limited test' of the screening procedures in both countries, the GAO analysts looked at UNHCR case files on ten selected cases. For Hong Kong, five of the cases were referred by Boat People SOS and the other five by the Lawyers Committee for Human Rights. All ten of the Indonesian cases were referred by Boat People SOS. After reviewing the files in Hong Kong, GAO concluded that 'the Hong Kong government and UNHCR officials' decisions appeared to be reasonable in nine of the ten cases we examined. In the tenth case we identified information that we believe should have been factored into the decision. UNHCR agreed and subsequently granted the individual mandate refugee status.... A UNHCR official acknowledged judgmental errors in this case.'[51]

Following an examination of the UNHCR files in Indonesia, GAO officials came to similar conclusions. Of the ten cases, five rejection decisions were deemed 'reasonable and consistent with screening criteria'. In two cases, the screening decisions appeared to have been incorrect but both were among the cases mandated by UNHCR during its 1995 review of the Indonesian programme. Of the three remaining cases, one had fled Galang for Australia before his case was appealed (Australian authorities granted him refugee status), the second 'appeared to be reasonably adjudicated', and in the third case GAO 'raised questions that resulted in UNHCR's mandating the individual'.[52]

Recognizing that a review of 20 non-randomly selected cases is hardly conclusive, the GAO's 'limited test' is still suggestive of two things: both that screening decisions, for the most part, were reasonable and consistent with established criteria and that the process left meaningful room for error.

Unaccompanied Minors

In its August 1988 *Guidelines on Refugee Children*, UNHCR defined unaccompanied minors as persons under the age of 18

> who are separated from both parents and are not being cared for by an adult
> who, by law or custom, has responsibility to do so. Action to assist such children
> must take into account the many different reasons that may have caused them to
> become 'unaccompanied'. Children may have been accidentally separated,
> abducted, or orphaned. They may have run away, been abandoned, or live
> independently with or without their parents' consent. Some may have become
> street children in larger urban areas. Some children may have been sent to the
> country of asylum by parents who have remained in their country of origin, whilst
> others may be children left in the country of asylum by parents who have returned
> home or resettled elsewhere. In conflict situations, children may have been
> separated as a result of conscription. Children may have become separated as a
> result of their being removed by aid workers. Different causes of separation have
> different implications for the care of the child and the potential for family
> reunion.[53]

Unaccompanied minors are among the most vulnerable of refugee and
asylum-seeker populations and the UNHCR guidelines recognized that they
should be 'first among the first' to receive protection and care. It was with
this in mind that UNHCR submitted a 'Note on Unaccompanied Minors'
to the coordinating committee for the CPA conference, proposing that
Special Committees be established in each country of first asylum to decide
on a case-by-case basis what solution would be in the best interest of each
unaccompanied minor. Members of the Special Committees were to include
representatives of the host government, UNHCR, and other appropriate
agencies with child welfare expertise. UNHCR recommended that these
committees be given the task of carrying out a refugee status determination
for all children under 16 and then deciding on a solution that was deemed
to be in the best interest of the child.

'The cardinal principles governing the handling of unaccompanied minors',
stated the Note, 'are the best interests of the child and the unity of the family.
In most cases, these objectives are compatible. Where they are not, the best
interests of the child should be the guiding principle.' In reaching decisions
on a solution for these children, UNHCR reiterated, speed was of the essence
as 'prolonged residence in camps is potentially harmful to unaccompanied
minors, even more so than to adults and accompanied children.'[54]

As of March 1989, when the regional cut-off dates went into effect, there
were more than 2,100 Vietnamese unaccompanied minors in Southeast Asian
camps. Under the terms of the CPA, these were to be resettled overseas. By
November 1990, nearly 18 months after the CPA went into effect, the
caseload of new, post-deadline unaccompanied minors stood at 5,000
regionwide and the Special Procedures were coming under intense criticism.
A UNHCR update noted that after an 'extremely slow start' caused largely

by difficulty in recruiting qualified caseworkers, about 20 per cent of the minors had gone through initial interviewing and documentation but only about 10 per cent of the cases had actually been submitted to a Special Committee. Of these, only four children actually had left the camps of first asylum, two volunteering to return to Vietnam and two departing for resettlement.[55]

That same month, at a meeting in New York with voluntary agency representatives, Sergio Vieira de Mello reported a cordial exchange of views on developments in Rwanda, Cambodia, Western Sahara and South Africa. The conversation then turned to the CPA and the issue of unaccompanied minors. Dawn Calabia, then with the USCC, accused UNHCR headquarters of being unable to answer even 'basic' questions and acting 'in a secretive manner' about the Special Procedures. Julie MacDonald of the LIRS said her agency had offered UNHCR's Hong Kong office the services of a child specialist free of charge but had received no reply. Processing of unaccompanied minors was occurring at what she termed 'geological speed'. Furthermore, she was convinced that UNHCR was biased regarding the best interest of the children and 'determined, as a rule, to recommend repatriation.' Because of this bias and the extraordinary slowness of the process, MacDonald concluded that as far as unaccompanied minors were concerned, UNHCR had become an 'agent of harm'.[56]

At the meeting, Vieira de Mello denied the charges of bias, saying this was 'totally contrary to UNHCR's impartial approach to this and other CPA components and in no way reflected humanitarian doctrine of the office'. Still, if bias meant a presentiment that the large majority of unaccompanied minors were not refugees and their best interests would be served by sending them home to their parents in Vietnam, then the accusation was not unfounded.

In an article for *Refugees* magazine, UNHCR's senior regional social services officer, Christine Mougne, had written

> The problem is that many of the unaccompanied children now living in camps and detention centers around Southeast Asia, in conditions ranging from difficult to dangerous, are there because their parents chose to send them with a view to their own resettlement.... For most children ... whose parent or parents have remained in Vietnam, it is likely that the decision will be to return them to their families in the country of origin. This is in line with all internationally accepted child care principles.[57]

The worry that unaccompanied minors, especially Vietnamese ones, were being sent out by parents to 'anchor' resettlement for other family members was a long-standing one. The premise of the 'anchor case' argument was as follows: beginning in April 1982, the US government halted resettlement of all cases without previous links, family or professional, to the United States, a pattern later adopted by other resettlement countries. But in 1983, out of humanitarian concern for what it considered a population at risk, the United States indicated that it was prepared to resettle all unaccompanied minors who had links to the United States and 50 per cent of those who did not. Thus, a family in Vietnam with no previous connections to the United States (or elsewhere) could establish a link by sending a minor child, sometimes with an older relative as chaperone.

No clear statistical evidence seems to exist as to just how many unaccompanied minors later were joined in resettlement countries by other family members. Mougne and others in UNHCR felt the numbers were significant. Child psychologist and pediatric psychiatrist, Nguyen Ba Thien, who has worked with Indochinese minors resettled in France since the earliest days of the exodus said, 'The first aim in sending the children was for them to get an education. Maybe in some cases, parents intended to join them later on.' Since 1989, she noted that most of the unaccompanied minors 'came from very poor villages in North Vietnam, where there are no schools'.[58]

Others saw the issue more strictly in political terms. A Vietnamese expatriate organization in San Diego, California called Aid to Refugee Children Without Parents protested any repatriation of minors to Vietnam on the grounds that

> the parents of the children who are returned and the children themselves will be subjected to overt as well as subtle forms of discrimination and persecution.... Faced with the prospect of seeing their children forced to live under communism, parents have chosen to send their children away despite the dangers to the children, the political repercussions for the entire family if the children are caught by the communist security forces, the cost of financing an escape, and above all the trauma of separation.[59]

The San Diego group's bias clearly was in favour of ongoing resettlement in the United States. 'The people who know what is in the best interests of the children,' it insisted, 'are not "specialists" outside the country, but the parents who sent the children out' in order to see them resettled.

There was an ironic consonance between the UNHCR view and that of organizations like Aid to Refugee Children Without Parents: each in its own way linked the best interests of the unaccompanied minors in the camps with the parents left behind in Vietnam. The links between the children and their parents, however, were often circuitous and a challenge to discern. One report noted that 'A very common reason for leaving Vietnam, expressed by unaccompanied minors in the first asylum camps, was to escape a traumatic family situation caused by a family breakdown.'[60] A study carried out in the Hong Kong camps by the International Catholic Child Bureau (ICCB) noted that unaccompanied minors

> report significantly higher numbers of deceased parents than the accompanied children. It is known that many of these reports are inaccurate, and in part reflect the perception that such a statement enhances the chances of resettlement. In approximately half of these statements, the children report that the death occurred since their arrival in Hong Kong.... An added dimension to the family situation of the ... unaccompanied children is that 32% of them report that they did not

live with their parents prior to departure.... The 'attachment' of these children to their parents may well have been poor, and intervening events will have done nothing to improve this. One girl interviewed, when asked if she wrote to her divorced mother replied, 'Why should I write to her? She abandoned me'.[61]

In July 1992, Nordic Assistance to Repatriated Vietnamese (NARV), a consortium of five Nordic voluntary agencies, reached an agreement with UNHCR to coordinate a reintegration programme for unaccompanied minors returning to Vietnam. In their home assessments and monitoring visits, NARV caseworkers found that of those unaccompanied minors who returned by early 1995, 78.2 per cent with both parents, 10.3 per cent with at least one parent, and 9.5 per cent were living with grandparents or other relatives. 'Only a fraction of the unaccompanied minors who claimed to be orphans in the camp', NARV concluded, 'were genuine orphans.'[62]

Whether they were orphans or not, and whether sent by their parents to escape communism, get an education, or anchor a case for future migration, the unaccompanied minors in the first asylum camps were deeply vulnerable young people. Those that were screened in or otherwise recommended for resettlement – roughly 28 per cent of the caseload – moved on to start new lives, but those recommended for repatriation mostly remained in the camps. An evaluation of the NARV programmes cited three main reasons for this:

> By far the most important was the expectations from their parents who had sent them away to reach a Western country. Unless they received a letter from their parents telling them to come home, few would dare return. In addition, a fear of coming home as a drop out and a 'nobody' with nothing to do kept many from volunteering to return. The third was the apathy that took hold of the camp population. Each new day in the camp was not so much a result of a decision to stay but of avoiding the decision to go home.[63]

The impact of long-term detention on all children, and especially the unaccompanied ones, was staggering, according to Margaret McCallin, who drafted the report on children in detention in Hong Kong for the International Catholic Child Bureau. She wrote that

> the principal effects characterizing the majority of the children in the sample are depression and anxiety. They are typically sad, lacking in energy and disinterested in what is going on around them. Their daily lives are overwhelmingly characterized by fears for their personal safety. They suffer from psychosomatic symptoms of anxiety and are restless and have problems concentrating. Memories of distressing events they have experienced intrude upon their thoughts. They feel that they do not have enough help or guidance and express a need for affection. It is not surprising, therefore, that for most children the future seems hopeless.[64]

The list of insults and traumatic experiences was long and painful: sexual assault, physical assault, bullying/threatening, forced separation from family and friends, prostitution, witness to suicide, witness to murder, substance abuse, hunger strike, demonstrations and riots, tear gassing, forced relocation (from one camp to another), weapons searches, gang warfare, and general physical violence in the camp. The children interviewed, on average, had experienced more than three of these events.[65]

McCallin recommended several steps to improve conditions in the camps, including training for paraprofessionals working with victims of physical and sexual abuse, enhanced educational opportunities including sexual education and self-protection, and the creation of 'safe spaces' for children in the detention centres. As much as the unaccompanied minors needed a sense of community, however, the ICCB suggested that the most urgent priority was to get them out of the camps. Here, McCallin noted, 'There is a certain inconsistency in the position which, recognizing the child's immaturity, demands special procedures to determine the status of children, and yet allows a child to veto return by refusing assent.' She cautioned that 'the use of force in any repatriation exercise may do irreparable harm to children who are already "psychologically wounded". This must always be the last resort.'[66] And yet, every day that went by in the detention centres inflicted its own punishment on innocent children.

If there is any consensus at all on the CPA's Special Procedures for unaccompanied minors, it is that they failed to treat this vulnerable population as 'first among the first', instead, as one UNHCR official put it, 'The minors were kept waiting longer than anyone else. It was an unintelligible process. The mantra was that unaccompanied minors were better off in Vietnam. Their parents were telling them to lie in order to get out. The kids were being torn apart. Children need prompt screening followed by prompt resettlement or prompt return.'[67]

The Special Procedures, in the end, did not appear to be in the best interests of the children they were intended to serve. The delays were so lengthy, in fact, that by the end of 1993, more than 2,600 minors who had arrived in camps under the age of 16 had 'aged out', putting them into the normal status determination procedures for adults. For the majority of minors, who were not recommended for resettlement, the delays had kept them pinned down in such a dangerous and unhealthy environment, it was a very real question whether they were capable of making a rational decision about their future. Indeed, from their perspective, it was hard to see what choices they had at all. The camp authorities and UNHCR were pressing them to repatriate, which their family members in Vietnam and neighbours in the camp actively opposed. The pressure from the Vietnamese community, meanwhile, was to hold out for resettlement, which was not a real possibility. Either way, they could not win. As psychologist Nguyen Kim Ba Thien said, 'These children were sent on a dangerous mission and failed. They were abandoned to do a difficult job alone and feel rejected by their families. They have failed and been failed by all sides. This leaves a feeling of bitter revolt.'[68] In this feeling, at least, they were not alone.

Repatriation

In March 1989, a group of 75 Vietnamese returned home from the camps in Hong Kong, the first organized voluntary repatriation to Vietnam in at least ten years. By the end of that year, about 800 more had followed suit. Faced with the arrival of 34,000 new asylum seekers in 1989 alone, however, the Hong Kong authorities took little encouragement at the pace of voluntary return. The June 1989 agreement had stated that 'If, after the passage of reasonable time, it becomes clear that voluntary repatriation is not making sufficient progress towards the desired objective, alternatives recognized as being acceptable under international practices would be examined.' Though many saw the timing as quite unreasonable, Hong Kong took steps to exercise its alternatives and start forcing people home before the year was out.

On 12 December 1989, under cover of darkness, more than 100 Hong Kong police and prison guards escorted a group of 51 Vietnamese men, women, and children across the tarmac of Kai Tak Airport to a waiting Cathay Pacific jet. At 5:09 a.m., the plane lifted off for Hanoi. This first exercise of what the Hong Kong government chose to call 'mandatory repatriation' launched a wave of international protest. A White House spokesman said that the United States 'deeply regrets' the incident while Senator Claiborne Pell, chairman of the Senate Foreign Relations Committee, said simply, 'It's a disgrace.' British Foreign Secretary Douglas Hurd insisted that the forced return was necessary as a deterrent 'to show people who may even now be planning to come in the spring, when the winds change and the season begins, that it is not a happy voyage'.[69]

Witnesses in Hanoi said the returnees looked tired and depressed as they were driven from the airport to a reception centre six miles away where they stayed temporarily before returning to their home provinces of Haiphong and Quang Ninh. While Britain maintained that the involuntary move had been cleared with Vietnam, Foreign Minister Nguyen Co Thach suggested otherwise: 'Now we are checking with these 51 people,' he said. 'If there are any who are against repatriation, we will ask the British to take them to Hong Kong. If they refuse ... we will stop our cooperation for receiving the voluntary returnees.'[70]

At a CPA steering committee meeting held in Geneva in January 1990, the US delegation insisted on a one-year moratorium on further involuntary return. After that, said Deputy Assistant Secretary of State Robert Funseth, the United States was prepared to accept involuntary return of the screened-out, but only on the condition that there were no volunteers waiting to return and that international monitors were present on both ends of the mandatory return process.[71] Hong Kong's Legislative Council responded by calling for an end to first asylum until forced returns could resume.[72]

As tensions simmered in the Hong Kong camps, the moratorium held for most of 1990. Then, on 23 September 1990, Britain and Vietnam announced that they had reached a new agreement on the return of 'those who, while not volunteering to return, are nevertheless not opposed to going back'. UNHCR, furthermore, agreed to play an 'active role fully compatible with its humanitarian mandate'.[73] The United States offered no objection to this new arrangement, though it remained opposed to the use of force. In the end, only 23 people could be found willing, or at least not opposed, to jump through these semantic hoops and, by 1991, Hong Kong's 'non-objectors scheme' was a non-issue. The agreement did have one powerful effect, however, and that was to heighten anxieties in the camps. In an internal memorandum, a JVA official in Hong Kong said that

> The asylum seekers are either misinformed and confused about the terminology or believe that this is only a smokescreen for an attempt to implement forced repatriation. It is to be expected that activities such as hunger strikes, demonstrations, and suicide attempts will occur in different detention centres to protest the forced repatriation and the unjust screening policies.[74]

The memorandum also noted that Hong Kong had a new Refugee Coordinator, Clinton Leeks, 'who is known for being a hard liner and who is expected to be less accommodating than the previous coordinator, Mike Hanson.' The press were now 'unofficially' restricted from entering the detention centres and 'tougher measures are being applied toward agencies and workers who need to have access to the detention centers on a daily basis'.

Following a brief lull at the beginning of the year, Vietnamese asylum seekers once more began pouring into Hong Kong by the middle of 1991. Some refugee officials blamed the new outflow on a Voice of America broadcast in March, which aired a proposal by conservative US Congressman Robert Dornan to the effect that Vietnamese boat people should be resettled in Kuwait to help rebuild the country after the Iraqi invasion.[75] By September, Hong Kong was housing more than 64,000 Vietnamese, the highest total in its history. Referring to the screened-out population, Clinton Leeks said, 'We have 19,000 illegal immigrants who ... are going to have to go home. Not just voluntarily, they're going to have to go home.'[76]

On 27 September 1991 – just days after the voluntary repatriation programme celebrated the return of the 10,000th Vietnamese from Hong Kong – officials from the British, Hong Kong and Vietnamese governments, together with UNHCR, announced yet another agreement on repatriation. Following several days of meetings in Hanoi, the parties issued a joint statement concurring that 'the cash payment provided to those returning to Vietnam has become an incentive for departure rather than return'.[77] All new arrivals in first asylum countries as of that date would no longer be eligible for the UNHCR *per capita* cash grant of up to $360. The new amount was set at $50 per person and that only for the most deserving cases. The statement also noted an 'agreement in principle on the need to implement measures to achieve an accelerated rate of return'. Although details were sketchy, speculation was rampant that this meant Vietnam had dropped its long-standing objection to forced repatriation. Not necessarily, said a Foreign Ministry spokeswoman in Hanoi. Her government preferred 'better, appropriate ways'.[78]

On 21 October 1991, Britain, Hong Kong and Vietnam signed an agreement on the 'orderly return' of some 222 boat people who were found to have entered Hong Kong previously, returned to Vietnam, and then left again. These so-called 'double-backers' were suspected of re-entering the camps in order to receive another round of repatriation assistance. On 29 October the British and Vietnamese governments announced they had reached a much broader agreement, one that would encompass all of the existing 19,000 screened-out cases and any new arrivals who were rejected for refugee status.

Also in October, the warring parties to the long-running Cambodian conflict agreed in Paris to a peaceful power-sharing arrangement, pending UN-sponsored elections. Days later, US Secretary of State James Baker announced that his government was prepared to seek normal relations with Vietnam. Monthly arrivals in Hong Kong had totalled 2,893 in September 1991. In October, they dropped to 492 and, by November, they had fallen to only 7. Whether cowed into surrender by the new cutbacks in reintegration aid and the new threats of forced return, or coaxed into staying by the new prospects for economic opportunity, Vietnamese finally stopped fleeing their country by boat. The exodus was over.

In the Hong Kong camps, however, resistance to repatriation was building, particularly in Whitehead which then housed 25,000 people. Additional police units with full anti-riot gear were deployed amidst threats of widespread demonstrations and mass suicide attempts. On 10 November Hong Kong police and security officers forced 59 Vietnamese, including two women injected with sedatives, onto a transport plane bound for Hanoi. By the end of 1995, Hong Kong sent back just over 2,100 people under the Orderly Return Programme (ORP). 'We have never seen ORP as a main means of return,' said Hong Kong Refugee Coordinator Brian Bresnihan. 'It is a stick to encourage them to go home voluntarily but it must be regular enough to menace the population.'[79] Because of the heavy security involved, ORP flights averaged about 60 people and were carried out roughly six times per year. This created in the camp a cycle that one UNHCR official described as 'two months of silence, one day of violence, two months of silence, one day of violence'. The years following witnessed a rising tide of tension and violence in the Hong Kong detention centers, sparked by the overcrowded, prison-like conditions; the in-camp rivalries and conflicts; cutbacks in camp services; and the systematic use of mandatory return as a spur to voluntary repatriation.

In September 1993, UNHCR's representatives and chiefs of mission in Southeast Asia met in Jakarta to review progress on the CPA. More than 44,000 Vietnamese had returned home, screening was coming to an end and the exodus from Vietnam had slowed to a trickle. A confidential discussion paper drafted for the meeting by the UNHCR Hong Kong office, then headed by Robert van Leeuwen, noted that despite the 'evolving conditions' in Vietnam tens of thousands of screened-out Vietnamese remained in detention and refused to go home. Reintegration programmes were beginning to wind down in Vietnam and the Indochinese refugee issue was no longer as high on the political agendas of key governments. 'Time is and has been the worst enemy of those who still remain,' stated the paper. 'There is an urgent need to act.'[80]

In a section titled 'What is to be done?' the confidential paper outlined a course of action to bring the CPA to a rapid close. First, screening should be completed as quickly as possible and new arrivals should be 'summarily returned' unless there was an obvious basis for granting asylum. 'Further agreements ... on non-voluntary return of non-refugees', the Hong Kong office recommended, 'should be promoted and implemented.' The main thrust of the paper, however, was on eliminating what many UNHCR officials had come to refer to as 'stay factors' in the camps.

'The number of NGOs and their activities in first asylum camps should be *sharply reduced* [sic]', the discussion paper recommended, and 'all assistance activities which contribute to expectations of permanence of life in detention should cease.' Moreover, 'UNHCR should sharply reduce its presence ... with respect to non-refugees refusing to return' and 'further reductions in assistance to returnees should be announced' in the camps.

Not all of these recommendations were endorsed by the other UNHCR representatives and some were never implemented, but changes already were under way and the message was unmistakable: conditions in the camps must be made ever more onerous until people were driven to return home. UNHCR-supported cutbacks around the region included reductions in medical and counselling services, new restrictions on freedom of movement in and around some camps, elimination of income-generating activities and reductions in employment opportunities, and limits on monthly remittances from overseas.

Perhaps the most dramatic and the most controversial change, however, was the elimination of all educational programmes above the primary level (grades 1–5). The move was greeted by almost universal protest and derision from the voluntary agencies. 'The UNHCR decision to cut secondary education was stupid and irresponsible,' said Louise MacPherson, a teacher with International Social Services in Hong Kong's infamous Whitehead camp. 'I don't believe in cutting education for children. This flies in the face of everything the UN says about education and poverty. Volrep numbers didn't go up after the cutback. It only made a lot more hard feelings in camp.'[81] Jackie Lindgren, who worked in the Hong Kong camps for several years, first for Caritas then as an education officer for UNHCR, said 'I defended my programmes. Adult education was the only place where we had funding for adolescents and secondary schools. The loss of adult ed lost the unaccompanied minors programmes. The worst group in terms of violent behaviour was the late adolescent single men.' In the end, she said, 'it was really dishonest not to have the courage to say "Go", rather than pressing people in so many ways…. If they want people to be unproductive and fight in order to make them go back, then they should state that.'[82]

As one Vietnamese detainee said, referring to an undefined 'they', which could mean UNHCR, the Hong Kong authorities or the world at large:

> They don't want hope to remain in us. They want everybody to go back to Vietnam. They don't want us to be happy or to do anything. Just live and eat and nothing else and don't do anything else. So they won't help us. And the most important thing to them is voluntary repatriation, do you see? And that is why they don't want to let us do anything.[83]

For Quentin Dignam, SJ, regional director for Jesuit Refugee Service/Asia-Pacific (JRS), the trade-off was clear: UNHCR, under pressure from the international community (and especially the United States) to promote voluntary return, had opted to impose harsh conditions in the camps in order to compel people to volunteer.

> We accept the use of proportionate and necessary force in the direct process (e.g. assembly, transit, boarding) of moving people back to Vietnam under the ORP. We view this as a legitimate – if regrettable – process of deportation. We welcome proportionate measures to prevent coercion by some asylum seekers against others. But we strongly oppose the practice of harassment, coercion and deliberate deprivation of services and assistance (including food, shelter, access to medical care) applied with the aim of having asylum-seekers 'volunteer' to return.[84]

One of the forms of harassment practised by Hong Kong's Correctional Services Department in the name of security was periodically to 'decant' Vietnamese from one camp to another or from one section to another. At dawn on 7 April 1994, an estimated 1,200 riot police moved into Whitehead's Section 7 to break up a long-running but peaceful demonstration and to move the 1,500 protesters to another camp at High Island. Tensions had been running high in the camps ever since February when, at the fifth meeting of the CPA Steering Committee in Geneva, participants had agreed to try to empty the camps by the end of 1995 or sooner if possible. The Steering Committee had noted 'with appreciation' the 60,000 Vietnamese who had returned home voluntarily since 1989 but 'nevertheless, expressed the feeling that additional arrangements were now appropriate to expedite the return of all non-refugees from camps in the region'. The committee, furthermore, 'recognized that orderly return programmes can have a beneficial impact on the voluntary repatriation programme' and noted that Indonesia had reached its own ORP agreement with Vietnam on 2 October 1993.

For the residents in the camps, it was now clear that involuntary return was no longer an isolated phenomenon in Hong Kong but now enjoyed regional and international sanction. The United States might express a *pro forma* caution against the use of force but no longer stood in opposition. The demonstrations and hunger strikes in Whitehead, according to one participant, represented 'our only possible hope' to stir international attention.[85] As another detainee described the events of 7 April,

> Over 500 tear gas canisters, a pepper-fog machine, and hundreds of mace cans were deployed by 1,250 armed tactical forces, backed with 2 armoured personnel carriers and a helicopter. Yet the 'threat to security' against which this impressive show of force was massed was none other than 1,500 defenseless men, women, and children who the powers that be had decided to move to another camp without prior warning. Our situation is so desperate: At least 170 people, including children, sustained injuries in the raid, and even now people are still suffering from breathing problems, chest pains, bruising and burns. Our sleep is disturbed by the cries of our children reliving the raid in their nightmares, and many families have been split up, the fathers sent to Upper Chimawan camp for their part in the 'unrest' where they may be held for up to six months without any judicial process. But why did the government resort to this heavy-handed military-style operation? We believe they did so because they wanted to demonstrate to all the boat people that force could be used against any of us at any time without justifiable cause, and that our protests against unfair screening and forced repatriation were nothing more than futile. But what else can we do?[86]

For many observers, including some UNHCR officials, that was the turning point. From then on, any last semblance of mutual trust and communication between camp administrators and 'inmates' was lost, replaced by open hostility or sullen silence. Following Hong Kong and Indonesia, the remaining countries of asylum – Philippines, Malaysia, and Thailand – eventually signed tripartite ORP agreements with Vietnam and UNHCR. These agreements – under which UNHCR provided some logistical support and funding for transportation costs – 'do not envisage the use of force', as one UNHCR report said. 'As a matter of policy, UNHCR does not participate in movements that involve force.'[87] By the time of the sixth CPA Steering Committee in March 1985, however, no country other than Hong Kong had elected to try an ORP exercise. Meeting participants 'recognized the appropriateness of timely implementation of the orderly return programmes in safety and dignity' but experience in Hong Kong had shown that this was a complex, costly and controversial job. The end of the CPA, they suggested, might not come in 1995.

Further delays occurred when, on 8 June 1995, the US House of Representatives passed a bill prohibiting the use of American funds for Vietnamese and Laotian repatriation unless the President could certify that no genuine refugee had been wrongly screened out. The legislation, introduced by Republican Congressman Chris Smith, also authorized funding for additional resettlement of Indochinese refugees in the United States above and beyond existing CPA commitments. Opponents of Smith's bill, which included UNHCR and the Clinton Administration, blamed the legislation for stirring up violence in the camps and warned it could prompt renewed boat flows from Vietnam. No new exodus took place, however, and the camp violence had far deeper and more tangled roots than could be blamed on any one element. Certainly, the legislation had a dampening impact on return to Vietnam, though numbers had been declining since the beginning of 1995. Here again, the decision to remain was complex, and according to a report by Jesuit Refugee Service,

> is influenced especially by persistent false hopes of resettlement, by pressures from family and community members in Vietnam and in third countries, by inconsistent and ambivalent policies on the part of governments and UNHCR, and by the psychologically disabling effects of camp life which make free and informed decision-making difficult.[88]

Missing from that list, of course, was the fear of persecution upon return. Immigration authorities and UNHCR insisted that such fear was not well-founded, but anyone who worked in or even visited the camps knew there was fear all the same. 'It will be some time', predicted the JRS report at the end of 1995, 'before the people return voluntarily or otherwise to Vietnam.'

The Smith amendment never became law though it did serve to galvanize thinking in the United States about what might be done outside the multilateral bounds of the CPA both to promote voluntary return, avoid further violence in the camps and, at the same time, offer a last chance at resettlement for some screened-out groups of lingering US concern. Out of this was born what first was known as Track II and, later, Resettlement Opportunities for Vietnamese Returnees (ROVR). Under this programme, begun in late April 1996, any Vietnamese who was in a first asylum camp as of 1 October 1995 and who had already returned to Vietnam, or who registered for voluntary return by 30 June 1996, could be eligible for an interview with an INS officer *in Vietnam*.[89] Despite substantial confusion and suspicion on the part of camp residents, nearly 9,000 people registered by the deadline, which also marked the official end of the CPA.

On 25 June 1996, UNHCR and Malaysian officials gathered for a ceremony marking the closure of Sungei Besi, the last camp for Vietnamese boat people in Malaysia. Beginning in April, the Malaysian government had launched a series of 'orderly returns' by ship back to Vietnam, successfully emptying the camp and enabling it to become the first of the asylum countries to end its involvement with the Indochinese. Singapore followed two days later with the return of the remaining 103 people in Hawkins Road camp. On 30 June UNHCR ceased funding for Vietnamese boat people throughout the region, with the exception of Hong Kong which still held 15,000 in its detention centres.

Indonesia and Thailand did not manage to empty their remaining Vietnamese camps by the deadline, although each moved aggressively on involuntary repatriations in the latter half of 1996, sending back 1,500 and 2,000 people respectively. On 29 June, during Thailand's first ORP exercise, one Vietnamese man died, apparently of head injuries sustained from falling off a roof where he had fled to avoid camp security, and another 60 people were injured, some from self-inflicted knife wounds. Despite allegations of excessive force being used by Thai authorities and the fact that UNHCR officials were not permitted access to the camp during the operation, UNHCR agreed to contribute to the costs of the involuntary movement as they were contractually obligated.

In February 1996, the Philippines had attempted the first ORP flight outside of Hong Kong. According to a report from Boat People SOS,

> CNN footage, pictures in the local press and eye-witness accounts have established beyond dispute that force had been used in the military operation leading to the 14 February repatriation. Filipino marines and the national police had twice raided Palawan Camp to round up asylum seekers. During the second round-up, the marines laid siege to the Van Duc Buddhist Temple, assaulted the asylum seekers, including women and children, and desecrated the temple. The 150 asylum seekers rounded up for deportation were detained in squalid conditions and received threats from top [Filipino military] officials. On the day of the repatriation, 89 boat people were dragged to the runway, escorted by armed marines. Those who resisted were severely beaten or roughed up by the military guards. At least 18 boat persons have suffered injuries, including one miscarriage, as a result of the incident.[90]

The exercise prompted President Fidel Ramos, following strong appeals from the Catholic Church, to reverse government policy and allow the 2,700 Vietnamese still in Palawan camp to remain in the Philippines, at least until they chose to go home voluntarily.

The rounds of violence and silence continued in the Hong Kong camps until only a residual caseload of several hundred refugees remained. On 30 June 1997 the CPA formally and finally came to an end when the British colony reverted to Chinese hands.

The CPA and Laotians

After the intensive scrutiny given to the Vietnamese boat people in the planning and implementation of the CPA, the Laotians seemed scarcely an afterthought. The language in the draft declaration ran to a mere paragraph:

> In dealing with Laotian asylum seekers, future measures are to be worked out through intensified trilateral negotiation between UNHCR, the Lao People's Democratic Republic and Thailand with the active support and cooperation of all parties concerned. These measures should be aimed at:
>
> (a) Maintaining safe arrival and access to the Lao screening process;
> (b) Accelerating and simplifying the process for both the return of the screened-out and voluntary repatriation to the [LPDR] under safe, humane and UNHCR-monitored conditions.
>
> Together with other durable solutions, third-country resettlement continues to play an important role with regard to the present camp populations of the Laotians.[91]

Several factors conspired to make the Laotian issues little more than a footnote in the proceedings. First, Laotian asylum seekers were confined to

Thailand alone; this was not a matter of regional concern. Second, by 1989, only the United States remained as a significant country of resettlement; the Laotians were a matter of US interest but of scant international concern. Third, Laotian arrivals had not surged in recent years; there was no sense that the Laotians constituted a new crisis, only an unresolved old problem. And finally, screening for Laotian asylum seekers had been operational in Thailand since 1985 and, since 1986, the LPDR had permitted the 'orderly' return of both voluntary repatriates and screened-out.[92]

But by late 1988, the Lao border screening programme was in a state of near-collapse, due to a lack of systematic access on the part of the Hmong, rampant extortion on the part of local Thai officials, and intransigence and suspicion on the part of the Lao government in vetting applications for return. The CPA procedures brought new structure and accountability to the process and, not coincidentally, an increase in voluntary repatriation to Laos. They also brought new charges of UNHCR complicity in forced return.

From 1985 to 1989, the screening process was run by Thailand's Ministry of Interior with no formal appeal procedure available to UNHCR. About 90 per cent of the 31,000 people who got into the screening process were approved. Following the CPA, UNHCR and MOI worked out new procedures consistent with those applied regionally to Vietnamese asylum seekers. UNHCR was permitted to observe interviews, to query the applicants themselves, and to appeal decisions of the Thai screening committee. It took until the end of 1990, however, to put these procedures fully in place.

In all, since October 1989, a total of 10,005 Laotians were interviewed, of whom 4,918 (or 49 per cent) were screened in and 4,473 (45 per cent) were screened out, with the remainder pending or otherwise closed. Ironically, more than half of the people screened under the CPA guidelines were Hmong who had entered Ban Vinai and had been living there as 'illegals' for several months, or even years, prior to the implementation of the CPA. Had they been willing or able to present themselves for an interview earlier, their chances of acceptance would have been nearly double what they experienced in the CPA era.

One major reason for the decline was the fact that Thai MOI officers generally no longer considered the presence of close relatives in a resettlement country sufficient grounds, in and of itself, for approval. Hmong had to demonstrate a link to the pre-revolutionary government or armed forces, association with a foreign embassy or international organization, or evidence of participation in activities 'deemed to be antagonistic and adversary to the communist government'.[93]

In addition, both MOI and UNHCR officials looked more closely at issues of credibility and at what one UNHCR monitor called the 'time lapse of persecution'. Generally, this meant that the Hmong had to present credible reasons not only as to why they feared persecution upon return to Laos but why it had taken them so long to leave. As an example of a time lapse deemed unacceptable, one observer said, 'a 50 year old woman who fled to Phou Bia in 1975, then fled to a forest area with a group of Hmong after her husband was killed during a Pathet Lao attack in 1985, did not receive UNHCR support [for her appeal] because she lived without incident from 1985–88 and fled to Thailand only to avoid the hardship of living in the forest'.[94] UNHCR did not agree with Thai screening committee rejections in every case, however: its legal officers supported the appeals of at least 233 individuals, of whom the screening committee reversed its decision on 216.

But broadly speaking, as the border screening programme became more accountable under the CPA, it became somewhat less accommodating. Even as approval rates declined, Thai officials stepped up their efforts to get the screened-out to go home. Ever since October 1986, when the Lao government had signed an agreement with UNHCR to take back rejected asylum seekers, the MOI had undertaken periodic deportations of screened-out Laotians, including more than 300 in 1989 and 1990. In the pre-dawn hours of 18 January 1991, armed Thai security guards assembled a group of 59 screened-out Hmong and Mien in Chiang Kham camp and ordered them on to buses for a trip to the border town of Nong Khai and eventual repatriation. According to one reliable report, 'this was not well accepted by the screened out and there was some rough treatment, threatening with guns by Thai guards and people were literally pushed on the bus'.[95]

The action prompted a flurry of protests from the expatriate Hmong community as well as human rights groups in the United States. MOI defended itself by saying that if advanced notice had been given to the group pending deportation, they all would have slipped out of camp and disappeared. UNHCR termed the move voluntary because, by the time the group reached Nong Khai, the people had calmed down and were willing to return. The medical coordinator for Médecins Sans Frontières, who accompanied the buses to Nong Khai, attested to the 'excellent' work of two Hmong field officers employed by UNHCR in calming people's fears, but the line between voluntary and involuntary seemed thin indeed.

In fact, it is not clear why, in this and other cases, UNHCR felt it necessary to insist that all returns to Laos were voluntary. The terms spelled out by the CPA called for 'the return of the screened-out and voluntary repatriation to the [LPDR] under safe, humane and UNHCR-monitored conditions'. Moreover, in the tripartite meetings between Laos, Thailand and UNHCR that began in 1989, the three parties had agreed that 'those considered to be refugees and asylum seekers returning under the programme will do so on a voluntary basis, whereas those rejected in the screening process will be returned without the use of force in safety and dignity'.[96]

On 23 May 1991 another group of 93 screened-out Hmong from Chiang Kham were returned to Laos, along with 43 refugees repatriating voluntarily. UNHCR listed the entire movement in its official statistics as a voluntary repatriation, although in a letter to MOI it noted that the LPDR 'has approved the movements of Laotian voluntary repatriation candidates and screened-outs', thus appearing to make a clear distinction between the two.[97] In its own reporting on the events, the US Embassy in Thailand simply noted that 'the Ministry of Interior escorts were unarmed and the returnees, who were noticeably fewer than the 134 originally scheduled for repatriation, were relaxed and had all their belongings intact. The repatriation was carried out without incident'.[98]

At the end of 1991, Thai officials suspended further deportations of screened-out Laotians, opting instead to try to persuade them to volunteer. Until December 1991, screening for the highland Lao had taken place in Chiang Kham camp while lowlanders were screened in Nong Saeng, a detention centre in the northeastern city of Nakhon Phanom. In January 1992, MOI announced that all screening was to be centralized in Nong Saeng. Then, in August and early September that same year, MOI moved a group of more than 5,000 formerly 'illegal' residents of Ban Vinai to Na Pho, prompting alarms from the Hmong community in the United States that the group was the victim of a 'bait and switch' and would be forced back to Laos.

In mid-July 1992, frustrated at the slow pace of voluntary repatriation, MOI announced that the screened-out Hmong in Na Pho would be sent to Nong Saeng unless they signed up for voluntary return. On that date, according to eyewitnesses in the camp, a group of about 1,500 to 2,000 Hmong demonstrated in front of the UNHCR office in Na Pho. Some carried signs saying, 'No need to go to Nong Saeng. No need to go to Laos. Request to UNHCR-MOI for humanity.'

'The demonstrators began showing up at about 10:15 in the morning,' said Hans Willman, the local UNHCR camp officer. 'We usually have about 20 guards in the camp and three policemen. By about 11:30, there were 40 to 50 uniformed men standing just inside the gate, carrying bamboo shields and batons. There were no guns and they stayed in the background.' The Thai camp commander, Sati Phonyiam, 'handled the situation well', Willman said. 'He told the group to go home, in exchange for which he would meet with their designated leaders. By 2:00 p.m., the group had dissipated.'[99] Later, Sati met with leaders of the screened-out, who submitted a petition outlining 18 conditions for their return to Laos. Willman's account later was confirmed in confidential interviews with the Hmong leadership in camp.

But within 24 hours, a group called the Lao Human Rights Council, headed by Pobzeb Vang, was circulating reports in the Hmong community in the United States that 1,300 Thai troops had entered Na Pho camp to arrest the Hmong and force them back to Laos. 'I have to believe this is deliberate misinformation,' Willman said. 'Communication back and forth with the United States is very easy.'

In the week following the demonstration, all of the Ban Vinai screened-out group signed up for voluntary repatriation. 'We signed so that we would not be sent to Nong Saeng,' one Hmong put it simply, 'but we still don't trust the Lao government and we still don't want to go back.'

'It is a tactical move,' one MOI official said of the decision to transfer the screened-out Hmong to Nong Saeng. 'The problem that we face right now is this,' said Prapakorn Smiti, then deputy director of MOI's Operations Centre for Displaced Persons. 'We transferred all unauthorized Hmong to Na Pho. Genuine [refugee] cases we transfer to Phanat Nikhom if they want to resettle. If they are genuine and don't want to resettle, they stay in Na Pho. But if they are screened-out, they should go to Nong Saeng. When we tried to move people before, UNHCR asked for a delay of one month in order to promote voluntary repatriation. They had no success so we had to make some decisions.... We have got to start moving people'.[100]

Notes

1 Author's interview with Nguyen Thi Anh (pseudonym), Sungei Besi Camp, Malaysia, 29 September 1995.

2 The cut-off date for Thailand and Malaysia was 14 March 1989, 17 March 1989 for Indonesia, and 21 March 1989 for the Philippines. Hong Kong had preceded the four ASEAN countries by nine months, establishing a cut-off date of 16 June 1988.

3 Sadako Ogata, 'Refugees in Asia: From Exodus to Solutions,' The Charles Rostov Annual Lecture in Asian Affairs, 27 November 1995, Johns Hopkins University, School of Advanced International Studies, Washington, DC.

4 *Draft Declaration and Comprehensive Plan of Action, Approved by the Preparatory Meeting for the International Conference on Indochinese Refugees, 8 March 1989.*

5 Lawrence S. Eagleburger, *Indochina Refugee Situation: Toward a Comprehensive Plan of Action* (Washington DC: US Department of State, Bureau of Public Affairs, June 1989)

6 Author's interview with Eric Morris, Kuala Lumpur, April 1990.

7 In Court Robinson, 'Malaysia Pushes Off 6,500 Vietnamese Boat People,' *Refugee Reports*, Vol. 11, No. 5, 18 May 1990.

8 *Ibid.*

9 *Ibid.*

10 *Ibid.*

11 *Ibid.* One of the alternative solutions to involuntary return of the screened-out involved placing them in a regional holding centre. But the idea never materialized as no country in the region proved willing to host such a facility. A proposal to use Guam was rejected by the US government as it was likely to create a powerful magnet effect.

12 UNHCR Press Release, 'Rescue at sea: a maritime tradition to be upheld', 10 April 1990.

13 In May 1985, the Disero programme was supplemented by the RASRO programme, under which resettlement commitments were shared out more equitably between 16 countries (8 maritime and 8 non-maritime).

14 Author's interview with Michael Someck, Geneva, September 1990.

15 *Draft Declaration and Comprehensive Plan of Action.*

16 Author's interview with Allan Jury, Tokyo, 27 October 1995.

17 UNHCR, *Note on the Work of the Coordinating Committee for the International Conference on Indochinese Refugees*, A/CONF.148/4, 30 May 1989. Annex V, p. 32.

18 Stephen D. Goose and R. Kyle Horst, 'Amerasians in Vietnam: Still waiting', *Indochina Issues*, No. 83 (August 1988), p. 3.

19 *Ibid.*

20 Amnesty International, ASA 41/05/81. Cited in Asia Watch and Committee to Protect Journalists, *Still Confined: Journalists in 'Re-education' Camps and Prisons in Vietnam* (New York: April 1987), p. 27.

21 Author's interview with Diem Ngoc Nguyen, St Paul, Minnesota, 1 May 1996.

22 *Bangkok Post*, 2 September 1988.

23 Author's interview with former senior US refugee official, Washington, DC, 15 April 1996.

24 Unclassified Department of State cable, Bangkok 38486, 30 July 1989.

25 *San Jose Mercury News*, 14 January 1990.

26 Author's interview with Diem Ngoc Nguyen.

27 See Leonard Davis, *Hong Kong and the Asylum Seekers from Vietnam*.

28 Author's interview with Mike Hanson, Hong Kong, 8 November 1995.

29 Cable from UNHCR Hong Kong to Sergio Vieira de Mello, Head of Regional Bureau for Asia and Oceania, 9 June 1988.

30 Statement of an Understanding reached between the Hong Kong Government and UNHCR concerning the Treatment of Asylum Seekers arriving from Vietnam in Hong Kong, 20 September 1988.

31 Author's interview with Mike Hanson, Hong Kong, 8 November 1995.

32 Anne Wagley Gow, *Protection of Vietnamese Asylum Seekers in Hong Kong: Detention, Screening and Repatriation* (Berkeley: Human Rights Advocates, 1991), p. 5.

33 Lawyers Committee for Human Rights, *Uncertain Haven: Refugee Protection on the Fortieth Anniversary of the 1951 United Nations Refugee Convention* (New York: 1991), p. 19. See also Lawyers Committee for Human Rights, *Inhumane Deterrence: The Treatment of Vietnamese Boat People in Hong Kong* (New York: 1989).

34 In addition to *Inhumane Deterrence*, the 1989 report from the Lawyers Committee for Human Rights, see also Janelle Diller, *In Search of Asylum: Vietnamese Boat People in Hong Kong* (Washington, DC: Indochina Resource Action Center, November 1988).

35 Asia Watch, *Indefinite Detention and Mandatory Repatriation: The Incarceration of Vietnamese in Hong Kong* (New York and Washington, DC: December 1991), p. 6.

36 *Draft Declaration and Comprehensive Plan of Action.*

37 Regional Meeting of Senior Government Officials of First Asylum Countries and UNHCR on Appeals Procedures Under the CPA, Manila, 3–5 March 1992.

38 Memorandum from Anne Wagley Gow to Robert van Leeuwen, 17 June 1990.

39 UNHCR Memorandum, 'Mr. W. Collins' Survey on Vietnamese Boat People', 9 April 1990. The study found that 57 per cent of respondents in Thailand reported 'bad family status'. No data were presented for Malaysia.

40 Memorandum from Anne Wagley Gow to Robert van Leeuwen, 17 June 1990.

41 Author's interview with Erika Feller, Kuala Lumpur, 25 September 1995.

42 UNHCR, *Refugee Status Determination and Special Procedures under the Comprehensive Plan of Action* (Kuala Lumpur: November 1992).

43 *Ibid.*

44 Author's interview with Erika Feller.

45 NSW Refugee Fund Committee, *Report on Corruption in the Screening Process Under the Comprehensive Plan of Action in Galang Camp, Indonesia* (Cabramatta: August 1994).

46 US General Accounting Office, *Vietnamese Asylum Seekers: Refugee Screening Procedures Under the Comprehensive Plan of Action* (Washington, DC: GAO, October 1996),

p. 16.

47 UNHCR, *The Comprehensive Plan of Action: A Regional Approach to Improving Refugee Protection* (Geneva: July 1995), p. 3.

48 Author's interview with Nguyen Dinh Thang, Washington, DC, 12 April 1996.

49 Author's interview with Che Nhat Giao, Palawan, 25 November 1995.

50 GAO, *Vietnamese Asylum Seekers: Refugee Screening Procedures Under the Comprehensive Plan of Action*, pp. 6–7.

51 *Ibid.*, pp. 7, 12.

52 *Ibid.*, p. 16.

53 UNHCR, *Guidelines on Refugee Children*, August 1988, p. 27.

54 'Note on Unaccompanied Minors', submitted by UNHCR to the Coordinating Committee for the International Conference on Indochinese Refugees, Geneva, 25 and 26 May 1989, p. 21. While special procedures originally were conceived for the unaccompanied minors in the first asylum countries, UNHCR also noted that there might be other vulnerable persons who by reason of their inability to comprehend or articulate their claims for refugee status or because of other exceptional circumstances, required a consideration of issues that went beyond the refugee claim in order to determine an appropriate durable solution. This could include people with severe mental or physical disabilities as well as those who had suffered extremely traumatising experiences.

55 UNHCR, 'Regional Update on Special Procedures and Identification of Issues for Discussion', November 1990.

56 Cable from Sergio Vieira de Mello to UNHCR Geneva, 19 November 1990.

57 Christine Mougne, 'Difficult decisions', *Refugees*, November 1989, p. 13.

58 Author's interview with Nguyen Kim Ba Thien, Paris, 29 February 1996.

59 Aid to Refugee Children Without Parents, *Unaccompanied Minors: They Should Not Be Repatriated to Vietnam* (San Diego: ARCWP, May 1990), pp. 5–6.

60 John Kelly, *Evaluation Report: Nordic Assistance to Repatriated Vietnamese Family Reunification Programme for Unaccompanied Minors*, April 1994. p. 23.

61 Margaret McCallin, *Living in Detention: A Review of the Psychosocial Well-Being of Vietnamese Children in the Hong Kong Detention Centers* (Geneva: International Catholic Child Bureau, 1993), pp. 12–13. Of the unaccompanied minors arriving in Hong Kong in 1990/1, 22 per cent reported their mother was deceased and 30 per cent reported their father was deceased. Of the accompanied children arriving in the same period, 4 per cent reported a deceased mother and 3 per cent a deceased father. The fact that 32 per cent of unaccompanied minors reported they did not live with their parents prior to departure, if even partly accurate, may be a more telling insight into the motivations to leave (or be sent out of) Vietnam. Overall, of the 603 children interviewed, both accompanied and unaccompanied, 19 per cent reported that their parents were living separately, either divorced, remarried, or in some other arrangement.

62 Irene Mortensen, *Final Report: Achievements of the NARV Programme, October 1992–April 1995* (Nordic Assistance to Repatriated Vietnamese, 1995) p. 6. The NARV consortium included the Norwegian Refugee Council, the Danish Refugee Council and the Finnish Refugee Council, Radda Barnen, and Diakonia.

63 Kelly, *Evaluation Report: Nordic Assistance to Repatriated Vietnamese*, pp 26–27.

64 McCallin, *Living in Detention*, p. 15.

65 *Ibid.*, p. 18–19.

66 *Ibid.*, p. 26.

67 Author's interview with Daniel Alberman, London, 25 February 1996.

68 Author's interview with Nguyen Kim Ba Thien.

69 See *Refugee Reports*, Vol. 10, No. 12 (29 December 1989), p. 1.

70 *Ibid.*, pp. 1–2.

71 Sheila Rule, 'US softens its stance on return of the boat people in Hong Kong', *New York Times*, 25 January 1990.

72 *Hong Kong Standard*, 26 January 1990.

73 *Washington Post*, 24 September 1990.

74 JVA Hong Kong, Memorandum from Duyen Nguyen, 'Summary of recent developments in Hong Kong', 14 November 1990.

75 Sheryl WuDunn, 'Plan for boat people cheers Hong Kong', *New York Times*, 7 June 1991. The plan referred to in the headlines was not Dornan's Kuwait resettlement idea but an agreement by the United States to support the non-voluntary return of boat people to a special internationally managed camp in Vietnam. That plan never materialized.

76 *Agence France-Presse*, 26 September 1991 (FBIS-EAS-91-187).

77 Socialist Republic of Vietnam, Permanent Mission to the UN, 'Joint Press Statement of the British, Hong Kong, Vietnam and Representatives of UNHCR and IOM', 27 September 1991.

78 Neil Lewis, 'Fallout expected in Hanoi refugee issue', *New York Times*, 4 October 1991.

79 Author's interview with Brian Bresnihan, Hong Kong, 9 November 1995.

80 Office of the Chief of Mission Hong Kong, 'Discussion Paper prepared for the UNHCR Regional Meeting of Representatives and Chiefs of Mission on Implementation of the CPA', Jakarta, 1 September 1993.

81 Author's interview with Louise MacPherson, Hong Kong, 7 November 1995. This last point was supported by a UNHCR field officer in Whitehead who declined to be identified: 'It's irrational to try to stabilize an unnatural situation but the cuts have increased the siege mentality. The demonstrations are increasingly against *us*', as opposed to the Hong Kong government or Vietnam.

82 Author's interview with Jackie Lindgren, London, 25 February 1996.

83 Cited in Refugee Concern Hong Kong, *Defenseless in Detention: Vietnamese Children Living Amidst Increasing Violence in Hong Kong* (Kowloon: RCHK, June 1991), p. 111.

84 Quentin Dignam, SJ, letter to the author, 20 February 1996.

85 In *Refugee Concern Newsmagazine*, Issue 2 (June/July 1994), p. 1.

86 *Ibid.*, p. 7.

87 UNHCR Information Bulletin, *The Comprehensive Plan of Action*, August 1995, p. 3.

88 Jesuit Refugee Service, *Concerns and Recommendations: Displaced Vietnamese, Laotians and Cambodians in Hong Kong and Southeast Asia* (Bangkok: JRS, 28 December 1995) p. 2.

89 The selection criteria were quite similar to the category groups outlined in the 1983 INS Worldwide Guidelines and focused on former re-education camp prisoners and family, persons with civil or military service with the South Vietnamese government, religious leaders and ethnic minorities. See *Refugee Reports*, Vol 17, No. 5 (31 May 1996), p. 16.

90 Boat People SOS, *The Role of UNHCR in the Forced Repatriation Operation in the Philippines* (Merrifield, Virginia: Boat People SOS, February 1996), p. 1.

91 *Draft Declaration and Comprehensive Plan of Action*.

92 On 6 October 1986, UNHCR and the LPDR signed an *aide-memoire*, under which the Lao government agreed to accept back screened-out Lao if they returned 'in an orderly manner'. Author's interview with Darioush Bayandor, Paris, 27 February 1996.

93   The quote is from a UNHCR translation of a Thai Cabinet decision enacted in 1977 but not enforced until screening began in 1985.

94   From a 13 August 1992 internal memorandum written by a JVA official, Jack Price, following in-depth analysis of 31 screened-out cases of former Ban Vinai illegals, including interviews with two UNHCR monitors handling the appeals process. Overall, Price commented, 'UNHCR's decisions do not seem unfair or arbitrary so much as they seem overly rigid at times.'

95   Handicap International, Confidential Note for the File, 29 January 1991.

96   *Outline of the Plan for a Phased Repatriation and Reintegration of Laotians in Thailand*, Fourth Session of the Tripartite Meeting (LPDR/RTG/UNHCR), Luang Prabang, 27–29 June 1991.

97   UNHCR letter to Nivat Pibul, Director, Operations Centre for Displaced Persons, 14 May 1991.

98   'Reports on Results of Investigations of Allegations Concerning the Welfare of Hmong Refugees and Asylum Seekers in Thailand and Laos', prepared by the Refugee and Migration Affairs Unit, US Embassy, Bangkok, Thailand, June 1992.

99   Author's interview with Hans Willman, Na Pho Camp, Thailand, 11 August 1992.

100 Author's interview with Prapakorn Smiti, Bangkok, 14 August 1992.

—

CHAPTER 9

Roads Back Home

Return to Laos

In the midddle of 1992, declared by UNHCR to be the 'Year of Voluntary Repatriation', Kasidis Rochanakorn sat in his office overlooking Bangkok's sluggish canals and stagnant traffic, pondering another sort of exercise in immobility. A Thai national and career UNHCR official, Kasidis had started with the agency in 1979, working first with Vietnamese boat people in Laem Sing, then helping to set up Khao I Dang and other Cambodian holding centres on the border. Now, many years later, he was back on the Indochinese refugee detail, this time working on Laotian issues. Since 1975, UNHCR figures showed him, more than 300,000 Laotians had passed through the Thai camps on their way to resettlement overseas while only 10,000 had gone home. Roughly 50,000 highland and lowland Lao remained in camps in Thailand, about the same number that had entered in the first year of the exodus.

'One could easily say that the problem with lowland Lao refugees in Thailand is virtually resolved,' Kasidis said. New arrivals had declined to a handful and only about 6,000 lowland Lao remained in Thailand, most of whom had elected for repatriation. Increasing numbers of some highland Lao groups – the Mien, Htin, and others – were returning home as well. 'Overall, the picture for Lao repatriation is very good,' he said. Here Kasidis frowned, then smiled quizzically and threw up his hands. 'The Hmong, of course, are the exception.'[1]

While change, both dramatic and incremental, had come to Southeast Asia in the previous two decades, it was slow in coming to the Laotian camps. Now time was catching up on the Hmong; for many, that was an unsettling, even ominous, prospect. Most of the 45,000 Hmong then in the camps remained unreconciled either to going back to Laos or to living in the United States. Some were still at war with the Lao socialist government and others were simply at odds with their circumstances. But the unavoidable reality for the Hmong was that time was running out for them in Thailand.

In June 1991, at the fourth in a series of meetings between Thailand, Laos and UNHCR, the three parties had agreed to a newly invigorated repatriation initiative. During the start-up phase, from July 1991 to May 1992, an anticipated 5,000 to 6,000 would return home. In Phase II, from June 1992 to May 1993, repatriation gradually would increase so that, by the end of 1994, Thailand hoped that virtually all the Laotian refugees would have resettled elsewhere or gone home.

In fact, by the middle of 1992, fewer than 2,000 Laotians had returned to Laos during Phase I. Of these, only one quarter were Hmong, and of those, only 100 repatriated voluntarily – the rest went home in accord with the promise of the tripartite arrangements that 'those rejected in the screening process will be returned without the use of force in safety and dignity'.[2]

The reasons for the disappointing showing were numerous: attacks by Laotian resistance forces near resettlement sites in Laos, backtracking and intransigence by LPDR officials, funding shortfalls on the part of UNHCR, and general reluctance on the part of the Laotian refugees in Thailand – especially the Hmong – to go home. At the fifth tripartite meeting between Thailand, Laos, and UNHCR held in Rayong, Thailand in July 1992, the Thai government's impatience was evident. 'The Laotian refugees have been residing in Thailand for a long time,' said General Charan Kullavanijaya, Secretary-General of Thailand's National Security Council. 'We have to reaffirm our principle that all refugees have to return home or be resettled in third countries. Thailand will not house them.'[3]

The Thai delegation reiterated its position that Ban Vinai, for more than a decade the largest camp for highland Lao in the country, would close by the end of 1992, and that Chiang Kham camp would be closed by the end of 1993.

'The clock is ticking,' said Dennis Grace, Joint Voluntary Agency Representative in Thailand, in 1992. 'So far, the Hmong have been no-shows for voluntary repatriation. How do you go from 100 Hmong to 10,000 in the next twelve months? Probably half the Hmong in Thailand want to go back to Laos, but without some success stories on the repatriation side, a good percentage of people may end up backing into the United States. It won't be forced but it won't be what they want either.' Without some dramatic breakthroughs on repatriation, Grace warned, 'We are going to get ourselves into an unhappy endgame with the Hmong.'[4]

One of the frustrations for those promoting voluntary repatriation to Laos was the fact that, as of June 1992, there were 2,000 Laotians in Thailand, including about 700 Hmong, who had applied to go back but were awaiting for approvals or return schedules from the Laotian side. Several developments, all on the Lao side, contributed to building this backlog in Thailand. In a report prepared for the fifth tripartite meeting, the UNHCR branch office in Laos said funding shortfalls and staff shortages created 'longer delays in processing applications and organizing movements'.

Another 'major factor in determining the speed of repatriation movements,' the report noted, 'is the special procedure for vetting applications to four provinces in Laos'. Beginning in November 1991, officials in four provinces – Vientiane, Sayaboury, Bokeo, and Oudomxay – had required that all applications for repatriation needed provincial as well as central government approval before any returnees are permitted to settle there.[5] The introduction of these 'special procedures', some observers noted, corresponded with stepped-up guerrilla activity in the four provinces. 'The resistance has been successful in rekindling the fears of the Lao government about repatriation,' said a US official.[6]

New concerns about the returnees also persuaded the Lao Ministry of Foreign Affairs to withdraw four potential sites in Vientiane and Xieng Khouang provinces from a list of proposed sites for group settlement. In their joint statement following the fifth tripartite meeting, Thailand, Laos and UNHCR said they were all of the view 'that repatriates should be prepared to return to areas suggested by the Laotian government, in the case that they are not able to return to the locations which they previously chose'.[7]

Even as UNHCR worked on the Lao side to remove the bottlenecks to return, it continued to pitch repatriation in the camps. From 1 January 1992 the assistance package had been increased to a cash grant of $120 per person and the provision of 18 months of rice. Voluntary organizations in the camps were encouraged to reorient their programmes toward preparing people for eventual return. Advocates of safe repatriation for the Hmong stepped up the search for a dramatic breakthrough, the heretofore missing ingredient that would instil confidence in the camps that the Hmong were welcome back home. On 1 March 1991 some of the camp leadership in Ban Vinai sent a letter to UNHCR in Geneva indicating an interest in returning as a group. In Chiang Kham, another group of 1,000 were in discussion with the UNHCR camp representative about settling outside Vientiane in two villages of 500 each.

One of the complaints the Hmong had against repatriation had been the roadblocks erected by the Lao authorities, hindering return to former villages in the mountainous highlands. Those who had returned in the 1980s had gone back as individual families or in small clusters of 50 to 100. Many observers hoped that the prospect of establishing a Hmong returnee village large enough to provide a sense of community (and strength in numbers) would breathe new life into the Hmong repatriation programme. 'The Hmong are not going to be able to select every repatriation site,' concluded a delegation from the Women's Commission for Refugee Women and Children in 1991. 'But when they see a large group resettled in an area with arable land, and access to other services and markets, some of their fears will be allayed.'[8]

Vue Mai, a camp leader in Ban Vinai since 1980 and a former member of the resistance forces, was one of the principal signatories of the March 1991 letter to UNHCR, proposing terms for Hmong repatriation. In fact, he had helped draft an earlier letter, stating four conditions for returning to

Laos, which the UNHCR representative in Ban Vinai had rejected, according to one observer, because they were 'too militaristic, too political and were not in accord with international law'. UNHCR and the Thai Ministry of Interior then offered to draft another letter, which became a 10-point plan for Hmong group repatriation. The gist of the changes was to drop demands for a multi-party democracy in Laos and focus on such things as a renewed declaration of amnesty and guarantees of arable land and water at the returnee sites.[9]

When UNHCR Bangkok received this new letter – which had been endorsed by Vue Mai and his counterpart in Chiang Kham camp, Ka Toua Thao – the agency passed the document on to the LPDR for consideration. Said Vue Mai later,

> When the Thai and Lao governments decided that the refugees had to go home, I wanted to help. The Lao came to talk to me about repatriation and I agreed that people who didn't want to resettle in the United States – old people, long-stayers, people addicted to opium – should have the opportunity to return. There will also be many people who will not be eligible for resettlement in the United States – those without relatives, polygamists, opium addicts. These people too, I think, will be willing to go back but they don't know where they will live.
>
> I have promoted the idea to the Thai Ministry of Interior and the Lao government that they should allow the Hmong to go back in a group with their leaders, that they should allow us to build a 'model village' with schools, hospitals, jobs. I would like to build this project near the city of Vientiane. Up to 10,000 Hmong could live together. If they would let us do this, I think many Hmong would go back. But if the Lao government tries to put us in the jungle, isolated, without houses, then the Hmong won't go back.[10]

But as Vue Mai and other members of the refugee camp leadership were negotiating terms for return, other Hmong groups in exile were intent on pushing a more political agenda. In January 1991, the Lao Human Rights Council in the United States sent a 15-point letter to UNHCR, reiterating the demand for a change in government in Laos before Hmong repatriation could go forward. In June 1991, at a Hmong national conference held in Washington, DC, the Democratic Chaofah Party, a militant resistance group, submitted a statement saying 'we propose to not repatriate our fellow refugees until the minority puppet installed government of Vietnam in Vientiane has agreed to change its system of single party rule to a system of democratic multi-party rule'.[11]

When Vue Mai returned to Thailand after attending the conference, he did not return to Ban Vinai. 'There are lots of people who are willing to go back' to Laos, he said, 'but they are not willing to say so publicly. If they do, several things happen: MOI comes and says they must sign a paper that they could go back within a few days. The other thing is they get pressure from people in the camps. I had a firebomb thrown at my house for talking about voluntary repatriation in Ban Vinai. I felt it was no longer safe to stay there. Two groups want the refugees to stay in Thailand. One is the resistance, and they are getting money from overseas to help in this effort.

The other is local Thai officials who are also making money off the camps. Neither wants the camps to close'.[12]

But the camps did close, Ban Vinai in December 1992 and Chiang Kham at the end of the following year. Vue Mai's dream of 10,000 Hmong returnees living together outside of Vientiane never came to pass. He returned voluntarily to Laos in November 1992. Ten months later, on 11 September 1993, he left his house in Vientiane after a brief phone conversation with a Lao-speaking woman. He has never been heard from since. Several theories have developed as to his disappearance, none of which has been proven or disproven. As *Philadelphia Inquirer* reporter Marc Kaufman described these theories,

> Lao officials, downplaying the incident, emphasize Vue Mai's mercurial character, saying he had many girlfriends and personal enemies. American and UN officials generally blame the Hmong resistance, suggesting that Gen. Vang Pao was desperate to retain his power by keeping the Hmong from following Vue Mai back to Laos. The Hmong resistance denies any involvement and accuses the Lao government of arresting Vue Mai.[13]

Though the incident had a temporarily chilling effect on repatriation (and continues to provoke strong reactions in the Hmong-American community), voluntary movements back from Thailand averaged more than 4,800 people annually between 1992 and 1994. By the end of 1995, counting the 3,000 Laotians who returned from China's Yunnan province, repatriations to Laos since 1980 have totalled just over 27,000. Of those who returned from Thailand, better than 80 per cent overall (and 65 per cent of all highland Lao) enjoyed refugee status in Thailand and thus were not obliged to return except voluntarily. About 4,400 returnees, of whom about 3,400 were Hmong, were screened-out asylum seekers. Many of these returned voluntarily as well, although some did not. Since 1980, it is estimated that anywhere from 12,000 to 20,000 Laotians returned spontaneously from the camps in Thailand.

Return and rural settlement

Basically, three options were available to returnees who wished to repatriate to Laos under UNHCR auspices:

1 They could return as individuals to any village where they had friends or relatives;

2 They could return in small groups (5 to 20 families) to villages which had volunteered to receive them; or

3 They could return as part of a larger rural group settlement, whose location and infrastructure was established by UNHCR in cooperation with the Lao government and NGO partners.[14]

Since 1993, more than half of all returnees (and 60 per cent of the Hmong) chose to return to one of the 29 rural settlement sites throughout the country. There were also four small group sites and 60 villages that have received returnees. The provinces of Bolikhamxay and Bokeo remained closed to individual Hmong repatriations. In May 1995 Vientiane municipality also closed its doors to individual Hmong applications, 'due to the crowded conditions in villages accepting returnees'.[15]

All returnees were given the same standard assistance package consisting of a cash grant equivalent to $120 as well as an 18-month rice ration. Other standard assistance provided prior to departure from Thailand included agriculture and carpentry tools, vegetable seeds and mosquito nets. In addition to this, each returnee family going to the rural settlement sites received a home plot of 800 to 1,600 square metres, cultivation land of from one to two hectares, and housing materials. Most of the rural settlement sites were also provided with water supply systems, roads and primary schools.

The first group settlement site was established as early as July 1986 in Bokeo province to accommodate some 500 Mien who wished to return together. By the end of 1989, however, only three more sites had opened up, offering space for an additional 350 people altogether. Though several new sites were added each year, it was not until early 1992 – ironically, just when the approach was proving so unworkable in a Cambodian context – that the group settlements began to hit their stride in Laos. This was partly a result of new interest in repatriation in the Thailand camps, partly a result of new donor interest, especially from the United States, and partly due to a more productive working relationship that was forged between local UNHCR staff and their Lao government counterparts.

Essentially, five steps were involved in the preparation of rural settlements: after potential sites were proposed by local and central authorities, a UNHCR technical team made a preliminary assessment in conjunction with the Ministry of Labour and Social Welfare (MLSW). The basic characteristics that UNHCR looked for in a viable site were relatively easy access to nearby towns and communication networks, access to reasonably flat arable land, potential sources of domestic water, and availability of land for village development. Once UNHCR was satisfied on a preliminary basis that the site had potential, a more detailed investigation followed, involving demarcation and cadastral surveys. The product of these surveys, according to UNHCR field officer Michael Zwack,

> is a set of maps which define the site's boundaries, identify outstanding physical features, delimit occupied and cultivated areas within the project boundaries and proposes both a village layout and agricultural land allocation system. These maps, along with the report of the detailed investigation are provided to the camps in Thailand as promotional materials for the recruitment of repatriates to the proposed site. Only when a group has indicated their interest by submitting their volrep [voluntary repatriation] applications through UNHCR Bangkok can serious expenditure on a site be undertaken.[16]

Once a group had expressed an interest in a site, it took anywhere from four months to one year to lay the groundwork. The final step was the actual movement back across the Mekong. Back in Laos, the new arrivals are welcomed with a two- to three-day 'orientation about the Lao political and legal systems ... by local authorities'.[17] Once past the speeches, returnees were given the remainder of their cash grant and transported to their new site, where they would begin the arduous task of starting over.

Laos is a small, poor, landlocked country with *per capita* income estimated at $180 in 1990. Although a population of 4.3 million in a total area of 231,000 square kilometres gives an overall density figure of 18.6, only about 4 per cent of land in Laos is considered arable. The competition for lowland cultivation land is intense. In the wake of market reforms begun in 1986, so too is competition in the non-agricultural sector.[18]

Given this, it is hard to say how economically viable the returnee communities will prove to be, although it is a positive sign that only about 8 per cent of those initially settling in rural settlement sites had migrated elsewhere, against about 20 per cent of individual returnees, while an equal or larger number of people had moved in. The best sites, according to one UNHCR monitor, were those with 'adequate land with room to expand if the population grows, locations close to Thailand for trade and business, good irrigation, and a population appropriate to the site, neither too large nor too small.'[19]

Of all these, he insisted that good irrigation was 'the most important'. But irrigation systems take time to implement, and not all the sites have received the facilities they were promised. Another 'fundamental problem that a lot of sites face is insufficient agricultural land', according to Bruce Shoemaker, director of the Consortium, a US NGO with programmes in Laos, Cambodia and Vietnam.

> It is less than what [returnees] were led to believe they would have. This is a dynamic in all of the sites where the Consortium has worked: the shrinkage of land from what is promised to what is allocated. At Nan district in Luang Prabang, people are ending up with less than one hectare [per family]. They were promised twice that. The reality is that it is not there to give away. It was unrealistic to expect that land would be available for all returnees.[20]

With all the resources available for the settlement sites, Shoemaker said, 'you would expect more results'. He said the organization had experienced some success with small-scale income generation but real community development took time. Still, he felt that local authorities generally see the sites as a 'worthwhile endeavour' and that many returnees are 'happy to be back. For the vast majority of people, their concerns are not issues of political freedom or repression. Their main concerns are food security and malaria.'

As part of its mandate in Laos, UNHCR has carried out missions throughout the country to visit repatriates, monitor their living conditions, health and welfare and investigate any allegations of mistreatment. Monitors are usually accompanied by a government official but often conduct interviews alone and are permitted to do so when they request it. Since July 1995, the UNHCR monitoring staff in Laos was enhanced by two Hmong-speaking expatriates (one Thai and one American). In general, UNHCR officials say that 'the physical security of returnees is not an issue in Laos. More frequently, returnees are concerned about reestablishing their lives and feeding their families.'[21] But monitors visit each of the rural settlement sites at least once a year and make periodic spot checks on individual returnees throughout the country. UNHCR staff have also undertaken over 30 investigations into allegations of human rights abuses against returnees since 1992. Of these, it confirmed one arrest, though the person in question was not executed as alleged but released after a two-month jail term. In addition to Vue Mai, whose disappearance remained still unexplained by early 1997, UNHCR was also seeking information about another returnee, Bouavanh Phothirath, who had been an active Christian evangelist since his return, but disappeared in May 1994.

One of the newest settlement sites, Ban Na Saat in Khammoune province, opened for business in February 1995. By the end of the year, it had a population of about 400 Hmong and 150 lowland Lao. UNHCR had helped to construct three kilometres of internal roads on the site as well as a brand-new school, but permanent housing was only just going up and agricultural land remained a promise. 'This is a very mixed group,' said Fai Zoua Vue, assistant village leader of the Hmong in Ban Na Saat. 'There are people from Ban Vinai, Chiang Kham, Na Pho. We have screened-in and screened-out.' The screened-out 'came back voluntarily' he said, then added, 'We had no choice to go anywhere else so we chose to come back.' He was not sure how many Hmong would remain at Ban Na Saat but he said, 'We are satisfied with the site. The Hmong are confident we can adjust.'[22]

Return to Cambodia

In September 1980, UNHCR had opened a small, two-person office in Phnom Penh and announced the establishment of a programme of humanitarian assistance for Cambodian returnees, then estimated at 300,000 (including 175,000 returning from Thailand). The programme was to provide basic food assistance, seeds, tools, and household goods to returnees in five frontier provinces. But the effort proved to be about a decade premature. Although talks sputtered on and off for many years, UNHCR was unable to find common ground between Bangkok and Phnom Penh and organized return from the Thai border camps went nowhere.

Then, in 1991, the political landscape shifted dramatically and UNHCR's repatriation plans, three years in development, swiftly took shape. One month after a peace agreement was signed in Paris on 23 October 1991, UNHCR signed a tripartite Memorandum of Understanding with the Thai government and the Cambodian Supreme National Council (SNC). The 29-point document detailed the specific responsibilities of the three contracting parties involved in the Cambodian repatriation and, among other things, reiterated a commitment to have all the refugees back from Thailand in time to vote. In November, UNHCR took over responsibility for the border camps from UNBRO. Denied recognition as refugees for so long, the Cambodian displaced persons finally won that status, but only in the context of return.

At the end of 1991, UNHCR's planning objectives were to transport 250,000 returnees across the border while another 100,000 were expected to return home spontaneously. Movements were expected to begin in April 1992 and take six months to complete. The total caseload included an estimated 85,000 families with more than 21,000 especially vulnerable individuals (EVIs) – incuding female heads of household, elderly, handicapped, chronically sick and mentally ill. UNHCR had outlined five essential preconditions for safe return to Cambodia:

1   overall peace and security in the country;
2   provision of adequate agricultural settlement land for the returnees by the government of Cambodia;
3   demining of settlement land by the government of Cambodia and the United Nations;
4   repair of major repatriation roads and bridges; and
5   strong funding support from the donor countries.[23]

During the same period, UNHCR had commissioned Halo Trust, a British non-profit organization, to conduct a survey of the mine problem in potential areas of returnee settlement. The news was discouraging: out of 70,000 hectares surveyed, Halo Trust found that 30,200 hectares were 'probably clear of mines', 28,200 hectares were 'probably mined', and 11,200 hectares were 'heavily mined'.[24]

While the land and mine surveys were going on in Cambodia, UNHCR undertook a pre-registration of residents in the UN-assisted border camps. Of the 315,000 who registered, 90 per cent said they wished to return with UNHCR. Extrapolating from this data, UNHCR estimated that 330,000 Cambodian refugees would return under UN auspices. More than 57 per cent (189,200 people) chose Battambang province as their preferred destination; another 14 per cent chose the new province of Banteay Meanchey. More than 11 per cent asked the UN to choose a province for them. Others selected a province but left the choice of district to UNHCR and so on. 'Altogether,' said UNHCR in its January 1992 summary of the pre-registration results, 'almost 41 per cent of all respondents left the choice of destination to UNHCR, whether at sub-district, district, or provincial level, testifying to the extent to which links with home have been severed for the border population.'

That was a plausible conclusion at the time, but given the relative speed and ease with which many returnees reconnected with family members following the collapse of the land option, another conclusion presents itself: by November and December 1991, the border population was aware that UNHCR was offering two hectares of land per family. Thousands chose Battambang for that very reason, given its fertile soil and proximity to Thailand. Many who gave their choice to the UN likewise may have opted to forgo return to their place of origin – and likely family reunification – in hopes that UNHCR would give them better land somewhere else.

With a total population of 363,000 Cambodian refugees and displaced persons, of whom about 330,000 expressed a wish to return under UN auspices, UNHCR now figured it would take nine months, instead of six, to transport this much greater number of people from Thailand to Cambodia. A repatriation process that was both larger and longer would also cost more money. By January 1992, the UN had raised virtually all of the $33 million sought for the preparatory phase. But actual movements were a matter of two months away and the budget for the operations phase was under revision.

It was not just the budget UNHCR was revising in January but key aspects of the plan itself. Throughout much of 1991, UNHCR had been deeply worried at the prospect of massive spontaneous returns following the signing of the peace agreement. As late as November of that year, the agency was devising contingency plans to find some way to protect and assist up to 100,000 spontaneous returnees. By January 1992, the pre-registration showed that all but about 30,000 Cambodians wished to return in an organized manner under UNHCR auspices. The worry by this time was whether the agency could deliver on its promises of safe return – with a house and farmland at the choice of destination – for 330,000 people.

It was also clear that not everyone wanted to go back to live under the State of Cambodia (SOC) government. About 10 per cent of those who wished to return with UNHCR said they preferred resettlement in faction-controlled areas. This would require opening new border crossing points and reception centres and certifying conditions for safe and voluntary return to these areas.

There was another problem: in all of its planning, UNHCR had staked the safety – the very possibility – of repatriation on demining of reception centres, access roads, and settlement areas. By January, the agency knew it would be lucky to get two out of three. Prompted by UNHCR, the Thai engineering battalion that was repairing Highway 5 did use mine-sniffing dogs to clear several hundred hectares of land east of the road in Banteay Meanchey and Battambang. But, generally speaking, instead of any actual demining of rural settlement sites, UNHCR had to settle for 'verification of land presumed not to have been mined'.[25]

'Given the number of persons to be moved, the physical obstacles and the political parameters,' UNHCR warned the donor countries, 'it is clear that for many of the returnees who wish to be settled on land, a transitional period may be inevitable.'[26] In late 1991, UNHCR had distributed flyers and shown a video in the border camps highlighting the promise of two hectares of land at each returnee family's destination of choice. By 1 February the agency had begun to hedge on that promise: 'In some provinces, particularly Battambang, not enough land has yet been identified.... At this stage, and depending on your preference, either suitable land will be identified for you in the near future or UNHCR will seek non-agricultural alternatives for you.'[27]

By March 1992, as the first convoys prepared to roll across the border, it was apparent that few of UNHCR's preconditions for safe return were in place. Roads and bridges were ready, but very little else. Only two of the six reception centres were completed, the UN Transitional Authority in Cambodia was barely operational, demining was almost nonexistent, sporadic violence still flared about the country, and land for the returnees was all but impossible to secure. A survey of the four northwestern provinces conducted by the Cambodian Red Cross (CRC) in early March had identified suitable land for only a few thousand families.[28]

On 30 March 1992, the first UNHCR repatriation convoy, carrying 525 people, crossed the Aranyaprathet–Poipet bridge bound for the reception centre in Sisophon, where they were welcomed by Prince Norodom Sihanouk and a host of dignitaries and journalists. The next day, another 400 people were bussed farther on down Highway 5 to Otaki reception centre in Battambang. But by the end of April fewer than 6,000 refugees had been repatriated; the plan called for the movement of 10,000 people per week if everyone was to be home in time for the elections.

The problem was not lack of interest in repatriation; most returnees were eager to get back home. Nor, as often hampers UNHCR repatriation programmes, was there a crippling lack of funds. By early April, donor countries had contributed nearly $55 million to the UNHCR operation. Trucks, buses, and computers were running with remarkably few breakdowns. But having offered returnee families two hectares of land at their choice of destination, UNHCR found it could not deliver on its promise. Worse yet, many of those who were moving into the UN settlements were not staying long. By early May, UNHCR had moved about 1,000 families into settlement sites in Battambang where agricultural land and/or housing plots had been set aside for returnees. By June, half of them had moved on, looking for relatives or a more favourable location.

The UN repatriation plan had to change. On 13 May 1992, UNHCR published an information update for distribution in the border camps. Suitable land, it said, 'will probably not be in the province of your choice.... As many people want to return to areas where not enough land is available – particularly in Battambang – UNHCR is going to provide you with additional options.' Those who wanted land, either to farm or to build a house on, would have to wait in camp until it became available. For those who wanted to return quickly, UNHCR was offering 'reintegration money'.

UNHCR's options package ultimately offered the following choices:

Option A (Agricultural Land): This assistance package included up to two hectares of agricultural land per family, a housing plot, wood for construction of a house frame, US$25 to buy thatch and bamboo, a household/agricultural kit (including water buckets, mosquito nets, various handtools, and a blue plastic sheet), and WFP food for 400 days.

Option B (House): Included a plot of land for a house, wood for construction of a house frame, US$25 to buy thatch and bamboo, a household/agricultural kit, and food for 400 days (reduced to 200 days if a returnee chose to settle in the Phnom Penh area).

Option C (Cash): Included reintegration money of $50 per adult and $25 per child under 12, a household/agricultural kit, and food for 400 days (200 days in Phnom Penh area).

Option D (Income generating tools): This option, intended to promote non-agricultural employment alternatives, was considered for several months then scrapped as too complicated.

Option E (Employment): Returnees who were offered jobs with UNTAC or other organizations in Cambodia while they were in the Thai camps would receive reintegration money (same amounts as for Option C) and food for 400 days (200 days in Phnom Penh) but no household/agricultural kit.

Option F (Family reunion): This option was intended for families of soldiers or Option E returnees who had preceded them into Cambodia. It included reintegration money and food for 400 days (200 days in Phnom Penh).

Option G (Spontaneous return): Refugees who chose to go back on their own and registered with UN camp officers before their departure would be eligible for 400 days of food in Cambodia (200 days in Phnom Penh).[29]

Out of 362,000 Cambodians who returned from Thailand on UNHCR voluntary repatriation convoys, only 2,435 returnee families (10,261 persons) chose Option A, scarcely 3 per cent of the total. Just over half of these were resettled in Battambang province. A total of 9,177 families (24,147 persons) selected Option B, the housing package, without farmland and without cash.

In an August 1992 information bulletin, UNHCR had called the housing settlements programme 'the heart and soul of the repatriation operation … [and] the most visible symbol of stability for returnees'.[30] The truth of that statement was short-lived at best. By the end of that month, nearly 90 per cent of all returnee families were taking Option C, the cash option, and setting out for home, or the closest thing to it they could find.

Praised as the salvation of Cambodian repatriation or pilloried as a shortsighted buy-out, Option C became the option of choice for more than 85 per cent of returnees. Repatriations jumped from 4,800 in April 1992 to 13,000 in May, nearly 20,000 in June, and averaged 30,000 returns per month from July to the end of 1992. Through the first quarter of 1993, nearly 40,000 returnees crossed the border each month, leaving about 25,000 to straggle home in April.

Option C's primary benefit to UNHCR – though more of a mixed blessing for the returnees – was that it removed the onus of finding housing or agricultural land for returnees and put the choice of destination, along with some cash, back into the hands of the refugees. In so doing, it enabled UNHCR to accelerate the pace of repatriation and meet the election deadline. Option C's primary benefit to returnees – although this, too, had its downsides – was that it both encouraged and necessitated family reunification. Previous surveys had attested to the refugees' tenuous links to their places of origin, their loss of contact – often for more than a decade – with family members still in country. But returnees showed a remarkable capacity to find their way back to long-lost relatives. Some sent out advance 'scouts' from the camps. Others relied on the tracing services of the ICRC, which was permitted to operate inside Cambodia from 1989. But many simply relied on the 'grapevine' and a kind of homing instinct to get back to their places of origin or wherever a relative had last been seen. Although it is not possible to equate the choice of Option C automatically with family reunification, it is likely that the majority of returnees who selected Option C found relatives in Cambodia.[31]

The shift away from settlement sites and toward village-based family reunification – the new 'heart and soul' of Cambodian repatriation – meant that week after week, month after month, returnee families left the reception centres and the food distribution points and disappeared into thousands of towns and villages throughout the country. The new measure of success for repatriation was precisely *not* that returnee homes were easy to see but that they became increasingly hard to find.

In a 1993 report, UNHCR noted that 'The mobility of the returnees, their success in linking up with relatives, and their even distribution over the countryside created favourable conditions for the start of the reintegration process.'[32] Mobility, on the other hand, also made monitoring all the more difficult. Once returnees left the reception centres, it became very difficult to say where they ended up, even initially. Although patterns of secondary migration have been hard to track closely, it is estimated that at least 20 per cent of all returnees have moved at least once since reaching their initial 'final destination'.[33]

The great disadvantage of the cash option was that it lacked any guarantee of land, either for a house or for agricultural use. As such, it lacked any guarantee of stability or durability. UNHCR clearly was mistaken in building its initial repatriation plan around the promise of land for everyone. But over time, the assistance packages seemed to grow less and less substantial. Land for tilling had been replaced by wood for housing and dollar bills for anything and everything. The question was: For how many returnees would the paper money vanish into thin air?

'No-Gos' and 'O-Zones'

The new options brought important flexibility to the repatriation process. It was no longer necessary for returnees to go where UNHCR or the local authorities could find them land. They could go where they chose, whether to look for family, land, work, or simply a bit of peace. With the collapse of the land plan, UNHCR now was urging people to go home. But what if home was in a minefield, or somewhere equally insecure?

In the registration conducted in the border camps at the end of 1991, nearly 60 per cent of the refugees who signed up to return with UNHCR indicated a preference to repatriate to Battambang province. The single most popular district for returnees in all of Cambodia was Rattanak Mondol, in the province's westernmost reaches. A total of 26,734 border residents – 8.5 per cent of all registered returnees – expressed a preference for Rattanak Mondol.

'This popularity is not inexplicable,' according to a November 1992 report drafted by the private relief agency, World Vision. Rattanak Mondol 'has an extremely rich agricultural heritage, being one of the nation's centers of commercial agriculture in the 1960s'. Returnees no doubt were attracted by the prospect of two free hectares of such fertile farmland. 'The district also lay on the prosperous trade route to Pailin and Thailand,' the report noted, 'the gem wealth of Pailin and the productivity of the surrounding forests are still a strong pull factor.... The mere proximity to Thailand may also be a pull factor for returnees who are sensibly concerned about the lack of any real peace at this time.'[34]

But what the border camp population may not have known at the time of registration was that Rattanak Mondol was now one of the most heavily mined areas in Cambodia. Between October 1989 and March 1991, the district was a battleground between the Khmer Rouge guerrillas and the Phnom Penh forces, both seeking to extend or consolidate territorial control in the wake of the Vietnamese withdrawal in September 1989. By early 1991, the entire population of 14,500 had fled toward Battambang city for temporary safety and shelter, most houses and government buildings had been damaged or destroyed, and anywhere from 50–80 per cent of all cultivable land had been lost to landmines or unexploded ordnance.[35]

In January 1992, before they were even aware of the UNHCR registration figures, Cambodian authorities reported that Rattanak Mondol had no capacity to absorb returnees. Officially, the 4,782 people registered as district residents in December 1991 were considered internally displaced and district authorities were expecting another 2–3,000 internally displaced families to return from Battambang city. Rattanak Mondol had become the poorest district in the province, in part because it was the most heavily mined. It could not accommodate even a few returnees, the authorities argued. They did not know it was facing a potential population increase of over 500 per cent!

When UNHCR announced in February 1992 that 26,700 people had registered to settle in Rattanak Mondol, provincial and district authorities dutifully identified seven resettlement locations with a total area of 5,650 hectares. 'However,' noted one report, 'all of these sites are currently mined, and will require a long time to demine.'[36] But a concerted, internationally supervised effort to demine in Rattanak Mondol did not get under way until the middle of 1993, at the very end of the movement phase. In the meantime, UNHCR realized, something had to be done to try to keep returnees out of danger zones like Rattanak Mondol.

On 27 July 1992, a returnee collecting firewood at the foot of Tippadey Mountain in Battambang province stepped on a mine and lost part of his leg. According to UNHCR, this was the first mine casualty among the returnee population. Following the accident, UNHCR began to centralize a list of what it had begun to call 'no-go' areas: specific districts throughout the country where UNHCR discouraged repatriation. In an October 1992 information bulletin, UNHCR laid out its policy:

> Some of the returnees want to return to their villages of origin which are considered as 'no-go' areas by UNHCR for various reasons: security risks, the presence of mines, difficulty of access, high incidence of malaria and other health hazards, lack of potable water, and sanitation problems. Despite such obstacles, some returnees insist on proceeding to these areas, pointing out they have relatives who could facilitate their reintegration. In such cases, UNHCR organizes comprehensive briefings and interviews in the camps in Thailand for groups or individuals concerned, advising them of the risks involved and counselling them to consider other destinations. Under the principle of free choice and freedom of movement embodied in the Paris peace agreement, returnees who pursue their request to proceed to the difficult places despite UNHCR warnings are taken to the nearest 'go' district.[37]

By then, the 'no-go' list included part or all of about 64 districts in 20 provinces throughout Cambodia. In light of UNHCR's abortive efforts to secure any significant demining in Rattanak Mondol until mid-1993, the district remained on the 'no-go' list for the entire movement phase. But migrations into Rattanak Mondol continued throughout 1992 and 1993. By the end of the repatriation convoys in May 1993, a total of 2,700 returnees were living in the district. Most of them had registered their final destination in a nearby 'go' district then moved down Route 10. Some came from other provinces, looking for land or a livelihood. Five months later, in October 1993, district officials counted 4,657 returnees out of a total population of nearly 22,000. And in April 1994, district figures showed that while the local population remained relatively stable at 17,400, the number of returnees had climbed to more than 6,000.

UNHCR officials in Battambang believe that most of the 'second wave', post-movement phase returnee migrations were motivated by a search for land or livelihood. As Paul Davies writes in *War of the Mines*, however, the cost of extracting these riches could be terribly high:

> in the absence of any large-scale demining effort by the UN or other demining agencies, the civilian population of Rattanak Mondol was left with two stark 'choices' in order to survive, both of which involved taking enormous risks with landmines. The first of these 'choices' was to clear the land of mines – either by themselves or by employing ex-soldiers.... [M]ost resorted to the second 'option', which involved entering known mine-risk areas to cut and gather wood, bamboo, and other natural resources. These activities, which had previously been regarded as a useful supplement to incomes gained primarily from agriculture, became for many the only source of livelihood.[38]

From 1979 to February 1993, mines killed 281 people in Rattanak Mondol. These are just the official figures; the real death rate no doubt is much higher. One adult male in seven in the district has been killed or injured by a landmine in the last decade. One person in 90 is an amputee, more than four times the national average. Mines are the leading cause of disability and among the top three causes of death in the district. 'Mines', Davies writes, 'have produced a medical, social, and economic state of emergency in Rattanak Mondol.'[39]

Based on information from the registration completed in January 1992 and from lists submitted by Khmer Rouge administrators in Site 8 and Site K, UNHCR officials had concluded that more than 14,000 people in the border camps wished to return to areas controlled by the Khmer Rouge. Under the terms of its own mandate, the agency felt obliged to honour a returnee's choice of destination so long as it was made voluntarily and in full knowledge of the facts. As an UNTAC component, moreover, UNHCR was commited to treating each of the factions in a neutral and unbiased manner. Furthermore, UNHCR had taken the position that repatriation to faction-controlled zones served to break down internal frontiers.

Throughout 1992, UNHCR had been in discussions with Khmer Rouge representatives in the camps and in Cambodia to explore the prospects of repatriation to Khmer Rouge areas. As the year wore on, and the Party of Democratic Kampuchea (DK) escalated its challenges to the peace process, the prospects for UNHCR-sponsored repatriation diminished, even as the stakes grew higher.

Phase 2 of the ceasefire as spelled out in the Paris peace agreements called upon all four factions to disarm and demobilize 70 per cent of their armed forces. By late June 1992, the State of Cambodia, FUNCINPEC, and the KPNLF had begun to comply but the DK refused, calling first for a dismantling of the Hun Sen regime and verification of a Vietnamese withdrawal from Cambodia. On 22 July the UN Security Council passed a resolution requesting the Secretary-General to ensure that 'international assistance to the rehabilitation and reconstruction of Cambodia from now on only benefits the parties which are fulfilling their obligations under the Paris Agreements and cooperating fully with UNTAC.'[40]

UNHCR laid down several conditions to be met before it would encourage repatriation to DK territory: access by UNHCR and its implementing partners; access by other UNTAC components, specifically civilian police; and certified demining of the settlement area. In return, UNHCR was prepared to assist with road and bridge construction, to transport returnees to the site, and to guarantee them food rations and reintegration assistance. By the end of 1992, UNHCR had found only one site that would meet these conditions. It was the former village of Yeah Ath, south of Highway 5 in Banteay Meanchey.

On 15 December UNHCR Special Envoy Sergio Vieira de Mello met with Hun Sen, the State of Cambodia's Prime Minister, and asked for SOC cooperation in taking the returnees back into DK zones. 'Mr Hun Sen stated that this was a difficult problem,' according to a UNHCR report on the meeting. 'He was not against returns to DK area via SOC territory but asked for caution and stressed that the DK should not profit from those movements by legitimizing its presence and administrative authority.'[41] He also told Vieira de Mello that SOC had claimed the territory near Yeah Ath as its own following the Paris peace agreements.

On 18 December Vieira de Mello met in Sisophon with 14 high-ranking SOC officials – including the Vice-Minister of Defence, the Governor of Banteay Meanchey, and a general of the Cambodian People's Armed Forces (CPAF) – 'to explain', as Vieira de Mello put it, 'exactly what we would be doing and to seek their respect of the status quo' in the area. A similar meeting was held with Khmer Rouge officials. The Cambodian armed forces agreed to stay on the northern side of the Kuttasat bridge and the Khmer Rouge had agreed to keep their soldiers at a military base south of Yeah Ath.

On 13 January UNHCR escorted a convoy of 252 Site 8 residents across the border to the Sisophon reception centre, where they were registered by the Cambodian Red Cross and issued UNTAC voter ID cards. The next day they were trucked back down Highway 5 to the SOC-controlled village of Kuttasat. They crossed the bridge (which UNHCR had completed just that morning) over the Kuttasat canal and rode about 5 more kilometres to the Yeah Ath settlement site. The Vice-Governor of Banteay Meanchey, Ith Loeur, accompanied de Mello to Yeah Ath, where he shook hands with Long Norin and watched the arrival and unloading of the first convoy.

For several months, there was peace and Yeah Ath became something of a showcase settlement site, whose component parts UNHCR could never quite assemble in SOC areas. The Khmer Rouge offered a substantial tract of fertile, unmined land for housing and agriculture; the residents built their own houses, pagoda, and a small school. The international community also made substantial investments: a new access road, bridges, wells, and school buildings.

In all, according to UNHCR statistics in mid-June, 2,714 residents of Yeah Ath had come directly from the border camps, including 2,345 from

Site 8 and the remainder from Khao I Dang and Site 2. Another 3,729 returnees transferred to Yeah Ath having first repatriated to other locations.

In late April and again in mid-May CPAF soldiers raided Yeah Ath. Following the attack on 15–16 May more than 1,000 Yeah Ath residents are believed to have fled the area. Sporadic conflict continued for several months. By late September, UNHCR statistics kept by the field monitor in Yeah Ath showed a population of 6,743. The actual number of full-time residents was probably no more than half of that. As security continued to unravel in Yeah Ath, more and more families moved to nearby villages and towns but kept their ration book registered in Yeah Ath in order to maintain a claim on their land.

Toward the end of September 1993 the UNHCR field assistant in Yeah Ath reported that orders had come from the Khmer Rouge leadership in Pailin to evacuate the population to Phnom Malai. Four Khmer medics left Yeah Ath for security reasons. Officials in WFP, CRC, and even UNHCR itself began to mull ideas for an alternative evacuation route. In the end, the residents of Yeah Ath made their own way out. On 5 October Khmer Rouge soldiers attacked the Cambodian National Armed Forces checkpoint in Kuttasat and killed three soldiers alleged to be exacting especially heavy 'taxes' from travellers. On 6 October the Cambodian national forces retaliated with a round of shelling close by Yeah Ath and a raid that left one section leader dead. On 7 October several former settlers said they were approached by the Khmer Rouge and encouraged to establish a new settlement deeper into DK territory. 'The soldiers came and said, "No more Yeah Ath",' one man said. Citing various concerns – malaria, lack of medical care, loss of food rations, and fear of military conscription – the great majority chose instead to move to the government side.

Within a matter of days, more than 3,000 people had fled Yeah Ath for the safety of the Sisophon reception centre and more than 1,000 were scattered in nearby villages. It is believed that between 500 and 700 people remained behind in Yeah Ath.

Interviews with a number of former residents suggested that they came to Yeah Ath for the land. More than any other single factor, the promise of fertile, unmined, free land was what brought people to Yeah Ath – directly from the border camps or through secondary migration – and kept them there in the face of growing insecurity. Another reason some people chose Yeah Ath appears to be that they had no place else to go. Several returnees said the UNHCR announcements in Site 8 had encouraged people without relatives to consider going to Yeah Ath. And, although UNHCR officials may be reluctant to admit it, the UNHCR presence in Yeah Ath – along with assistance and UNTAC security – was another draw factor. For better or worse, UNHCR was an integral part of Yeah Ath – its creation, its brief success, and, to an extent, its undoing.

'The UN informed us that if we had no relatives in Cambodia, we could live in a neutral camp under UN auspices,' one returnee said. He had lived in Site 8 since early 1985 and repatriated directly to Yeah Ath in mid-January. 'I knew very clearly about Yeah Ath from the UN but I didn't know it was in a Khmer Rouge area. When I arrived, I was worried about security.'[42]

Despite the painstaking negotiations UNHCR undertook and the understandings it had reached with CPAF or the National Army of Democratic Kampuchea to leave Yeah Ath alone, the territory lay on a fault line between two increasingly hostile camps. It was hardly neutral territory and all too soon became a no-man's-land. 'Yeah Ath was untenable,' said Scott Leiper, then Cambodia director for the WFP. 'The situation was bound to change. The DK could not continue to hold it without a fight and the government could not take it over without a fight.' UNHCR was 'absolutely correct', Leiper said, in maintaining UNTAC's policy of neutrality toward the four factions. But Yeah Ath 'is also a casualty of this policy,' he said. In the end, 'the bridge reinforced the boundaries'.[43]

Final days on the border

By the end of January 1993, repatriation was entering its final stages. Only two camps remained. The population in Site 2 had dropped below 100,000 and was emptying fast, and Khao I Dang stood at 7,000. The problem was that as many as half of the remaining Khao I Dang people did not want to return.

The November 1991 Memorandum of Understanding between Thailand, Cambodia and UNHCR had provided for consultations between the contracting parties to find 'acceptable solutions for any exceptional cases involving individuals who, due to the particularities of their situations, might not be able to return to Cambodia'. Thailand already had spelled out its position on the 'refuseniks' and any other residual caseload: if UNHCR wished to protect them, it should transfer them first to reception centres inside Cambodia. UNHCR had rejected that proposal but was vague as to its own plans for those who spurned voluntary return.

On the morning of 28 January Thai border authorities met with UNHCR officials and informed them of their plan to close Khao I Dang by the end of February. They made the same announcement to camp residents that afternoon. Anyone who had not returned to Cambodia before Khao I Dang closed would be moved to Site 2. In the meantime, Thai officials said, the camp market and video parlours were to close and curfew moved up from 10:00 pm to 8:00 pm. The intent was very clear: to separate the Khao I Dang 'resistance' from its base camp.

From March 1992 to the end of January 1993, voluntary returns from Khao I Dang had averaged about 1,000 per month. In February, 5,604 people left the camp for Cambodia. 'When repatriation came, we did not sign up,' one of the KID returnees said. 'My father wanted to stay until the last convoy. We felt that security in Cambodia was not so good.' But the young man, Yang Yathana, went back on his own in October to look for family and scout out locations. 'I found family in Kompong Thom and Kompong Cham', he said. 'We chose to go back to Kompong Cham because it's safer.'

About 800 KID residents chose to move to Site 2 instead, where UNHCR placed them in newly constructed housing in Section 99. On 3 March the last convoy of 199 returnees left Khao I Dang and the camp – first opened on 21 November 1979 – was officially and finally closed. In his speech at the closing ceremony, Sergio Vieira de Mello called Khao I Dang a 'powerful and tragic symbol' of the Cambodian exodus and the international humanitarian response. UNHCR's 'prime objective and eventual achievement', he said, was 'to create a camp that was neutral, where people of all political affiliations could seek refuge'. At the same time, 'Khao I Dang also became a gateway for resettlement in third countries.'[44]

Part of the tragedy of Khao I Dang, and part of its power, the UNHCR's special envoy for repatriation suggested, derived from what he had elsewhere called 'excessively generous humanitarian policies in terms of resettlement and assistance provided'.[45] From 1975 to 1992, more than 235,000 Cambodian refugees in Thailand were resettled overseas, including 150,000 in the United States. Although officially the camp was closed to new arrivals in 1980, successive waves of illegal entrants had bribed their way past the Thai guards, some hiding for years in underground holes and behind false partitions before they were registered and ultimately permitted to seek resettlement themselves.

'I cannot but share the misgivings of a former colleague,' de Mello said at the camp's closing, 'when he said many years ago that he "could never quite see how we were contributing to the solution of Cambodia's problem by flying its few remaining qualified people to new homes thousands of miles away."' It was no surprise, then, to UNHCR that virtually all the 'refuseniks' were from Khao I Dang. They were, so to speak, dinosaurs, vestiges of an outmoded international response, clinging forlornly to the hope of resettlement and unable to reconcile themselves to a new future in Cambodia.

In the end, about 600 people, most of them former residents of Khao I Dang, refused to return to Cambodia. After UNHCR had reviewed their cases and concluded that they had no well-founded fear of persecution in Cambodia, the Thai military rounded them up and drove the angry and unwilling returnees to the Sisophon reception centre. Some protested their return by damaging the buses, trying to set fire to a UNHCR vehicle, and threatening violence to several workers in the reception centre. Fortunately, the incident ended without injury and by the next morning, UNHCR officials began the thankless job of reconciling people to their involuntary return. By early June 1993, all of the centres were empty. The movement phase, finally, was over.

Sisophon had hosted the triumphant return of the first convoy in March 1992 with flag-waving crowds and warm welcomes from Prince Sihanouk. The final, violence-marred movement was an unbecoming end to repatriation but an ironically apt baptism for Sisophon's second life as a centre for internally displaced persons.

Reintegration

By September 1993 UNTAC's transitional mandate had expired and, by November, virtually all of its more than 22,000 civilian and peacekeeping staff had left Cambodia. In April 1994, the 400 days of food rations provided to returnees by the WFP had come to an end. Although it maintained a sub-office in the troubled northwestern provinces into mid-1995 and a liaison office in Phnom Penh beyond that, UNHCR's substantial presence had scaled back from 250 people at the peak of the movement phase to 10 at the end of 1995. Its role shifted primarily to monitoring the security situation as well as the social and economic reintegration of the returnees. But what exactly did reintegration mean in the context of Cambodian repatriation? Once defined, how was it measured? And who was responsible for seeing that it happened?

In all of their agreements, programme descriptions, and discussions on reintegration, it is telling that neither UNHCR nor UNDP offered much of a definition of the term. Either everybody assumed a common understanding of the concept or nobody much wanted to be held accountable to specifics. Dictionary definitions of integration talk of combining parts into a whole, or bringing different racial or cultural groups into equal membership of society. Reintegration, then, has to do with making disparate parts whole again or disparate groups equal again. For purposes of repatriation, a working definition would be that reintegration is achieved when returnees have reached parity with the local population in terms of basic living conditions and means to self-sustainability.

This definition – benchmark may be the better term – confronts two painful moral dilemmas. The first is that while no one would argue that any individual or family has reintegrated if they are failing to sustain themselves, on an aggregate level, if that is the condition of a significant percentage of the local population, then some corresponding level of failure must be built into any realistic programme goals for returnee reintegration. The second is that repatriation from the border camps to Cambodia was bound to bring about a deterioration in basic levels of health care and sanitation for many returnees, leading to an increase in mortality rates and a lower quality of life in Cambodia than in the camps. In September 1992, Dr Robert Overtoom, at the time a UNHCR medical adviser, compiled a list of vital statistics on Cambodia and the border camps (see table on p. 252).[46]

A mortality rate in Cambodia of 17, Overtoom pointed out, 'means that in a city of 100,000 there are on average 1,700 deaths per year and that is 142 deaths per month.... So, if 200,000 refugees are repatriated, the Cambodian mortality rate would "allow for" 284 deaths among the returnee population per month.'[47] Among a full complement of 362,000 returnees, that would be 512 deaths per month. This is not to say that a mortality rate of 17 was 'acceptable' or that vigorous efforts should not have been made to reduce it. Nevertheless, those were the local conditions to which refugees returned and into which they would, perforce, reintegrate.

Table 9.1 Birth and Mortality Rates in the Border Camps and in Cambodia, 1992

	Border camps	*Cambodia*
Crude birth rate per 1,000 per year	50	39
Mortality rate per 1,000 per year	5.7	17
Infant mortality rate per 1,000 per year	38	132
Child mortality rate	na	206

Overtoom could have mentioned other statistics: that only 27 per cent of one-year-olds in Cambodia were immunized against childhood diseases, that only 12 per cent of the rural population had access to safe drinking water, that 53 per cent of the population had access to health services, that on the 1990 Human Development Index, Cambodia ranked 140th out of 160 countries.[48]

In this light, it was the role of the UN agencies and their implementing partners to try to raise the living standards of local communities while cushioning the 'fall' of the returnees. Parity, ideally, would be reached on a middle ground. That ground, like so much of the real estate in Cambodia, proved elusive and hard to reach. 'The Cambodians used to say at the border,' said Sr. Joan Healy, an Australian development worker, 'that when they returned home, 30 per cent would succeed, 30 per cent would fail, and the rest would have to struggle very hard.' Given the realities, that was probably optimistic. But without reintegration, Healy noted, 'repatriation would not be a durable solution, merely a relocation exercise'.[49]

'The debate begins,' said a UNHCR report in March 1992, 'as to how far UNHCR's responsibility extends towards the returnees, and how repatriation can jumpstart reconstruction without sucking UNHCR into a development role.'[50] The debate was older than Cambodian repatriation, of course, but the questions had never had so much riding on them. On 14 January 1992, UNHCR signed a Memorandum of Understanding with UNDP, under which UNHCR agreed to concentrate on meeting the immediate reintegration needs of returnees and the communities in which they were settling, while UNDP would work to 'bridge the initial reintegration phase with longer term regional integrated rural development'.[51] UNDP's Office for Project Services (OPS) was designated the implementing agency for longer-term reintegration; OPS, in turn, established the Cambodian Resettlement and Reintegration (CARERE) programme. Other UN partners in repatriation included WFP, UNICEF, the World Health Organization (WHO), and the International Labour Organization (ILO).

To complement the repatriation effort, one of UNTAC's seven components was rehabilitation. In many ways, its mandate was the most breathtakingly ambitious (and naive) of them all. At the Paris conference on Cambodia in October 1991, the participants had signed not only a peace agreement but a Declaration on the Rehabilitation and Reconstruction of Cambodia. Long-term reconstruction was to await the election of a sovereign Cambodian government but in the rehabilitation phase – coterminous with the peacekeeping operation – 'particular attention will need to be given to food, security, health, housing, training, education, the transport network and the restoration of Cambodia's existing basic infrastructure and public utilities'.[52] In short, get the country up and running again within 18 months.

In April 1992, UN Secretary-General Boutros Boutros-Ghali appealed to donor nations for voluntary contributions of $593 million (above the assessed contributions of $1.9 billion for the peacekeeping operations) to support rehabilitation efforts. In June 1992, at the Ministerial Conference on the Rehabilitation and Reconstruction of Cambodia held in Tokyo, 33 donor countries led by Japan and the United States pledged $880 million in recovery aid.[53]

Although the rehabilitation component was not entirely without success, it was hampered by what one observer called 'exceptionally poor planning and administrative confusion … losing two directors within months through resignation or dismissal'. Moreover, 'judged against its original mandate to "benefit all areas of Cambodia, especially the disadvantaged and reach all levels of society", the component fell far short of its goals. Less than $100 million of the $880 million pledged was disbursed before the elections, and most of that was directed to the [returning] refugees'.[54]

As of early 1993, in other words, more than 75 per cent of rehabilitation funding was being concentrated on only 4 per cent of the population. Repatriation, it seemed, was not simply jumpstarting the engine of reconstruction. It was driving the bus.

QIPs

One of the programmes that UNHCR and UNDP agreed to manage jointly was QIPs, Quick Impact Projects, intended to 'further anchor repatriation as a durable solution by maximizing the returnees' chances of reintegration into their communities'.[55] The projects – ranging from latrine construction to roads, bridges, wells, and health centres – were designed to have a visible outcome, usually within six months, and to be sustainable. In all, UNHCR spent $9.5 million on some 80 projects covering 10 sectors of assistance countrywide. Among the projects were the repair or construction of 238 kilometres of road, 22 bridges, 64 hospitals and clinics, and 376 schools. QIPs also funded preparation of 14,000 hectares of land and distributed seeds to 76,000 vulnerable families.

In the first two months of the QIPs program, from June to July 1992, UNHCR allocated more than US$500,000 for 14 quick impact projects. The smallest QIP was a grant of $5,800 to build 270 pit latrines in the Chamkar Samrong settlement site in Battambang. The largest grants of about $69,000 each went to upgrade hospitals in Siem Reap, to teach literacy to demobilized soldiers, to increase production of artificial limbs in Pursat and Siem Reap, and to construct concrete footings for 3,000 returnee houses in Banteay Meanchey and Siem Reap.

In July 1992, UNHCR's chief of mission in Phnom Penh, Anne-Willem Bijleveld, newly arrived from Geneva, called a one-month moratorium on approval of new QIPs proposals 'to permit some consolidation and review'.[56] The UN's 1990 Inter-agency Mission Report had urged that reintegration assistance 'should not unduly privilege returnees nor distance them from their home communities of return'. UNHCR's initial approach, officials agreed, focused too much on emergency needs in the fragile settlement sites, trying to anchor them, in effect, with concrete feet. Too little was being done to promote sustainable community development and self-sufficiency.

In late July 1992, UNHCR issued a one-page list of criteria for new QIPs proposals. New projects 'should be oriented in such a way as to be incorporated into [post-election] government infrastructures and services ... or directly or indirectly improve the employment and production capacities of communities or groups of individuals'. Any emergency assistance to meet immediate reintegration needs of returnees would be considered under separate project funds.

One of the problems in the initial implementation of QIPs was that funding and staffing problems had delayed CARERE's deployment of its technical teams, the provincial support units (PSUs). Scheduled to be in place by June 1992, the first PSU was not operational in Banteay Meanchey until August. (The Battambang PSU opened in September and Pursat in October; for reasons of both security and funding, the Banteay Meanchey office covered Siem Reap until July 1993.) The technical advice and coordination that UNHCR had envisioned, therefore, was not available at the field level until several months later.

'UNHCR is not a development agency and we don't pretend to be,' programme officer Daniel Le Blanc said. 'Because QIPs was not a project well defined beforehand, there was an initial period of a few months where everyone struggled.' Gradually, as CARERE became operational in the field, the UNDP side was able to give more advice and support on the QIPs programme as well as to formulate a more detailed workplan of its own for reintegration, though it remained painfully short of funds.

By the end of 1992, the QIPs programme had funded 33 projects totalling $3.4 million. Of this, UNHCR gave more than $700,000 to CARERE to repair 52 kilometres of road in Banteay Meanchey and to construct 35 primary schools (25 in Banteay Meanchey and 10 in Pursat). Another $614,000 went to Australian Catholic Relief to implement a Family Food

Production programme. The five-month project provided vegetable seeds, water jars, and basic extension training services to 10,000 returnee, internally displaced, and other vulnerable families in the four northwestern provinces.

In March 1992 a UNDP mission headed by former UNBRO director Winston Prattley had proposed a rural integration strategy linking QIPs with broader and longer-term plans for rural development and rehabilitation. Among the many recommendations in the report were proposals for QIPs totalling more than $63 million. Agricultural projects predominated, with $20 million to provide rice seed, draught animals, tractors, and fertilizer to returnees and IDPs. Education-related QIPs to the tune of $13 million were proposed, including $4.3 million to convert the reception centres into technical schools.

The sums proved far higher than donors were willing to give (or UNHCR was prepared to administer) for QIPs, but the Prattley Report serves as a telling reminder of how grand were the early visions for repatriation and how critically land figured in the designs for successful rural reintegration. Working under the assumption that land would not be available in the northwest to every returnee family who wanted it, the Prattley Report had urged that a contingency plan be developed

> to accommodate a substantial percentage of the returnee population who are widely expected to seek refuge, support, and employment on at least an interim basis in one or other of the urban centers of Sisophon/Monkol Borei, Battambang, Pursat, or Siem Reap.[57]

In February 1993, however, UNHCR reported 'no significant problem of migration towards the cities and towns. To date, there has been no substantial need to provide reintegration assistance to returnees in urban and peri-urban areas.'[58] At the same time, UNHCR statistics for May 1993 showed more than 60,000 returnees – 15 per cent of the total – registered at food distribution points in the four urban centres mentioned above. Commented Vieira de Mello at the end of 1992, 'We can employ people, including returnees, for relatively short periods of time, but the lasting economic reintegration of those opting for non-agricultural activities in rural or urbal areas is something that worries me.'

Ironically, one of the most frequently voiced criticisms of QIPs is that they were too quick. The six-month time-frame for implementation of projects was too rigid and left no margin for error or delays. More damagingly, UNHCR had obligated all of its QIPs money by the end of the movement phase in June 1993. This forced the agency to try to anticipate all of the immediate reintegration needs of returnees while they were still benefiting from the 400 days of WFP food aid.

CARERE

With a population estimated at 390,000 prior to repatriation and returnees estimated at 93,000, Banteay Meanchey province experienced, on a *per capita* basis, possibly the most significant impact of any province in Cambodia.

During the course of the movement phase, moreover, internally displaced persons in Banteay Meanchey numbered 38,400, nearly a quarter of the countrywide total. When CARERE opened its first provincial office in Banteay Meanchey on 1 August 1992, chief technical adviser Toni Stadler made contact with the local administrative officials from the provincial governor to the commune chiefs as well as with other UN, international, and non-governmental organizations working in the area. Together, they identified priorities, taking into account CARERE's approach to reintegration and development:

1 there are urgent needs that must be met, particularly in the area of infrastructure, before most other activities can be undertaken;

2 whatever work is done must have a long-term impact and be directly linked to activities to be undertaken in the future in the context of an overall integrated approach;

3 direct participation by the beneficiaries as well as by relevant local authorities is a must; and

4 projects must be sustainable, easily replicable, and not lead to long-term dependency on external support.[59]

CARERE combined UNDP resources with funds from UNHCR and several governments (particularly the Netherlands, Japan and Finland) to launch programmes in target communities in Banteay Meanchey, Battambang and Pursat. The idea was to link mutually supportive activities like agricultural production, job creation, education, transport and communication, health, and social services in particular communities while advocating the same approach on a provincial basis. CARERE projected a first-year budget of $31.2 million. Instead, it was given $7.9 million for the first six months.

The first thing CARERE did in Banteay Meanchey was to build roads. 'Poor roads lead to poor towns,' the CARERE workplan stated. 'Roads ... are a precondition for the successful development of all sectors.'[60] From September 1992 to August 1993, CARERE work crews completed 155 kilometres of roads, the benefits of which – aside from the obvious one of facilitating travel and transport – were manifold, Stadler suggested. CARERE roads connected villages and communities controlled by all four of the former political factions so, to some extent, they promoted reconciliation. Road construction also offered six months of employment at $1 per day to more than 6,000 local people, including many returnees and internally displaced persons. Moreover, 'road construction has enormous potential for irrigation,' Stadler said, 'since bridges and roads can also serve as dams. We will try to exploit that.'

In conjunction with local authorities and non-governmental organizations, CARERE also built schools, dug wells, developed agricultural extension programmes and even supported demining efforts. The CARERE programme in Banteay Meanchey was widely credited with ameliorating tensions between returnees and the local population, and in helping significant numbers of internally displaced people to return to their homes. CARERE's legacy in other provinces was much more patchy, however, as the programme fell victim to funding shortfalls, staff turnover, and bureaucratic inertia. In July 1993, UNDP assumed the lead role in coordinating and funding the reintegration programme.

WFP

In December 1990, the World Food Programme signed a Memorandum of Understanding with UNHCR to provide food assistance to Cambodian returnees. On 1 April 1993, WFP assumed responsibility from UNHCR for the distribution of food aid to the returnees and has integrated delivery with its other programmes in Cambodia. Of all the food aid that WFP distributes in Cambodia, WFP country director Scott Leiper pointed out, 65 per cent goes to returnees though they comprise only about 4 per cent of the population. Food for returnees, moreover, has been an entitlement, guaranteed for their first 400 days back in country.

WFP's approach to returnees post-400 days was firm but not unbending: 'While returnees would no longer be entitled to food assistance after 400 days,' said a WFP report in February 1993, 'it is expected that the most vulnerable could, if necessary, continue to be assisted for a time by other food aid programs operating in the country.'[61] These programmes, all operated by WFP, include aid to internally displaced persons, vulnerable groups, demobilized soldiers, and food-for-work projects.

In late 1991, USAID gave WFP $5 million to launch a programme to assist vulnerable individuals and families throughout Cambodia who were being assisted through WFP's programmes for returnees and internally displaced persons. The criteria for vulnerability that evolved throughout 1992 came to include rural and urban poor, hospital patients, orphans, prison inmates, residents of handicapped centres, and, in some cases, victims of natural disasters. WFP estimated that more than 400,000 people in 17 provinces and Phnom Penh received distributions of food aid through the Vulnerable Groups Programme (VGP) in 1992.

In 1993, WFP requested another 20,000 metric tons of rice to assist the 'poorest of the poor in targetted food deficit areas of the country'.[62] During the 'lean season' of July to December 1993, WFP distributed food rations to 350,000 rural poor and other vulnerable populations. Of VGP beneficiaries registered in the northwestern provinces, 8.5 per cent were returnees.

In 1994 and 1995, WFP dropped the categorical designations – internally displaced person, returnee, and vulnerable groups – and instead targeted geographical areas marked by severe rice production deficits and high concentrations of returnees and internally displaced people. Although WFP continued to provide food aid to newly displaced persons, it sought increasingly to use food assistance as a tool for development through income generation, training, and labour-intensive community work.

Anticipating the end of returnee food rations in mid-1994, WFP conducted a survey in the latter half of 1993 to assess the living conditions of returnee families and to identify how many might face difficulties living on their own resources. From May to November 1993, WFP teams interviewed 7,524 returnees in 15 provinces who were coming to an end of their 400 days of food. Based on a points system that considered land availability, income and possessions, WFP gave each family a score on a 'Wealth index' scale. Families that scored fewer than two points were considered 'at risk', two points were 'needy', three points 'marginal', four points 'fair', and five or more points 'good'.

Families that scored two points or fewer on the 'wealth index', and, moreover, were headed by single women, handicapped or otherwise disabled men, or elderly men, were classified by WFP as 'vulnerable'. Overall, this group comprised 31 per cent of the total. 'Application of the findings to the returnee population as a whole,' concluded the WFP survey, 'would imply the continued vulnerability of 25,682 families, or approximately 120,700 persons, at the end of the planned assistance program.' Other findings from the WFP survey included the following:

- Households headed by single women accounted for 20 per cent of the total and 53 per cent of families with a wealth index of less than three.

- 73 per cent of all returnee families scored fewer than three points on the wealth index, thus placing them in the categories of 'needy' or 'at risk.'

- 12 per cent of all returnee families reported having access to land for rice cultivation. 87 per cent of returnees who chose either Option A (agricultural land) or Option B (house and housing plot) reported that they still had no access to land.

In a summary report to donors on the Cambodian repatriation food resupply operation, WFP noted that, in two years, it distributed more than 85,000 metric tons of rice, fish, vegetable oil, and salt to 372,000 returnees. This food aid, the donor report argued, 'has been one of the most crucial factors in the returnee reintegration process and is often overlooked'. The food rations 'provided critical time to concentrate on resettlement and reintegration … and meant that any income derived by returnees during the reintegration period was able to be used for non-food investments'. The report further noted that while support from relatives has played an important role in reintegration, the 400 days of food aid meant that returnees 'were either able to contribute to the extended family outcome or at least able to reduce the burden they represented to their relatives by covering their own food needs'.[63]

This meant, of course, that if returnees had not successfully reintegrated within their first 400 days back home, the task might only become harder.

WFP estimated that about 50 per cent of all returnees 'have achieved a minimum level of food security either through their own means or through support from extended families'. Another 15 per cent 'are probably living at subsistence levels, and the ending of the food assistance will provide an added incentive to actively pursue income-generating activities'. The 5 per cent who were living in settlement sites 'may have to consider secondary migration. Continued food assistance would only prolong such decisions.' This left roughly 30 per cent of returnees 'who will face hardships after the end of food assistance'.

Two studies conducted in Battambang province in 1994 tend to bear out WFP's predictions. A survey of nearly 400 local and returnee families conducted by Chulalongkorn University's Indochinese Refugee Information Centre found that 34 per cent of returnee families were living 'hand to mouth', which involved 'foraging for food, or performing menial, short-term labor and spending the day's pay on food'.[64] Another contemporaneous study carried out by World Vision Australia concluded that about 40 per cent of some 300 families studied were 'not managing' which their report described as 'an inability to meet basic daily needs and ... characterized by foraging and inconsistent labour activities'. The World Vision Australia study recommended, among other things, that 'land access and land use are clearly the most essential long term determinants of development and progress'.[65]

Return to Vietnam

In June 1992, in the early days of Cambodian repatriation, a group of several thousand Cambodians in Site 2 held a demonstration demanding $700 per person in repatriation money. They looted UN offices, threatened staff members and camp residents, and set fire to several buildings. Convoy movements out of Site 2 were halted for two weeks. UNHCR officials suspected that in addition to 'real demonstrators' who were concerned about the adequacy of the assistance package, the disturbances were caused by 'political agitators' from the factional administrations who wanted to discredit and disrupt the UN plan and thus persuade people to move into the 'liberated zones' along the border.[66]

But the 'real demonstrators' had a real complaint: Vietnamese returnees were getting $360 per adult in cash against their $50 per adult (and $25 for children under 12). On top of this, the European Community had just launched a large-scale assistance programme for returnees that would pump more than $50 million into the local economy. UN officials on the border published flyers explaining that Cambodian returnees got a good deal more than their Vietnamese counterparts in terms of in-kind assistance like housing, food and land, so the total packages were roughly equivalent. Privately, however, some acknowledged the disparities. 'Let's face it,' said one later, 'the Cambodians by and large were eager to go home and the Vietnamese were not. Given that, who do you think would be offered the greater enticements?'[67]

Since 1989, more than 80,000 Vietnamese boat people have returned home, in a repatriation programme that has generated arguably more coverage, more controversy and more international contributions (at least on a *per capita* basis) than any other in UNHCR history.

Framework

When UNHCR first established an office in Hanoi in late 1974, its earliest projects focused on the reintegration of displaced people and included such things as animal husbandry, agricultural extension and vocational training. But the growing boat exodus, coupled with an influx of more than 100,000 refugees from Cambodia, forced the agency to put off any plans for reintegration and concentrate on securing asylum for those who had entered the country and orderly alternatives for those who sought to leave it. It was not until the end of 1988 that UNHCR was able to sign an official agreement with the Socialist Republic of Vietnam for the return and reintegration of those who left.

The Memorandum of Understanding of 13 December 1988 between the SRV and UNHCR spelled out four basic guarantees:

- Vietnam would ensure that voluntary return from the countries of first asylum would take place 'in conditions of safety and dignity in conformity with national and international law. This would include the waiver of prosecution and of punitive and discriminatory measures.'

- The government of Vietnam would 'ensure that such persons would be allowed to return to their place of origin ... [or] ... to a comparable place of their choice subject to the approval of the local authorities.'

- In the exercise of UNHCR's traditional monitoring functions, Vietnam promised to 'allow UNHCR full access to the returnees'.

- In order to help people 'resume normal life in the shortest possible time', it was agreed that appropriate reintegration assistance would be made available to the returnees.[68]

Vietnamese repatriation, not surprisingly, began slowly. Fewer than 1,000 boat people returned in 1989, all but a handful of them coming back from Hong Kong, where the reality of screening had had a year to settle on the camp residents. The pace picked up slightly in 1990, with 6,300 returnees, but these numbers were dwarfed by the more than 100,000 clandestine departures in the same two years. UNHCR's efforts in this country were concentrated more on stopping the flow outward than on settling those who were trickling homeward.

In 1990, UNHCR launched a multi-media mass information campaign to generate a new awareness in Vietnam of the now more stringent terms of asylum in the region. Short-wave broadcasts over Voice of America and BBC networks, newspaper articles and video presentations all pitched the same message to would-be boat people: think again. The journey is hard and the hope of resettlement slender at best.

Although the Vietnamese authorities were not involved directly in the UNHCR information campaign, they formulated their own on a parallel track. In July 1990, the Council of Ministers issued a number of directives to 'completely resolve this [illegal departure] problem from its roots'. Among its initiatives, the council promised to expand the ODP and increase the pace of acceptance of voluntary returnees. Furthermore, it urged 'cadres of all levels at localities that have numerous escapees' to increase their responsibilities 'in the area of propaganda, education, taking care of the people's needs, resolve their employment issues, assist families to overcome their problems, and increase the effectiveness of measures designed to prevent the illegal departure'. Specifically, it called on local officials

> to severely punish the instigators and the organizers, apprehend and prosecute according to the Law (including applying monetary penalties) those who had attempted to escape several times and who did not repent even after re-education and persuasion; to strongly increase our propaganda efforts and counsel people not to leave the country because of the dangers that entail [sic] and because of the difficulties in obtaining resettlement in another country.[69]

In some respects, the mass information campaign may have worked too well. Said one local UNHCR staffmember in Hanoi,

> When we started the repatriation programme, returnees received $360 per person, plus housing, work tools and some medicine. When people heard about the program, they realized that this was a large sum – a family of five would get $1,800. This was good money. In 1990–91, a lot of people showed up in Hong Kong with an application in their pocket to return. Some people who repatriated returned to Hong Kong as double-backers.[70]

In September 1991, UNHCR and the Vietnamese government made a joint announcement that anyone arriving in first asylum camps after that date would not be eligible for any repatriation assistance. The following month, for the first time since the beginning of the CPA, more Vietnamese returned voluntarily than fled by boat. Not coincidentally perhaps, the ODP was enjoying its most productive year ever, helping more than 86,450 Vietnamese to emigrate safely and legally. The boat exodus declined from 70,000 in 1989 to 32,000 in 1990 and 21,000 the following year. In late October, shortly after the the British and Vietnamese governments announced an agreement on an 'orderly return programme,' boat departures essentially stopped. The exodus, at long last, was over but the work of repatriation was really just beginning.

Reintegration

In September 1990, aware that it had no clear mandate to assist or monitor screened-out asylum seekers upon their return home, UNHCR solicited a letter from UN Secretary-General Javier Pérez de Cuellar, who wrote to Thorvald Stoltenberg and 'requested him, independent of his mandate as the UN High Commissioner for Refugees, to serve on an exceptional basis as my Special Representative to coordinate and monitor the returnees program to Vietnam'.[71]

In general, returnees to Vietnam were met upon arrival in Hanoi or Ho Chi Minh City by UNHCR staff. After a brief stay in a reception centre, the returnees moved back home, which usually meant their last address of record before they left the country. To help with their reintegration, UNHCR provided a cash grant of $240–360 to each returnee, paid in instalments through the government's Ministry of Labour, War Invalids, and Social Affairs (MOLISA).[72]

Beginning in 1992, as the pace of repatriation picked up (as well as the international contributions), UNHCR established a micro-projects programme to improve the material conditions of the communities to which the former boat people were returning. In three years, UNHCR spent over $6 million on some 300 small-scale projects throughout the country, including everything from health, education and water to vocational training and income generation.

In the first year, two-thirds of micro project funding was devoted to income generation, which mainly involved giving money to state sector enterprises to hire returnees. UNHCR repatriation monitors encountered two sorts of problems with this approach. First, working through the state sector meant encountering, as one monitor put it, 'bankruptcies, fraud, and corruption'. Second, others suggested, returnees were not attracted to the state enterprises, because of the low pay and often rigid bureaucracy, preferring instead to work in private enterprise or even start their own businesses.

So, said field monitor Goran Rosen, 'UNHCR started to think in other terms: infrastructure, roads, schools, dikes. These had community benefits and they were easier to monitor and created better cooperation with the local authorities. They offset the costs that local communities incurred with returnees.'[73] By 1994, water, education and infrastructure projects made up better than 90 per cent of micro project funding and income generation had dwindled to 4 per cent of the annual budget. The job of helping returnees find work had been handed over to another entity, the European Community International Programme (ECIP), which had more money and more expertise for the task.

As the boat people crisis escalated in Hong Kong in 1989–91, the British government searched for both carrots and sticks that might either pry or entice people out of the camps and back to Vietnam. Endymion Wilkinson, a senior European Community official and a British citizen, took the lead in developing and promoting the idea of a large-scale aid package, funded by the EC and focusing on returnee communities.[74] The first phase of ECIP started up in Ho Ch Minh City, Quang Ninh, and Haiphong provinces with a budget of $12 million and a timetable of seven months. From June 1992 to November 1994, however, the programme expended $100 million on repatriation and reintegration efforts, the centrepiece of which clearly was the small business loan scheme.

During the main phase of its programme, the ECIP made over 56,000 loans of between $300 and $20,000 (the average was $900) to returnees and locals alike. 'We applied the 50 per cent rule,' said former international programme director, Iain Francis: '50 per cent of our clients had to be returnees and 50 per cent could be locals. This rule applied to all components to reduce divisiveness.' The highest proportion of loans went to fishing and transport projects, followed by agriculture and aquaculture. 'We initially tried to lend money to businesses to employ returnees,' said Francis, 'but returnees generally preferred to set up their own businesses. We came back to loaning to returnees to set up businesses as equity holders. We were very pessimistic about this at the beginning. We thought these people were unbankable. It turned out to be very much the opposite. This was a middle-class clientele with entrepreneurial characteristics. They were a fragment of the frustrated entrepreneurial class.'

Overall, a remarkable 88 per cent of these loans were repaid. This, according to Francis, 'was unexpectedly good'. There was, he added, one unfortunate reason for this success:

Conspicuously, it was the better off who tended to benefit rather than the poorer. The poor needed a joint liability approach. Loans under $300 were not collateralized but were undersigned by 'mass organizations' – women's unions, peasants unions – or by groups of returnees. But these proved inefficient. The bank generally insisted on the house of the borrower as collateral. That bias against the poor persisted. The beneficiaries remained primarily the better off, the most resourceful.[75]

Still, said Francis, 'I think the programme succeeded in many ways in spite of itself. An extraordinarily high proportion of family businesses are still flourishing.... The negative aspects of targeting assistance have to be brought out. But we created the whole private-sector loan infrastructure. The whole growth of a market economy is dependent on the sweeping away of the bureaucratic class and the ascendancy of an entrepreneurial class.'

World Vision, working with returnees in Vietnam under a grant from the US government, conducted a survey of 360 returnees in 1996. The survey found that, of all the reintegration initiatives, 'small business enterprise had the greatest impact. It helped to pull a lot of people out of the debt cycle. Small business training is also necessary – bookkeeping, marketing, pricing, etc.'[76] One World Vision official noted that the new market economy offered unprecedented opportunities for those with good health, good ideas, and a modicum of capital. But, she added, 'a lot of people are getting blown out of the water in the new economy. One of the bad by-products of the market economy is that health care, education, and day care are all declining. The public sector is shrinking and qualified people are getting into business. This leaves single mothers, the sick and the handicapped all the more vulnerable'.[77]

The original plan was for ECIP to phase out by the end of 1994. But when the deadline came, more than half of the anticipated 80,000 returnees still were in the camp so the EC pledged to put another $15 million into a 'bridging programme' to focus not only on small and medium-sized enterprise development but also on the vulnerable populations left in the camps – unaccompanied minors, female-headed households and the chronically ill.

Monitoring

In the December 1988 Memorandum of Understanding, Vietnam gave UNHCR assurances that it would have full access to the returnees and that they would be treated humanely and not subjected to intimidation or harassment. In the early years of repatriation, according to Goran Rosen, a Vietnamese-speaking Swede who has worked for UNHCR since 1989,

> There used to be much stricter controls on monitoring. We used to have the Ministry of Labour plus the Ministry of Foreign Affairs plus the Ministry of Interior coming along with us. That was just from Hanoi. The people's committees added one or two people at the province level, then the district officers, then the commune. We were often 20 people coming into a poor returnee's house. You can imagine what the interview was like. It was terrible.[78]

Despite limited staffing, occasional travel restrictions and the difficulty in speaking with returnees outside of earshot of Vietnam's ubiquitous bureaucracy, UNHCR field officers managed to see 60 per cent of all returnees in 1989 and nearly half of those who came back in 1990. Gradually, monitoring became more routine. By 1990, said Rosen, the number of accompanying government officials

> was down to one or two total. Now it is still that way more or less [although] many local officials prefer to leave us alone; it is more and more relaxed. When there are sensitive issues, they know that it is a strength to discreetly let us be alone with the returnees. We leave name cards. Returnees sometimes come in the evening to our hotels or they send letters. It is sometimes hard to find privacy from neighbours but you learn how to make it happen.[79]

But as the number of returnees steadily increased, UNHCR found that it had to become more systematic in its approach to monitoring. Although returnees by and large left from and returned to coastal areas throughout the country and 80 per cent were concentrated in eight provinces, there were at least some returnees in all of Vietnam's 53 provinces and significant concentrations in the north, south, and central regions. Likewise, although nearly 40 per cent of all returnees went back to cities or townships with populations of more than 100,000 (making the Vietnamese repatriation experience a distinctly more urban phenomenon than its Laotian and

Cambodian counterparts), returnees also could be found in the remotest mountain villages and border zones.

To make monitoring all the more complex, an estimated 20–25 per cent of all returnees have moved at least once since repatriating. Most of these, according to one UNHCR monitor, have gone to look for employment in the cities and towns.[80] 'The policy is that people must return to the address cleared by the Ministry of Interior,' said Dirk Hebeker. 'Even if that is a New Economic Zone and their family is still there, then that is where they must return.' But there is no longer a policy of forced movement to the NEZs and little control on movements out. 'Often returnees will go there to register for their *ho khau* [family registration card],' Hebeker said, 'then de-register and move somewhere else.'

By 1995, UNHCR employed seven full-time, expatriate, Vietnamese-speaking monitors, four based in Hanoi and three in Ho Chi Minh City. Since 1989, UNHCR monitors have conducted more than 360 missions, visiting roughly 25 per cent of all returnees, some of them more than once.

The highest priority for the monitoring missions, according to UNHCR, is 'to investigate all allegations regarding either protection or reintegration related issues'. These allegations might have been brought to UNHCR's attention by the returnees themselves, their relatives or neighbours, UNHCR offices overseas, governments and their representatives, non-governmental organizations and expatriate pressure groups or the international media. Out of 2,500 'problem cases' identified by UNHCR between 1989 and 1995, about 1,100 were identified as priority monitoring cases (of these, UNHCR interviewed 1,050). Other vulnerable categories identified for additional attention included unaccompanied minors, victims of violence, single mothers, medical and psychiatric cases, ethnic minorities (Nung and Chinese), religious groups (Ching Hai and Catholics) and arrest cases.[81]

UNHCR officials argue that returnees to Vietnam have been monitored more intensively and extensively than any other group of returnees anywhere in the world. In addition to checking on allegations of harassment and persecution, monitors made home visits to provide advice and counselling and, where possible, make referrals for assistance. 'The cumulative experience of many thousands of monitoring visits,' summarized one UNHCR report, 'has led the UNHCR to perceive a gap, ironically, between its mandated function – international protection – and the demands placed upon it by returnees for economic assistance. While protection issues remain at the core of its tasks and receive most attention from outside observers, the vast majority of returnees, facing no protection problems whatsoever, request UNHCR attention, advice and assistance only to improve their economic situation.'[82]

The difficulties returnees have encountered in resuming their former lives include delays in payments of repatriation grants, trouble in getting houses back that have been confiscated by the authorities, and problems in reacquiring family registration cards or other official identification. But

UNHCR officials categorically insist that 'monitoring has revealed no indication that returnees have been persecuted'.[83] Critics from several human rights organizations and overseas Vietnamese groups disagree. Some of the most contentious cases involved those returnees who are arrested following their return.

According to UNHCR interpretations, in signing the 1988 Memorandum of Understanding, the 'waiver of prosecution' agreed to by the Vietnamese government gave returnees a *de facto* amnesty from prosecution under Article 89 ('Illegal immigration/emigration or illegal stay abroad') and Article 85 ('Fleeing and/or remaining abroad with the aim to oppose the people's authority') of the Socialist Republic of Vietnam (SRV) Penal Code.[84] But the government gave no such amnesty for Article 88, 'Organizing and/or forcing others to flee to a foreign country and/or remain abroad illegally.'[85] Nor did the provisions of the Memorandum spell out any automatic waiver of prosecution for other crimes or offences committed either before leaving or after returning to Vietnam.

As of the middle of 1995, UNHCR was aware of 88 returnees who had been arrested and detained on criminal charges since 1989, and MOI officials had given verbal indications that the number ran as high as 200. An internal evaluation conducted by UNHCR's Division of International Protection, while calling the overall work of the monitoring team 'impressive', nevertheless said the country office 'lacks the most rudimentary documentary evidence relating to arrest, trial and sentence, and imprisonment.... This situation is compounded by difficulties in obtaining access to the individuals concerned, a still only nascent concept of the rule of law, and the only partial compliance of the Vietnamese authorities' in notifying UNHCR in advance of return of cases where they were not willing to waive prosecution 'due to allegations of a serious common crime'.[86]

By the middle of 1996, UNHCR monitors had identified 106 arrest cases, of whom they had visited 80. Again, the agency insisted that in none of the cases monitored could the arrest and sentence be attributed to state persecution. Again, critics disagreed. One example cited was a September 1995 article in a weekly newspaper published by the Security Police in Haiphong titled, '79 political suspects identified among 1,432 people repatriated to Hai Phong'. In the article, which UNHCR confirmed to be genuine, the Haiphong police said they had

> collected complete dossiers on 79 political suspects and arrested three members of the reactionary organization, New Democracy. Based on these findings, the PA16 Bureau of Haiphong Police Department has taken measures in order to control this caseload and has proposed legal action to be taken in a timely manner towards those reactionary elements for whom sufficient evidence with regard to their criminal activities was found.[87]

In April 1996, UNHCR followed up on the report first by interviewing the chief of the Haiphong police department who claimed the article was 'intentionally exaggerated' in 'typical tabloid fashion'. Apparently, encouraged to find their own sources of revenue in the new market economy, police departments have discovered that crime tabloids 'are big money makers as they are filling a pent up demand for never reported stories about crime, gore, corruption and other misdeeds'. The police chief acknowledged that two, not three, arrests had been made. One man had been arrested in January 1994 for smuggling and had been released after less than two years' imprisonment. The other man, arrested for 'fraud involving private property' was still in prison. UNHCR interviewed this second man, who confirmed that he had borrowed a friend's motorcycle, pawned it, then lost the money gambling. UNHCR monitors said he 'gave an unambiguous "no"' when asked if his arrest had anything to do with his having been an asylum seeker in Hong Kong or a member of the New Democracy Movement.[88]

Was UNHCR naive or even duplicitous in so readily accepting the explanation of the chief of police and dismissing the concerns about possible persecution, as overseas Vietnamese groups assert? Would these expatriate organizations accept the findings of UNHCR as fair and impartial if they were true? And what insights, if any, does this case offer on the prospects of the many screened-out returnees who came from black-listed families?

According to UNHCR monitor, Dirk Hebeker, 'the *ly lich xau* [bad family background designation] is not fully eradicated yet but it has become more of a provincial issue. In some locations, it has been completely eliminated. In other cases, you get a bad feeling. Some people speak out and say they are really screwed because their grandfather fought with the French or their father with the Americans.'[89] Goran Rosen added: 'It is now possible to talk about black-listed families. The French period is a non-issue in the north. The *ly lich ba doi* [three-generation history] was officially abolished in 1987. For sensitive occupations – police and military – they still use a simplified form. But no matter what the rules and regulations, reality provides a lot of flexibility. Up to a point. You have to behave. There are not many taboos left: (1) you don't say anything bad about Ho Chi Minh; and (2) you don't advocate a multi-party system.' But, he added, 'Even if you live in this country for years and years, like I have, don't take anything for granted.'[90]

Notes

1 Author's interview with Kasidis Rochanakorn, Bangkok, July 1992.
2 UNHCR, *Outline of the Plan for a Phased Repatriation and Reintegration of Laotians in Thailand*, Fourth Session of the Tripartite Meeting, 27–29 June 1991, p. 5.
3 In Court Robinson, '"Unhappy Endgame": Hmong Refugees in Thailand,' *Refugee Reports*, Vol. 13, No. 8 (28 August 1992), p. 2.
4 *Ibid.*
5 UNHCR, *Background Information Note on the Situation of Lao Refugees and Asylum Seekers and Status of Voluntary Repatriation Program*, prepared for the Fifth Session of the Tripartite Meeting (LPDR/RTG/UNHCR), Rayong, July 1992.
6 Court Robinson, 'Unhappy endgame', p. 7.

7 UNHCR Information Note, Bangkok, 20 July 1992.

8 Women's Commission for Refugee Women and Children, *Repatriation and Reintegration: Can Hmong Begin to Look Homeward?* (New York: 1991), p. 11.

9 Unpublished, undated report from the Hmong/Highlander Development Fund, Washington, DC.

10 Author's interview with Vue Mai, Bangkok, July 1992.

11 Democratic Chaofah Party, Sayaboury, Laos [*sic*], undated manuscript.

12 Author's interview with Vue Mai.

13 See Marc Kaufman, 'Casualties of peace', *The Philadelphia Inquirer*, 27 February 1994.

14 UNHCR, 'Repatriation Information for Returnees to the Lao PDR', 18 September 1995.

15 *Ibid.*

16 UNHCR Branch Office in LPDR, 'Group Settlements: Site Selection and Preparation', July 1993.

17 *Ibid.*

18 *Ibid.*

19 Author's interview with Khun Prachuap, Vientiane, 7 December 1995.

20 Author's interview with Bruce Shoemaker, Vientiane, 10 December 1995.

21 UNHCR Information Bulletin, 'Laos', April 1996.

22 Author's interview with Fai Zoua Vue, Ban Na Saat, 12 December 1995.

23 UNHCR, 'Summary of Revised Operations Plan (Cambodia Portion)', 7 November 1991.

24 UNHCR, 'Cambodia Land Identification for Settlement of Returnees, November 4–December 17, 1991', PTSS Mission Report 91/33, p. 13.

25 UNHCR Fundraising Document, 22 January 1992.

26 *Ibid.*

27 UNHCR, 'Information Update on Voluntary Repatriation', 1 February 1991.

28 Specifically, the CRC found suitable land for 3,360 families in Battambang, 1,300 in Pursat, 700 in Banteay Meanchey, and 359 in Siem Reap. The CRC survey also provisionally identified land in the east for 472 families in Kompong Speu province, 271 in Kompong Cham, and 271 in Takeo.

29 Prior to repatriation, UNHCR had estimated that anywhere from 30,000 to 100,000 Cambodian refugees might repatriate spontaneously. Statistics at the end of the movement phase in May 1993 record 22,035 spontaneous returnees, of whom 5,306 registered with UNHCR and were eligible for assistance. It is questionable how many of the remaining 16,729 were real people and not a statistical figment.

30 UNHCR, 'Information Bulletin No. 6: Cambodia Repatriation Operation', 3 August 1992.

31 In informal interviews with more than 50 Option C families in 1992–93, the author found that 85 per cent had located relatives and in most cases were living with or near them. In a 1994 survey of 139 returnee families in Battambang province, conducted for Chulalongkorn University's Indochinese Refugee Information Centre (IRIC), the author found that 75 per cent of Option C families were living in the same village as their relatives.

32 'United Nations Joint Appeal for the Reintegration Phase of the Cambodian Repatriation Operation', February 1993, p. 7.

33 In April 1993, UNHCR staff in Battambang province conducted an informal survey of 1,050 families in the districts of Banan, Rattanak Mondol, Sangke, and

Moung Russei. The survey gave a secondary migration rate of just over 20 per cent. Most of those had moved somewhere else within the province. One frequently cited reason for moving was 'poor living conditions'. One year later, the IRIC survey found a secondary migration rate of nearly 20 per cent among returnees living in Battambang town, Sangke district, and Banan.

34 This is taken from a World Vision returnee reintegration program proposal of 11 February 1992.

35 For a full discussion of landmines in Rattanak Mondol (and throughout Cambodia), see Paul Davies, *War of the Mines: Cambodia, Landmines and the Impoverishment of a Nation* (London: Pluto Press, 1994), with photographs by Nic Dunlop.

36 *Ibid.*

37 UNHCR, 'Information Bulletin No. 7: Cambodia Looking to the Future', Phnom Penh: 28 October 1992.

38 Davies, *War of the Mines*, p. 49.

39 *Ibid.*, p. 59.

40 United Nations, *Security Council Resolution 766* (S/RES/766), 21 July 1992.

41 UNHCR, 'Cambodia Repatriation Operation: Situation Report No. 29', 14–21 December 1992.

42 Author's interview with Keo Chanda, Sisophon, 14 November 1993.

43 Author's interview with Scott Leiper, Phnom Penh, 17 November 1993.

44 Statement by Sergio Vieira de Mello at the closure of Khao I Dang, 3 March 1993.

45 Author's interview with Sergio Vieira de Mello, 17 December 1992.

46 The border camp data was from UNBRO, Overtoom noted, and the Cambodian data was from a software program, PC Globe, but was 'consistent with UNICEF's figures'. Personal communication.

47 Overtoom noted that the mortality rates in the camp were artificially low due to an under-reporting of deaths: 'If the death was not reported, the relatives collected the rice ration until the camp closed or the next headcount was held.' Still, the mortality rates in Cambodia were more than twice that in the camps.

48 Figures are from UNICEF, Cambodia.

49 Comments made by Sr. Joan Healy on 22 September 1992 at a meeting of the Coalition for Peace and Reconciliation (CPR), Aranyaprathet, Thailand.

50 UNHCR, 'Cambodian Repatriation Operation, Situation Report No. 3', 29 February to 7 March 1992.

51 United Nations, 'Outline of Memorandum of Understanding of Cooperation between the United Nations Development Program and the United Nations High Commissioner for Refugees', (Draft), 22 November 1991.

52 'Declaration on the Rehabilitation and Reconstruction of Cambodia', in *The United Nations and Cambodia, 1991–1995* (New York: United Nations Department of Public Information, 1995), p. 148.

53 *Ibid.*, p. 21. The figure is misleading in that more than $100 million of the $880 million had already been pledged for repatriation and reintegration-related activities.

54 Michael W. Doyle, *UN Peacekeeping in Cambodia: UNTAC's Civil Mandate* (Boulder, Colorado: Lynne Rienner Publishers, 1995), p. 50. See also Jarat Chopra, *United Nations Authority in Cambodia* (Providence, Rhode Island: Thomas J. Watson, Jr. Institute for International Studies, 1994). Chopra (p. 71) notes that rehabilitation 'was the only component without its own personnel deployment at the provincial level.'

55 UNHCR, 'Quick Impact Projects, Project Summary', Phnom Penh: 1 April 1993.

56 UNHCR, 'Cambodia Repatriation Update No. 8', 18–27 July 1992.

57 Prattley Report, p. 73.

58 'United Nations Joint Appeal for the Reintegration Phase of the Cambodian Repatriation Operation', February 1993. p. 14.

59 UNDP/Office for Projects Services, 'CARERE Workplan: September 1992–February 1993'.

60 UNDP/OPS, 'CARERE Workplan', *op. cit.*

61 UN Joint Appeal, *op. cit.*, p. 18.

62 UNTAC, 'Donors Review Meeting: 25 February 1993, Addendum: Specific Programmes and Appeals, Annex IV' (Phnom Penh: February 1993).

63 World Food Programme, *Donor Report: Cambodia Repatriation Food Resupply Operation* (Phnom Penh: February 1994).

64 Court Robinson, *Rupture and Return: Repatriation, Displacement and Reintegration in Battambamg Province, Cambodia* (Bangkok: Chulalongkorn University, 1994), p. 2.

65 Paul Davenport, Sr. Joan Healy and Kevin Malone, '*Vulnerable in the Village': A Study of Returnees in Battambang Province, Cambodia with a Focus on Strategies for the Landless* (World Vision Australia, 1995), pp. 3, 5.

66 UNHCR–Aranyaprathet, 'Situation Report No. 1: Cambodian Repatriation Operation', 1–30 June 1992.

67 Author's interview with Jahanshah Assadi, Melbourne, 24 July 1996.

68 Quotes from the 13 December 1988 Memorandum of Understanding are from UNHCR Information Paper, 'UNHCR Monitoring of the Repatriation and Reintegration of CPA Returnees to Vietnam' (Hanoi, 2 February 1996).

69 Council of Ministers, 'Directives from the Chairman of the Council of Ministers: In Reference with the Dealing with the Illegal Departures People' (Hanoi, 20 August 1990).

70 Author's interview with Son, Hanoi, 20 March 1996. UNHCR statistics show that of the 12,196 people who returned to Vietnam in 1991, 2,229 had been in the first asylum camps for less than 60 days and another 4,618 for less than 120 days. It is likely that most of these people never had a final screening decision rendered.

71 Pérez de Cuellar cited this 14 September 1990 letter in a letter of 4 October 1991 to High Commissioner Sadako Ogata renewing the request.

72 In September 1993, UNHCR reduced the repatriation grant from $360 to $240 per person.

73 Author's interview with Goran Rosen, Hanoi, 23 March 1996.

74 Author's interview with Iain Francis, Hanoi, 19 March 1996.

75 *Ibid.*

76 Author's interview with Kathryn Munnell, Hanoi, 22 March 1996.

77 *Ibid.*

78 Author's interview with Goran Rosen.

79 *Ibid.*

80 Author's interview with Dirk Hebeker, Hanoi, 21 March 1996.

81 *Ibid.*

82 UNHCR Information Paper, 'UNHCR Monitoring of the Repatriation and Reintegration of CPA Returnees to Vietnam'.

83 UNHCR Information Bulletin, 'The Comprehensive Plan of Action', August 1995.

84 UNHCR Information Paper, 'UNHCR Monitoring of the Repatriation and Reintegration of CPA Returnees to Vietnam'.

85 Translation supplied by UNHCR Branch Office, Hanoi.
86 UNHCR Internal Memorandum, 'Vietnam Mission Report', 20 July 1995.
87 UNHCR translation, cited in Council of Vietnamese Refugee Supporting Organizations in Australia, *UNHCR's Failures in the Comprehensive Plan of Action: A Factual Presentation, Part II: Repatriation* (Cabramatta, July 1996).
88 Letter 4 April 1996 from Henry Domzalski, Senior UNHCR Legal Advisor, Bureau Chief for Asia and Oceania to Mr Martin, cited in *ibid.*
89 Author's interview with Dirk Hebeker.
90 Author's interview with Goran Rosen.

CHAPTER 10

Aftermath

Even at a quick glance, the cumulative UNHCR statistics on Indochinese do not add up. Boat and overland arrivals of Vietnamese, Cambodians and Laotians in UNHCR-assisted camps totalled 1,440,000 from 1975 to mid-1997, of whom 1,315,000 were resettled in third countries. Just over 525,000 Indochinese, however, returned home under UNHCR auspices during that 22-year span. How could 400,000 more people leave the camps than arrived there in the first place? Not even an abnormally high birth rate could account entirely for this discrepancy. The answer is found in the Cambodian numbers. Of the 240,000 Cambodians who entered Khao I Dang camp (or its precursors), all but about 5,000 were resettled. Most of the 390,000 Cambodians who returned under UNHCR auspices never officially arrived in a UNHCR camp. For virtually all of their time on the border, they had been 'displaced persons' in camps run by the UN Border Relief Operation. Denied refugee status for so long, they were permitted to become former refugees upon their return home.

UNHCR's final figures, moreover, do not register the 134,000 Vietnamese who were evacuated to the United States in 1975 or the 263,000 Vietnamese refugees who fled to China in 1978–9. One should also add the 320,000 refugees who fled from Cambodia into Vietnam during 1975–8 as well as the more than 600,000 people who left Vietnam directly via the Orderly Departure Programme. Thus, even the most conservative figures show total departures from Cambodia, Laos and Vietnam in the past 22 years surpassing 3 million people. This does not count the hundreds of thousands more who were displaced at one time or another inside their countries or who slipped clandestinely across a border, nor does it account for the tens of thousands who died in the attempt to flee.

As the numbers suggest, the scope and multiplicity of the Indochinese exodus fundamentally challenged not only UNHCR's capacity but its mandate to respond. Depending on the times and circumstances, the Indochinese came to be called evacuees, displaced persons, refugees, asylum seekers, immigrants and illegal aliens. In each instance, UNHCR was called upon to say whether populations under that name were of concern to the organization or not. In each instance, it might be said that UNHCR grew or shrank, but it was never the same again.

Looking back at the massive human migrations in the last quarter century in Southeast Asia, the question arises: how has UNHCR changed in the light of its responses to the Indochinese exodus? To try to answer this question, it might be helpful to examine it by reviewing the three durable solutions UNHCR historically has been obligated to pursue on behalf of refugees and asylum seekers – resettlement in a third country, local integration in the country of first asylum, and voluntary repatriation. Underpinning the search for more durable solutions lies the elusive search for what has sometimes been termed a 'non-durable non-solution', temporary asylum.

Resettlement

In 1979 and 1980, at the peak of the Indochinese refugee outflows, resettlement was being offered to nearly every Vietnamese and Laotian who entered a UNHCR-administered camp, and to a significant percentage of Cambodians as well. Largely because of this massive international commitment, third-country resettlement was available to 1 in every 20 of the world's refugees. By 1994, that ratio had fallen to 1 in 418. In that same year, UNHCR's programme budget for resettlement worldwide amounted to only $7.2 million out of a total budget of $1.4 billion, a mere half of one percent. Although many factors contributed to the declining importance of resettlement as a durable solution, one UNHCR assessment in 1994 pointed the finger squarely at the Indochinese programme:

> The long-term impact of fifteen years of UNHCR involvement in the Southeast Asia operation – during which large numbers of staff saw themselves as unwilling participants in an 'automatic resettlement machine' – has been a widespread sense of disenchantment with the concept of resettlement. Many of the mid-ranking and senior UNHCR staff who served in Southeast Asia now seriously question the appropriateness of resettlement as a durable solution for refugees. The disenchantment with resettlement has had a negative effect on UNHCR's capacity to effectively perform resettlement functions.[1]

The 1995 issue of UNHCR's *The State of the World's Refugees* reiterated the view that the Indochinese experience somehow debased the coin of resettlement:

> The Vietnamese program has in many ways cast a long shadow over the role of resettlement as a solution and a means of protection. There is now general agreement that the decision taken in 1979 to offer resettlement to the boat people arriving in Southeast Asia acted as a 'pull factor', helping to create an unmanageable exodus of people, an increasing number of whom left their homeland for economic and social reasons, rather than to escape from persecution. As a result of this experience, one can assume that the industrialized states will be wary about making an open-ended commitment to the resettlement of an entire refugee population in the foreseeable future.[2]

As if to confirm that assumption, one senior immigration official from an industrialized state (in this case, Canada) called resettlement 'the narcotic of cures. It is expensive, addictive and, in the long run, destructive.'[3]

Certainly, there is general agreement in most Western capitals that what began as an essential durable solution for Indochinese became part of the problem, both by perpetuating an outflow of people in search of permanent exile and by hampering the search for other durable solutions, namely local settlement or voluntary repatriation. In 1984, the 35th Session of UNHCR's Executive Committee adopted a set of Principles for Action in Developing Countries. Among the conclusions of this committee of sovereign governments was that 'refugee problems demand durable solutions' but it went on to prioritize these: voluntary repatriation was the 'best solution,' local settlement was second best, and resettlement in third countries was 'least desirable'.[4] A later Executive Committee report went on to call third-country resettlement 'the solution of last resort'.[5] This hierarchical ranking of 'voluntary repatriation on top, followed by local settlement, then resettlement at the bottom', as one senior UNHCR official put it, is 'thanks primarily to the Indochinese exodus'.[6]

In 1990, UNHCR's resettlement section was incorporated into the Division of International Protection, a move that created both positive and negative perceptions. On the one hand, noted the 1994 UNHCR assessment, it 'reinforced the focus on resettlement as a tool of protection'. On the other hand, the report suggested, 'the low authority level of the Section within the Division ... combined with the marginal nature of resettlement within the organization as a whole, has meant that resettlement has not received the attention and support required to ensure appropriate and consistent policy implementation'.[7]

But has the Indochinese exodus only cast a shadow over the role of resettlement or does it also shed light on what remains, even in diminished status, a critical resource in the search for a durable solution to temporary exile? There is general agreement that the international response to the Indochinese refugee crisis was a one-off experience, that third-country resettlement may never again be offered so unequivocally to so many people over so long a time. Nevertheless, the lessons of this experience offer a variety of insights into the still timely question, as David Martin phrases it, 'In what circumstances is foreign relocation the indispensable solution to the individual's need?'[8]

The resettlement of Indochinese refugees performed many functions over its twenty year span – family reunification programme, burden-sharing device, even a foreign policy tool to embarrass and isolate the communist governments – but its most enduring role was as a vital *quid pro quo* to secure asylum. 'Resettlement was an essential component of protection,' said Michael Myers, a key aide to Senator Edward Kennedy. 'Without it, we would have had no impact on first asylum.'[9]

For one full decade, from 1979 to 1989, international resettlement commitments maintained a fragile equilibrium in the Southeast Asian camps, slightly outpacing new arrivals but not by so much as to trigger new outflows. This was the device US officials often referred to as 'managing down the programme', under which, the thinking went, ultimately the Indochinese countries would exhaust their stock of refugees before the resettlement countries ran out of admissions numbers or the asylum countries ran out of patience. Despite the growing misgivings that resettlement was, in part, perpetuating a need for more resettlement there seemed to be no way off the treadmill that did not risk losing asylum and, in doing so, losing lives.

The agreements reached in Geneva in 1979 finally and tragically came undone off the coasts of Thailand in early 1988 when Thai authorities pushed back thousands of Vietnamese asylum seekers. The new compact of the Comprehensive Plan of Action introduced regional status determinations and the return of the screened-out; yet it maintained, even strengthened, the international commitments to resettle refugees. It is possible, in hindsight, to question the wisdom of an arrangement that purchased asylum with resettlement but it is impossible to question its necessity in 1979 or the difficulty of altering its terms so long as the flows continued. Resettlement not only provided the ultimate form of protection for hundreds of thousands of Vietnamese, Cambodians and Laotians but it preserved the opportunity of asylum for hundreds of thousands more, many of whom were waiting only for an opportunity to go home safely.

The Indochinese exodus also introduced a new form of resettlement – direct departure by way of the ODP. Controversial at first, ODP proved to be an invaluable component of the international response, offering not only an alternative to dangerous, clandestine flight but safe and legal migration for several special – and especially vulnerable – populations, including former re-education camp prisoners, Amerasians, and their accompanying family members. Such a mechanism may never again involve as many as 30 countries or move more than 600,000 people in a 15-year span but direct departure programmes cover an important middle ground between normal migration and refugee resettlement. Whether provided on a bilateral basis or multilaterally through UNHCR auspices, programmes like the ODP offer a bridge to the outside for certain vulnerable populations within a state and, as happened with the United States and Vietnam, may help to build a bridge of communication between two otherwise estranged nations.

Almost from the beginning of the exodus, there was talk of local settlement for at least some of the Laotian refugees in Thailand. A US Senate report noted in 1978 that 'the Thai government has always recognized the need for some local settlement and has agreed, in principle, with the UNHCR's proposals for the local settlement of refugees; the only question is timing'.[10] Twenty years later, local settlement of Laotians had amounted to little more than a token gesture (though some estimates suggest that as many as 50,000 Laotians have settled spontaneously in Thailand).

Although local integration was not offered (except informally) to

Laotians, it would be misleading to think that it did not occur for Indochinese refugees. While third-country resettlement obviously garnered the lion's share of international attention, it should not be forgotten that more than a quarter of a million Vietnamese were offered local settlement in China while 10,000 Khmer Muslims were permanently settled in Malaysia. Both populations appear well integrated and reasonably self-sufficient.[11] The Vietnamese flight into China was not the first refugee movement from one communist state to another. That distinction, at least in Asia, belongs to the Cambodians who fled the Pol Pot takeover in 1975 by escaping into Vietnam and Laos. But China's resettlement of 260,000 Vietnamese certainly is the largest ever undertaken by a socialist state and offered UNHCR an opportunity to establish a presence in the world's most populous country.

In its 1996 edition of the *Resettlement Handbook*, UNHCR reiterated the 'last resort' viewpoint in stating that 'The decision to resettle is taken in the absence of other durable solutions and when there is no alternative and lasting way to guarantee the legal or physical security of the person concerned.'[12] That view was challenged by, among others, John Fredriksson, former Washington representative of the Lutheran Immigration and Refugee Service, who argued that 'UNHCR speaks primarily of resettlement as an instrument of protection while ignoring the equally important aspect of resettlement as a tool to achieve durable solutions in specific circumstances.' Resettlement, says Fredriksson, can be an effective 'tool of international solidarity'.[13]

By late 1997, official UNHCR pronouncements on resettlement had taken on a more positive, expansive tone. The 1997 version of *The State of the World's Refugees*, for example, commented that 'Unfortunately, the notion that resettlement can act as a 'pull factor' for economic migrants continues to obscure the vital role which resettlement can play in the protection of refugees who, for one reason or another, cannot remain safely in their country of first asylum.'[14] The UNHCR report noted that the organization helped to resettle only 27,000 refugees in 1996, but also outlined four reasons why refugees need to be resettled.

First and foremost, resettlement still represents 'a vital method of protection for those whose safety and security can not be guaranteed in their country of first asylum'. This might include people threatened with expulsion or forced repatriation as well as those facing a threat of arbitrary detention. Second, resettlement can be an effective way to help those with 'special humanitarian needs' that cannot be met in the country of first asylum. This might include people with life-threatening medical conditions, mental problems or physical disabilities; victims of torture and rape and other severely traumatized refugees; and refugees who wish to be reunited with family members living elsewhere. Third, resettlement may be necessary for those who have 'no other way of finding a lasting solution to their plight'. Fourth and finally, UNHCR acknowledged that 'there is a growing consensus that resettlement represents an important means of sharing responsibility for the global refugee problem'. By alleviating the refugee burden on poorer countries, third-country resettlement serves as a 'positive gesture of solidarity' on the part of wealthier nations.[15]

One role that resettlement could have played more aggressively in Southeast Asia was as a stimulus to local integration, particularly where an ethnic or religious affiliation existed between refugees and their country of asylum. Otherwise, all but the most strident critics of the various Indochinese resettlement initiatives would have to agree that the efforts were both necessary and effective for all the reasons outlined above. In the end, it might be said that over-reliance on third-country resettlement for Indochinese has instructed policy makers and field workers alike on the proper scope of this durable solution. To say that it is always the 'solution of last resort' is an over-correction of the imbalance. Rather, permanent resettlement in a third country will remain the best – indeed, only – solution for that small percentage of the world's refugees who cannot go home and cannot find even temporary safe asylum.

There is another important function of resettlement that should not be overlooked. As one Western government official put it, the resettled refugee represents a 'window to UNHCR'.[16] In other words, the refugee that one sees at home puts a human face on the work that the United Nations and other humanitarian organizations are doing on the other side of the world. This, of course, presumes that the face of the refugee does not prompt reactions of nativism and heterophobia. Resettlement, at heart, is a quite intimate process, opening its participants to new and sometimes painful discoveries about themselves and others. If the process proves ultimately more enriching than antagonizing, however, then sponsors, local service providers, community leaders, and resettled refugees themselves could prove to be key supporters of the international refugee regime. In this light, the massive Indochinese programmes of the last 25 years have left resettlement not a spent force but a latent energy.

Repatriation

Asked what UNHCR had learned about repatriation from the Indochinese experience, Sadako Ogata replied succinctly, 'that it is very difficult'.[17] It can also be a long time coming. Vietnam backtracked on its 1975 offer of repatriation and it would be 13 years before an agreement was reached on voluntary return *en masse*. Laos had a repatriation agreement first, in 1980, but was the last country to witness a dramatic gain in momentum. The breakthrough for Cambodia came in conjunction with the October 1991 peace agreement. Within six months, packed buses were moving in almost daily convoys across the border. Each of the Indochinese repatriation programmes proved different from the other and, in its own way, different from anything UNHCR had been involved with before.

In 1955, accepting UNHCR's award of its first Nobel Prize for peace,

High Commissioner van Heuven Goedhart suggested that 'Voluntary repatriation is no longer of great importance.'[18] By 1975, in the wake of the US evacuation from Indochina, UNHCR's third High Commissioner, Prince Sadruddin Aga Khan, saw repatriation as an essential tool for resolving the budding refugee problem. In 1981, when UNHCR won a second Nobel Prize, primarily for its work with Vietnamese boat people, voluntary repatriation still was not of great importance, certainly not in Southeast Asia. By the 1990s, however, repatriation was a growth industry. Indeed, from 1991 to 1996, roughly nine million refugees returned home, against only 1.2 million in the previous five years.[19] Likewise, repatriation accounted for 15–20 per cent of UNHCR expenditures in the 1990s, against less than 5 per cent in the 1970s and 1980s.[20]

As the sheer size of repatriation grew, so did the scope of UNHCR's involvement in return and reintegration. In August 1980, however, High Commissioner for Refugees Poul Hartling had submitted a Note on Voluntary Repatriation to UNHCR's Executive Committee which concluded that 'voluntary repatriation, whenever feasible, is the most desirable solution for refugee problems'. The roles for UNHCR outlined by the Note included making 'appropriate arrangements for establishing the voluntary character of repatriation', taking 'appropriate measures to ensure that refugees are fully informed of the situation in their countries of origin', and facilitating 'the provision of formal guarantees for the safety of returning refugees and/or the promulgation of amnesties by the countries of origin'. Finally, the Note stated that 'it may also be necessary to envisage appropriate arrangements to facilitate the reintegration of returning refugees into the society of their country of origin. Such arrangements may be of particular importance in the case of large-scale repatriation movements.'[21]

Throughout the 1980s, UNHCR became ever more focused on the necessity of reintegration for returnees. By the turn of a new decade, UNHCR operations in countries of origin had expanded considerably and repatriation programmes 'were a far cry from the days when refugees were provided with transport back to their own country and largely left to fend for themselves.'[22] In early 1980, Zia Rizvi, UNHCR's regional coordinator for Asia, defended the agency's role in helping people return across the volatile Thai–Cambodian border by saying that 'the conditions prevailing in the country to which the individual wishes to return are immaterial'.[23] Ten years later, the conditions in the Indochinese countries of origin – from infrastructure to economic opportunities – were one of UNHCR's major preoccupations. Still, a UNHCR policy paper in 1990 stated that the organization's protection and assistance role in the country of origin 'should not be envisaged as extending beyond three to six months' after the refugees had returned.[24] All three Indochinese repatriation exercises would push the envelope and redefine the state of the art.

In the case of Cambodia, the imperatives of the peace process and the election timetable called for a rapid mobilization of resources to move more than 360,000 people back to their country within twelve months. For the first eighteen months of the operation, logistics dominated and it was not until the newly elected government took office in September 1993 that UNHCR could concentrate on much more than immediate transitional assistance in the form of cash payments, housing kits, and quick impact projects. By that time, the mandate for returnee reintegration (and the money) had been turned over to the UNDP and its Cambodian resettlement and reintegration projects.

The success of the Cambodian repatriation operation lay in the capacity of the UN plan to enable more than 360,000 people – including 75,000 residents of Khmer Rouge encampments – freely to leave their border camps and travel safely to a destination of their choice inside Cambodia. The operation managed to avoid any number of 'doomsday scenarios' although the ultimate viability of returnee households remained a question mark even after several years. The only nationwide survey of returnees, which was conducted in late 1993 by the World Food Programme, found that nearly 74 per cent of all returnee families interviewed were still 'needy' or 'at risk' due to lack of resources, and nearly 39 per cent were vulnerable because they were headed by women, handicapped, or elderly.[25] Returnee vulnerability was exacerbated further by ongoing fighting between rival political factions, the ongoing terrorism of the Khmer Rouge, the presence of landmines throughout the country and the pressure for cultivable land in the northwest. In July 1997, a coup led by Hun Sen ousted his co-prime minister, Norodom Ranariddh, from the fragile coalition government. In the scattered fighting that ensued, another 65,000 Cambodian refugees fled once again into Thailand.

The return of 107,000 Vietnamese and 27,000 Laotian refugees and asylum seekers in some ways offered a study in contrasts with the Cambodian repatriation. While the Cambodian operation was widely hailed as a logistical and political triumph and its failures in reintegration have been the stuff of fairly limited debate, the international protests and spasmodic camp violence that erupted over CPA screening and repatriation controversies have overshadowed a story of steady, often painstaking, achievements in Laos and Vietnam in establishing programmes for reintegration assistance and monitoring.

On a *per capita* basis, the reintegration assistance available to Laotian and Vietnamese returnees significantly exceeded not only that for their Cambodian counterparts but virtually all other large-scale repatriation programmes to date. If one counts the repatriation allowances, the in-kind assistance, QIPs, small business loans from the European Community programmes, and various kinds of help from NGOs, reintegration aid totalled around $1,000 per person. UNHCR, moreover, is undoubtedly correct in stating that 'monitoring efforts in Vietnam are by far the most complex, far reaching and systematic individual case follow-up of any repatriation operation to date'.[26]

It might be argued that all this was simply excessive, symptomatic of the same unbalanced international preoccupation with Indochinese that generated such massive resettlement commitments while most of the world's refugees languished in long-term asylum. On the other hand, it might also be asked whether such inequities – at least in the context of repatriation and reintegration – suggest that other returnee populations need more resources rather than that the Indochinese needed much less. Asked this question, High Commissioner for Refugees Ogata replied, 'It is quite possible that the Indochinese displaced attention and resources from other populations. The big operations do take a lot of attention and money but you do get attention and money to do other things. You have to be a credible agency and credibility is based on conspicuous programmes and, of course, conspicuous successes.'[27]

Given the longevity and the seeming intractability of the Indochinese exodus and the deep political rifts that shaped and sustained it, the most remarkable success of Indochinese repatriation may be that it happened at all. And given the international attention that the Indochinese garnered throughout the course of their exodus, the amount of money spent on their return is not surprising. The most important achievements of the Indochinese repatriation programmes, however, may be among the least conspicuous – the many family reunions that occurred, the many small businesses that were established, the protection problems that did not arise because monitoring was, by the end, widespread and systematic. Similarly, the failures of repatriation will not all be as obvious as Yeah Ath, UNHCR's ill-fated effort to build a returnee community in Khmer Rouge territory. Many difficult questions have been raised by Inodchinese repatriation: under what circumstances, if any, should UNHCR involve itself in involuntary return? How long should a returnee remain of concern to the international community? How is reintegration measured and what responsibilities does UNHCR have if it is not achieved? Are QIPs compatible with sustainable community development? What is the right mix of money, food and in-kind assistance? One must hope not only that answers will be found but that they are not as long in coming as was repatriation itself.

Asylum

Looking back over the last 25 years, the Indochinese refugee crisis may well be remembered for the comprehensive solutions it engendered: the 1979 international conference that generated massive resettlement commitments, the 1989 CPA that sought a balance between resettlement and return, and the 1991 Cambodian peace agreement that laid the foundation for repatriation from the border. For those who lived it, however, and lived through it, the Indochinese exodus probably will be remembered most vividly as a crisis in asylum and an enduring search for even temporary terms of refuge.

The 1979 international response to Indochinese refugees involving blanket refugee status and virtually automatic resettlement for those in UNHCR camps was a response not so much to conditions inside Vietnam, Cambodia and Laos but to the onerous conditions of flight and asylum. As one senior UNHCR official argued, 'the flood of people, the pushbacks, the piracy, the attacks, the robbery, the killing, the rape, the machine-gunning of boats, the breakdown of the obligation to rescue people at risk on the high seas, the threats of closure of territorial waters – we faced a problem so peculiar, so specific, and so dramatic that we had to act in this way.'[28]

The promise of eventual resettlement worked – however imperfectly – to preserve asylum for roughly a decade. But by 1989, with the outflow of Vietnamese boat people rising after a ten-year decline, new terms became necessary to shore up regional and international commitments. The CPA introduced screening and repatriation into the equation but the old guarantees of third-country resettlement for *bona fide* refugees persisted. The countries of first asylum, with the exception of Singapore, agreed to conduct the status determinations and, with the significant exception of Malaysia, continued to permit boats to land. But it is difficult to call what they offered asylum when all that was available was temporary confined transit.

It has been suggested that, over time, the Vietnamese came to be seeking not asylum but resettlement; but, in truth, they could not have had one without the other. In Southeast Asia, it was not possible for an Indochinese refugee to seek and enjoy asylum unadorned. Even if the refugee did not necessarily seek it – as the Hmong experience shows – resettlement was the necessary consequence of the search for safe haven. Of course, resettlement was what the Vietnamese themselves overwhelmingly preferred to life in the camps, though that was probably the least of the reasons why they were given it.

Alan Simmance, a former UNHCR official with substantial experience in Asia, made this observation of the Indochinese crisis and the international response: 'Two concepts left behind – international burden-sharing and temporary asylum – proved a mixed legacy, both capable of being applied either to great humanitarian advantage or as an easy excuse to shift the responsibility and avoid the blame.'[29] The evidence suggests that the legacy of the Indochinese crisis in Asia is, at best, mixed.

In 1975, when the Indochinese exodus began, no countries in Asia were signatories to the 1951 Convention on the Status of Refugees or its 1967 Protocol. As of the end of 1997, the list was still relatively short: China, Japan, the Philippines, Fiji, Papua New Guinea, South Korea and, most recently, Cambodia. In his book, *The Status of Refugees in Asia*, Thai legal scholar and human rights advocate Vitit Muntarbhorn notes that while virtually every country in Asia has been either a producer or receiver of refugees, or both, since the Second World War, few have seen fit to accede to international refugee laws. 'The simple answer,' he suggests, 'would be political expediency.'

However, the reasons for non-accession are complex and should be seen in the light of a general reluctance to accede to all international instruments concerned with human rights.... Dominant in the minds of Asian states is the national security factor and the fear that accession to these instruments would oblige them to accept an unlimited number of refugees for long-term settlement. This apprehension is not easily dispelled.[30]

In April 1981 Japan acceded to the 1951 Refugee Convention, followed by China in 1982, although only Japan introduced implementing legislation in the form of the Immigration Control and Refugee Recognition Act of 1982. Article 32 of China's 1982 Constitution acknowledges only that 'The People's Republic of China may grant asylum to foreigners who request it for political reasons.' As Muntharbhorn indicates, however, 'That law has not generally been invoked for the large-scale influx of Indochinese cases.'[31]

In 1981, the Philippines became the first member of the Association of Southeast Asian Nations to accede to the 1951 Refugee Convention, and remains the only member to do so. It is probably no coincidence that the Philippines was also the only ASEAN country never to have pushed back Vietnamese boats. Thailand, Malaysia, Indonesia, and Singapore all systematically pushed refugees away from their borders at various points in the history of the exodus; tiny Brunei, after gaining independence from the British in 1984, refused to let any more boats land. In recognition of the leading role the Philippines has played in refugee matters in the region, the country was made a member of the Executive Committee of UNHCR in 1990. Spurred by the strong advocacy of the Catholic Church, the Philippines finally agreed to offer local settlement to about 2,500 screened-out Vietnamese living in Palawan who refused to return to Vietnam. Again, it was the only country in the region to make such an offer.

It is no secret that UNHCR would like to see more countries in Asia follow the example of the Philippines. As one UNHCR official put it, 'We hope we have inculcated in these governments the norms and standards of status determination and the possibility of a normal presence for UNHCR.'[32] But not even the Philippines has passed implementing legislation to make screening for refugee status available as a matter of due process. The offer of local settlement to the Palawan Vietnamese, government officials have suggested, was an exceptional gesture to close the chapter on the Indochinese and is not necessarily permanent. Other countries in the region are even more guarded about the prospects of status determination as a normal procedure. Witness the following comment from a senior Malaysian official:

> We have not really framed any law in response to refugees. In our classification, only Vietnamese are refugees. All the rest are illegal immigrants, of whom we have more than one million. Basically, every Malaysian has an identity card. Anyone who does not is a suspect.... We do not want to expand this thing any more than is necessary. One might argue that the Indochinese are a unique case.... First asylum countries are experiencing hospitality fatigue. I do not see any of the countries taking resettlement cases.[33]

In fact, Malaysia did take a number of resettlement cases. Some of the earliest boat people to arrive in Malaysia in 1975 were not Vietnamese at all but Cambodian Muslims fleeing the ethnic cleansing of the Pol Pot regime. By the end of the year, 1,275 Khmer Muslims had arrived, some by boat and some overland through Thailand. The government first put them in a camp but later decided to offer them permanent resettlement. In 1980, UNHCR made a grant of $2.1 million to the Malaysian Muslim Welfare Organization (PERKIM) to help with their integration. By 1992, Malaysia had resettled 10,000 Khmer Muslims, most of them from refugee camps in Thailand.

Malaysia, moreover, has been a long-time haven to more than 50,000 Filipino Muslims fleeing ethnic strife in Mindanao and, more recently, offered temporary haven to about 400 Bosnian Muslims. But, PERKIM's director stressed in 1995,

> I don't think this country is interested in proclaiming itself as a haven for Muslims around the world.... The government will not accede to the Refugee Convention but it needs to recognize that selected groups are in need of protection and assistance. Sri Lankans, Burmese Rohingyas, Bosnians have a case. There are also others who are not Muslims but who say their lives are in danger. Do we treat them simply as illegals and deport them? Generally, the government does not do this but they have not recognized them as refugees either.... There is no policy, no standard operating procedure. It is all dealt with on a case-by-case basis.[34]

In September 1992, while it was still under UN transitional authority, Cambodia acceded to the 1951 Refugee Convention along with a slew of other UN agreements. It is disappointing but perhaps not surprising that the government has failed to introduce any implementing legislation; indeed a new immigration law passed by the National Assembly in late August 1994 not only makes no mention of refugees or asylum but provides for the prompt expulsion of anyone without a residency permit and raises the prospect of crackdowns on ethnic minorities and foreign residents living in Cambodia, particularly ethnic Vietnamese. The absence of a nationality law, an accountable security force, or an independent judicial system rendered enforcement of this law problematic at best.[35]

Cambodians may be forgiven for holding a somewhat jaded view of refugees. After all, they have witnessed at first hand how a humanitarian regime can be manipulated to foment violence and prolong suffering even if it served (for some) useful political ends. Thailand, similarly, appears to have derived little positive resolve from its experience with Indochinese refugees, save to try not to repeat it. As one Thai academic and former government adviser said of the Cambodian refugees,

> We treated them in a not very ideal manner. We should not expect gratitude. Certainly we should not expect them to compromise their national interests. The Thai people were not so idealistic. The target was to get these people out of the country. As to what happens to them after they go home, the Thai people don't care. It is a general feeling among the Thai people that it is a different age. We should no longer have to bear this burden. There is no longer patience. The logical consequence is to push them back as quickly as possible.[36]

Still, consequences are not always logical or predictable, especially in matters of refugee policy, and it bears noting that, by May 1998, Thailand was patient host to nearly 90,000 Cambodian refugees. Hopes of their voluntary return hinged upon free and fair elections in Cambodia scheduled for July 1998.

Vitit Muntarbhorn notes that 'There is neither an Asian Convention on Refugees nor an Asian Convention on Human Rights. Rules of law at the regional level, arising from treaties, do not exist for the protection of refugees.' He adds however, that 'certain principles ... have emerged from the region, with at least persuasive force'.[37] In August 1966, an intergovernmental body, the Asian-African Legal Consultative Committee (AALCC), met in Bangkok where it came up with a non-binding set of agreements on refugees, which came to be known as the Bangkok Principles.

The committee's definition of a refugee is strikingly similar to that of the 1951 Convention. Vitit comments, moreover, that the Principles contain an article on asylum that represents 'a more progressive step in the protection of refugees' than the 1951 Convention. Article II accepts the position that 'A State has the sovereign right to grant or refuse asylum' then tempers this by saying:

1   The exercise of the right to grant such asylum to a refugee ... shall not be regarded as an unfriendly act, [and]

2   No one seeking asylum ... should except for overriding reasons of national security or safeguarding the population be subject to measures such as rejection at the frontier, return or expulsion.[38]

In 1987, the AALCC adopted an addendum to the Bangkok Principles elaborating on the need for international solidarity and burden-sharing. Among the points added was

The principles of international solidarity and burden-sharing should be seen as applying to all aspects of the refugee situation, including the development and strengthening of the standards of treatment of refugees, support to States in protecting and assisting refugees, the provision of durable solutions and the support of international bodies with responsibilities for the protection and assistance of refugees.[39]

These statements are neither explicit nor binding in their commitments to protection of asylum seekers. Thus far, as Vitit observes, the Bangkok Principles 'have not been very influential'. Is it reasonable to hope that ASEAN – which in 1997 formalized the memberships of Vietnam, Laos, Cambodia and Burma – will seek to harmonize regional policies on migration by incorporating international standards and procedures for status determination? Probably not, just as it is unlikely that the international community ever again will seek to secure asylum in Asia with large-scale resettlement elsewhere. The CPA may be too comprehensive, costly and complex to replicate but if Asian countries wish to do more than simply respond case by case, crisis to crisis, they could do worse than beginning with the Bangkok Principles. Asylum need not be regarded as an unfriendly act. Indeed, as Andrew Shacknove points out, it can be quite a friendly one:

Asylum is a global regime from which all States benefit in extreme times only if each contributes when it can. A sustained commitment to asylum on a global level is the only means of preserving the institution of asylum in whichever States find themselves geographically proximate to a refugee emergency. This is a matter not just of normative values such as solidarity or burden-sharing but of international order.[40]

Asylum, in other words, may be likened to an investment, deposited in times of plenty and drawn on in times of need.

A New Paradigm?

During the first 40 years of UNHCR's history, the strictures of the Cold War and the dictates of the donor countries confined the agency to an approach that was largely 'reactive, exile-oriented and refugee-specific'.[41] A refugee must first have crossed an international border before UNHCR could get involved; the burden of solutions fell most heavily on countries of asylum and resettlement rather than on the country of origin; and, with few exceptions, the beneficiaries of UNHCR's services were those who fell within the defined limits of the 1951 Convention.

In the 1990s, a new paradigm has begun to emerge, which UNHCR has characterized as 'proactive, homeland-oriented and holistic'. The proactive posture, sometimes called 'preventive protection' might include such activities as 'monitoring and early warning, diplomatic intervention, economic and social development, conflict resolution, institution building, the protection of human and minority rights, and the dissemination of information to prospective asylum seekers'.[42]

Central to the notion of preventive protection is the concept of state responsibility: a country that generates refugees must be held accountable to take the corrective actions needed for them to return home again safely. Corollary to the right to leave one's country and seek asylum elsewhere are the 'right to return' and the 'right to remain'. The search for durable solutions within this paradigm necessarily takes on a homeland orientation. What this has meant for UNHCR is an expanding operational presence in countries of origin, working to create the conditions for safe return.[43]

The new holistic approaches have seen the involvement of a wider array of organizations and institutions – from the UN Security Council to the World Bank and from developmental NGOs to the armed forces – in seeking cures to the problem of forced migration. It has also seen the transformation of UNHCR 'from a refugee organization into a more broadly-based humanitarian agency'.[44]

In 1957, for the first time, the UN General Assembly authorized UNHCR to use its 'good offices' to assist Chinese refugees in Hong Kong even though they were not 'of concern' to the agency.[45] Two years later, another UN resolution extended the use of UNHCR's 'good offices' to all refugees 'who do not come within the competence of the United Nations'. In 1975,

Resolution 3454 of the General Assembly affirmed 'the essentially humanitarian character of the activities of the High Commissioner for the benefit of refugees and displaced persons'.[46] Despite this gradual expansion of its mandate and organizational scope, in 1975 UNHCR still had the features of what one knowledgable observer called 'a small, narrow, legalistic, non-operational organization'.[47] Four years later, everything changed.

As Leo Cherne, chairman of the International Rescue Committee, later wrote:

> If there ever was a watershed year that has changed the scope, dimension, and complexity of refugee emergencies it is 1979–1980. During this period, the phenomenon of Vietnamese boat people fleeing persecution by the hundreds of thousands was followed immediately by the flight of more than 2 million Afghans following the Soviet invasion of their country. These, in turn, were followed by the tragedy of Cambodia, as hollow-eyed survivors of Pol Pot's 'social experiments' staggered into Thailand by the thousands, only, in too many cases, to die. In short order came the Mariel Cubans, with thousands taking the opportunity flee Castro's Cuba by boat, the plight of fewer but no less compelling numbers of Haitians, Salvadorans, Guatemalans, and Nicaraguans. Then nature, political manipulation, and ruthless military action combined to provoke the exodus of hundreds of thousands of Ethiopians, first to Somalia and Djibouti and then to the Sudan.[48]

UNHCR's annual budget doubled in size from 1978 to 1979, then doubled again to nearly $500 million in 1980. More than half of this amount went to Asia. The Indochinese crisis, more than any other, put UNHCR on the map.

In 1986, six years after UNHCR had begun running Khao I Dang and other refugee camps in Thailand, High Commissioner for Refugees Jean Pierre Hocké wrote a memorandum to his staff titled 'The Operational Role of UNHCR':

> Since occasionally one hears the phrase, 'UNHCR is not operational,' I would like to make it clear, both that we are operational and that there are specific ways in which we discharge our operational responsibilities. UNHCR is operational in the same way that a general, or turn-key, contractor is operational. We are fully responsible and accountable to the international community and the refugees for operations during the full life cycle of a refugee situation – all the way from early warning/contingency planning through lasting solutions to the plight of refugees.[49]

By 1990, as it neared its 40th birthday, UNHCR had grown into a worldwide organization with a staff of over 1,500 and a budget of more than half a billion dollars. It was also an agency in deep financial and institutional crisis. As a report by the Lawyers Committee for Human Rights noted, 'During 1989, governments refused for the first time in 40 years to approve the agency's requested budget. Instead, they forced the UNHCR to cut its programmes by 25% and reduce staff by 15%. The impact has been devastating.'[50]

Some blamed the Western donor governments and their growing

preoccupation with the rising tide of asylum seekers on their doorstep. Others put the blame on UNHCR's Hocké for fiscal mismanagement and a weakened commitment to protection. Hocké resigned in October 1989 and after a brief 11-month term by Thorvald Stoltenberg, Mrs Sadako Ogata was appointed High Commissioner by the General Assembly in December 1990.

According to Dr Michel Bonnot of Action Humanitaire, UNHCR took a 'big step' toward righting itself by getting involved in humanitarian assistance to Kurdistan in 1991,

> when we saw one million people escaping their country because they were afraid of being gassed or killed by the Republican Guard of Saddam Hussein. More than 100,000 people had fled in 1988 for similar reasons. France proposed to the UN Security Council a resolution that international relief and intervention superceded the right of sovereignty. Resolution 688 passed on April 5, 1991.... President George Bush made a statement that Kurdish refugees must be assisted inside their own country, not like in Indochina. That was a new concept.[51]

After mounting international dismay at UNHCR's conspicuous absence in Kurdistan, Ogata 'accepted the criticism and moved her agency to respond', said Bonnot. 'We see this new approach now in Bosnia and Rwanda. The UNHCR decision to protect humanitarian convoys inside Yugoslavia and its role as head agency in that operation was another important step in the expansion of UNHCR.' Now Bonnot sees another problem for the agency:

> In 1988–89, UNHCR was a completely bankrupt operation with a staff in deep malaise. The operations in Kurdistan and Bosnia re-established them. Now, more and more, the world is asking UNHCR to do jobs where it must play the role of policeman: to take people back to Vietnam because they are not refugees, to prevent freedom of migration in order to prevent ethnic purification. But UNHCR cannot guarantee security in Vietnam, or Rwanda, or Bosnia. And can it play the role of doctor, advocate, and policeman all at the same time?

Even as UNHCR's mission and modes of operation continue to evolve and expand, some observers ask if the world is not entering an era of the 'shrinking refugee' where harmonization of asylum policies has toughened restrictions on entry and diminished commitments to grant safe haven, whether temporary or permanent.[52] Can the right to seek and enjoy asylum flourish alongside the right to remain? Have approaches grown so holistic that they are not sufficiently refugee-specific? Has UNHCR grown large, to some degree, at the expense of its principal client, the refugee in search of protection? In a more specific regional context, Southeast Asia has shown great innovation and cooperation in getting people home, but what will be the nature of the response in the face of the next exodus? What new ground has been gained in Asia, if any, in the search for mutual commitments on asylum?

The lessons from the Indochinese crisis and the international response are at once encouraging and disheartening. In the wake of such mass upheaval, it seems a victory of sorts – howsoever small or Pyrrhic it may feel – that by the end of 1997, virtually all of the refugee camps in Southeast

Asia were closed and their former occupants either had gone on to start new lives in other countries or had returned home. What began in the stark polarities of the Cold War has ended two decades later in relative peace and stability. Mass exodus and exile has been transformed into large-scale return. And a small, legalistic, non-operational agency has evolved into a world-wide organization with a budget in excess of $1 billion and a capacity to respond swiftly and professionally to complex humanitarian emergencies.

The closing of refugee camps and detention centres throughout the region, and the safe repatriation of more than 500,000 people, is cause for satisfaction, but the images of joyful family reunion in Cambodia must be balanced with the lines of new Cambodian refugees straggling towards the Thai border and the panic-stricken faces of deportees herded aboard the airplanes in Hong Kong. It is not inappropriate that the last Indochinese camps to close in Southeast Asia under the CPA were Nakhon Phanom in Thailand and Whitehead in Hong Kong, the one a legacy of the dubious 'humane deterrence' policy and the other a steel and barbed-wire cage in the middle of one of the wealthiest enclaves on earth. Both of these, however one may gloss the terms, were UNHCR camps.

In a 1995 speech, Mrs Ogata concluded that 'the protection of victims of conflict and the search for solutions will continue to be necessary on the Asian continent' and offered these thoughts, drawing on the lessons from Indochina:

- the international refugee protection regime in Asia needs to be strengthened... Asian states will hopefully overcome their traditional reluctance to accede to the 1951 Convention and its 1967 Protocol.

- Asylum must remain a possibility even if it is not permanent.... Temporary refuge should, however, not be made conditional by countries of first asylum on any particular solution, especially resettlement in third countries.

- There is a need to affirm the non-political nature of asylum and the humanitarian character of refugee camps and settlements.

- The capacity of local governments to assure emergency assistance in case of massive internal and external displacement must be enhanced.

- An effective and early international presence in countries of asylum as well as of origin should help governments to safeguard the rights of refugees and internally displaced persons alike and to facilitate their early return and reintegration.

- The international community must insist on the responsibility of countries of origin to create the political and practical conditions necessary for the safe return of refugees and internally displaced persons at the earliest possible stage.

- Finally, the responsibility of countries of origin must be matched, through an integrated approach, by the commitments of the international community to help these countries solve their problems.

'In Asia too,' Madame Ogata concluded, 'the end of the Cold War has transformed humanitarian action, and is prompting new strategies and possibilities for the prevention and resolution of problems of forced displacement. Humanitarian action can, however, not be a substitute for political determination. At the end of the day, it is the commitment of governments to ensure economic progress, stability and democratic governance for all, that matters most.'[53]

Although, by mid-1998, Thailand was host to 115,000 Burmese refugees and nearly 90,000 new Cambodian refugees, overall refugee numbers in the region are the lowest they have been in a quarter of a century. Once the epicentre of the refugee universe, Southeast Asia has become a relatively quiet backwater. But the political and human rights crisis in Burma shows no signs of resolution, peace continues to evade Cambodia, and North Korean refugees have begun to trickle into China searching for food and respite from the hardships in their country. When a new crisis breaks, what will be the terms of refuge offered?

At the end of 1997, the government of the Hong Kong Special Administrative Region announced that it was scrapping the 'first asylum' policy that had been in place for Vietnamese asylum seekers since May 1975. In the future, announced Secretary for Security Peter Lai, 'there would be no special treatment for Vietnamese illegal arrivals in Hong Kong. They would be treated in the same way as are illegal arrivals from any other country.' A report in a Chinese government newspaper, *China Daily*, stated that any future Vietnamese arrivals 'will be screened for refugee status under internationally recognized standards' but gave no indication as to who would do the screening or whether asylum would be granted to *bona fide* refugees.[54]

The thrust of the international agreements on Indochinese refugees, in 1979 and again in 1989, was to pass ultimate responsibility for asylum seekers from the country of first asylum onto other countries or onto international organizations. As Alan Simmance suggested, that can serve as a model either of sharing the burden or of passing the buck. 'First asylum' is now at an end in Asia but, new paradigms notwithstanding, it is an open question whether asylum in Asia will be unconditional or largely unavailable.

Conclusion

More than 25 years ago, before the Indochinese exodus had begun to spill much across international boundaries, a distinguished migration scholar, Egon Kunz, noted that 'In traditional parlance migration is based on push and pull factors. The "push" factor of the old home environment provides the future migrant with causal motivations to leave the old country, and the "pull" factor of the country of choice provides him with purpose and a wish to migrate.'[55] In formulating a conceptual model for the movements of refugees, Kunz modified this approach to propose a 'push-pressure-pull model of refugee kinetics'.[56] According to this theory, refugees are pushed out of their countries by violence or political upheaval to find themselves in a place of temporary refuge. In seeking asylum, Kunz suggested, the refugee finds that 'He has arrived at the spiritual, spatial, temporal and emotional equidistant no man's land of midway-to-nowhere and the longer he remains there, the longer he becomes subject to its demoralizing effects.'[57]

As the marginal conditions of asylum and camp life work their dispiriting effects, Kunz theorized, refugees come under intense pressure to get on and go somewhere else. They might be pulled onward to an offer of resettlement overseas (which Kunz suggested was often 'more the taking of a plunge than an enthusiastic reaction to a pull') or they might feel pressure to return home or even to stay in place. In proposing his model, Kunz said he used the term *kinetics* rather than the more general term *dynamics* because the latter term,

> when used in social sciences suggests the existence of an inner self-propelling force. In the writer's view, this inner force is singularly absent from the movement of refugees. Their progress more often than not resembles the movement of the billiard ball: devoid of inner direction their path is governed by the kinetic forces of inertia, friction and the vectors of outside forces applied on them.[58]

The Indochinese exodus has confirmed all too painfully the demoralizing effects of long-term confinement and offered all too many examples of the brutal and indifferent forces that buffet refugee lives. At the same time, the Indochinese asylum seekers themselves have taught the world another, perhaps more durable, lesson: that refugees, in the end, are not billiard balls. Their paths are not devoid of inner direction but reflect complex patterns of volition and choices made in the face of bad odds.

In the last quarter of a century, the international refugee regime has moved from a bias toward exile and resettlement to a bias toward prevention, containment and return.[59] UNHCR, meanwhile, finds itself called to protect and assist an increasingly bewildering array of internally displaced persons, war-affected populations, asylum seekers, stateless persons and returnees. Of the 22 million people assisted by UNHCR in 1996, scarcely more than half were refugees in the legal sense of the word.[60] While that may indeed give evidence of an era of the 'shrinking refugee', it also suggests an era of expanded opportunity to assist and protect displaced populations in ever more unorthodox situations.

The Indochinese refugee crisis and the international response gave witness to the innovative capacities of the traditional durable solutions of resettlement, repatriation and even local integration but it also demonstrated their limitations. No one solution works for everyone and not all solutions are durable. Even temporary asylum is a solution, if it offers refugees the vital space needed to regather themselves and ponder their choices. More than a century ago, someone observed that 'There is no greater curse in the world for any cause than a demoralized emigration and the handling of its affairs is the most thankless task on this earth.'[61] But refuge, however brief or hard-won its terms, has a value beyond price. It is still a matter of life itself.

Notes

1 UNHCR, 'Resettlement in the 1990s: a review of policy and practice', an evaluation summary prepared by the Inspection and Evaluation Service for the Formal Consultations on Resettlement, 12–14 October 1994, Geneva. p. 1.

2 UNHCR, *The State of the World's Refugees: In Search of Solutions* (Oxford University Press, 1995), p. 92.

3 Author's interview with Mike Molloy, Toronto, 26 April 1996.

4 In Barry Stein, 'Refugee aid and development: slow progress,' in Adelman, *Refuge Policy: Canada and the United States*, p. 152.

5 UNHCR, *The State of the World's Refugees: In Search of Solutions,* p. 92.

6 Author's interview with Erika Feller, Kuala Lumpur, 25 September 1995.

7 UNHCR, 'Resettlement in the 1990s', pp. 9–10.

8 David Martin, 'The refugee concept: on definitions, politics, and the careful use of a scarce resource', in Adelman, *Refuge Policy: Canada and the United States*, p. 39.

9 Author's interview with Michael Myers, Washington, DC, 19 April 1996.

10 US Congress, Senate, Committee on the Judiciary, *Humanitarian Problems of Southeast Asia, 1977–78,* p. 16.

11 A 1984 survey conducted by UNHCR and PERKIM in Malaysia found that 57 per cent of the working-age Khmer Muslim population were in the labour force and the mean household income was M$527, which was lower than the mean income for urban Malaysian households but higher than the national average of M$355 for Malaysian rural households. About 86 per cent of Cambodian families were settled in rural areas. See UNHCR, *Socio-Economic Survey of Khmer Muslim Refugees in Malaysia* (Kuala Lumpur: 1984).

12 UNHCR, *Excerpts from the Resettlement Handbook, 1996 Version* (Geneva: UNHCR Division of International Protection, June 1996), p. II/1.

13 John Fredriksson, 'Revitalizing resettlement as a durable solution', *World Refugee Survey 1997* (Washington, DC: US Committee for Refugees, 1997), p. 51.

14 UNHCR, *The State of the World's Refugees: a Humanitarian Agenda* (Oxford University Press: 1997), p. 86.

15 *Ibid.*, pp. 88–9.

16 UNHCR, 'Resettlement in the 1990s: A Review of Policy and Practice', p. 1.

17 Author's interview with Sadako Ogata, Geneva, 15 February 1996.

18 Cited in Lawyers Committee for Human Rights, *The UNHCR at 40: Refugee Protection at the Crossroads* (New York: Lawyers Committee for Human Rights, 1991), p. 28.

19 UNHCR, *The State of the World's Refugees: A Humanitarian Agenda*, p. 143.

20 *Ibid.*, p. 167.

21 In Coles, *Voluntary Repatriation*, Annex B, p. 8.

22 UNHCR, *The State of the World's Refugees: In Search of Solutions*, p. 47.

23 In Shawcross, *The Quality of Mercy*, p. 312.

24 Cited in UNHCR, *The State of the World's Refugees: A Humanitarian Agenda*, p. 165.

25 See Robinson, *Something Like Home Again: The Repatriation of Cambodian Refugees.* p. 2.

26 UNHCR, *The Comprehensive Plan of Action, 1989–1995: a Regional Approach to Improving Refugee Protection.*

27 Author's interview with Sadako Ogata, Geneva, 15 February 1996.

28 In UNHCR, *The State of the World's Refugees: In Search of Solutions*, p. 208.

29 Alan Simmance, 'The international response to the Indochinese refugee crisis',

paper presented at the International Seminar on the Indochinese Exodus and the International Response, 27–28 October 1995, Tokyo, Japan.

30 Vitit Muntarbhorn, *The Status of Refugees in Asia*. (Oxford: Oxford University Press: 1992), p. 33.

31 *Ibid.*, pp. 61–62.

32 Author's interview with François Fouinat, Geneva, 17 June 1997.

33 Author's interview with A. Ganapathy, Kuala Lumpur, 28 September 1995.

34 Author's interview with Lt Col Hj Abdul Kadir Abdul Hamid, Kuala Lumpur, 28 September 1995.

35 The last Cambodian nationality law, promulgated on 30 November 1954, stipulated that 'anyone with at least one Cambodian parent was to be regarded as a Cambodian citizen, as was anyone born in Cambodia with at least one parent also born in the country'. Ramses Amer, 'The ethnic Vietnamese in Cambodia: a minority at risk?', p. 214.

36 Author's interview with Khien Theeravit, Bangkok, August 1995.

37 Muntarbhorn, *The Status of Refugees in Asia*, p. 45.

38 *Principles Concerning Treatment of Refugees*, Eighth Session of the Asian-African Legal Consultative Committee, Bangkok, August 1966.

39 *Status and Treatment of Refugees*, Twenty-Sixth Session of the Asian-African Legal Consultative Committee, Bangkok, January 1987.

40 Shacknove, 'From asylum to containment', p. 530.

41 UNHCR, *The State of the World's Refugees: In Search of Solutions*, p. 30.

42 *Ibid.*, p. 43.

43 *Ibid.*, p. 47.

44 *Ibid.*, p. 48.

45 Yefime Zarjevski, *A Future Preserved*, p. 16. At the time, Taiwan was recognized by the UN as the legal government of China. Thus, the refugees theoretically had the protection of the Chinese government and, as such, were not considered to be 'of concern' to UNHCR.

46 *Ibid.*, p. 17.

47 Author's interview with Dennis Gallagher, Washington, DC, 15 April 1996.

48 Foreword to W. R. Smyser, *Refugees: Extended Exile* (New York: Praeger Publishers, 1988), p. ix.

49 UNHCR Inter-Office Memorandum No. 62, 'The Operational Role of UNHCR', To All Substantive Officers at Headquarters, All Representatives, Chargés de Mission, and Correspondents, From the High Commissioner, 2 July 1986.

50 Lawyers Committee for Human Rights, *The UNHCR at 40: Refugee Protection at the Crossroads*, p. 15.

51 Author's interview with Michel Bonnot, Paris, 29 February 1996.

52 Tom Farer, 'How the international system copes with involuntary migration: norms, institutions and state practices', in Michael S. Teitelbaum and Myron Weiner, eds, *Threatened Peoples, Threatened Borders: World Migration and US Policy* (New York: W.W. Norton and Company, 1995). pp. 275–80.

53 Sadako Ogata, 'Refugees in Asia: from exodus to solutions', The Charles Rostov Annual Lecture on Asian Affairs, Johns Hopkins University, School of Advanced International Studies, 27 November 1995.

54 *China Daily*, 9 January 1998.

55 E. F. Kunz, 'The refugee in flight: kinetic models and forms of displacement', *International Migration Review*, Vol. 7, No. 2 (Summer 1973), p. 131.

56 *Ibid.*, p. 134.

57 *Ibid.*, p. 133.
58 *Ibid.*, p. 131.
59 See T. Alexander Aleinikoff, 'State-centered refugee law: from resettlement to containment', in E. Valentine Daniel and John Chr. Knudsen, eds, *Mistrusting Refugees* (Berkeley: University of California Press, 1995), p. 257.
60 UNHCR, *The State of the World's Refugees: A Humanitarian Agenda*, p. x.
61 In Kunz, 'The Refugee in Flight: Kinetic Models and Forms of Displacement', p. 133.

Appendix 1 Cumulative Indo-Chinese Arrivals, Departures and Residual Caseload, 1975–1997

Refugees and asylum seekers	Countries/territories of asylum	Arrivals in countries of first asylum — Arrivals in UNHCR camps	Departures from countries of first asylum — Resettlement	Repatriation	Cumulative departures	Residual caseload
From Vietnam	Hong Kong	195,833	138,545	66,696	205,241	2,069
	Indonesia	121,708	111,876	12,672	124,548	18
	Japan	11,071	10,350	1,300	11,650	23
	Korea	1,348	1,387	0	1,387	0
	Macau	7,128	7,708	0	7,708	7
	Malaysia	254,495	248,781	9,130	257,911	16
	Philippines	51,722	49,559	2,502	52,061	31
	Singapore	32,457	32,364	106	32,470	5
	Thailand (boat)	117,321	108,121	11,751	119,872	80
	Thailand (land)	42,918	37,752	5,064	42,816	39
	Other countries	3,227	3,486	101	3,587	0
Total Vietnamese		**839,228**	**749,929**	**109,322**	**859,251**	**2,288**
From Cambodia	Thailand	237,398	235,083	389,178	624,261	0
	Other countries	2,164	410	2,093	2,503	2
Total Cambodians		**239,562**	**235,493**	**391,271**	**626,764**	**2**
From Laos	Thailand (highland)	146,784	140,200	13,362	153,562	1,513
	Thailand (lowland)	213,146	183,907	10,529	194,436	
Total Laotians		**359,930**	**324,107**	**23,891**	**347,998**	**1,513**
Grand Total		**1,438,720**	**1,309,529**	**524,484**	**1,834,013**	**3,803**

Note: The figure for Cambodian repatriation from Thailand includes 367,040 Cambodians who were not counted as arrivals in UNHCR camps but returned under UNHCR auspices in 1992–3.
Source: UNHCR.

Appendix 2 Cumulative Indo-Chinese Resettlement Statistics, 1975–97

Countries of Resettlement	Resettlement from countries of first asylum					Orderly Departure Programme		Total
	Vietnamese Boat people	Vietnamese Land people	Laotian Lowland	Laotian Highland	Cambodian	Vietnamese	Cambodian	
Australia	108,808	2,344	8,949	1,290	16,309	46,711	1,296	185,700
Belgium	1,729	323	977	12	745	3,106	151	7,043
Canada	100,012	3,118	16,301	973	16,819	60,285	4,670	202,178
Denmark	4,592	117	0	12	31	2,298	20	7,070
Finland	1,813	52	6	0	37	736	0	2,644
France	21,421	5,663	26,005	8,231	34,364	19,264	4,234	119,182
Germany	15,489	1,360	1,681	25	874	12,067	124	31,620
Japan	6,388	86	1,254	19	1,061	1,757	162	10,727
Netherlands	7,332	2,234	33	0	465	1,980	58	12,102
NewZealand	4,476	483	1,283	67	4,426	1,140	1,469	13,344
Norway	5,950	118	2	0	128	3,998	50	10,246
Sweden	5,857	163	26	0	19	3,079	195	9,339
Switzerland	5,814	426	568	25	1,638	1,064	79	9,614
United Kingdom	19,329	96	346	0	273	4,842	108	24,994
United States	402,382	22,568	122,249	129,085	150,241	458,367	2,507	1,287,399
Others	6,526	601	4,227	461	8,063	2,815	268	22,961
Total	**717,918**	**37,752**	**183,907**	**140,200**	**235,493**	**623,509**	**15,391**	**1,954,170**

Note: The Vietnamese total for the US Orderly Departure Program includes 39,495 Amerasians, 140,857 re-education camp prisoners and their families, and 117,520 resettled through other programmes.
Source: UNHCR

Appendix 3 Thai–Cambodian Border Populations: 1975–1993

End of year	North	Central	South	Subtotal	UNHCR Camps	Grand total
1975					9,777	
1976					10,954	
1977					15,029	
1978					15,173	
1979	73,000	291,500	31,500	396,000	135,744	531,744
1980	33,100	92,601	38,500	164,201	147,059	311,260
1981	26,300	137,495	44,160	207,955	97,804	305,759
1982	32,004	144,037	11,400	187,441	83,951	271,392
1983	49,915	154,537	21,025	225,477	56,299	281,776
1984	49,270	170,378	21,318	240,966	41,619	282,585
1985	54,583	168,256	14,630	237,469	31,761	269,230
1986	62,877	178,540	15,233	256,650	26,949	283,599
1987	74,937	193,220	22,357	290,514	22,974	313,488
1988	65,057	216,052	19,607	300,716	17,152	3 17,868
1989	69,498	184,252	16,525	270,275	17,230	287,505
1990	71,010	219,043	18,809	308,862	15,097	323,959
1991	77,106	255,163	20,186	353,799	14,975	368,774
1992	0	112,506	0	112,506	6,816	119,322
1993	0	0	0	0	0	0

Note: Population figures for the North, Central, and South sectors of the border count border camp residents only. Non-residents and 'hidden border' figures are not included.

Source: UNHCR, UNICEF, World Food Programme, UN Border Relief Operation U

Bibliography

Selected interviews

Dato Abdullah bin Samsuddin, Sungei Besi Camp, Malaysia, 27 September 1995.
Rafael Abis, Pillar Point Camp, Hong Kong, 9 November 1995.
Cecilia Abraham, Kuala Lumpur, 30 September 1995.
Morton Abramowitz, Tokyo, 27 October 1995.
Howard Adelman, Toronto, 26 April 1996.
Daniel Alberman, London, 25 February 1996.
Corazón Alma de León, Manila, 21 November 1995.
Jim Anderson, St. Paul, Minnesota, 29 April 1996.
Gervais Appave, Canberra, 26 July 1996.
Bill Applegate, Manila, 22 November 1995.
Evan Arthur, Canberra, 25 July 1996.
Jahanshah Assadi, Melbourne, 24 July 1996.
Robert Bach, Washington, DC, 17 April 1996.
Pam Baker, Hong Kong, 7 November 1995.
Danilo Bautista, Singapore, 2 October 1995.
Darioush Bayandor, Paris, 27 February 1996.
Michel Bonnot, Paris, 29 February 1996.
Brian Bresnihan, Hong Kong, 9 November 1995.
Sten Bronee, London, 21 February 1996.
Sandy Buchan, London, 21 February 1996.
Dominique Buff, Aranyaprathet, Thailand, 6 August 1987.
Dawn Calabia, Washington, DC, 15 April 1996.
Gerry Campbell, Ottawa, 23 April 1996.
Can Le, Ottawa, 23 April 1996.
Margaret Carpenter, Washington, DC, 16 April 1996.
Alexander Casella, Geneva, 15 February 1996.
Che Nhat Giao, Palawan, 25 November 1995.
Chen Hui Hua, He Cheng, China, 1 November 1995.
Paul Chin, Singapore, 2 October 1995.
Dick Clark, Washington, DC, 17 April 1996.
Anne Convery, Washington, DC, 12 April 1996.
Robert Cooper, Jakarta, 10 October 1995.
Dale de Haan, Washington, DC, 17 April 1996.

Robert DeVecchi, New York, 10 April 1996.
Marion Dewar, Ottawa, 22 April 1996.
Henry Domzalski, Geneva, 20 February 1996.
Doua Thao, Kilometre 52, Laos, 7 December 1995.
Glen Dunkley, Geneva, 13 February 1996.
Fai Zoua Vue, Ban Na Saat, Laos, 12 December 1995.
Erika Feller, Kuala Lumpur, 25 September 1995.
Rosalind Finlay, London, 22 February 1996.
François Fouinat, Geneva, 12 February 1996, 17 June 1997.
Iain Francis, Hanoi, 19 March 1996.
Robert Funseth, Washington, DC, 15 April 1996.
Dennis Gallagher, Washington, DC, 15 April 1996.
A. Ganapathy, Kuala Lumpur, 28 September 1995.
Dennis Grace, Bangkok, 18 September 1995.
Mike Hanson, Hong Kong, 8 November 1995.
Lennart Hansson, Bangkok, 21 October 1995.
Abdul Kadir Abdul Hamid, Kuala Lumpur, 28 September 1995.
Carl Harris, Bangkok, 18 January 1996.
Scott Heatherington, Ottawa, 23 April 1996.
Dirk Hebeker, Hanoi, 21 March 1996.
Erna Henriksen, Nakorn Phanom, 13 December 1995.
Pao 'Paul' Herr, Bangkok, 4 June 1996.
Ha Duong Hui, Song Be, Vietnam, 26 March 1996.
Ivor Jackson, Geneva, 16 February 1996.
Udo Janz, Geneva, 12 February 1996.
Allan Jury, Bangkok, February 1988; Tokyo, 27 October 1995.
Henry Kamm, Paris, 28 February 1996.
Kasidis Rochanakorn, Bangkok, July 1992.
Margaret Kemp, London, 22 February 1996.
Keo Chanda, Sisophon, 14 November 1993.
Khammouane Souphantong, Vientiane, 7 December 1995.
Khien Theeravit, Bangkok, 3 August 1995.
Thida Khus, Phnom Penh, 28 August 1995.
Elizabeth Kirton, Savannakhet, 10 December 1995.
Latda Pathamavong, Vientiane, 8 December 1995.
Herman Laurel, Manila, 22 November 1995.
Lay Ka Khin, Hong Kong, 9 November 1995.
Datin Ruby Lee, Kuala Lumpur, 28 September 1995.
Clinton Leeks, Hong Kong, 10 November 1995.
Lee Pao Xiong, St. Paul, Minnesota, 29 April 1996.
Julian Lefevre, Hanoi, 22 March 1996.
Scott Leiper, Phnom Penh, 17 November 1993, 30 August 1995.
Li Chong Sheng, Guangxi Province, China, 4 November 1995.
Jackie Lindgren, London, 25 February 1996.
Shep Lowman, Washington, DC, 18 April 1996.
Luu Van Tanh, Ho Chi Minh City, 25 March 1996.
Louise MacPherson, Hong Kong, 7 November 1995.
Tom Malia, Bangkok, 20 December 1995.
Antonio Manguiat, Manila, 23 November 1995.
Maligna Saignavongs, 8 December 1995.

Pat Marshall, Ottawa, 22 April 1996.
Susan Forbes Martin, Washington, DC, 15 April 1996.
May Phoung, Ho Chi Minh City, 25 March 1996.
Dennis McNamara, Geneva, 14 February 1996.
Mike Molloy, Toronto, 26 April 1996.
Merida Morales-O'Donnell, Manila, 21 November 1995.
Eric Morris, Kuala Lumpur, April 1990.
Steve Muncy, Manila, 23 November 1995.
Kathryn Munnell, Hanoi, 22 March 1996.
Michael Myers, Washington, DC, 18 April 1996.
Adnan Nala, Galang, Indonesia, 7 October 1995.
Anthony Newman, Hanoi, 20 March 1996.
Nguyen Diem Ngoc, St. Paul, Minnesota, 1 May 1996.
Nguyen Dinh Thang, Washington, DC, 12 April 1996.
Nguyen Huu Dung, Hanoi, 19 March 1996.
Nguyen San Duy, Toronto, 27 April 1996.
Nguyen Thu Huu, Ho Chi Minh City, 28 March 1996.
Nguyen Kim Ba Thien, Paris, 29 February 1996.
Nguyen Thi Anh (pseud.), Sungei Besi Camp, Malaysia, 29 Sepember 1995.
Nhung Bui, London, 22 February 1996.
Sadako Ogata, Geneva, 15 February 1996.
Murray Oppertshauser, Toronto, 26 April 1996.
Père Parais, Paris, 27 February 1996.
Sr. Pascale Le thi Triu, Manila, 21 November 1995.
Andy Pendleton, Bangkok, 8 February 1996.
V.C. Phillips, Sungei Besi Camp, 27 September 1995.
Prapakorn Smiti, Bangkok, 14 August 1992.
Quy Dam, St. Paul, Minnesota, 29 April 1996.
Goran Rosen, Hanoi, 23 March 1996.
Lionel Rosenblatt, Bangkok, 19 January 1996.
Sakorn Boongullaya, Bangkok, 23 October 1995.
R. Sampatkumar, Geneva, 15 February 1996.
Suon Sandab, Khao I Dang Camp, 9 August 1987.
Eric Schwartz, Washington, DC, 17 April 1996.
Andrew Shacknove, Oxford, 20 February 1996.
Bruce Shoemaker, Vientiane, 10 December 1995.
Frank Sieverts, Washington, DC, 11 April 1996.
Ian Simington, Canberra, 25 July 1996.
Alan Simmance, Geneva, 12 February 1996.
Guy Simon, Paris, 26 February 1996.
Soesanto Mangoensadjito, Jakarta, 5 October 1995.
Enny Soeprapto, Jakarta, 6 October 1995.
Stephen Solarz, Washington, DC, 18 April 1996.
Michael Someck, Geneva, September 1990.
Julia Vadala Taft, Washington, DC, 16 April 1996.
Rick Towle, London, 26 February 1996.
Tran Van Mao, Galang Camp, Indonesia, 7 October 1995.
Tran Van Tinh, Hanoi, 20 March 1996.
Patrick Van de Velde, Bangkok, 9 August 1995.
Alan Vernon, Geneva, 16 February 1996.

Hong-Bich Huynh Vernon, 16 February 1996.
Sergio Vieira de Mello, 17 December 1992.
Vilay Chaleunrath, Washington, DC, 16 April 1996.
Vue Mai, Bangkok, July 1992.
Susan Walker, Bangkok, 6 July 1993.
Gerald Walzer, Geneva, 19 February 1996.
Jean-Noel Wetterwald, Jakarta, 5 October 1995.
M. Wihm, Paris, 27 February 1996.
Hans Willman, Na Pho Camp, Thailand, 11 August 1992.
Roger Winter, Washington, DC, 17 April 1996.
Xu Li Hua, Guangong, 1 November 1995.
Dato Yaacob Bin HJ Daud, Kuala Lumpur, 25 September 1995.
William Boua Yang, Bangkok, 4 June 1996.
Yang Dao, St. Paul, Minnesota, 1 May 1996.

Books and articles

Adelman, Howard (1982) *Canada and the Indochinese Refugees*, L.A. Weigl Educational Associates, Regina.
Adelman, Howard (1991) 'Canadian refugee policy in the postwar period: an analysis', in Howard Adelman (ed.), *Refugee Policy: Canada and the United States*, York Lanes Press, Toronto.
Aid to Refugee Children Without Parents (1990) *Unaccompanied Minors: They Should Not Be Repatriated to Vietnam*, ARCWP, San Diego.
Aleinikoff, T. Alexander (1995) 'State-centered refugee law: from resettlement to containment', in E. Valentine Daniel and John Chr. Knudsen, eds, *Mistrusting Refugees*, University of California Press, Berkeley.
Amer, Ramses (1991) *The Ethnic Chinese in Vietnam and Sino-Vietnamese Relations*, Forum, Kuala Lumpur.
Amer, Ramses (1994) 'The ethnic Vietnamese in Cambodia: a minority at risk?' *Contemporary Southeast Asia*, Volume 26, Number 2.
Amnesty International (1985) *Background Paper on the Democratic People's Republic of Laos Describing Current Amnesty International Concerns.*
Ashworth, Georgina (1979) *The Boat People and the Road People*, Quartermaine House, London.
Asia Watch and Committee to Protect Journalists (1987) *Still Confined: Journalists in 'Re-education' Camps and Prisons in Vietnam*, Asia Watch, New York.
Asia Watch (1991) *Indefinite Detention and Mandatory Repatriation: The Incarceration of Vietnamese in Hong Kong*, Asia Watch, New York.
Baker, Reginald P. and David S. North (1984) *The 1975 Refugees: Their First Five Years in America*, New Transcentury Foundation, Washington.
Banister, Judith and Paige Johnson (1993) 'After the nightmare: the population of Cambodia', in Ben Kiernan (ed.), *Genocide and Democracy in Cambodia*, Yale University Southeast Asian Studies, New Haven.
Barber, Martin (1987) 'Operating a United Nations program: a personal reflection', in Barry S. Levy and Daniel C. Susott (eds), *Years of Horror, Days of Hope: Responding to the Cambodian Refugee Crisis,* Associated Faculty Press, New York.
Barber, Martin (1987) 'Resettlement in Third Countries Versus Voluntary Repatriation', in Levy and Susott, *Years of Horror, Days of Hope.*
Barnes, Thomas J. (1977) *Of All the 36 Alternatives: Indochinese Resettlement in America*,

Department of State, Senior Seminar in Foreign Policy, Washington.

Becker, Elizabeth (1986) *When the War Was Over: The Voices of Cambodia's Revolution and its People*, Simon and Schuster, New York.

Benoit, Charles (1981) 'Vietnam's "boat people"', in David W.P. Elliot (ed.), *The Third Indochina Conflict*, Westview Press, Boulder.

Boat People SOS (1996) *The Role of UNHCR in the Forced Repatriation Operation in the Philippines*, Boat People SOS, Merrifield.

Bui Tin (1995) *From Cadre to Exile: Memoirs of a North Vietnamese Journalist*, Silkworm Books, Chiang Mai.

Bui Van Luong (1959) 'The role of friendly nations', in Richard A. Lindholm (ed.), *Vietnam: The First Five Years*, Michigan State University Press, East Lansing.

Bulk, Jack D. (1996) 'American Hmong on the move', in *Hmong Forum*, January.

Burrows, Robert (1994) *Displacement and Survival: United Nations Border Relief Operation for Cambodians in Thailand*, UNBRO, Bangkok.

Caplan, Nathan, John K. Whitmore and Marcella H. Choy (1989) *The Boat People in America: A Study of Family Life, Hard Work, and Cultural Values*, University of Michigan Press, Ann Arbor.

Castles, Stephen and Mark J. Miller (1993) *The Age of Migration: International Population Movements in the Modern World*, The Guilford Press, New York.

Catholic Office for Emergency Relief and Refugees (1986) *Report of Survey of Refugee Needs and Problems in Ban Vinai Refugee Camp, Thailand 1985-1986*, COERR, Bangkok.

Cerquone, Joseph (1986) *Refugees from Laos: In Harm's Way*, US Committee for Refugees, Washington.

Chanda, Nayan (1986) *Brother Enemy: The War After the War*, Harcourt Brace Jovanovich, New York.

Chandler, David (1991) *The Tragedy of Cambodian History*. Yale University Press, New Haven.

Chang, Pao-min (1982) *Beijing, Hanoi, and the Overseas Chinese*, University of California, Berkeley.

Chopra, Jarat (1994) *United Nations Authority in Cambodia*, Thomas J. Watson, Jr Institute for International Studies, Providence.

Coles, Gervase (1985) *Voluntary Repatriation: A Background Study*, prepared for the Round Table on Voluntary Repatriation, San Remo, Italy.

Committee for the Coordination of Services to Displaced Persons in Thailand (1977) 'Seminar on Displaced Persons in Thailand, Nakorn Pathom, September 22 1977', CCSDPT, Bangkok.

Committee for the Coordination of Services to Displaced Persons in Thailand (1981) *1981 Annual Conference on Displaced Persons in Thailand*, CCSDPT, Bangkok.

Committee for the Coordination of Services to Displaced Persons in Thailand (1982) 'Group discussion of policy implementation for displaced persons from Kampuchea', in *1982 Annual Conference on Indochinese Displaced Persons in Thailand*, CCSDPT, Bangkok.

Conroy, Thomas P. (1990) *Highland Lao Refugees: Repatriation and Resettlement Preferences in Ban Vinai Camp, Thailand*, Ford Foundation, Bangkok.

Cooper, Robert (1986) 'The Hmong of Laos: economic factors in refugee exodus and return', in Hendricks, Downing, and Deinard (eds), *The Hmong in Transition*.

Cornelius, Wayne A., Philip L. Martin, and James F. Hollifield (eds) (1994) *Controlling Immigration: A Global Perspective*, Stanford University Press, Stanford.

Council of Vietnamese Refugee Supporting Organizations in Australia (1996)

UNHCR's Failures in the Comprehensive Plan of Action: A Factual Presentation, Part II: Repatriation, Council of Vietnamese Refugee Supporting Organizations in Australia, Cabramatta.

DPA Consulting Ltd (1982) *Evaluation of the Indochinese Refugee Group Sponsorship Program*, Prepared for Employment and Immigration Canada, Ottawa.

Dacyl, Janina Wiktoria (1992) *Between Compassion and Realpolitik: In Search of a General Model of the Responses of Recipient Countries to Large-Scale Refugee Flows with Reference to the South-East Asian Refugee Crisis*, University of Stockholm, Stockholm.

Davenport, Paul, Sr. Joan Healy, and Kevin Malone (1995) '*Vulnerable in the Village': A Study of Returnees in Battambang Province, Cambodia with a Focus on Strategies for the Landless*, World Vision Australia, Phnom Penh.

Davies, Leonard (1991) *Hong Kong and the Asylum-Seekers from Vietnam*, Macmillan, London.

Davies, Paul and Nic Dunlop (1994) *The War of the Mines: Cambodia, Landmines and the Impoverishment of a Nation*, Pluto Press, London.

Dawson, Mark (1993) *Flight: Refugees and the Quest for Freedom. The History of the International Rescue Committee 1933–1993*, IRC, New York.

Delworth, W.T. (1980) 'Vietnamese refugee crisis 1954/55' in Howard Adelman (ed.), *The Indochinese Refugee Movement: The Canadian Experience*, Operation Lifeline, Toronto.

Desbarats, Jacqueline (1987) 'Population Relocation Programs in Socialist Vietnam: Economic Rationale or Class Struggle?' *Indochina Report*, No. 11.

Dia Cha and Jacquelyn Chagnon (1993) *Farmer, War-wife, Refugee, Repatriate: A Needs Assessment of Women Repatriating to Laos*, Asia Resource Center, Washington, DC.

Diller, Janelle (1988) *In Search of Asylum: Vietnamese Boat People in Hong Kong*, Indochina Resource Action Center, Washington.

Doyle, Michael W. (1995) *UN Peacekeeping in Cambodia: UNTAC's Civil Mandate*, Lynne Rienner Publishers, Boulder.

Duke, Karen and Tony Marshall (1995),*Vietnamese Refugees Since 1982*, HMSO Books, London.

Eagleburger, Lawrence S. (1989) *Indochina Refugee Situation: Toward a Comprehensive Plan of Action*, US Department of State, Bureau of Public Affairs, Washington.

Fall, Bernard B. (1967) *Hell in a Very Small Place: The Siege of Dien Bien Phu*, J. B. Lippincott, Philadelphia.

Farer, Tom (1995) 'How the international system copes with involuntary migration: norms, institutions and state practices', in Michael S. Teitelbaum and Myron Weiner (eds), *Threatened Peoples, Threatened Borders: World Migration and U.S. Policy*, W. W. Norton and Company, New York.

Fenton, James (1993) 'The Fall of Saigon', *The Best of Granta Reportage*, Granta Books, London.

Finck, John (1986) 'Secondary Migration to California's Central Valley', in Hendricks, Downing, and Deinard, *The Hmong in Transition*.

Forbes, Susan S. (1985) *Adaptation and Integration of Recent Refugees to the United States*, Refugee Policy Group, Washington.

Fredriksson, John (1997) 'Revitalizing resettlement as a durable solution', *World Refugee Survey 1997*, US Committee for Refugees, Washington.

Freeman, James M. (1989) *Hearts of Sorrow: Vietnamese-American Lives*, Stanford University Press, Stanford.

French, Lindsay, Barnabas Mam and Tith Vuthy (eds) (1990) *Displaced Lives: Stories of Life and Culture from the Khmer in Site II, Thailand*, International Rescue Committee, Bangkok.

Godley, Michael (1980) 'A summer cruise to nowhere: China and the Vietnamese Chinese in perspective', *The Australian Journal of Chinese Affairs*, No. 4.

Goose, Stephen D. and R. Kyle Horst (1988) 'Amerasians in Vietnam: still waiting', *Indochina Issues*, No. 83, August.

Gow, Anne Wagley (1991) *Protection of Vietnamese Asylum Seekers in Hong Kong: Detention, Screening and Repatriation*, Human Rights Advocates, Berkeley.

Grant, Bruce (1979) *The Boat People: An 'Age' Investigation*, Penguin Books, Harmondsworth.

Hafner, James A. (1985) 'Lowland Lao and Hmong refugees in Thailand: The plight of those left behind', *Disasters*, Vol. 9, No. 2.

Haines, David W. (ed.) (1985) *Refugees in the United States: A Reference Handbook*, Greenwood Press, Westport.

Haines, David W. (ed.) (1989) *Refugees as Immigrants: Cambodians, Laotians, and Vietnamese in America*, Rowman and Littlefield Publishers, Totowa.

Hale, Samantha (1993) 'The Reception and Resettlement of Vietnamese Refugees in Britain', in Vaughan Robinson (ed.) *The International Refugee Crisis: British and Canadian Responses*, Macmillan Press, London.

Hall, Kari Rene (1992) *Beyond the Killing Fields*, Aperture, Bangkok.

Hamilton-Merritt, Jane (1993) *Tragic Mountains: The Hmong, the Americans and the Secret Wars for Laos 1942–1992*, Indiana University Press, Bloomington and Indianapolis.

Hawthorne, Lesleyanne (ed.) (1982) *Refugee: The Vietnamese Experience*, Oxford University Press, Melbourne.

Heder, Stephen (1980) *Kampuchean Occupation and Resistance*, Asian Studies Monograph No. 027, Institute of Asian Studies, Chulalongkorn University, Bangkok.

Heder, Stephen (1983) 'Kampuchea: From Pol Pot to Pen Sovan to the villages', in Khien Theeravit and MacAlister Brown (eds) *Indochina and Problems of Security and Stability in Southeast Asia*, Chulalongkorn University Press, Bangkok.

Hein, Jeremy (1995) *From Vietnam, Laos and Cambodia: A Refugee Experience in the United States*, Twayne Publishers, New York.

Hendricks, Glenn L., Bruce T. Downing and Amos S. Deinard (eds) (1986) *The Hmong in Transition*, Center for Migration Studies, New York.

Hickey, Gerald Cannon (1993) *Shattered World: Adaptation and Survival Among Vietnam's Highland Peoples During the Vietnam War*, University of Pennsylvania Press, Philadelphia.

Hitchcox, Linda (1988) 'Britain and the Vietnamese refugees', in Supang and Reynolds (eds), *Indochinese Refugees: Asylum and Resettlement*.

Holborn, Louise W. (1975) *Refugees: A Problem of Our Time*, Scarecrow Press, Metuchen.

Hollifield, James F. (1994) 'Immigration and republicanism in France: The hidden consensus', in Cornelius, Martin, and Hollifield (eds) *Controlling Immigration: A Global Perspective*.

Isaacs, Arnold R. (1984) *Without Honor: Defeat in Vietnam and Cambodia*, Vintage Books, New York.

Jensen, Leif (1991) 'Secondary earner strategies and family poverty: immigrant–native differentials 1960–1980', *International Migration Review*, Vol. 25, Spring.

Jesuit Refugee Service (1995) *Concerns and Recommendations: Displaced Vietnamese, Laotians and Cambodians in Hong Kong and Southeast Asia*, JRS, Bangkok.

Jones, Peter R. (1982) *Vietnamese Refugees: A Study of Their Reception and Resettlement in the United Kingdom*, Home Office, London.

Kamm, Henry (1984) 'Vietnam's refugees sail into heart of darkness', *New York Times*, 4 July 1984.

Karnow, Stanley (1992) 'In Orange County's Little Saigon, Vietnamese try to bridge two worlds', *Smithsonian*, Vol. 23, No. 5 (August).

Kaufman, Marc (1994) 'Casualties of peace', *The Philadelphia Inquirer*, 27 February.

Kelly, Gail Paradise (1977) *From Vietnam to America: A Chronicle of the Vietnamese Immigration to the United States*, Westview Press, Boulder.

Kelly, John (1994) *Evaluation Report: Nordic Assistance to Repatriated Vietnamese Family Reunification Program for Unaccompanied Minors*, Nordic Assistance to Repatriated Vietnamese (NARV).

Kiernan, Ben (1985) *How Pol Pot Came to Power*, Verso, London.

Kim Ha (1983) *Report on the Vietnamese Land Refugees: The Journey Through Cambodia and Life in the Refugee Camps*, Boat People SOS Committee, San Diego.

Kopsak Chutikul (1988) 'Thai Perspectives on the Influx of Vietnamese Boat People', Thai Ministry of Foreign Affairs, Bangkok.

Kosol Vongsrisart, Vanchai Julsukont, Cletus Rego and Jack Reynolds (eds) (1980) *The Indochinese Refugees (Thailand)*, Office for Human Development of the Federation of Asian Bishops' Conferences, Bangkok.

Kunz, E. F. (1973) 'The refugee in flight: kinetic models and forms of displacement', *International Migration Review*, Vol. 7, No. 2, Summer.

Lacey, Marilyn (1987) 'A case study in international refugee policy: lowland Lao refugees', *People in Upheaval*, Center for Migration Studies, New York.

Lawyers Committee for Human Rights (1989) *Forced Back and Forgotten: The Human Rights of Laotian Asylum Seekers in Thailand*, Lawyers Committee for Human Rights, New York.

Lawyers Committee for Human Rights (1989) *Inhumane Deterrence: The Treatment of Vietnamese Boat People in Hong Kong*, Lawyers Committee for Human Rights, New York.

Lawyers Committee for Human Rights (1991) *Uncertain Haven: Refugee Protection on the Fortieth Anniversary of the 1951 United Nations Refugee Convention*, Lawyers Committee for Human Rights, New York.

Lawyers Committee for Human Rights (1991) *The UNHCR at 40: Refugee Protection at the Crossroads*, Lawyers Committee for Human Rights, New York.

Layton-Henry, Zig (1994) 'Britain: the would-be zero-immigration country', in Cornelius, Martin and Hollifield (eds), *Controlling Immigration: A Global Perspective*.

Lee, Gary Y. (1982) 'Minority policies and the Hmong', in Martin Stuart-Fox (ed.) *Contemporary Laos: Studies in the Politics and Society of the Lao People's Democratic Republic*, University of Queensland Press, Queensland.

Lewins, Frank and Judith Ly (1985) *The First Wave: The Settlement of Australia's First Vietnamese Refugees*, George Allen and Unwin, Sydney.

Liu, William T., Maryanne Lamanna and Alice Murata (1979) *Transition to Nowhere: Vietnamese Refugees in America*, Charter House Publishers, Nashville.

Loescher, Gil and John A. Scanlan (1986) *Calculated Kindness: Refugees and America's Half-Open Door 1945–Present*, Free Press, New York.

Loescher, Gil (1993) *Beyond Charity: International Cooperation and the Global Refugee Crisis*, Oxford University Press, New York and Oxford.

Long, Lynellyn D. (1993) *Ban Vinai: The Refugee Camp*, Columbia University Press, New York.

Lynch, James F. (1989) *Border Khmer: A Demographic Study of the Residents of Site 2, Site B and Site 8*, Ford Foundation, Bangkok.

Martin, David (1991) 'The refugee concept: on definitions, politics, and the careful use of a scarce resource', in Adelman (ed.), *Refuge Policy: Canada and the United States*.

Martin, Marie-Alexandrine (1984) 'The Vietnamisation of Kampuchea: a new model of colonialism', *Indochina Report*, October.

Martin, Susan Forbes (1992) *Refugee Women*, Zed Books, London.

Mason, Linda and Roger Brown (1983) *Rice, Rivalry, and Politics: Managing Cambodian Relief*, University of Notre Dame Press, Notre Dame.

McCallin, Margaret (1993) *Living in Detention: A Review of the Psychosocial Well-Being of Vietnamese Children in the Hong Kong Detention Centers*, International Catholic Child Bureau, Geneva.

Migration and Refugee Services, US Catholic Conference (1986)*The Orderly Departure Program: The Need for Reassessment*, USCC, Washington.

Mortensen, Irene (1995) *Final Report: Achievements of the NARV Program, October 1992– April 1995*, Nordic Assistance to Repatriated Vietnamese.

Mougne, Christine (1989) 'Difficult decisions', *Refugees*, November.

NSW Refugee Fund Committee (1994) *Report on Corruption in the Screening Process Under the Comprehensive Plan of Action in Galang Camp, Indonesia*, NSW Refugee Fund Committee, Cabramatta.

Narisa Chakrabongse (1986) *The Affected Thai Village Program: 1978–1986*, Ford Foundation, Bangkok.

Nayaporn Penpas (1987) *Khambanyai Ruang Panha Phuopayop Lae Pholopniikhaomuang* (A Lecture on the Problem of Displaced Persons and Those Who Flee into the Country), *Sathaban Jitwittaya Khwammankhong*, Institute of Security Psychology, Bangkok.

Nguyen Khac Vien (1985) 'Those who leave', in *Southern Vietnam: 1975–1985*, Foreign Languages Publishing House, Hanoi.

Nguyen, San Duy, Terence Cooke and Tran Q. Phung (1983) *Refugee Needs Asssessment*, Ottawa–Carleton SEA Refugee Project, Ottawa.

Nhat Tien, Duong Phuc and Vu Thanh Thuy (1981) *Pirates on the Gulf of Siam*, Boat People SOS Committee, San Diego.

Niksch, Larry A. (1981) 'Thailand in 1980: confrontation with Vietnam and the fall of Kriangsak', *Asian Survey*, Vol. 21, No. 2.

North, David S., Lawrence S. Lewin and Jennifer R. Wagner (1982) *Kaleidoscope: The Resettlement of Refugees in the United States by the Voluntary Agencies*, report prepared for the Bureau for Refugee Programs, US Department of State.

Olson, Clifford (1981) *Associations and Committees Serving Voluntary Agencies at the Country Level: a Study of Eight Organizations in Five Countries*, International Council of Voluntary Agencies.

O'Sullivan, John (1981) *Thailand: Medical Care for Lao Refugees in Ubon Camp, 1978– 1979*, International Disaster Institute, London.

Pack, Mary E. (1988) *The Human Dimension of Longterm Encampment: Vietnamese Boat Refugees in First Asylum Camps*, Ford Foundation, Bangkok.

Pai Yang and Nora Murphy (1993) *Hmong in the 90s: Stepping Towards the Future*, Hmong American Partnership, St Paul.

Pasuk Phongpaichit and Sungsidh Piriyarangsan (1994) *Corruption and Democracy in Thailand*, Chulalongkorn University, Bangkok.

Ponchaud, François (1977) 'Indochinese Refugees in Thailand', International Catholic Migration Commission.

Poole, Peter A. (1970) *The Vietnamese in Thailand: a Historical Perspective*, Cornell University Press, Ithaca.

Pranee Saipiroon (1982) *ASEAN Government's Attitudes Toward Regional Security: 1975–1979*, Institute of Asian Studies, Chulalongkorn University, Bangkok.

Refugee Concern Hong Kong (1991) *Defenseless in Detention: Vietnamese Children Living Amidst Increasing Violence in Hong Kong* (Kowloon: RCHK).

Renard, Donald A. (1987) 'The last bus', *The Atlantic Monthly*, October.

Reynell, Josephine (1989) *Political Pawns: Refugees on the Thai-Kampuchean Border*, Refugee Studies Program, Oxford.

Rizvi, Zia (1995) 'The Indochinese refugee exodus: comments on some specific aspects', *Report of the International Seminar on the Indochinese Exodus and the International Response, October 27–28 1995*, UNHCR and Ministry of Foreign Affairs Japan, Tokyo.

Robinson, W. Courtland (1988) 'Vietnamese refugees in Thailand face first asylum crisis', *Refugee Reports*, Vol 9, No. 2 (February).

Robinson, W. Courtland (1988) 'The Vietnamese refugee crisis in Thailand continues to elude solutions', *Refugee Reports*, Vol 9, No. 3 (March).

Robinson, W. Courtland (1988) 'Laotian refugees in Thailand: the Thai and US response 1975–1988', in Joseph J. Zasloff and Leonard Unger (eds) *Laos: Beyond the Revolution*, St. Martin's Press, New York.

Robinson, W. Courtland (1990) 'Malaysia pushes off 6,500 Vietnamese boat people', *Refugee Reports*, Vol. 11, No. 5 (May).

Robinson, W. Courtland (1990) 'Pirate attacks on Vietnamese refugees grow more vicious', *World Refugee Survey – 1989 in Review*, US Committee for Refugees, Washington.

Robinson, W. Courtland (1992) ' "Unhappy endgame": Hmong refugees in Thailand', *Refugee Reports*, Vol. 13, No. 8 (August).

Robinson, W. Courtland (1993) *Something Like Home Again: The Repatriation of Cambodian Refugees in Thailand*, US Committee for Refugees, Washington.

Robinson, W. Courtland (1994) *Rupture and Return: Repatriation, Displacement and Reintegration in Battambang Province, Cambodia*, Institute of Asian Studies, Chulalongkorn University, Bangkok.

Robinson, W. Courtland (1996) *Double Vision: A History of Cambodian Refugees in Thailand*, Institute of Asian Studies, Chulalongkorn University, Bangkok.

Robinson, Vaughan (1989) 'Up the creek without a paddle? Britain's boat people ten years on', *Geography*, Vol. 74, No. 325 (October).

Robinson, Vaughan (1993) 'North and South: resettling Vietnamese refugees in Australia and the UK', in Richard Black and Vaughan Robinson, *Geography and Refugees: Patterns and Processes of Change*, Bellhaven Press, London.

Rogers, Rosemarie and Emily Copeland (1993) *Forced Migration: Policy Issues in the Post-Cold War World*, Tufts University, Medford.

Rogge, John (1992) 'Return to Cambodia', in Frederick C. Cuny, Barry N. Stein and Pat Reed (eds), *Repatriation During Conflict in Africa and Asia*, Center for the Study of Societies in Crisis, Dallas.

Shacknove, Andrew (1993) 'From asylum to containment', *International Journal of Refugee Law* Vol. 5, No. 4, Oxford University Press, Oxford.

Shawcross, William (1984) *The Quality of Mercy*, Simon and Schuster, New York.

Simmance, Alan (1995) 'The international response to the Indochinese refugee crisis', *Report of the International Seminar on the Indochinese Exodus and the International Response, 27–28 October 1995*, UNHCR and Ministry of Foreign Affairs Japan, Tokyo.

Smyser, W. R. (1988) *Refugees: Extended Exile*, Praeger Publishers, New York.

Sobel, Lester A. (ed.) (1979) *Refugees: A World Report*, Facts on File, New York.

St Cartmail, Keith (1983) *Exodus Indochina*, Heinemann, Auckland.

Stein, Barry (1983) 'The commitment to refugee resettlement', *The Annals of the American Academy of Political and Social Science*, Vol. 467 (May).

Stein, Barry (1991) 'Refugee aid and development: slow progress', in Adelman (ed.) *Refuge Policy: Canada and the United States.*

Stone, Scott C. S. and John E. McGowan (1980) *Wrapped in the Wind's Shawl: Refugees of Southeast Asia and the Western World*, Presidio Press, San Rafael.

Strand, Paul and Woodrow Jones, Jr (1985) *Indochinese Refugees in America: Problems of Adaptation and Assimilation*, Duke University Press, Durham.

Strauch, Judith (1980) 'The Chinese Exodus from Vietnam: Implications for the Southeast Asian Chinese', *Cultural Survival*, Occasional Paper 1, December.

Sukhumbhand Paribatra (1987) *From Enmity to Alignment: Thailand's Evolving Relations with China*, Institute of Security and International Studies, Chulalongkorn University, Bangkok.

Supang Chantavanich and Bruce Reynolds (1988) (eds) *Indochinese Refugees: Asylum and Resettlement*, Chulalongkorn University, Bangkok.

Sutter, Valerie O'Connor (1990) *The Indochinese Refugee Dilemma,* Louisiana State University Press, Baton Rouge.

Tapp, Nicholas (1986) 'The Hmong of Thailand: Opium People of the Golden Triangle', *Anti-Slavery Society and Cultural Survival*, Report No 4.

Teitelbaum, Michael S. (1983) 'Tragic choices in refugee policy', in J. M. Kitagawa (ed.) *American Refugee Policy*, Winston Press, Minneapolis.

Tenhula, John (1991) *Voices from Southeast Asia: The Refugee Experience in the United States*, Holmes and Meier, New York.

Terry, Lui Ting (1983) 'Undocumented migration in Hong Kong', *International Migration Review*, Vol. 21, No. 2.

Thion, Serge (1988) 'Indochinese refugees in France: solidarity and its limits', in Supang and Reynolds (eds), *Indochinese Refugees: Asylum and Resettlement.*

US Catholic Conference (1986) *The Orderly Departure Program: The Need for Reassessment*, USCC, Washington.

US Committee for Refugees (1984) *Vietnamese Boat People: Pirates' Vulnerable Prey*, USCR, Washington.

Van-es-Beeck, Bernard J. (1982) 'Refugees from Laos: 1975–1979', in Martin Stuart-Fox (ed.), *Contemporary Laos: Studies in the Politics and Society of the Lao People's Democratic Republic*, University of Queensland Press, St Lucia.

Vitit Muntarbhorn (1980) 'Displaced persons in Thailand: legal and national policy issues in perspective', *Round Table of Asian Experts on Current Problems in the International Protection of Refugees and Displaced Persons*, International Institute of Humanitarian Law, Manila.

Vitit Muntarbhorn (1982) 'Displaced persons in Thailand: legal and national policy issues in perspective', *Chulalongkorn University Law Review*, Vol. 1.

Vitit Muntarbhorn (1992) *The Status of Refugees in Asia*, Oxford University Press, Oxford.

Viviani, Nancy (1988) 'Indochinese refugees and Australia', in Supang and Reynolds, *Indochinese Refugees: Asylum and Resettlement.*

Wain, Barry (1979) 'The Indochina refugee crisis', *Foreign Affairs*, Fall Issue.

Wain, Barry (1981) *The Refused: The Agony of the Indochina Refugees*, Simon and Schuster, New York.

Warner, Roger (1995) *Back Fire: The CIA's Secret War in Laos and Its Link to the War in Vietnam* Simon and Schuster, New York.

Wiesner, Louis A. (1988) *Victims and Survivors: Displaced Persons and Other War Victims in Viet-Nam 1954–1975*, Westport Press, New York.

Women's Commission for Refugee Women and Children (1991) *Repatriation and Reintegration: Can Hmong Begin to Look Homeward?* Women's Commission for Refugee Women and Children, New York.

Young, Stephen B. (1983) 'Who is a refugee? A theory of persecution', in Lydio F. Tomasi (ed.), *In Defense of the Alien, Volume V, Refugees and Territorial Asylum*, Center for Migration Studies, New York.

Zarjevski, Yefime (1988) *A Future Preserved: International Assistance to Refugees*, Pergamon Press, Oxford.

Zasloff, Joseph (1981) 'The Economy of the New Laos, Part II: Plans and Performance', *AUFS Reports,* No. 45.

Zolberg, Aristide R., Astri Suhrke and Sergio Aguayo (1989) *Escape from Violence: Conflict and the Refugee Crisis in the Developing World*, Oxford University Press, Oxford.

Zubrzycki, Jerry (1981) 'International migration in Australasia and the South Pacific', in Mary M. Kritz, Charles B. Keely, and Silvano M. Tomasi (eds), *Global Trends in Migration: Theory and Research on International Population Movements*, Center for Migration Studies, New York.

Zucker, Norman L. and Naomi Flink Zucker (1987) *The Guarded Gate: The Reality of American Refugee Policy*, Harcourt Brace Jovanovich, San Diego.

Government and international documents

'Agreement between the United Nations High Commissioner for Refugees and the Government of the Kingdom of Thailand, December 22 1975'.

British Home Office (1985) The Government Reply to the Third Report from the Home Affairs Committee Session 1984–85 HC 72-I, *Refugees and Asylum, with Special Reference to the Vietnamese*, Her Majesty's Stationery Office, London.

Congressional Research Service (1979) *World Refugee Crisis: The International Community's Response*, US Government Printing Office, Washington.

Employment and Immigration Canada, Program Evaluation Branch (1982) *Evaluation of the 1979–80 Indochinese Refugee Program* Employment and Immigration Canada, Ottawa.

Employment and Immigration Canada (1986) *Sponsoring Refugees: Facts for Canadian Groups and Organizations*, Employment and Immigration Canada, Toronto.

Office of the Special Representative of the Secretary-General of the United Nations for the Coordination of Cambodian Humanitarian Assistance Programmes (1992) *Cambodian Humanitarian Assistance and the United Nations 1979-1991*, OSRSG, Bangkok.

Socialist Republic of Vietnam, Permanent Mission to the UN (1991) 'Joint Press Statement of the British, Hong Kong, Vietnam and Representatives of UNHCR and IOM', 27 September 1991.

Thailand, Ministry of Foreign Affairs (1980) *The Vietnamese Acts of Aggression against Thailand's Sovereignty and Territorial Integrity*, MFA, Bangkok.

Thailand, Ministry of Foreign Affairs (1985) *Documents on the Kampuchean Problem: 1979–1985*, MFA, Bangkok.

Thailand, Ministry of Interior (1978) *A Call for Humanity: Displaced Persons from Indochina in Thailand* Operation Center for Displaced Persons, Bangkok.

Thailand, Ministry of Interior (1980) *Too Long to Wait: Displaced Persons from Indochina in Thailand*, MOI, Bangkok.

Thailand, Ministry of Interior (1981) *An Instrument of Foreign Policy: Indochinese Displaced*

Persons, MOI, Bangkok.

Thailand, Joint Operations Center, Supreme Command, 'The Assistance Plan for Thai Villagers Affected by Kampuchean Migration into Thailand', Undated mimeograph.

United Nations (1992) *Security Council Resolution 766* (S/RES/766), 21 July 1992.

— (1993) *United Nations Joint Appeal for the Reintegration Phase of the Cambodian Repatriation Operation.*

— (1995) *World Population Prospects, The 1994 Revision,* United Nations, New York.

— (1995) *The United Nations and Cambodia 1991–1995,* United Nations Department of Public Information, New York.

UN Border Relief Operation (UNBRO) Monthly Reports 1982–1991.

United Nations Childrens Fund (UNICEF) (1979) 'Joint UNICEF/ICRC Emergency Relief for Kampuchea', Information Note by the Executive Director, 2 November 1979.

UN Development Program and UN High Commissioner for Refugees (1991) 'Outline of Memorandum of Understanding of Cooperation between the United Nations Development Program and the United Nations High Commissioner for Refugees', (Draft), 22 November 1991.

UN Development Programme/Office for Projects Services (1993) 'CARERE Workplan: September 1992–February 1993', UNDP, Phnom Penh.

UN High Commissioner for Refugees (1978) 'Report on UNHCR Activities in the LPDR in 1977', February 1978, Vientiane.

— (1978) Cable from UNHCR Regional Office Malaysia, to UNHCR Geneva, 13 November 1978, Kuala Lumpur.

— (1978) Cable from UNHCR Geneva to UNHCR Regional Office Malaysia, 14 November 1978, Geneva.

— (1979) Note for the File, 'Meeting with Representatives of Interested Governments on Refugees and Displaced Persons in Southeast Asia', 16 January 1979.

— (1979) 'Report on UNHCR Activities in the LPDR in 1978', February 1979, Vientiane.

— (1979) Letter from Poul Hartling to missions of Executive Committee countries in Geneva, 22 March 1979.

— (1979) 'Note by the High Commissioner for the Meeting on Refugees and Displaced Persons in Southeast Asia, 9 July 1979'.

— (1979) *Handbook on Procedures and Criteria for Determining Refugee Status under the 1951 Convention and the 1967 Protocol relating to the Status of Refugees,* Geneva.

— (1979) 'Meeting on Refugees and Displaced Persons in Southeast Asia, Convened by the Secretary-General of the United Nations at Geneva on 20 and 21 July 1979, and Subsequent Developments', 7 November 1979.

— (1980) 'Report on UNHCR Activities in the LPDR in 1979', February 1980, Vientiane.

— (1980) *Report on UNHCR Assistance Activities in 1978–1979 and Proposed Voluntary Funds Program and Budget for 1980.*

— (1980) 'On the Proposal for the establishment of a procedure for the Determination of Refugee Status in Thailand', Internal memorandum by Ivor Jackson, 7 August 1980, Geneva.

— (1981) 'Screening of Lowland Lao', Note for the File, 23 February 1981, Bangkok.

— (1982) 'Zia Rizvi Briefing at Australian Embassy, Thursday, 20 May 1982.' Bangkok.

— (1984) *The Nansen Medal and its Recipients: Thirty Years in Retrospect,* Geneva.

— (1984) *Socio-Economic Survey of Khmer Muslim Refugees in Malaysia*, Kuala Lumpur.
— (1984) 'Push-backs and other measures against Lao asylum-seekers', Note for the File, 8 October 1984, Bangkok.
— (1985) 'Hmong pushed back to Paksane', Note for the File, 1 March 1985, Bangkok.
— (1986) Inter-Office Memorandum No. 62, 'The Operational Role of UNHCR', To All Substantive Officers at Headquarters, All Representatives, Chargés de Mission, and Correspondents, From the High Commissioner, 2 July 1986, Geneva.
— (1988) *Collection of International Istruments Concerning Refugees.* UNHCR, Geneva.
— (1988) *Guidelines on Refugee Children*, UNHCR, Geneva.
— (1988) Memorandum from Dennis McNamara, Deputy Director, Division of Refugee Law and Doctrine, to G. Arnaout, Director, Division of Refugee Law and Doctrine, 11 March 1988. Geneva.
— (1988) Cable from UNHCR Hong Kong to Sergio Vieira de Mello, Head of Regional Bureau for Asia and Oceania, 9 June 1988, Hong Kong.
— (1988) 'Statement of an Understanding Reached between the Hong Kong Government and UNHCR Concerning the Treatment of Asylum Seekers Arriving from Vietnam in Hong Kong, 20 September 1988.'
— (1989) *Draft Declaration and Comprehensive Plan of Action, Approved by the Preparatory Meeting for the International Conference on Indochinese Refugees, March 8 1989.*
— (1989) 'Survey V: VBP [Vietnamese Boat People] New Arrivals', April 1989, Kuala Lumpur.
— (1989) *Note on the Work of the Coordinating Committee for the International Conference on Indochinese Refugees*, A/CONF.148/4, 30 May 1989. Annex V.
— (1989) 'Note on Unaccompanied Minors', Submitted to the Coordinating Committee for the International Conference on Indochinese Refugees, Geneva, 25 and 26 May 1989.
— (1990) 'Mr. W. Collins' Survey on Vietnamese Boat People', Internal memorandum, 9 April 1990, Hong Kong.
— (1990) Press Release, 'Rescue at Sea: A Maritime Tradition to be Upheld', 10 April 1990, Geneva.
— (1990) Memorandum from Anne Wagley Gow to Robert van Leeuwen, 17 June 1990, Hong Kong.
— (1990) 'Regional Update on Special Procedures and Identification of Issues for Discussion', November 1990, Kuala Lumpur.
— (1991) 'Information Update on Voluntary Repatriation', 1 February 1991, Geneva.
— (1991) Letter from UNHCR Branch Office, Thailand to Nivat Pibul, Director, Operations Center for Displaced Persons, 14 May 1991. Bangkok.
— (1991) *Outline of the Plan for a Phased Repatriation and Reintegration of Laotians in Thailand*, Fourth Session of the Tripartite Meeting (LPDR/RTG/UNHCR), Luang Prabang, 27–29 June 1991.
— (1991) 'Summary of Revised Operations Plan (Cambodia Portion)', 7 November 1991, Bangkok.
— (1991) 'Cambodia Land Identification for Settlement of Returnees, 4 November–17 December 1991', PTSS Mission Report 91/33, Geneva.
— (1992) 'Cambodian Repatriation Operation, Situation Report No. 3', 29 February–7 March 1992, Aranyaprathet.
— (1992) 'Cambodian Repatriation Operation, Situation Report No. 6', 1–30 June 1992, Aranyaprathet.

— (1992) *Background Information Note on the Situation of Lao Refugees and Asylum Seekers and Status of Voluntary Repatriation Program*, Prepared for the Fifth Session of the Tripartite Meeting (LPDR/RTG/UNHCR), Rayong, July 1992.

— (1992) 'Cambodia Repatriation Update No. 8', 18–27 July 1992, Aranyaprathet.

— (1992) 'Information Bulletin No. 6: Cambodia Repatriation Operation', 3 August 1992, Phnom Penh.

— (1992) 'Information Bulletin No. 7: Cambodia Looking to the Future', 28 October 1992, Phnom Penh.

— (1992) 'Cambodia Repatriation Operation: Situation Report No. 29', 14–21 December 1992, Aranyaprathet.

— (1992) *Refugee Status Determination and Special Procedures under the Comprehensive Plan of Action*, UNHCR, Kuala Lumpur.

— (1992), *The State of the World's Refugees: In Search of Solutions*, Oxford University Press, Oxford.

— (1993) 'Quick Impact Projects, Project Summary', 1 April 1993, Phnom Penh.

— (1993), 'Group Settlements: Site Selection and Preparation', July 1993, Vientiane.

— (1993) 'Discussion Paper prepared for the UNHCR Regional Meeting of Representatives and Chiefs of Mission on Implementation of the CPA', 1 September 1993, Jakarta.

— (1993) *The State of the World's Refugees: The Challenge of Protection,* Penguin Books, New York.

— (1994) *Refugee Children: Guidelines for Protection and Care*, UNHCR, Geneva.

— (1994) *Resettlement in the 1990s: A Review of Policy and Practice*, An Evaluation Summary prepared by the Inspection and Evaluation Service for the Formal Consultations on Resettlement, 12–14 October 1994, Geneva.

— (1995) 'Vietnam Mission Report', Internal Memorandum, 20 July 1995, Geneva,

— (1995) 'Repatriation Information for Returnees to the Lao PDR', 18 September 1995, Vientiane.

— (1995) *The Comprehensive Plan of Action 1989–1995: A Regional Approach to Improving Refugee Protection*, UNHCR, Geneva.

— (1995) Information Bulletin, *The Comprehensive Plan of Action*, UNHCR, Geneva.

— (1996) *UNHCR Monitoring of the Repatriation and Reintegration of CPA Returnees to Vietnam*, UNHCR, Hanoi.

— (1996) Information Bulletin, 'Laos', April 1996, Geneva.

— (1996) *Excerpts from the Resettlement Handbook, 1996 Version*, UNHCR Division of International Protection, Geneva.

— (1997) *The State of the World's Refugees: A Humanitarian Agenda*, Oxford University Press, Oxford.

UN Transitional Authority in Cambodia (1993) *Donors Review Meeting: February 25 1993, Addendum: Specific Programs and Appeals, Annex IV*, Phnom Penh.

US Central Intelligence Agency (1978) *The Refugee Resettlement Problem in Thailand*, National Foreign Assessment Center, Washington.

US Congress, Senate Committee on the Judiciary (1974) *Relief and Rehabilitation of War Victims in Indochina: One Year After the Ceasefire*, A Study Mission Report Prepared for the Use of the Subcommittee to Investigate Problems Connected with Refugees and Escapees, 93rd Congress, 2nd Session.

— (1975) *Indochina Evacuation and Refugee Problems, Part II: The Evacuation*, Hearings before the Subcommittee to Investigate Problems Connected with Refugees and Escapees, 15, 25 and 30 April 1975, 94th Congress, 1st Session.

— (1976) *Aftermath of War: Humanitarian Problems of Southeast Asia*, A Staff Report

Prepared for the Use of the Subcommittee to Investigate Problems Connected with Refugees and Escapees, 94th Congress, 2nd Session.

— (1978) *Humanitarian Problems of Southeast Asia 1977–78*, 95th Congress, 2nd Session.

— (1982) *Refugee Problems in Southeast Asia 1981: Staff Report,* 97th Congress, 2nd Session.

— (1985) *U.S. Refugee Program in Southeast Asia: 1985*, Report Prepared for the Use of the Subcommittee on Immigration and Refugee Policy, 99th Congress, 1st Session.

US Congress, House Committee on Foreign Affairs (1982) *Piracy in the Gulf of Thailand: a Crisis for the International Community*, 97th Congress, 2nd Session.

US Department of Health Education and Welfare (1976) *Report to Congress*, 15 June 1976.

US Department of Health and Human Services, Office of Refugee Resettlement (1995) *Report to the Congress: FY 1994 Refugee Resettlement Program*, HHS, Washington, DC.

US Embassy, Thailand (1992) 'Reports on Results of Investigations of Allegations Concerning the Welfare of Hmong Refugees and Asylum Seekers in Thailand and Laos', Prepared by the Refugee and Migration Affairs Unit, Bangkok.

US General Accounting Office (1977) *Domestic Resettlement of Indochinese – Struggle for Self-Reliance*, GAO, Washington.

— (1979) *The Indochinese Exodus: A Humanitarian Dilemma*, GAO, Washington.

— (1980) *Indochinese Refugees: Protection, Care and Processing Can Be Improved*, GAO, Washington.

— (1996) *Vietnamese Asylum Seekers: Refugee Screening Procedures Under the Comprehensive Plan of Action*, GAO, Washington.

US National Security Council (1983) 'Refugee Policy and Processing Refugees from Indochina.' National Security Decision Directive No. 93, White House, Washington, 13 May 1983.

World Food Programme (1982) *Kampuchean Emergency Operation: An Information Note*, WFP, Rome.

— (1994) *Donor Report: Cambodia Repatriation Food Resupply Operation*, WFP, Phnom Penh.

Newspapers, periodicals and radio broadcasts

Agence France-Presse, 26 September 1991, (FBIS-EAS-91-187).

Asiaweek, 26 December 1980–2 January 1981.

Bangkok Domestic Service, 13 June 1980, (FBIS-APA-80-116), 18 June 1980 (FBIS-APA–80–120).

Bangkok Post, 3 September 1975, 7 September 1975, 7 September 1978, 5 December 1978, 12 December 1978. 12 June 1979, 18 July 1979, 20 October 1979, 11 June 1980, 13 June 1980, 17 June 1981, 13 July 1984, 2 September 1988.

Bangkok World, 25 April 1979, 16 May 1979.

Boston Globe, 17 March 1985.

China Daily, 9 January 1998.

Christian Science Monitor, 11 May 1976.

Far Eastern Economic Review, 25 May 1979, 29 June 1979, 3 August 1979, 17 July 1981, 5 June 1985.

Hanoi Domestic Service, 18 June 1980 (FBIS-APA-80-120).

Hong Kong Standard, 26 January 1990.

International Herald Tribune, 26 June 1979, 3 July 1980, 5 July 1984.

Keesing's Contemporary Archives, 1975.

The [Bangkok] Nation, 14 May 1978, 30 November 1978, 15 December 1978, 20 April 1979, 19 June 1979, 11 June 1980, 25 July 1981, 8 July 1987, 21 July 1988.

New York Times, 28 December 1975, 4 July 1984, 25 January 1990, 7 June 1991, 4 October 1991.

Operation Lifeline Newsletter, No. 2, 30 July 1979.

Phnom Penh Domestic Service, 20 June 1980 (FBIS-APA-80-121).

Refugee Concern Newsmagazine, Issue 2, June/July 1994.

Refugee Reports, Vol. 10, No. 12, 29 December 1989. Vol 17, No. 5, 31 May 1996.

Refugees, September 1987.

SPK, 13 June 1980 (FBIS-APA-80-116).

San Jose Mercury News, 14 January 1990.

Vietnam News Agency, 5 June 1978, 6 June 1978.

Voice of Democratic Kampuchea, 22 June 1980 (FBIS-APA-80-124).

Washington Post, 22 November 1983, 12 August 1986, 22 March 1987, 24 September 1990.

Washington Times, 30 March 1987.

The Weekend Observer, 26 November 1988.

Speeches and unpublished manuscripts

American Refugee Committee, February 1980 Survey in Ban Vinai, Mimeograph.

Ashe, Robert 'Cross-Border Feeding', Mimeographed report, 8 July 1980.

Greve, Hanna Sophie 'Kampuchean Refugees, "Between the Tiger and the Crocodile"', PhD. Dissertation, University of Bergen, 1987.

Greve, Hanna Sophie (1987) 'Evacuation Sites for Kampucheans in Thailand: Virtual Concentration Camps Under International Auspices?' Mimeograph, 9 September 1987.

Heder, Stephen 'Kampuchea, October 1979–August 1980: The democratic Kampuchea resistance, the Kampuchean countryside, and the Sereikar', Unpublished manuscript.

Khachadpai Burusapatana, Speech presented at the Public Affairs Institute Seminar on Refugee Research, Pattaya, Thailand, 28–29 March 1986.

Kumin, Judith. 'Orderly departure from Vietnam: a humanitarian alternative?' Ph.D. Dissertation, The Fletcher School of Law and Diplomacy, June 1987.

McNamara, Dennis 'The politics of humanitarianism: a study of some aspects of the international response to the Indochinese refugee influx (1975–1985)', unpublished manuscript.

Maat, Bob 'The weight of these sad times: end of mission report on the Thai–Kampuchean border, 8 December 1979–30 April 1989', unpublished manuscript.

Niland, Norah. 'The politics of suffering: the Thai–Cambodian border, a case study on the use and abuse of humanitarian assistance', Masters Thesis, University of Dublin, 1991.

Ogata, Sadako, 'Refugees in Asia: From Exodus to Solutions', The Charles Rostov Annual Lecture in Asian Affairs, 27 November 1995, Johns Hopkins University, School of Advanced International Studies, Washington, DC.

Sibley, John and Jean, 'Report from Ban Vinai, No. 3', 5 December 1979.

Wright, Alan G. 'A Never ending refugee camp?: The explosive birth rate in Ban Vinai', 1986.

Index

2,000 Programme 150
Abrahams, Cecilia 128
Abramowitz, Morton 49, 73, 161-2
Action Humanitaire 287
Adelman, Howard 139, 142
Afghan people 286
Aga Khan, Prince Sadruddin 7, 21-4, 70, 105, 109
Agency for Volunteer Service 202
Aid to Refugee Children Without Parents 212
Alberta 141
Algeria 146
Amar, Francis 49
American Council for Nationalities Service (ACNS) 130
American Fund for Czechoslovak Refugees 130
American Refugee Committee (ARC) 89-90
Amin, Idi 7, 139
Amnesty International 103-4, 119, 195
Anti-Piracy Agreement (APA) 167
Appave, Gervais 183
Argentina 127
Arizona 132
Ashe, Robert 79
Asia Watch 201
Asian-African Legal Consultative Committee (AALCC) 284
Association of Southeast Asian Nations (ASEAN) 50-1, 53, 55, 57-8, 66, 78-9, 153, 162, 183, 282, 284
asylum 3, 8, 42-3, 51-2, 54-6, 58-9, 69, 72-4, 79, 84, 105, 113-14, 116-17, 128, 134, 138, 142-5, 150, 152-3, 155, 161-4, 168-9, 173, 175-6, 178-83, 187-94, 198-224, 235, 260-2, 267, 272-90
Atkey, Ron 140
atrocities 32-3, 43, 47, 49, 61, 92-5, 104, 119-20, 166, 169
Australia 2, 5, 24, 47, 52, 54, 74, 80, 96, 127, 143, 146, 151-5, 165, 171, 174-5, 179-80, 183, 187, 190, 192, 194; Refugee Status Review Committee 155
Australian Catholic Relief 254
Austria 7

Baba, Abdul Ghafar 190
Bailey, Colonel Jack 167-8
Baker, James 217
Baker, Reginald 132
Bali 50, 53
Ban Laem 45
Ban Me Thuot 17
Ban Na Saat 238
banditry 2, 92

Bangkok 1-2, 8, 10, 15, 24, 46, 49, 69, 75, 80, 82, 119, 165, 182, 195, 231, 234, 236
Bangkok Post 46, 109
Bangkok Principles 284
Bangladesh 7, 127
Banteay Meanchey 239-40, 247, 254-7
Barber, Martin 69-70, 77
Barnes, Thomas J. 131-3, 143-6
Barnes, Walter 138
Bataan Island 55, 194
Battambang 45-6, 48, 239-42, 244, 254-6, 259
Becker, Elizabeth 67
Beddoes, Dick 140
Beihai 39
Bien Hoa province 41
Bihari people 7
Bijleveld, Anne-Willem 254
Birmingham 147, 149
Blatten, Werner 31, 106
Boat People SOS Committee 208-9, 222
boat people 28-32, 41-4, 46, 50, 55-62, 66, 96-7, 112-14, 134, 137-9, 152-3, 155, 161-76, 180-2, 187-94, 198-200, 205, 216, 220, 231, 260, 261-2, 272-3, 278, 281, 283, 286
Bokeo province 233, 236
Bolikhamxay province 236
Bona Yang 13-14
Bonnot, Michel 287
Borneo 190
Bosnia 283, 287
Botswana 145
Bouavanh Phothirath 238
Boutros-Ghali, Boutros 253
Bresnihan, Brian 217
Britain 16, 54, 59, 146-51, 175, 194, 207, 215-17, 261-2; Select Committee on Refugee Resettlement and Immigration (SCORRI) 150
British Broadcasting Corporation (BBC) 162, 261
British Council for Aid to Refugees (BCAR) 147
Brown, Roger 72
Brown, William A. 182
Brunei 282
Brzezinski, Zbigniew 67
Buchan, Sandy 149
Buddhism 2, 11, 14-15, 44, 94-5, 165
Bui Tin 41
Buriram 44
Burma 181, 284, 289
Bush, George 287

Calabia, Dawn 211
California 132-5, 138, 212

314